# MUSIC IN
# WORLD WAR II

# MUSIC IN WORLD WAR II

## Coping with Wartime in Europe and the United States

EDITED BY
PAMELA M. POTTER, CHRISTINA L. BAADE,
AND ROBERTA MONTEMORRA MARVIN

INDIANA UNIVERSITY PRESS

This book is a publication of

Indiana University Press
Office of Scholarly Publishing
Herman B Wells Library 350
1320 East 10th Street
Bloomington, Indiana 47405 USA

iupress.org

© 2020 by Indiana University Press

All rights reserved
No part of this book may be reproduced or utilized in any form or by any means, electronic or mechanical, including photocopying and recording, or by any information storage and retrieval system, without permission in writing from the publisher. The paper used in this publication meets the minimum requirements of the American National Standard for Information Sciences—Permanence of Paper for Printed Library Materials, ANSI Z39.48-1992.

Manufactured in the United States of America

Published with financial assistance from the General Publications Fund of the American Musicological Society, supported in part by the National Endowment for the Humanities and the Andrew W. Mellon Foundation, and from an SSHRC Exchange—Scholarly Publications Grant, awarded by McMaster University's Arts Research Board.

Library of Congress Cataloging-in-Publication Data
Names: Potter, Pamela Maxine, editor. | Baade, Christina L., editor. | Marvin, Roberta Montemorra, editor.
Title: Music in World War II : coping with wartime in Europe and the United States / edited by Pamela M. Potter, Christina L. Baade, and Roberta Montemorra Marvin.
Description: Bloomington : Indiana University Press, 2020. | Includes bibliographical references and index.
Identifiers: LCCN 2020007632 (print) | LCCN 2020007633 (ebook) | ISBN 9780253050250 (hardback) | ISBN 9780253050267 (paperback) | ISBN 9780253050274 (ebook)
Subjects: LCSH: World War, 1939-1945—Music and the war. | Music—Europe—20th century—History and criticism. | Music—United States—20th century—History and criticism. | Popular music—1941-1950—History and criticism. | Popular music—1931-1940—History and criticism. | Music—Political aspects—History—20th century.
Classification: LCC ML3917.E85 M875 2020 (print) | LCC ML3917.E85 (ebook) | DDC 780.9/04—dc23
LC record available at https://lccn.loc.gov/2020007632
LC ebook record available at https://lccn.loc.gov/2020007633

1 2 3 4 5 25 24 23 22 21 20

# CONTENTS

*Dedication*   viii

*Preface* / Roberta Montemorra Marvin   ix

Introduction: Music and Global War in the Short Twentieth Century / Pamela M. Potter   1

### PART I: *On the Airwaves and the Screen*

1. *Sandy Calling*: Forging an Intimate Wartime Public at the BBC Theater Organ / Christina L. Baade   27
2. "Alien" Classical Musicians and the BBC, 1939–1945 / Tony Stoller   56
3. Musical "Diplomacy" in American and Soviet World War II Films of the 1940s / Peter Kupfer   77

### PART II: *Opera, Theater Stage, and Concerts*

4. The Metropolitan Opera House and the "War of Ideologies": The Politics of Opera Publicity in Wartime / Christopher Lynch   111
5. Broadway Goes to War / Tim Carter   131
6. Throwing Some Light on the *Dunkelkonzerte*: Toward a New Image of Concert Life in Vienna, 1939–1944 / Nicholas Attfield   148
7. Before the End of Time: General Huntziger's Centre Musical et Théâtral / Christopher Brent Murray   172

### PART III: *National Imaginaries*

8. Swing in the Protectorate: Czech Popular Music under the Nazi Occupation, 1938–1945 / Brian S. Locke   199
9. A Musical Reeducation: Music-Making in America's German POW Camps and the Intellectual Diversion Program / Kelsey Kramer McGinnis   226

10. Bunkers, Cellars, and Acoustic Memory: Sonic Experiences of War and Surrender in Nazi Germany / Abby Anderton    246

Afterword: Trans/national Soundscapes in World War II / Annegret Fauser    263

*Selected Works*    275
*Index*    289

*Dedicated to our fathers and all others  
who experienced World War II*

Sewall B. Potter (1918–2013),
father of Pamela Potter

Anthony J. Montemorra (1920–2019),
father of Roberta Montemorra Marvin

# PREFACE

ROBERTA MONTEMORRA MARVIN

FOR MANY PEOPLE TODAY, World War II is a distant historical event, far removed from one's life experiences. We study the war as a historical phenomenon, but, in reality, we are not so far removed from the war that it does not have direct connections. That is indeed the case for two of the co-editors of this book—Pam and me—whose fathers were World War II veterans.[1] These personal connections are particularly apt when it comes to music in World War II. They provide additional motivation and inspiration to us in our attempts to capture our fathers' experiences or to imagine the sounds they heard, the sights they saw, the places they visited.

Pam's father, Sewall Bennett Potter (born Saul Bernard Podolsky), achieved the rank of sergeant in the US Army Air Forces as a radio and radar mechanic in the 64th Airdrome Squadron of the 474th Fighter Group. He served from May 12, 1942, to September 10, 1945, and shipped out to France on his twenty-sixth birthday, June 8, 1944, two days after D-Day. Having graduated from Boston Latin School and Harvard University with his classmate and fellow music major Leonard Bernstein, Saul visited Europe only once, spending time in England, France, Belgium, and Germany, where he was most impressed by the opportunity to retrace the steps of J. S. Bach in places such as Eisenach, Cöthen, and Leipzig. He also became painfully aware of the level of anti-Semitism in the US Army as General Dwight D. Eisenhower ordered troops to view the atrocities in Buchenwald and his comrades downplayed the severity of the carnage. The most dangerous situations he recalled were when he was required to fly in an aircraft that was being used for target practice. He would return home to earn a Ph.D. in musicology, courtesy of the GI Bill, working with the Austrian Jewish émigré Karl Geiringer at Boston University.

As Saul's daughter went into the "family business" of musicology, she enjoyed the rare privilege of having parents who actually understood what she was doing and who even showed an interest in reading her work. Even more than that, however, as she delved into her doctoral project on the history of German musicology surrounding the Nazi years, her father could directly relate to and validate her conclusions about the activities and ideologies of scholars he and other musicologists of his generation had been taught to revere. He even commented on the stark Germanocentrism of his own dissertation adviser Geiringer, in spite of the anti-Semitism that had driven the Austrian musicologist out of his homeland.

My father, Anthony Joseph Montemorra, also served in the US Army Air Forces for more than two and a half years (February 8, 1943, to November 7, 1945), earning the rank of staff sergeant. A decorated veteran, he served in the 85th Bomb Squadron, 47th Bomb Group, 12th Air Force, in the Po Valley in Italy as an airplane armorer gunner, where he manned a machine gun turret in an A-20 bomber during combat missions. He was wounded in action on March 11, 1945, when on his twenty-seventh combat mission his plane crashed behind enemy lines, after hitting a bridge in Noceto near Parma. The pilot was killed, but my father and the other surviving crew member, J. E. Fitzgerald, though injured, were able to walk several miles to a farmhouse in Collecchio, where partisans took care of their injuries and eventually managed to get them to the mountain town of Bardi. From there, they walked nearly a week, transported together with prisoners of war, to get back across enemy lines to Allied territory. My father was reported missing in action as of March 12.[2] Not until March 30 did the family receive notice that he had been found alive.[3]

The location of my father's crash becomes especially significant with regard to music and World War II, given that I conducted my dissertation research on Verdi in Parma. When my father came to visit me, we drove throughout the area trying to locate the bridge (we did) and the farmhouse (we were unsuccessful) and we spent time in Bardi with a map to try to retrace the route of his escape. This proved to be a cathartic experience for my father, and it was something that etched itself into my mind, making the connection between Italy, my father, and my music scholarship something quite special.

Both of our stories are testimony that the realities of war indeed live on in untold ways. Thus, acknowledgments are due first to our fathers, who instilled in us a firsthand appreciation for the significance of World War II and the experiences of those involved. Indeed, explorations and discussions of those everyday experiences, so many of which are addressed in the essays in this volume, help make history relevant and real. We cannot all benefit from those who were directly involved in the war, but we can gain insights into the deeper meanings of the arts as related to the horrors and uncertainties of war.

This project was inspired by conversations about the broader topic of music and politics. With specific interests in the World War II era, the editors decided to cast the net broadly, hoping to attract essays that provided snapshots of the uses of music in representative situations of the period worldwide. The group of essays that emerged turned out to be focused in geographical scope and refreshingly varied in engagement with a variety of repertoires. They take innovative approaches to music's function in coping with the conditions of life during wartime.

A project such as this reflects the labors of several people. We wish to thank Heidi Bishop, who, several years ago, planted the germ of an idea for a volume such as this one. At Indiana University Press, Janice Frisch and Allison Blair Chaplin have provided invaluable assistance in many ways, always responsive to our seemingly never-ending questions during the preparation of the manuscript. Thanks go as well to Roberta's brother, Donald Montemorra, who located family documents and edited the photograph of Anthony Montemorra. We could not have produced this volume without the diligent assistance of Lesley Hughes, who served as an exceptionally able editorial assistant during the final preparation of the manuscript, taking on countless tasks to make the manuscript presentable. Our gratitude also goes to our authors, whose dedicated scholarship and imaginative approaches to the topic have proven enlightening to all of us.

In an address titled "They Shall Have Music Wherever They Go," delivered in January 1943 at Town Hall in New York City, the conductor Serge Koussevitzky proclaimed:

> Music is a dominant need of our time.... To realize the full significance of music amid the profound calamities of the present war we must glance back into the history of the past.... As never before do we realize that art and culture are a stronghold against the aggressor and his devastating, demoralizing forces.... Let us write the hymns of freedom and victory; ... let us proclaim hatred for despotism and destruction; let us sing the song of love for mankind and faith in the ageless ideals of independence and democracy.[4]

The essays in this volume indeed capture the spirit behind these words. There remains much to be said about music in World War II, and our contribution is indeed a small one. We hope, however, that it will prompt ongoing inquiry into the role of the arts, music specifically, in the daily lives of those who experienced one of the most significant events of the twentieth century.

### NOTES

1. Gene Baade, the father of our other editor, Christina, was born in 1943. Given the family status, age, and work in reserve occupations of Christina's grandfathers (Walter Baade was a farmer in Oklahoma; Ernst Mueller was a

minister in Ontario), neither of them fought in World War II—although Ernst Mueller ministered to the refugees and immigrants who poured into Sudbury, Ontario, after the war.

2. Telegram dated March 23, 1945, from Adjutant General J. A. Ulio to my grandfather, Domenico Montemorra, in personal possession of my family.

3. Major General John K. Cannon to Domenico Montemorra, letter of March 30, 1945, in possession of my family: he "evaded capture behind enemy lines and fought his way back through unfamiliar terrain during several weeks of constant danger."

4. Cited from the version of Koussevitsky's address published in the *New York Times,* January 17, 1943.

ROBERTA MONTEMORRA MARVIN is Professor of Musicology and former Chair of the Department of Music and Dance at the University of Massachusetts Amherst. She is editor of several books and author of *The Politics of Verdi's Cantica* and *Verdi the Student – Verdi the Teacher,* as well as Associate General Editor for *The Works of Giuseppe Verdi.*

# MUSIC IN
# WORLD WAR II

# INTRODUCTION

## Music and Global War in the Short Twentieth Century

PAMELA M. POTTER

A CENTURY AGO, THE WORLD was reeling from a conflict such as never seen before. World War I, or the "Great War," transformed the century that followed in redrawing the maps of the world, redistributing global power, forming multinational alliances, and toppling centuries-old monarchies and aristocracies. The First World War was never envisioned to be the "first" but rather the "war to end all wars," yet in 1945, the conclusion of an even greater global conflict made it imperative once again to reconfigure the maps, alliances, and power relations that had futilely promised to secure world peace in 1919. The deployment of new technologies and effective rules of engagement intensified from the First World War to the Second World War, spreading death, destruction, and mutilation at unprecedented levels. The end of World War II in 1945 brought the additional responsibility of reckoning with the moral dimensions of the atrocities that unfolded, making it necessary to coin the terms *genocide* and *war crimes* and permanently associating the names of Hiroshima, Nagasaki, and Auschwitz with unimaginable suffering, death, and destruction.

As the global wars of the twentieth century fundamentally transformed national boundaries, power relations, systems of government, and global economies, so too did they deeply affect the ways in which populations responded to war. World War I introduced the concept of a "home front" by engaging civilians more directly in the war effort, a situation that would only intensify with the air wars of World War II. While nations continued to mourn their fallen, pledge loyalty to their leaders, revile their enemies, and praise their heroes, it became more difficult to ignore war's costs, as civilians witnessed firsthand how death, physical destruction, and population displacement affected their own communities. And while some technological advances had escalated the destructive impact of war, others created new media that offered glimpses of this carnage with uncompromising accuracy, as photography and film allowed those at home to experience combat vicariously in pictures, words, and sounds.

For many artists and writers, it was no longer acceptable or possible to idealize war, as in the past. Instead, they took it upon themselves increasingly to cast a blinding light on the devastating effects of modern warfare on human existence. In earlier eras, one might participate consciously or unconsciously in a mission to shield the public from fully fathoming the traumas of warfare. In the twentieth century, eyewitnesses to war gradually felt compelled to unleash a new wave of criticism that broke earlier codes of silence about what transpired on the battlefield. Although the World War I generation may have exhibited ambivalence or even enthusiasm at the start of the conflict, survivors documenting the cruelties of war after its conclusion mercilessly subjected their readers and viewers to the death, disfigurement, and deprivation it wrought. Writers expressed their horror in novels such as Erich Maria Remarque's *All Quiet on the Western Front* and in the poetry of Wilfred Owen and Siegfried Sassoon, while artists such as Wyndham Lewis, Paul Nash, John Singer Sargent, George Bellows, Georg Grosz, Otto Dix, Ernst Barlach, and Käthe Kollwitz graphically displayed the corruption, mutilation, and grief wrought by the Great War. What may have started as ambivalence in World War I grew into questioning any further involvement in subsequent global conflicts over the course of the century, reaching maximum volume in the anti-war protests of the Vietnam era and casting doubt on what had once inspired throngs of young men to march off to the battlefields in 1914.

Just like every military engagement that preceded them, the multinational wars of the twentieth century also had their own soundtracks. But unlike the marches, heroic symphonies, and grand operas that accompanied and memorialized wars in earlier times, twentieth-century wars gave rise to very different ways to accompany, comment on, and increasingly distract from surrounding atrocities. In Europe, music patronage prior to the end of World War I lay largely in the hands of the aristocracy, who had a vested interest in achieving victory and drew on all resources at their disposal, including musical ones, to support their military ventures. What we know of the music employed to accompany warfare of the past highlights the military bands, bugle corps, and the songs and strains accompanying soldiers marching in formation. The music of the home front seemed to be dominated by commissioned compositions, patriotic songs, somber musical homages to the dead, and opera stagings and symphonic odes rallying the spirit of patriotism and strengthening the resolve to defeat the enemy.[1] In the United States, the music of military units was similar to that employed in Europe, band music gained increased popularity among soldiers and civilians alike, and newly composed songs were performed and often also created by amateur musicians. In addition to parodies in the tradition of "Yankee Doodle" were patriotic tributes to specific battles, to noteworthy heroes, and to American values more generally, as well as expressions of homesickness, mourning of fallen soldiers, and the despair of separated families and lovers.²

While many of these trends persisted into the First World War, even the music accompanying that conflict started to show signs of pivoting toward distracting both soldiers and civilians from the grim realities of wartime. This escapist function took on even more importance in the course of World War II, fed by the increased access to radio, recordings, and film. After 1945, art music took a sharp turn to inspire a rich repertoire of anti-war sentiment, best known in Krzysztof Penderecki's *Threnody to the Victims of Hiroshima* and Benjamin Britten's *War Requiem*, while folk and popular music in the 1960s and 1970s witnessed the explosion of protest songs that drove the opposition to war in the United States and Europe. The music associated with war then transformed even more radically, such that it could no longer serve primarily to bolster a country's military engagement. By the end of the twentieth century, music had been used as a weapon in bringing the enemy to its knees in the Gulf War and compelling Manuel Noriega to turn himself over to US troops after being "bombarded" with heavy metal.³

What were the elements of twentieth-century warfare that turned music from a source of comfort and inspiration into a powerful instrument of protest and torture? To seek answers to this question, we must fill in some existing gaps in our knowledge about music's evolving role as a component of war; specifically, we need to deepen our understanding of music's functions in the Second World War. For reasons explored below, music scholarship focused much attention on the Cold War after the fall of communism, and the centennial commemoration of World War I has yielded important new materials and approaches, yet World War II has not been afforded the same comprehensive scrutiny. However, a better understanding of how music functioned during that conflict can reveal crucial links to the present. While some very important studies of music and the Second World War have appeared in the last few years, the essays in this volume look to many as yet underexplored aspects of music-making to identify defining moments in music's relation to war and its transition from supporting war efforts to opposing them. By the time German troops invaded Poland in September 1939, the shockwaves unleashed by the Great War and the Depression had already pointed to the need for distraction from the miseries of everyday life throughout Europe and the United States. Music was already well on its way toward redefining its role from that of an aid to war to that of a means to cope with war's disruption and devastation. A closer look at the musical experiences of World War II affords us a glimpse into how music changed from operating in step with the war to carrying on in spite of war.

As the essays in this volume demonstrate, an examination of the music that accompanied the daily activities of soldiers, civilians, and prisoners reveals important moments in music's evolving role in the twentieth century. For one thing, the burgeoning media of radio, recordings, and sound film made it possible for musical production and consumption during World War II to deviate from its earlier, longstanding commitment to bolstering the war effort. Instead, these outlets offered new forms of diversion, allowing those living through the war to find solace in music's capacity to invoke memories of peacetime. And although this war was waged along clear ideological lines, these technologies ironically internationalized music so much that any jingoistic attempts to distinguish between the musical cultures of "us" and "them" became increasingly challenging. Nevertheless, this did not stop music from functioning as a weapon, demonstrated foremost in the tenacity of prisoners to cling to the music of home as a defense against indoctrination by their captors. The first signs of using music as torture were also already evident during World War II, in the operations of concentration camps where prisoners were forced to entertain sadistic guards and even to accompany their own death marches. It was the conclusion of the conflict, however, that marked the most pivotal moment in music's redefined relationship to war, as the full effects of genocide and the ravages of nuclear devastation became known. The radical transformation of music into a vehicle of protest would come into full force only after the unprecedented horrors carried out during World War II could seep into the public consciousness. The shock from these revelations would galvanize the revulsion and cynicism toward war that would shape attitudes for subsequent generations.

While this volume does not make any pretense of providing a comprehensive overview of the subject, it does strive to raise new questions and point to new avenues for investigating the critical turning points in music's relationship to war between 1939 and 1945. Taken together, the essays gathered here aim to fill a gap first by providing missing information in our music-historical narrative about the role of music in World War II, and, second, by looking beyond the cultivation of music in established institutional settings to explore a wide range of organized as well as impromptu musical experiences among soldiers and civilians.

## THE SHORT TWENTIETH CENTURY AND MUSIC SCHOLARSHIP

An exploration of the role of music in World War II comes with a special set of challenges. While it may seem obvious, the first task in approaching this investigation is to examine what is meant by World War II itself, and where we situate its beginning, its end, and its placement in the broader sweep of history. Critics have increasingly pointed to the shortcomings of framing the conflict within the years

1939 to 1945, calling attention to a myopic European and American perspective that privileges the German invasion of Poland in 1939 as the start of the war and the bombing of Hiroshima and Nagasaki as its end but overlooks the ongoing conflicts that started much earlier and ended much later. Some historians have argued for marking the beginning of the war in 1931 with the Japanese occupation of northeastern China (a campaign that could even be traced back to the late nineteenth century) or in 1937 with the beginning of Chinese resistance against Japan. The start of the war could also arguably be moved to the Italian invasion of Ethiopia in 1935 or the Spanish Civil War in 1936, which engaged foreign soldiers from several countries, or conversely to the attack on Pearl Harbor in 1941. Similarly, for many regions of the world the year 1945 marked anything but an end to global conflict, as revolutions and wars surrounding the overthrow of European colonialism continued throughout Asia, Africa, and the Middle East for decades to come.[4]

Another approach suggests that what we identify as World War II was just one phase of a much longer event that defined most of the century. Historian Eric Hobsbawm famously popularized the notion of the "short twentieth century" that lasted from the onset of World War I in 1914 to the end of the Cold War in 1991. Hobsbawm's book *The Age of Extremes*, a sequel to his three-volume history of the long nineteenth century (from the French Revolution to World War I), applies concepts developed by the economic historian Ivan Berend that partition the short twentieth century into three periods, each marked by destabilization and crisis. The first period, the "Age of Catastrophe," signaled the end of bourgeois capitalism and was punctuated by a series of violent and transformative upheavals: the First World War, the Bolshevik Revolution, the Great Depression, the rise of Fascism and Nazism, and the Second World War. The second period, the "Golden Age," lasted from 1947 to 1973 and saw the rapid growth of capitalist nations as well as the modernization of the rest of the world through an integrated global economy. In the last period, the "Crisis Decades," income inequality started to plague capitalist societies, socialism struggled with a depressed standard of living, and the very foundations of modern society and its faith in science and technology were questioned. All in all, it was an era of contrasts, defined by war, violence, genocide, and famine, all residing alongside progress, population growth, and prosperity.[5] While just one phase of a much larger phenomenon according to this framework, the Second World War nevertheless marks an indisputable turning point, setting parameters for the new world order that would define the remaining years of the short twentieth century.

Music scholarship was slow to acknowledge the role of music in modern warfare, and the timing of its first forays into these areas coincided with a series of events that unwittingly drew attention to the beginning and end of the short twentieth century but overlooked the pivotal moment of World War II. Until the 1990s, the canon of twentieth-century music history barely acknowledged musical activities during the wars at all. Instead, textbooks adopted themes of progress and innovation as their narrative thread for constructing this history, invariably restricting their investigations to art music.[6] They reached back to the late nineteenth century to identify the roots of modernism and experimentation and to track their developments since 1900. Most accounts would then mark the dawn of twentieth-century music with "musical revolutions" and "-isms" (impressionism, expressionism, symbolism, exoticism, to name a few) that came on the scene prior to World War I, most notably in the works of Igor Stravinsky, Claude Debussy, and Arnold Schoenberg. They would invariably skip over the war years themselves to concentrate on the radical experiments of the 1920s that were, as many would now argue, actually cultivated in an atmosphere of war fatigue and cynicism. Similarly bypassing any musical activity during World War II, the narrative marked the next important phase with the postwar flurry of experiments dominating art music and pushing the limits of musical conventions to unforeseen levels. As a result, when it comes to both world wars, we are still most familiar with their musical legacies not through the soundtrack that accompanied the years of conflict, but rather through the postwar reactions that came with the revelations of the ever-mounting devastation wrought by each conflict.

This neglect of music and war would end as the short twentieth century was coming to a close, but an engagement with the music of World War II would not receive the full attention that the war's fiftieth anniversary might have anticipated. The years 1989 and 1995 would have offered occasions for music scholars to reflect on commemorating the beginning and end of the war, but these moments were overshadowed by the concurrent collapse of the Soviet Union and its satellites. The fall of the Berlin Wall in 1989 made any attempts to acknowledge the fifty-year anniversary of the war's outbreak almost irrelevant, and throughout the 1990s, there was far more urgency to reflect on the Cold War. In Germany in particular, the impetus to compare Germany's "two dictatorships"—Adolf Hitler's Reich and Communist East Germany—became a topic of investigation immediately after Germany's unification. No one could escape such self-examination, not even the musicology profession. In 1994, for instance, the Bach Society embraced the theme of "Bach under Two Dictatorships 1933–1945 and 1945–1989."[7] As a participant in the conference, I experienced firsthand the feeling among representatives from the besieged East that "victorious" Western scholars had, in their view, colonized the musical and academic institutions after driving out those with tainted communist allegiances of the past.[8]

The Cold War became an object of intense scrutiny because it ended so abruptly and called for immediate and serious reflection on how to deal with former adversaries on multiple levels. For one thing, it was impossible for scholars to resist the lure of open access to archives, especially those in the former Soviet Union, which could now unlock the secrets of politics and society under Communism. Most pressing, however, was the need to understand the cultural ramifications of the Cold War in order to face the challenge of bridging the cultural divide that had existed between NATO and Warsaw Pact nations for four decades. An impenetrable ideological barrier had been erected between those in Western democracies who saw themselves as preserving artistic freedom and experimentation and those who, in the name of socialism, reviled intellectualized "formalism" and strove to ensure that culture would belong to the masses. Over the course of the next two decades, the field witnessed an impressive outpouring of studies on music and the Cold War by a new generation of scholars, leading to the creation of a Cold War study group within the American Musicological Society in 2007. The explosion of Cold War music studies initially focused attention on art music, but the important work of dismantling Cold War stereotypes that tended to contrast a culturally "advanced" West with a "backward" East would accommodate more serious consideration for all music, including popular music, that did not conform to the prevailing Western canons of progress and narrow interpretations of modernism.[9]

The surge of interest in Cold War studies and its impact on music history was the first sign of acknowledging the outlines of the short twentieth century, but the inevitable engagement with the Cold War in the late 1980s and 1990s arguably took priority over any anticipated recognition of World War II commemorations, leaving a crucial gap in scholarship. By taking the year 1945 as their point of departure, many Cold War music studies rested on shaky assumptions about music and society leading up to 1945. Their focus took its cue from the creative fervor at Darmstadt, Paris, Columbia and Princeton universities, and elsewhere, rocked by the terror of nuclear war and inspired by a quest for peace that was harnessed by composers on both sides of the Iron Curtain, but these studies often failed to take into account the role of music in the very war that set the terms for the new world order in 1945. A lack of familiarity with politics and musical life before and during World War II at times left this field without a more informed context, leaving some to take at face value the disputed notion of a "zero hour" that claimed to reform all artistic enterprises after 1945 and to obliterate any fascist aesthetics that had previously prevailed.[10] In popular music studies as well, the emergence of rock and roll in the mid-1950s was often approached as something emerging ex nihilo, with only sketchy allusions to its wartime roots.

In the 2000s, attention to the other bookend of the short twentieth century would gather strength from the anniversary of World War I, as the politics of commemoration fostered a vibrant engagement with the interplay of music and war from 1914 to 1918. Research in the subject already had a solid foundation, as Glenn Watkins took the first step of surveying the music of World War I on an international scope, producing a work that stood as a model for understanding music's relationship to modern wars for many years thereafter. While most of his investigation focused on art music—both in service to the war and as a subtle commentary on the war—Watkins also examined popular song, jazz, and military music as powerful forces in sustaining the war effort.[11] That musicology would tend to privilege art music for some time should come as no surprise, as several generations of musicologists were trained exclusively in this domain. Musicology was beginning to acknowledge jazz and popular music as serious subjects of inquiry by this time, yet much of the interest in sheet music, recordings, popular songs, and performers of both world wars was being pursued outside the discipline.[12] Watkins clearly established the path for future studies to look at music and war in an international scope, even though the main focus of his work privileged Western Europe and the United States.[13] A conference volume that came out on the heels of Watkins's book successfully addressed the issue of incorporating other parts of Europe, branching out to include investigations of Russia, the Austro-Hungarian and Ottoman Empires, Spain, and Sweden.[14] A number of important contributions appearing in the next few years focused on the meaning of music and war in France, looking at art music and beyond and turning to popular culture, institutions, literary works, ephemeral literature, and musical as well as nonmusical artifacts to help reconstruct the everyday music-making and sonic experiences of war.[15]

Publications appearing around the World War I centennial have built on foundations established by earlier studies, looking for musical expressions in print sources and other material culture and broadening the scope of their investigations beyond well-known composers and institutions. Most of these publications have limited their investigations to individual countries but nevertheless have looked beyond art music compositions, musical tributes to the dead, and performances in concert halls and on opera stages to open up areas of investigation previously unimaginable in studies of music and war. These include a highly innovative examination of German postcards with musical themes that would have been exchanged between the battlefront and the home front[16] and a French exhibition that mines the artifacts of military music, song sheets, impromptu music-making at the front, and the spread of jazz, as well as the various sonic phenomena of the war in movie houses, medical interventions in hearing loss, and the role of silence.[17] Another collection coming out of France seeks to highlight lesser-known composers but also draws on such sources as private correspondence, memoirs, and newsletters to reconstruct musical activities at the battle lines and on the home front and to reveal how music-making provided a necessary distraction from the horrors of war for soldiers as well as civilians.[18] A special issue of *American Music* similarly considers the wartime careers of lesser-known composers and observes how they balanced musical obligations as songleaders and songwriters with their more serious compositional pursuits and how sheet music in Canada and Mexico negotiated complex national loyalties.[19] Christina Gier's monograph on American sheet music and recordings uses the material to explore how this music moved from promoting pacifism to supporting the war effort and recruitment, while also analyzing the content for what it can tell us about contemporary gender and race relations.[20]

There are also notable examples that take steps to broaden the scope of the subject both geographically and methodologically. The commemorative issue of the *Journal of Musicological Research* covers American, French, British, and German engagements in concert life, music at the front, music as an aid for recruitment and training, amateur music-making and its contributions to the war effort, settings of war-inspired poetry, and musical artifacts as private acts of mourning.[21] A special issue of the Belgrade-based journal *New Sound: International Journal of Music* not only took a corrective step in looking at wartime musical activities in countries that had previously received little attention (Serbia and Lithuania) but also accounted for the ways in which daily life had radically changed during the war years. That publication also moved toward situating World War I as the start of the short twentieth century in musical terms and surveying its impact over the next seven decades: the tradition of patriotic military music at the onset of the war, the changes brought by phonograph records in promoting international popular music (e.g., jazz and samba), and World War I allusions in heavy metal music.[22] Lastly, a collection of essays on popular song embraces the most comprehensive geographic coverage of the war theaters while also considering such aspects as patriotism, parody, gender, and the music business.[23]

At the time of this writing, Cold War music scholarship continues to be a robust field of inquiry, and we are still witnessing the impressive outpouring of studies on music and World War I.[24] Both of these events have generated an impressive body of work but at the same time have overshadowed direct engagements with that other pivotal moment in the short twentieth century, the Second World War.

## MUSIC IN WORLD WAR II: A MISSING LINK

In 1995, Leon Botstein's article "After Fifty Years: Thoughts on Music and the End of World War II" focused only marginally on the war years themselves, delving instead into questions about music's role in Nazi Germany, music in the concentration camps, and the overall legacy of modernism.[25] Botstein's interests were very much in keeping with the times, when the end of the Cold War and its comparisons to the end of the Third Reich discussed earlier coalesced with a heightened concentration of research into music and musicology under the Nazis (a project in which I was an active participant), music of the Holocaust, and the fate of exiled composers. As Botstein's observations imply, the more pressing task for musicologists at the time was to engage with the musical ramifications of policies emanating from Nazi Germany. Thus, instead of looking at music in World War II more broadly, the fifty-year mark inspired a closer look at the hardships endured by those terrorized by Nazi policies. This engagement was felt to be long overdue and generated entire subspecialties in music in the Holocaust, musicians in exile, and musical life in regions under German occupation.

Beginning in the 1980s, musicologists Fred Prieberg, Albrecht Dümling, and others had taken the bold steps of ending a tacitly imposed consensus of silence and opened the floodgates to scrutinizing musical activity in the Third Reich.[26] Their pioneering work was followed by an intense preoccupation with the victims of National Socialism that launched large and well-organized initiatives under the rubrics of "exile music," "degenerate music," and "suppressed music" and produced dozens of publications, exhibitions, and recordings. By the 1990s, musicologists were ready to tackle the grim task of exploring the music of the Holocaust, seeking to uncover the silenced art of those who desperately clung to the power of music to release them from their torment, first in the Nazi-sponsored Jewish Culture League and ultimately in the ghettos and camps. With the exception of continuous research in Russia on the folk and art music of the "Great Patriotic War," much of the work on wartime musical activity then concentrated on the German domination of France (in projects launched by Myriam Chimènes, Yannick Simon, Leslie Sprout, and Jane Fulcher), with some further investigations into the occupation of Belgium, Poland, Czechoslovakia, and Yugoslavia.

The importance of Nazi Germany for musicology is understandable, particularly if we take into account the vexing paradoxes this regime posed for the field. For more than a century prior to World War II, Germany had been recognized as the beacon of musical greatness, exporting a Germanocentric canon of music performance and education to many parts of the world. That Germany could devolve into a barbarity that would launch global war, exploit virulent racism and xenophobia, and ultimately carry out the slaughter of innocent civilians that would decimate Europe's Jewish population begged for answers to questions that were long overdue. And then there was the very nature of the war's end: the Allied defeat of the Axis nations carried with it a mission to eradicate the cultural legacies that presumably allowed such evil to thrive. Musicologists were less interested in trying to learn about the wartime music that might have played a role in inspiring such hatred and destruction; instead, much more value was placed on reanimating the silenced voices of the victims.

This did not mean that the musical dimensions of the war itself were completely neglected in those years, but much of the interest came from outside musicology. As the bibliography in the appendix to this volume illustrates, for some time prior to 2000 there had been considerable work on art music and popular music in the Second World War in several different fields—looking at the role of film, radio, recordings, and the music press, and to a lesser degree at music education and music scholarship—but this research remained decentralized. Since then, the study of music and World War II has yet to generate a full-fledged subdiscipline of musicology such as the Cold War has inspired, and—in contrast to World War I—no scholarly works have attempted to look beyond a single country's musical response to the war until now. All the same, the progress made in works dedicated to the music of World War II within specific national contexts has laid foundations for an international approach, while work on the histories of jazz, swing, and country music acknowledges the war period as a new era distinct from the Depression. If we look at a few of the prominent musicological monographs dedicated to the war that have appeared since 2000, we can observe how scholarship has sought to open inquiries into examining the impact of media, the integration of military and civilian efforts, the importance of diversion, the rise of popular music, the globalization of American culture, and the various roles music played in the war as a tool for diplomacy, indoctrination, resistance, and workplace productivity. Sherrie Tucker's pioneering investigation of all-female swing bands not only reanimated a forgotten demographic of widely popular ensembles that fell into obscurity after the war but also drew attention to the demand for entertainment and escape that characterized American musical tastes. Christina Baade's study of the BBC opened up another direction for understanding the role of music, exploring the many ways in which music broadcasting was harnessed to improve the morale of soldiers and civilians, increase productivity in factories, and offer diversion. In the process, ideals about the uplifting benefits of classical music had to give way to the popularity of dance music, jazz, and crooners, as BBC programmers wrestled with the incursion of American culture.[27]

Other work has turned to the realm of classical music, the wartime activities of composers, and the manipulation of music of the past toward serving patriotic aims. Annegret Fauser's comprehensive investigation of classical music in the United States surveys the institutions, government programs, and civilian and military engagement of composers and musicians, illustrating how classical music became a tool of ideology, diplomacy, even therapy, and how the quest for establishing an American musical identity had to negotiate ways to balance the contributions of European musical prototypes, American folk music, African American culture, and the recent influx of European exiles. Jane Fulcher's book on French classical music under Vichy and the German Occupation, her fourth monograph in a series exploring the politics and ideology of French musical life from the nineteenth century to the end of World War II, investigates the administrative changes following the German invasion and their effects on broadcasting, recording, education, and performance, and then follows the careers of Pierre Schaffer, Arthur Honegger, Francis Poulenc, and Olivier Messiaen in navigating the coexisting musical agendas of French and German leadership and the balancing act between resistance and collaboration.[28] Roberta Montemorra Marvin's study of Giuseppe Verdi's *Cantica* takes the investigation of art music in another direction, constructing a case study tracing the journey of Verdi's *Hymn of the Nations* (*Cantica—Inno delle nazioni*) from its original function as a tribute to Italian unification to its establishment as a "weapon of art" in World War II in the hands of Arturo Toscanini. Marvin analyzes how the conductor made no secret of his anti-Fascist position and used his international reputation to promote his politics, exploiting *Hymn of the Nations* first in a 1943 NBC radio broadcast and then in a propaganda film produced in collaboration with the US Office of War Information. Lastly, Leslie Sprout takes World War II as a starting point, tracing the wartime origins and postwar legacies of iconic works by Honegger, Stravinsky, Messiaen, Maurice Duruflé, and Poulenc. Her treatment examines the composers' interactions with Vichy, the Occupation, and the Resistance during the works' conception, and the truths and myths that shaped the postwar afterlife of each composition.[29]

As we commemorate the seventy-fifth anniversary of the end of World War II, there are compelling reasons why both a deeper and a broader investigation of its music is timely at this moment. Events unfolding in the late 1980s and 1990s may have left any potential to launch full-scale investigations of the music of World War II on its fiftieth anniversary in a state of limbo, but the new approaches pursued since then and the paths that have opened in redefining the relationship between music and war can only benefit our current investigation, as we find ourselves in a position to draw on approaches in music research that had not been available a quarter of a century ago. In particular, the examinations in this volume can take advantage of new tools that are essential to understanding the unique dynamics of music during the Second World War, applying methods advanced since the 1980s in areas such as sound studies, visual culture, popular music, material culture, film music, memory studies, and media studies. The progress made specifically in areas related to music and war is especially important to our endeavor. World War I commemorations have explored approaches that can be productively applied to World War II by exploiting untapped resources, adopting new methods, examining more diverse repertoires, and expanding the scope to include amateur as well as professional participation. Furthermore, the extensive body of work on the musical experiences of the victims of National Socialism provides sophisticated modes of inquiry into the roles of memory, displacement, community building, resistance, and escapism that could function among many other groups affected by the war. Both of these research areas have offered insights into the increasing importance of music as diversion, the sonic dimensions of warfare and incarceration, the precariousness of patriotism and national identity, and the importance of technology and material culture.

That being said, all of these innovative approaches need to be enhanced by the specific conditions of World War II. The purpose of this volume is to help forge the missing link between Cold War and World War I studies of music, but in a way that acknowledges the different tools required to comprehend how music and sound had taken on radically different functions by the time the Second World War began. To investigate the role of music in World War II, it no longer suffices to employ traditional musicological methods of examining art-music scores, because commissions from aristocratic patrons and institutions were no longer forthcoming as in wars past, and few composers and poets felt inspired to produce heroic and patriotic tributes on their own.

Not only did this war engulf a larger span of the globe than the First World War had, but, by the time it began in 1939, the nature of musical production, dissemination, and consumption had been radically transformed. Fauser pointed to a new direction for understanding the "sonic experience of war" by looking to the manner in which music was employed for war-related tasks in films, posters, books, newspapers, radio, and live performance. In addition, the unprecedented ways in which bombings, capture, and deportation brought the experience of war directly to civilians not only created a new sonic background of daily existence but also necessitated different types of musical diversion in shelters, bunkers, and camps. Understanding music in World War II requires investigating the powerful effects of technological advances on the impact of war, how these innovations transformed the war experience on the front and at home, and how changes to the ways of experiencing both war and music provided new avenues for forming communities and escaping reality.

The goal of *Music in World War II* is to apply these insights to an international and multidimensional examination of the musicscape of the war. The essays in this volume look to a broad range of media, venues for music-making, and repertoires, uncovering a prevailing tone of escapism as a replacement for the lofty, solemn, heroic, and celebratory mode of the "war music" of the past. Even in World War I, musical responses seemed to fit more comfortably into categories of promoting nationalism, denigrating the enemy, idealizing war and heroism, and bemoaning the fate of victims. The scholarship on music of the Great War could seek to demonstrate how composers, musicians, and songwriters became heavily engaged in rejecting the musical culture of the enemy and building a strong sense of national musical identity. But by the outbreak of World War II, these concerns had given way to other preoccupations. Following the end of World War I, survivors were caught up in coming to terms with the impact of the prolonged duration and global reach of the "war to end all wars"; the direct knowledge of the war's gruesomeness displayed by returning wounded veterans, narrative accounts, photographs, and film footage; the deprivation that came with the worldwide economic collapse; and the dangerous instability wrought by the fall of monarchies and the rise of dictatorships.

Simultaneously, the development of recording, broadcasting, and filming was starting to globalize and proliferate new forms of musical production and make them available to a diversifying mass of consumers. For several decades prior to World War II, rapid industrialization across Europe and the United States had led to radical demographic transformations that generated a completely new type of music public. As rural laborers and refugees fled to industrial centers to meet the need for cheap labor, new forms of entertainment venues and music industries arose to cater to emerging classes of consumers at all economic levels and with wide-ranging tastes. An industrial middle class amassed disposable income and sought to "better" itself through access to high culture, while state and educational interests felt the pressure to make this same high culture available to the uneducated with the purpose of "civilizing" and "uplifting" the faceless masses of workers, who were becoming increasingly diverse along national, ethnic, racial, social, and gender lines. But the simultaneous proliferation of other types of entertainment outlets—in the form of cabarets, vaudeville, band concerts, and amusement parks—stimulated a market to appeal to a broader range of tastes. Publishers and instrument makers—and eventually recording industries, broadcasters, and film studios—experienced a boom in these years, one that inspired both amazement and trepidation, motivating the Frankfurt School and especially Theodor Adorno to warn of the detrimental effects of an ever-growing "culture industry" on morale, self-worth, and individuality among the masses.

Technology was a central factor in drastically transforming both music and war by the time of the German invasion of Poland in September 1939. Sophistication in warfare had advanced well beyond the levels of World War I. The world knew all too well how the destructive capacities of weaponry had only increased with developments in waging battle in the air, on the sea, and on the ground. Advances in radar and communications, the transformation of aircraft from reconnaissance to artillery purposes, the introduction of armored tanks, and new missile and nuclear technologies had turned the two world wars into what Michael Howard called the "wars of the technologists," involving a far more complex interdependence of military and civilian support systems and expecting all members of society to do their part for the war effort as never before.[30]

Development of weapons and tactics after World War I already altered the sonic landscape on the battlefront and the home front. Particularly with the expanded deployment of air bombings, World War II created entirely new parameters for experiencing music and sound, subjecting civilians to the terrifying death knells of sirens and the deafening silences and muted rumblings of destruction that surrounded bunkers and bomb shelters.

Technology had its greatest musical impacts with the public access to radio, the expansion of the recording industry, and the invention of sound film, but these, too, changed the musical experience of war: instead of enhancing military efforts, media-generated music became an instrument of distraction. Despite the high-minded intentions of war offices and media administrators, efforts to use these media as sources of information, edification, and patriotism yielded to the public's desire to be transported to a time and place that would allow them to forget the war. Rather than dominating the musical offerings with edifying classical music or patriotically promoting the artistic achievements of domestic composers, radio programmers, record distributors, and film studios largely abandoned efforts to raise national consciousness and instead gave in to the demand for dancing, sentimentality, romance, and fantasy. With mounting competition from popular genres, opera houses and symphony orchestras had to find ways to repackage their traditional wares, sometimes enhancing them with technological gimmicks, sometimes touting their patriotic service to the war effort (even while continuing to program music originating from enemy countries).

The development of these media also had the unintended consequences of unprecedented exposure to American popular music throughout the world, frequently finding a following on enemy terrain. This went entirely counter to the hate campaigns operating within increasingly sophisticated propaganda mechanisms. Going beyond the propaganda of the First World War that characterized enemy soldiers and their leaders as subhuman beasts, such as the anti-German images of apes wearing the helmets of the Kaiser's army, the warring nations in World War II adopted even more vicious racist stereotypes of entire populations, including civilians, rendering them fair game for incarceration and, in the worst abuses, annihilation. But music—as a well-established international language— became one of the least effective tools for marking the enemy. During World War I, the Americans, French, and British already came to realize the futility of trying to demonize and suppress Austro-German music, because it had become the core repertoire of their own musical institutions, the foundation of their music education systems, and a model for their composers. This problem became even more complicated in World War II, as the flood of musicians escaping from Nazi discrimination posed the difficult question to the countries that took them in: were these German-speaking arrivals to be treated as enemies or asylum-seekers?

While it was tempting to engage their talents and publicize their sagas of escaping barbarism, were they not also importing the very culture that Allies should be intent on neutralizing, if not silencing all together? The same was true for Germany and German-occupied lands, where—rather than systematically suppressing imported American "mongrel" culture—those in charge turned a blind eye to its rising popularity and in some cases even promoted and reveled in its success.

## THE ESSAYS

The essays that comprise *Music in World War II* take into account the developments that transformed the musical experiences of war, and the authors represented in this volume apply a variety of methods to examine these experiences as broadly as possible. Although the essays offer a wider geographic diversity than did previous studies, they do not so much span the global breadth of the conflict as they do the breadth of musical experience. We do not offer in-depth studies of individual works of art music, in part because the volume of works created during the war as tributes to the war effort paled in comparison with all that had been produced during World War I, with the notable exception of the much-touted *Leningrad* Symphony by Dmitry Shostakovich (and to a lesser degree Sergei Prokofiev's opera *War and Peace*). Other considerations of the wartime behavior of "high culture" reveal instead how concert music had to find ways to compete for audiences and how practical concerns driving programming choices made it easier to supply program notes and advertising with wartime rhetoric than to scrap the products of enemy countries. A majority of the contributions explore the ways in which both old and new media had already transformed musical consumption and production in the years between the world wars. Radio was perhaps the most significant innovation, capable of bridging the combat front with the home front, but also balancing wartime restrictions on "enemy culture" (most notably in the case of jazz and swing) with giving the public the diversion they needed and supplying them with what they wanted to hear. Film provided one of the subtlest means for conveying messages of wartime ideology, and the recording industry presented a new way to experience music in the privacy of one's home, in bunkers, and in POW camps, offering creative ways to form communities. The turn toward escapism, however, was far more prevalent than the jingoism of earlier eras and could also be found in more traditional venues, such as musical theater, which thrived during the war by being ostentatiously evasive when it came to war-related themes.

Perhaps the most accessible source for music consumption during World War II was the radio. In response to war, broadcasters scrambled to transmit important information, enhance public education, and provide entertainment.

Two chapters examine the challenges and debates about music broadcasting at the BBC, one of the most storied broadcasting organizations in World War II. Christina Baade's chapter ("*Sandy Calling*: Forging an Intimate Wartime Public at the BBC Theater Organ") illustrates how music programming had become an unsuspecting ideological battleground, as administrators struggled to maintain a grip on music's powers of edification and uplift while dealing with the public's preference for light, sentimental music that was easy to listen to and that could also vicariously reunite soldiers with the loved ones they left behind. Tony Stoller ("'Alien' Classical Musicians and the BBC, 1939–1945") explores another dimension of ideological dilemmas within the BBC, as they had to address complex questions of how to handle the music of the enemy as the war progressed, a particularly vexing conundrum, since classical music repertoire was predominantly Austro-German and Italian. Realizing the impracticality of banning all German, Austrian, and Italian music, very few changes in programming took hold either during or after the war.

The challenge of identifying enemies and allies through their music is a common theme throughout several of the essays. The ambiguities in programming German, Austrian, and Italian music on the BBC posed fewer complications than did the situation at the Metropolitan Opera, as investigated by Christopher Lynch ("The Metropolitan Opera House and the 'War of Ideologies': The Politics of Opera Publicity in Wartime"), simply because opera productions had to be planned and budgeted years in advance. The cost and disruption of canceling the core repertoire of Italian and German works was unfathomable; the solution, instead, was to engage the community of refugees (conductors, musicologists, performers) to testify to the importance of the ideological war in which the United States was engaged and to use advertising and other supporting texts to employ rhetorical devices to convey the patriotic mission of the opera house. An equally daunting challenge existed for filmmakers who—prompted by government mandates—had to find subtle ways to enhance images of enemies as well as allies through musical scoring. Peter Kupfer ("Musical 'Diplomacy' in American and Soviet World War II Films of the 1940s") examines one of the biggest challenges posed to filmmakers and composers in the United States and the Soviet Union: trying to turn their ideological archrivals into sympathetic allies for the purposes of the war effort, only to completely undermine these efforts both musically and cinematically when the two resumed their adversarial relationship in the Cold War.

The globalization of music, combined with the demand for pure entertainment, served to further subvert any musical distinctions between "us" and "them," especially in the case of jazz and swing. As Brian S. Locke lays out in his investigation of the German occupation of Czechoslovakia ("Swing in the

Protectorate: Czech Popular Music under the Nazi Occupation, 1938–1945"), the brutality under Reinhard Heydrich and the retribution meted out after his assassination did not extend to suppressing even the music that Nazi propaganda had vilified as "degenerate" on the eve of the occupation. Quite to the contrary, the period of German occupation witnessed a flourishing of Czech swing that would come to be regarded nostalgically as the "Golden Years" after the Soviets introduced draconian measures to suppress "imperialist" American music during the Cold War. The thirst for pure entertainment also transformed the classical music experience in Vienna into a multimedia extravaganza, while simultaneously demonstrating how the *Anschluss* fostered an environment for Austrian music to thrive both economically and culturally. Nicholas Attfield ("Throwing Some Light on the *Dunkelkonzerte*: Toward a New Image of Concert Life in Vienna, 1939–1944") shows how the "dark concerts" were not the result of orders to darken concert halls during air raids, as is commonly assumed, but rather were an innovative theatrical stunt to make classical music concerts more entertaining. On Broadway as well, escapism proved to be more important than bolstering the war effort, as it became clear that any commentary on the war risked alienating audiences, and a safer route was to let pure entertainment prevail (Tim Carter, "Broadway Goes to War"). The war proved lucrative for the profit-driven industry of musical theater, whose audiences were swelled in part by soldiers enjoying a few final days in New York before shipping out to Europe.

The war also forced many civilians and soldiers alike to subsist in confinement, whether in camps, prisons, or air raid shelters. Three essays in this volume look at different circumstances in which such restrictions increasingly made music an essential component of daily existence. Although Olivier Messiaen's *Quartet for the End of Time*, written and performed in a POW camp, has been canonized as an act of resistance against Nazi inhumanity, Christopher Brent Murray's essay ("Before the End of Time: General Huntziger's Centre Musical et Théâtral") paints a very different picture of Messiaen's experiences. The essay reveals a musical vibrancy in the military unit to which the composer was assigned that persisted as its members were taken captive, released, integrated into Vichy society, and invited to participate in state-sponsored propaganda. Kelsey Kramer McGinnis ("A Musical Reeducation: Music-Making in America's German POW Camps and the Intellectual Diversion Program") reveals another side of POW existence, in which German prisoners in a camp in Iowa were allowed to run their own music programs that reinforced their loyalty to Germany and ties to home. Their presence in the surrounding community also gave Iowans direct contact with and a more human image of the enemy. Lastly, Abby Anderton ("Bunkers, Cellars, and Acoustic Memory: Sonic Experiences of War and Surrender in Nazi Germany") looks at a very different type of confinement in air raid shelters, bunkers, and cellars, where music took on a wide range of functions to divert attention from the rampant devastation outside their protective walls, to fill the dreaded silence, and to compete with the raw sounds of combat on city streets in the final stages of the war.

The topics covered in these essays represent both the current state of the field and promising new directions for the future. The emphasis on Europe and the United States reflects a state of scholarship in which World War II is a prominent operative concept in the study of music in Europe and North America, whereas a shortage of research focusing on Asian, African, and Middle Eastern contexts can be attributed to the longer histories of conflict and colonialism in those regions. As we solicited contributions, we started to recognize that by fixing World War II between the years 1939 and 1945 we were implicitly setting up our framework as a primarily European and American concern. However, a simple attempt to widen our scope to include musical experiences in other theaters of war between 1939 and 1945 would not do justice to the very different causes for which those nations and peoples were fighting. We also noted, nevertheless, that much of the work we were seeing was pushing the boundaries of traditional music research, even while operating within these geographic and chronological boundaries.

We also set our intention on highlighting innovative approaches to examining music's role in coming to terms with the conditions of war under various circumstances and covering topics that have up to now received little attention. In surveying the field, we came to realize that engagements with music of the Holocaust and music in exile had been actively ongoing since the 1980s, creating their own subdisciplines and generating vast amounts of scholarship, recordings, and performances. While none of the essays is devoted exclusively to music in Nazi concentration camps, however, the methods of incarceration introduced in World War II—POW camps, concentration camps, death camps, internment camps, and ghettos—held in common the ways that these settings brought civilians face-to-face with actual human beings they were supposed to hate, not pity. The use of concentration camp inmates as slave labor on the German home front occupied one end of this spectrum, while the mutually beneficial employment of POWs as farmhands in Iowa stood at the opposite end. Essays included here highlight the differences as well as the similarities among these environments, where music seemed to play a crucial role in maintaining ties to an idealized "home" and constructing notions of identity and community.

We envision these essays as a staging ground for investigations into the impact of new technologies, globalization, and the shifting relationship between music and war. We further anticipate that this collection will serve as a springboard for engagement with the musical and sonic dimensions of the war that will push beyond the limits of Europe and the United States and move in both directions beyond the years 1939 and 1945. The relationship between music and war has become something unrecognizable from what it was a century ago because the nature of both war and music has undergone such radical transformations. The war that marked the start of the short twentieth century gave rise to new forms of musical entertainment that have changed dramatically up to the present, and we see the work represented in this volume as a productive start to filling crucial gaps in tracking the transformation of music's role in wartime and its meaning for society.

## NOTES

1. See, for example, Jardin, ed., *Music and War in Europe from French Revolution to WWI*.
2. See the essays in Kraaz, ed., *Music and War in the United States*.
3. "Music Torture"; see also Cusick, "'You Are in a Place That Is Out of the World'"; Ross, "When Music Is Violence."
4. Weinberg, *A World at Arms*; Bayly, *Forgotten Wars*; Grosul, "Kogda nachalas' Vtoraya mirovaya voyna"; and Zhang, "Two Starting Points."
5. Hobsbawm, *Age of Extremes*, 1–17.
6. Morgan, *Twentieth-Century Music*; Salzman, *Twentieth-Century Music*; Watkins, *Soundings*; Simms, *Music of the Twentieth Century*.
7. *Bericht über die wissenschaftliche Konferenz anlässlich des 69. Bachfestes*.
8. The dialogue continued at the conference *Verfemte Musik* (Proscribed Music), shedding light on the complexities of comparing the two systems. Braun et al., eds., *Verfemte Musik*, 1–18; 284.
9. See Schmelz, "Introduction."
10. On the "zero hour," see Colpa, "Germany's 'Zero-Hour Myth'"; and Scherliess, ed., "*Stunde Null.*" See also Potter review of Monod, *Settling Scores*; and Potter review of Beal, *New Music, New Allies*.
11. Watkins, *Proof through the Night*.
12. Murdoch, *Fighting Songs and Warring Words*; Arthur, *When This Bloody War Is Over*; Brophy and Partridge, *The Long Trail*; Parker, *World War I Sheet Music*; Vogel, *World War I Songs*; Mullen, *The Show Must Go On!*; Wilson, *Soldiers of Song*; and Tyler, *Music of the First World War*. For further references to similar publications on World War II, see the Selected Works at the end of this book.
13. Historians at this time were already noticing the neglect of Eastern and Central Europe in studies of the culture of World War I; see Roshwald and Stites, eds., *European Culture in the Great War*.
14. Brüstle, Heldt, and Weber, eds., *Von Grenzen und Ländern, Zentren und Rändern*.
15. Sweeney, *Singing Our Way to Victory*; Fulcher, *The Composer as Intellectual*; Audoin-Rouzeau et al., eds., *La Grande Guerre des musiciens*; Moore, *Performing Propaganda*.
16. Giesebrecht, *Musik und Propaganda*.

17. Gétreau, ed., *Entendre la guerre*.
18. Doé de Maindreville and Etcharry, eds., *La Grande Guerre en musique*.
19. Magee, ed., "Special Issue: Music and the Great War."
20. Gier, *Singing, Soldiering, and Sheet Music*.
21. Kauffman, ed., "Special Issue: Music and the Great War."
22. "The early 20th century: an age of social, cultural, individual transitions and contradictions, and an age when these contradictions were big in size, loud in sound, fast in time. An age when people witnessed daily revolutions of nearly any sort: cars in the streets; one or two airplanes in the sky; psychoanalysis, department stores, great exhibitions; entire social (anthropological, in fact!) categories, like women or workers, claiming, shouting their right to play a role in society; artists of any field questioning nearly any existing preconception of what arts should look or sound like; capitalistic actions and socialist ideas reaching the dramatic, yet poignant, peak of their confrontation . . . and, along with all of this, phonographs, café chantants, noise-intoners, hexatonic scales, microtonal works. It was the age of wisdom, it was the age of foolishness. It was the epoch of belief, it was the epoch of incredulity.

"Then came the war, the Great War. The war that invented globality: the loudest and biggest of them all, but not the fastest. It was supposed to be the fastest, it ended up in a tragedy the world had not yet witnessed, and would hardly witness afterwards. And the contradictions went on: those who opposed the war, those who welcomed it; the artists who portrayed its tragedy, the artists who celebrated its grandeur; the social classes that profited from it, and the social classes that were sent to the Front." Martinelli, "Introduction," 30.
23. Mullen, ed., *Popular Song in the First World War*.
24. Recent work includes Brooks et al., eds., *Over Here, Over There*.
25. Botstein, "After Fifty Years."
26. Prieberg, *Musik im NS-Staat*; Heister and Klein, eds., *Musik und Musikpolitik im faschistischen Deutschland*; Dümling and Girth, eds., *Entartete Musik*.
27. Tucker, *Swing Shift*; Baade, *Victory through Harmony*.
28. Fauser, *Sounds of War*; Fulcher, *Renegotiating French Identity*. Fulcher's previous works are: *The Nation's Image*; *French Cultural Politics and Music*; and *The Composer as Intellectual*, cited above.
29. Marvin, *Politics of Verdi's* Cantica; Sprout, *Musical Legacy*.
30. Howard, *War in European History*, chapter 7.

## BIBLIOGRAPHY

Arthur, Max. *When This Bloody War Is Over: Soldiers' Songs of the First World War.* London: Piatkus, 2001.

Audoin-Rouzeau, Stéphane, Esteban Buch, Myriam Chimènes, and Georgie Durosoir, eds. *La Grande Guerre des musiciens.* Collection Perpetuum mobile. Lyon: Symétrie, 2009.

Baade, Christina. *Victory through Harmony: The BBC and Popular Music in World War II*. New York: Oxford University Press, 2012.

Bayly, Christopher Alan. *Forgotten Wars: The End of Britain's Asian Empire*. London: Allen Lane, 2007.

*Bericht über die wissenschaftliche Konferenz anlässlich des 69. Bachfestes der neuen Bachgesellschaft, Leipzig, 29. und 30. März 1994*. Leipziger Beiträge zur Bach-Forschung. Hildesheim: Georg Olms, 1995.

Botstein, Leon. "After Fifty Years: Thoughts on Music and the End of World War II." *The Musical Quarterly* 79, no. 2 (Summer 1995): 225–230.

Braun, Joachim, Heidi Tamar Hoffmann, and Vladimir Karbusický, eds. *Verfemte Musik: Komponisten in den Diktaturen unseres Jahrhunderts*. Frankfurt: Peter Lang, 1997.

Brooks, William, Christina Bashford, and Gayle Magee, eds. *Over Here, Over There: Transatlantic Conversations on the Music of World War I*. Urbana: University of Illinois Press, 2019.

Brophy, John, and Eric Partridge. *The Long Trail: What the British Soldier Sang and Said in the Great War of 1914–1918*. London: A. Deutsch, 1965.

Brüstle, Christa, Guido Heldt, and Eckhard Weber, eds. *Von Grenzen und Ländern, Zentren und Rändern: Der Erste Weltkrieg und die Verschiebungen in der musikalischen Geographie Europas*. Schliengen: Edition Argus, 2006.

Colpa, J. Alexander. "Germany's 'Zero-Hour Myth' as a Context for the Stylistic Evolution in the Orchestral Music of Wolfgang Fortner (1907–1987)." Ph.D. diss., New York University, 2002.

Cusick, Suzanne G. "'You Are in a Place That Is Out of the World'": Music in the Detention Camps of the 'Global War on Terror.'" *Journal of the Society for American Music* 2, no. 1 (2008): 1–26. Reprinted in *Transpositions* 4 (2014).

Doé de Maindreville, Florence, and Stéphan Etcharry, eds. *La Grande Guerre en musique: Vie et création musicales en France pendant la Première Guerre mondiale*. Brussels: Peter Lang, 2014.

Dümling, Albrecht, and Peter Girth, eds. *Entartete Musik: Eine kommentierte Rekonstruktion*. Düsseldorf: Service-Druck Kleinherne, 1988.

Fauser, Annegret. *Sounds of War: Music in the United States during World War II*. New York: Oxford University Press, 2013.

Fulcher, Jane F. *The Composer as Intellectual: Music and Ideology in France, 1914–1940*. Oxford: Oxford University Press, 2005.

———. *French Cultural Politics and Music: From the Dreyfus Affair to the First World War*. New York: Oxford University Press, 1999.

———. *The Nation's Image: French Grand Opera as Politics and Politicized Art*. Cambridge: Cambridge University Press, 1987.

———. *Renegotiating French Identity: Musical Culture and Creativity in France during Vichy and the German Occupation*. New York: Oxford University Press, 2018.

Gétreau, Florence, ed. *Entendre la guerre: silence, musiques et sons en 14–18*. Paris: Gallimard; Historial de la Grande Guerre, 2014.

Gier, Christina. *Singing, Soldiering, and Sheet Music in America during the First World War*. Lanham, MD: Lexington Books, 2017.

Giesebrecht, Sabine. *Musik und Propaganda: Der Erste Weltkrieg im Spiegel deutscher Bildpostkarten*. Beiträge zur Medienästhetik der Musik. Osnabrück: Electronic Publishing Osnabrück, 2014. 2nd ed., 2016.

Grosul, Vladislav Yakimovich. "Kogda nachalas' Vtoraya mirovaya voyna [When the Second World War Began]." *Novaya i Noveyshaya Istoriya* 2010, no. 3 (2010): 230–233.

Heister, Hanns-Werner, and Hans-Günter Klein, eds. *Musik und Musikpolitik im faschistischen Deutschland*. Frankfurt: Fischer, 1984.

Hobsbawm, Eric. *The Age of Extremes: A History of the World, 1914–1991*. New York: Pantheon Books, 1994.

Howard, Michael. *War in European History*. Oxford: Oxford University Press, 1976.

Jardin, Étienne, ed. *Music and War in Europe from French Revolution to WWI*. Turnhout: Brepols, 2016.

Kauffman, Deborah, ed. "Special Issue: Music and the Great War." *Journal of Musicological Research* 33, no. 1–3 (2014).

Kraaz, Sarah, ed. *Music and War in the United States*. New York: Routledge, 2019.

Magee, Gayle, ed. "Special Issue: Music and the Great War." *American Music* 34, no. 4 (Winter 2014).

Martinelli, Dario, ed. "Special Issue: Music around the First World War and Stevan St. Mokranjac." *New Sound: International Journal of Music* 44 (2014).

Martinelli, Dario. "Introduction." In Dario Martinelli, ed. "Special Issue: Music around the First World War and Stevan St. Mokranjac." *New Sound: International Journal of Music* 44 (2014): 29–32.

Marvin, Roberta Montemorra. *The Politics of Verdi's Cantica*. Royal Musical Association Monographs. Farnham, Surrey: Ashgate, 2014.

Moore, Rachel. *Performing Propaganda: Musical Life and Culture in Paris, 1914–1918*. Woodbridge: Boydell, 2018.

Morgan, Robert P. *Twentieth-Century Music: A History of Musical Style in Modern Europe and America*. New York: W. W. Norton, 1991.

Mullen, John. *Popular Song in the First World War: An International Perspective*. New York: Routledge, 2019.

———, ed. *The Show Must Go On! Popular Song in Britain during the First World War*. Surrey: Ashgate, 2015; originally published in French, 2012.

Murdoch, Brian O. *Fighting Songs and Warring Words: Popular Lyrics of Two World Wars*. London: Routledge, 1990.

"Music Torture: How Heavy Metal Broke Manuel Noriega." *BBC News*, 30 May 2017. Accessed February 27, 2018. http://www.bbc.com/news/world-latin-america-40090809.

Parker, Bernard S. *World War I Sheet Music: 9,670 Patriotic Songs Published in the United States, 1914–1920*. Jefferson, NC: McFarland, 2007.

Potter, Pamela M. Review of *New Music, New Allies: American Experimental Music in West Germany from the Zero Hour to Reunification*, by Amy Beal. *German Politics and Society* 25 (2007): 111–115.

———. Review of *Settling Scores: German Music, Denazification, and the Americans, 1945–1953*, by David Monod. *Central European History* 39, no. 2 (2006): 350–352.

Prieberg, Fred K. *Musik im NS-Staat*. Frankfurt: Fischer Verlag, 1982.

Roshwald, Aviel, and Richard Stites, eds. *European Culture in the Great War: The Arts, Entertainment, and Propaganda, 1914–1918*. Cambridge: Cambridge University Press, 1999.

Ross, Alex. "When Music Is Violence." *New Yorker*, July 4, 2016.

Salzman, Eric. *Twentieth-Century Music: An Introduction*. Prentice Hall History of Music Series. Upper Saddle River, NJ: Prentice Hall, 1967.

Scherliess, Volker, ed. *"Stunde Null": Zur Musik um 1945; Bericht über das Symposion der Gesellschaft für Musikforschung an der Musikhochschule Lübeck 24.–27. September 2003*. Kassel: Bärenreiter, 2014.

Schmelz, Peter. "Introduction: Music in the Cold War." *Journal of Musicology* 26, no. 1 (Winter 2009): 3–16.

Simms, Bryan. *Music of the Twentieth Century: Style and Structure*. New York: Schirmer, 1986.

Sprout, Leslie. *The Musical Legacy of Wartime France*. Berkeley: University of California Press, 2013.

Sweeney, Regina. *Singing Our Way to Victory: French Cultural Politics and Music during the Great War*. Hanover, NH: Wesleyan University Press, 2001.

Tucker, Sherrie. *Swing Shift: "All-Girl" Bands of the 1940s*. Durham, NC: Duke University Press, 2000.

Tyler, Don. *Music of the First World War*. Santa Barbara, CA: ABC-Clio, 2016.

Vogel, Frederick G. *World War I Songs: A History and Dictionary of Popular American Patriotic Tunes*. Jefferson, NC: McFarland, 1995.

Watkins, Glenn. *Proof through the Night: Music and the Great War*. Berkeley: University of California Press, 2003.

———. *Soundings: Music in the Twentieth Century*. New York: Schirmer, 1988.

Weinberg, Gerhard L. *A World at Arms: A Global History of World War II*. Cambridge: Cambridge University Press, 1994.

Wilson, Jason. *Soldiers of Song: The Dumbells and Other Canadian Concert Parties of the First World War*. Waterloo, ON: Wilfrid Laurier University Press, 2012.

Zhang, Haipang. "The Two Starting Points of World War II: A Reexamination from a Global Perspective." *Journal of Modern Chinese History* 10, no. 1 (2016): 52–66.

PAMELA M. POTTER is Professor of German and Music at the University of Wisconsin-Madison. She is author of *Most German of the Arts: Musicology and Society from the Weimar Republic to the End of Hitler's Reich* and *Art of Suppression: Confronting the Nazi Past in Histories of the Visual and Performing Arts* and editor (with Celia Applegate) of *Music and German National Identity*.

PART I

**ON THE AIRWAVES AND THE SCREEN**

ONE

## *SANDY CALLING*

Forging an Intimate Wartime Public at the BBC Theater Organ

CHRISTINA L. BAADE

ON DECEMBER 28, 1941, THE *Sunday Pictorial* published a profile of Sandy Macpherson, the British Broadcasting Corporation's resident theater organist, calling him "a radio fairy godfather." The profile offered a few tidbits about Macpherson—he was Canadian, "easy-going," and "quite unconceited and unawed by his fame"—but its main focus was on how, with the help of his theater organ, "radio's most human personality" could unite families separated by war through the magic of radio. Describing Macpherson as "probably the BBC's best contribution to the war so far," the article celebrated his requests or messages programs, in which listeners wrote in with a song request and a message for a family member in the hopes that Sandy would include it in one of his broadcasts, which were heard at home (*Sandy's Half-Hour*) and abroad (*Sandy Calling the Middle East, Sandy's Half-Hour for Canada, Sandy Calling India*).[1] The article opened with a vivid depiction of one such moment:

> Somewhere in the Middle East a soldier is listening to the camp's radio set, tuned in on Britain. He is listening with one ear to organ music, while he is writing a letter home. Then he sits bolt upright, for the quiet voice of the radio has given out his name.
>
> *I have a request for Gunner Smith from his wife and small daughter. The tune is "I'll Walk Beside You." And your wife hopes, Gunner Smith, that you'll have a happy birthday.*
>
> That is the sort of little human miracle that happens to dozens of families every week, and the man who is responsible is Sandy Macpherson, BBC organist.[2]

The power of Macpherson's broadcasts lay not simply in the connections they offered for those lucky enough to be selected, but in the public acknowledgment they represented for everyone separated by the war—demonstrating that the personal sensation of longing was also a public experience, a mark of participation in the nation's war effort.

The potency of Gunner Smith's story resided in what listeners had long understood: skillful broadcasters sounded like they were speaking directly to you, but it was an illusion—except when Sandy Macpherson actually *did* say your name. By the start of World War II, radio was established as a mass medium that offered an intimate listening experience. This duality was at the heart of radio's "intimate public," the term Jason Loviglio coined to describe the "new cultural space created by radio broadcasting," with its ability to cross between—and sometimes transgress—the boundaries of public and private. As Loviglio observed, "Radio voices were thrilling because they moved with impunity back and forth from private to public modes of performance"; however, that very movement also highlighted contestations over where the line between public and private should be drawn and who got to decide.[3]

As I show in this chapter, Macpherson's powerful appeal to wartime listeners was rooted in his ability to bridge modes of personal and public address in his radio performances, but his straddling of these modes also inspired intense ambivalence for leaders at the BBC and even the War Office. For the British, World War II itself was a moment when traditional boundaries between public and private were called into question—most strikingly when noncombatants became targets in the Blitz—but also in government measures that impacted everyday private life through rationing, national service, and propaganda, which suggested there was a proper way for citizens to *feel* about the war.[4] For his critics, the question was whether Macpherson and his organ encouraged the sort of public feeling—particularly among the forces—that would help Britain win the war. Would reminders of home stiffen the resolve of the fighting forces, or would they undermine their morale?

A corollary to these questions involved *how* longing could be expressed on the air, what emotional registers were acceptable in its expression, and who should be allowed to articulate it. In his broadcasts, Macpherson centered the often sentimental and clichéd words, voices, and musical choices of ordinary people—men, women, and even children—using the theater organ, an instrument that was closely associated with modern mass culture and, for some, overly emotional bad taste. By foregrounding popular song, ordinary voices, and "affective and emotional attachments," Macpherson's programs participated in another form of "intimate public," articulated by Lauren Berlant, which "operates when a market opens up to a bloc of consumers, claiming to circulate texts and things that express those people's particular core interests and desires"—in this case, ordinary Britons separated by war.[5] While sharing with Loviglio an interest in mediatized tensions between private and public, the locus of Berlant's intimate public was commercial entertainment, sentimentality, and public femininity—topics that became flashpoints in wartime debates about Macpherson, his messages programs, and cinema organs in general. It was not simply Macpherson's movement between a public and personal address that drove his popularity with listeners and, simultaneously, ambivalence from the BBC leadership; it was also the ways in which music and speech on his programs forged an intimate public in Berlant's sense.

Published in the last days of 1941, the *Sunday Pictorial* article captured a high point in Macpherson's wartime radio work. From the earliest days of the war, listeners and the more populist critics celebrated Macpherson's reassuring presence and provision of popular entertainment. Highbrows might chafe, but airing popular music and family messages seemed a sure way to boost morale—including that of Gunner Smith "somewhere in the Middle East." The *Sunday Pictorial*'s celebratory tone affirmed this approach, particularly with the still-fresh memory of the British army's success at Tobruk, Libya, where it had ended a 242-day siege on December 7 (a victory overshadowed by news of the Pearl Harbor attack). However, significant military setbacks in early 1942 raised fresh concerns about morale and the effects of sentimental music on the radio. In this climate—and with new leadership at the BBC (Sir Cecil Graves and Robert Foot became joint directors-general in January 1942; Arthur Bliss became the new Music Department head in April)—Macpherson's programs, the intimate public they fostered, and even the theater organ itself became subject to censure, despite their continued popularity among listeners. Throughout the war, Macpherson, his programs, and the theater organ continued to inspire both affection and animus—responses that hinged in no small part on the two notions of intimate public advanced by Loviglio and Berlant.

## "POPULAR ENTERTAINMENT FOR THE MASSES": THEATER ORGANS AT THE BBC

In December 1941, around the time that *Sunday Pictorial*'s readers learned about Gunner Smith, the composer and BBC Overseas Music Director Arthur Bliss penned some thoughts about the theater organ and its enthusiasts. In an early draft of what would become the BBC's new music policy, he wrote: "The delight Caliban takes in [the theater organ] is its evocative power to recall the hand-holding atmosphere of a cinema, where he can enjoy, suffer, and live vicariously. Certain successions of chords free the tear glands; the music starts a physical sensation of a cloying kind, offensive to a vigorous mind. The cinema organ exploits with skill its red plush quality.... It is a dope as insidious as opium."[6]

Infantilizing, emotional, and escapist, the theater organ embodied the worst of modern mass entertainment for Bliss, who would soon bring his musical standards and sense of mission to his new role as BBC director of music. Bliss did not spare those who liked the instrument: by citing "Caliban," the savage half-monster who inhabited Prospero's island in Shakespeare's *Tempest*, he not only underlined the baseness of their tastes but also cast them as antithetical to the BBC's mission of cultural uplift, which was symbolized by Prospero and the spirit Ariel, whose images stood in relief over the main entrance of Broadcasting House.[7]

Although Bliss's rhetoric situated the theater organ firmly within the "red plush" realm of the cinema, he was, in actuality, attacking a well-established component of BBC entertainment broadcasting. Critics might have considered the cinema organ to be the illegitimate sibling of the church organ, but, from the 1920s the BBC treated it as respectable popular entertainment that might become a gateway to "better," more serious musical fare. Indeed, cinema organs remained popular in the United Kingdom well into the sound film era, helped, in part, by the BBC's promotion and patronage. When, in 1936, the BBC acquired a state-of-the-art Compton organ, the *Times* of London described theater organs as *the* most popular entertainment offered by the BBC, outpacing dance bands and variety.[8]

Such an assertion may seem surprising, given the marginalization of theater organs in popular music histories.[9] However, with their streamlined consoles, "powerful pipework," and electronic circuitry, cinema organs embodied modern ideals of design and efficiency.[10] They first arrived in the United Kingdom from the United States in 1925, but the origins story went back to the nineteenth century.[11] According to Reginald Foort, who became the BBC's first resident theater organist, the instrument was born from an Anglo-American marriage between the "ideas and inventions" of the British church musician, organ builder, and electrical engineer Robert Hope-Jones and the industrial expertise of the Americans Farny and Howard Wurlitzer.[12] The Wurlitzers and other manufacturers promoted their organs as "one-man orchestras," which replaced the costs and hassles of employing an orchestra. Cinema and other venue owners would gain an instrument that offered a wide dynamic and timbral palette, abundant tuned percussion, special sound effects, and the distinctive flute-like Tibia Clausa, to which tremulant, a powerful vibrato, was almost always applied. As Foort explained, the cinema organ could "represent in turn a symphony orchestra, a cathedral organ, or a jazz-band. An almost lifelike reproduction in sound can be produced for any incident occurring on the screen, such as a baby crying, a barrel-organ, or a train starting. Sentimental love-scenes, dramatic outbursts, sinister villainies, sorrow, happiness, and the whole gamut of human emotions can be illustrated with equal facility."[13]

Whereas the theater organ's flexibility was celebrated by performers such as Foort, its sound effects and bricolage repertoire earned the enmity of others, such as the music-loving neighbor of the Maida Vale Palace, who the *Times* reported "did not like cinema music. One caught snatches of a Beethoven sonata, followed by 'The Girl I Left Behind Me,' and it was maddening."[14] Of course, cinema organists were not concertizing, nor were they guiding listeners in religious contemplation; rather, their job was to accompany silent films, and then, with the arrival of sound film, to engage a restive audience for a ten-minute interlude, using the right blend of familiarity, novelty, and showmanship. As the indefatigable Foort explained, "The cinema organ is designed . . . purely for the purpose of *entertaining an audience*."[15]

The sound of the theater organ carried powerful associations with the cinema, as physical space and as leisure pursuit. As Jackie Stacey and others have discussed, the cinema was an affordable luxury that offered a temporary escape into a glamorous world. Patrons experienced glamour not only through the filmic spectacle but also by occupying the space of the cinema, which offered a range of sensuous luxuries: marble entryways, solicitous ushers, plush seats, rich decorations, and even warmth—a delightful sensation, given the cost of heating and Britain's damp climate. Within this world of glamour and abundance, cinemagoers also experienced a sense of community and of membership in an intimate public built around the emotional language of Hollywood film. No wonder that cinema-going was such a popular activity during the interwar period—and even more so during the war—particularly among women.[16] For some, such as Bliss or the Maida Vale music lover, however, the theater organ's cinematic associations were a problem.

On radio, the sound of the cinema organ did not merely evoke the cinema as a site of pleasure, emotion, or escapism but it also dramatized the BBC's ability to take the radio microphone to venues beyond the studio. Theater organ broadcasting became a regular feature on the BBC during the late 1920s, at the same time that the Corporation expanded its Outside Broadcasting Unit (whose mobile units covered sporting and other events) and improved its relations with major variety syndicates. These broadcasts did not evoke the cinema in a generalized way; rather, the BBC's outside broadcasts featured particular organists playing particular organs at specific cinemas throughout the United Kingdom on an almost daily basis by the mid-1930s. Given the often-fraught relationship between the BBC, as the national broadcaster based in London, and the rest of the country, an airing by an organist at a cinema outside the capital was an easy (and inexpensive) way to promote regional representation and cater to local pride.

The difficulty was reconciling the tight scheduling of cinemas with that of the BBC. (It was not practical to broadcast when an audience was actually *in* the cinema.) In 1936, the BBC arrived at a partial solution when it invested in its own

Fig. 1.1. Reginald Foort and his Moller organ. Screenshot from British Pathé (1936).

£8,000 four-manual, British-made Compton organ; installed it in St. George's Hall, a former theater in central London that the BBC had acquired for variety broadcasting; and hired Foort (from a pool of 350 applicants) to serve as resident organist, a role that also involved administering all theater organ programming at the BBC.[17] John Watt, the BBC's director of the Variety Department (which was in charge of theater organ programming), was reluctant to hire Foort because he was already a "star personality," who might resist the administrative aspects of the job and, like the bandleaders Jack Payne and Henry Hall before him, use his BBC contract "to make a big name for himself."[18]

Watt's fears about Foort proved to be at least partially founded: the organist stayed with the Corporation for only two years and then departed to tour as a soloist in Variety, along with his gargantuan, yet portable, Moller organ (see fig. 1.1).[19] However, the Rugby- and Royal College of Music (RCM)-educated Foort, with his charisma, Englishness, and classical music credentials, had worked tirelessly in promoting theater organs as respectable popular entertainment on the BBC—paving the way for his Canadian-born successor, Sandy Macpherson. If, when the cinema organ was introduced to Britain in the mid-1920s, it was quite literally an American import, by the end of the 1930s it had become an appropriately ambivalent icon of British popular modernity for what Foort called "a more organ-minded country."[20]

By the start of the war, theater organs, played by Macpherson along with dozens of organists around the country, were fixtures in the BBC's entertainment offerings—in outside broadcasts, in recitals on the BBC's Compton, in variety shows, and as providers of incidental and "fill-up" music.[21] Though members of the BBC leadership might have been personally ambivalent about the theater organ, they recognized its importance, especially given growing pressures on the Corporation to be more responsive to popular tastes. As Watt explained to his superior, Basil Nicolls, the controller of Programmes, "There are lots of things we do in programmes that I personally do not like as entertainment to amuse me, but regard them as technical exercises in popular entertainment for the masses which we, as professional purveyors of entertainment should do, and do as well as they can be done."[22] The war would make this task more difficult—and more necessary—than ever.

## "HE HELD THE BBC FORT": MACPHERSON AS WARTIME PERSONALITY

In September 1939, a listener addressed a cheeky query to the BBC's official program guide, *Radio Times*: "We should like to know if you keep Sandy Macpherson chained up in the dungeons of the BBC. He always seems to be there when there is no one else to entertain us."[23] Macpherson spent the first month of World War II "on duty more or less continuously," making a total of fifty broadcasts of popular and light classical selections.[24] When Germany invaded Poland on September 1, 1939, Britain had prepared immediately for air raids: blackout regulations went into effect, cinemas and theaters were closed, and the BBC was reduced to a single national wavelength to prevent its transmitters from being used for navigation by the Luftwaffe. On September 3, the government declared war on Germany and "ordered the evacuation of over one million mothers, infants, and schoolchildren from London and other urban centers," and sent the British Expeditionary Forces to France.[25] Although the air raids did not materialize (it was still a year until the Battle of Britain and the Blitz), the nation was on edge, routines were disrupted, and millions turned to the radio as never before for information, comfort, and a sense of community.

The theater organ was ideally situated to help fulfill the BBC's wartime mandate of providing entertainment and diversion, as well as information and news.[26] During the war's early weeks, most of the BBC's Music and Variety Department staff (including musical ensembles) were evacuated to secret locations outside London, and external artists were subject to security vetting. Macpherson remained as one of the few providers of live entertainment, a role that drew on the theater organ's traditional role as a flexible "one-man orchestra"; his broadcasts in

September 1939 were fill-up music on a grand scale. For critics, from the popularly oriented Collie Knox of the *Daily Mail* to the classically oriented W. R. Anderson at the *Musical Times*, the BBC's emergency approach to entertainment was a failure, and the dominance of theater organ on the air encapsulated the BBC's inability to sustain its prewar standard—at a moment when such continuity would have comforted its audience. "Needing the refreshment of fine music, we found a cinema organist fix'd in his everlasting seat," Anderson wrote.[27]

For many, however, Macpherson's marathon at the organ was less a symptom of BBC failure than an admirable, even heroic, feat. In a profile published a few months later, the *Star* celebrated Macpherson's role during the early weeks of the war, declaring, "He Held the BBC Fort with 200 Broadcasts," and pointing to the enthusiastic response he had garnered from listeners—up to four thousand letters a week since the start of the war.[28] It was during the early weeks of the war that Macpherson, who had been the BBC's resident theater organist for less than a year (since November 1938), came fully into his own as a beloved radio personality, a wartime icon of constancy and comfort.[29] As "an elderly lady" told an interlocutor who asked whether she was lonely after self-evacuating to the country, "Sometimes, but I have two friends—the postman and Sandy Macpherson."[30]

On radio, stardom—or "personality"—was predicated on the ability of speakers to navigate radio's intimate public (in Loviglio's sense). The connection between broadcasters and listeners was forged as their voices moved between public and private modes of address; in contrast to being heard and seen by audiences in public cinemas or theaters, stars on radio were heard (usually) within the private spaces of the home. As Michael Thomas Carroll has argued, skilled broadcasters could "create a metaphysics of presence."[31] They developed a sense of intimacy with their listeners by nurturing a calm, conversational delivery on-air—reinforced, in many cases, when they encouraged and engaged with listener letters.[32] For critics, this intimacy was not just illusory, it was manipulative; thus, the guidelines for BBC newsreaders and announcers emphasized formality. Many production departments at the BBC, however, recognized the importance of "personality" at the microphone, as embodied by the beloved gardening expert C. H. Middleton, who pioneered a warm, extemporaneous style in his broadcasts beginning in 1931.[33]

Despite the Variety Department's receptiveness to "personality," live performances were a poor predictor of success on radio. In one scathing assessment of the top broadcasting bandleaders, Phyllis Frost criticized "half-hearted" and nervous announcing as well as "highbrowism"; what was required was a "bright and slightly intimate voice with plenty of personality."[34] Echoing Frost, Foort explained his own decision to avoid stilted oratory when he became resident theater organist: "'Reg,' I decided, 'you've got to talk to them just as though they were sitting in your own home. That's the only way you *can* talk . . . you're no actor.'"

He reported being "flabbergasted" by the results: "I found myself blossoming, willy-nilly, into a star."[35] Macpherson also had potential in this regard, as Watt noted at the start of his tenure: "He has a good personality, simple and straightforward, of the Foort–Middleton genre.... We want to exploit [Macpherson] naturally as an organist rather than as an announcer, but I believe that if he turns out right, we shall have a very good personality there."[36]

Macpherson arrived at the BBC having already developed a relatable public persona. According to fellow organist Quentin Maclean, Macpherson's friendly personality had been "inseparable" from the Empire Cinema in Leicester Square, London, where he had worked for ten years before joining the BBC.[37] In British cinemas, stardom was not limited to the screen: organists had their names displayed alongside those of movie stars on the marquee outside, while, inside, they rose illuminated from the pit in a wave of sound and dazzled audiences with their virtuosity. Broadcasting extended their celebrity, transforming them into stars in Richard Dyer's sense—consumable objects of desire, fascination, and identification for fans who collected their recordings, photos, and autographs. But it was not enough to inspire awe; the "paradox of the star" required that they be ordinary as well as extraordinary.[38] Thus, a key element of Macpherson's star persona was his friendliness, which many profiles reinforced by describing his Canadian origins and drawing liberally on stereotypes of (white settler) Canadians as a wholesome, cheerful, and outdoorsy people. In press accounts, the organist emerged as a "lanky, genial Canadian," who had "once worked in a lumber camp," knew how to "roll logs," and "like[d] a pint of beer, cigarettes, dogs, and fishing."[39] In wartime Britain, the relatable Canadian star also came to embody what would become a core value of the People's War—of ordinary people matter-of-factly stepping up to serve their country.[40]

Macpherson conveyed his relatable persona not only through his spoken delivery but also with his approachable, familiar repertoire and his tendency of rarely "playing *up* to the public instead of *down* to it," as one organist complained in *Kinematograph Weekly*.[41] Indeed, Macpherson's narrow repertoire of popular songs and inspirational melodies annoyed some listeners: early in the war, one correspondent complained, "We all know every note of Handel's Largo, the Holy City, and the Lost Chord; I presume that his music is not yet rationed."[42] Nevertheless, the formula remained popular. Another listener responded by urging Macpherson to "continue to fire away with Handel's Largo, the Holy City, and The Lost Chord—the majority of the British public is not so depraved that they cannot get inspiration from such fine themes."[43]

From the first weeks of the war, Macpherson's music and his on-air persona embodied the "simple British virtues" that would soon become central to ideologies of the People's War: according to the *Radio Times*, he displayed "dignity without ostentation, a wit that is dry and never caustic, and a cordial friendliness."[44] These qualities appealed deeply to many listeners during this anxious time. As one family wrote, "Sandy Macpherson's quiet voice is very reassuring at a time when our ears are on the alert for warning sirens."[45] The imaginative spectacle of Macpherson's broadcasts early in the war, when listeners so vividly imagined Macpherson holding down the fort, chained in the BBC dungeons, or "fixed in his everlasting seat," was one of steadfastness and intimacy, not glamour or expansiveness. Rather than guiding listeners out into Britain's cinemas—which, in any event, were closed—the microphone focused instead on Macpherson at the BBC theater organ. In a manner that recalled Berlant's intimate public (built around shared emotion and mass culture entertainment), Macpherson was able to foster an intimate public for the nation at war, using familiar popular songs and a friendly radio address. In his first Christmas message of the war, which was printed in the *Radio Times*, he invited his listeners into a community of mutual appreciation: "When I think of your patience, your fortitude, and your kindly endurance in listening to thirty-seven of my programmes in the first three weeks of the war, and then writing me letters of appreciation about them—well, I think you're marvellous. When I look around at the flowers, mufflers, handkerchiefs, cigarettes, fruit, and pots of jam you've sent me—most of them anonymously, so that I couldn't acknowledge them—well words fail me."[46]

In contrast to the boxes of cigars and cigarettes from music publishers that Macpherson reported each year to his supervisor, this list of gifts from listeners was more intimate, recalling what one might give a favorite uncle. (Were the mufflers hand knit? Were the handkerchiefs embroidered? Was the jam homemade?)[47] The gifts and letters demonstrated the emotional connection that Macpherson had fostered with his listeners, while his Christmas response captured an emotional register—of patience, fortitude, and endurance—that aligned closely with what the government considered to be good morale. If Macpherson could have such a powerful effect as a relief organist, what might he accomplish with programming dedicated to uniting this intimate wartime public?

### SANDY CALLING: FORGING AN INTIMATE WARTIME PUBLIC

Macpherson's friendly voice, familiar repertoire, and facility for interacting with his listeners found a new outlet in February 1940 with the debut of *Sandy's Half-Hour*, "a program of requests from men on active service."[48] During winter 1940, the British Expeditionary Forces were stationed in France, while at home the blackout and other war measures remained in force. In what was called the Bore War (and, later, the Phony War), boredom had replaced anxiety, and a significant concern for military leaders became how to keep the troops occupied and out of trouble. To sustain

Fig. 1.2. Sandy Macpherson's "gigantic post-bag." ("The Human Story behind Sandy's Half-Hour," *Radio Times* [5 April 1940]: 10.)

civilian and forces morale during the period, it was critical to keep listeners entertained and socially connected—and Macpherson's new weekly program promised to help on both fronts. Not only would Macpherson play popular requests, but the process of doing so involved a chain of correspondence: members of the forces would write in with requests, Macpherson would write back to inform them when their songs would be played, and they, in turn, could "write and tell the people at home when to listen." The series "should provide a wonderful link between our men in France and their people—not forgetting their girls—over here," the *Radio Times* opined.[49] Listeners responded with enthusiasm. By March, Macpherson was sometimes receiving as many "as many as 500 letters from the forces in one morning" and averaging more than a thousand request letters per week (see fig. 1.2).[50]

As a program that fused popular entertainment with morale building, *Sandy's Half-Hour* was ideally suited to the Forces Programme, which had started on an experimental basis in January 1940 and expanded to a full-day service in mid-February. The BBC promoted the Forces Programme as serving the British Expeditionary Forces, who needed light entertainment designed for shorter attention spans, but it also served as an alternative wavelength to the Home Service and became popular with home front audiences. Thus, both domestic listeners and soldiers stationed in France could hear *Sandy's Half-Hour* on the Forces Programme. Even after the retreat from Dunkirk in early June 1940, *Sandy's Half-Hour* remained in its weekly slot, continuing to relay messages and requests between families and the troops (and others in national service) who were stationed throughout the United Kingdom.

Over the next two years, *Sandy's Half-Hour* became the first of many wartime messages programs, which often featured women hosts (dubbed "radio girl-friends" by the producer Cecil Madden).[51] One Ministry of Information press release celebrated such programs as a comforting "life-line" between forces and their families back home.[52] Macpherson himself figured in three additional messages programs that could sometimes be heard domestically but also aired farther afield on the BBC's expanding overseas networks. Few documents provide precise reasons for why these "spin-offs" were created, but it is possible to deduce the impetus from when the programs were launched. The first was *Sandy's Half-Hour for Canada*, which first aired on June 9, 1940, on the Forces Programme and on the BBC's newly expanded shortwave North American Service (it aired every three weeks on both services). Although there was a limited number of Canadian forces stationed in Britain at that point in the war, the Dominion of Canada was becoming a key location in the Allied war effort: several thousand British children were evacuated to Canada in 1940, and Canada had been established as the main center for the British Commonwealth Air Training Plan (from which more than 130,000 air crewmen graduated over the course of the war).[53] By featuring Macpherson, the BBC's most visible Canadian, the BBC helped strengthen ties between Britain and a critical ally.

The next spin-off, *Sandy Calling the Middle East* (usually shortened to *Sandy Calling*) began broadcasting every two weeks in October 1940. Heard on the Forces Programme and on the BBC's expanding Middle East Service, *Sandy Calling* started soon after Italy invaded Egypt, where the British army was stationed. Whereas *Sandy's Half-Hour for Canada* was aimed at a varied audience of Canadians and Britons, civilian and military, *Sandy Calling* addressed a British forces audience almost exclusively. British troops were stationed throughout the Mediterranean, North Africa, and the Middle East in one of the largest and most crucial theaters of war for the British between late 1940 and 1943.

The last of the spin-offs, *Sandy Calling India*, began to air on the BBC overseas service by fall 1942, in response to a direct request for a messages program that the War Office had made in June.[54] The program served British soldiers stationed in India, whose numbers were being ramped up, both in response to the threat of Japanese invasion, following the disastrous fall of Burma in March 1942, and to serious concerns about India's independence movement, which grew in strength as Indian Army troops, factory goods, and food staples were shipped out to support Britain's war effort.[55] Only the latter concern materialized when on August 8, 1942, "the Indian National Congress called for civil disobedience to protest the colony's forced participation in [the war]," and British authorities responded by arresting "all the senior Congress leaders," including Mahatma Gandhi and Jawaharlal Nehru, an act that catalyzed the massive Quit India movement. In what Viceroy Leopold Amery described as "the most serious rebellion since 1857," the British "authorities arrested more than 90,000, and killed up to 10,000 political protesters."[56] Amid civil unrest and the conditions developing for a famine that would kill three million people in Bengal in 1943, British soldiers who had expected to fight the Japanese army instead found themselves enforcing imperial rule on civilians, a task distasteful to many.[57] Throughout this period, *Sandy Calling India* served these troops but did not air domestically until 1944 and received only limited coverage in the domestic press, reflecting the ambivalent place of India in the British wartime imaginary.

In his messages programs, Macpherson drew on the reputation for friendliness that he had developed early in the war, continuing to draw his British and Commonwealth listeners into an intimate wartime public built around the shared experience of separation and longing. Macpherson's musical choices played an important role in creating an atmosphere of reassurance, inclusivity, and togetherness, which he established by playing his signature tune, "I'll Play to You," a waltz of his own composition, at the start and close of virtually every broadcast. The title balanced the intimate singular and friendly plural address while the music offered listeners a calming sensation of repetition and enclosure with its predictable ABA structure, solid F-major theme, and regular place in the broadcast.[58]

Macpherson's signature tune reinforced his reassuring persona, but his focus on requests built an intimate wartime public through the shared vocabulary of popular and traditional songs. Requests, of course, provided an index not simply of what was popular but also of which songs were meaningful to his listeners, such as "the sailor who asks for 'Begin the Beguine' because that was the tune he and his sweetheart danced to the night they got engaged" or "the soldier who asks for 'I'll Remember' because it always makes him think of his wife and the two-month-old baby he has never seen."[59] As one May 1941 program for *Sandy Calling* showed, the requests ranged from folk songs ("My Bonny Lies over the Ocean,"

"Londonderry Air") to old music hall favorites ("I'll Be Your Sweetheart") to children's songs ("Horsey Horsey") to contemporary ballads ("Only Forever," "A Pair of Silver Wings").[60] According to the December 1941 *Sunday Pictorial* profile, the most requested song was the quasi-religious ballad, "I'll Walk beside You."[61] Many of these songs were what Vera Lynn described as "greeting card songs," which could convey emotional messages that few people could articulate in their own words.[62] Of course, in the case of Macpherson's messages programs, there was no Vera Lynn to sing the lyrics; the songs were familiar enough that listeners were already conversant with their lyrics, and the theater organ, with its sonic codes well established in the cinema, was ideal for conveying their emotional significance.

But Macpherson also recognized the value of the spoken word, and messages played a significant role in fostering his programs' "intimate personal appeal" (it is notable that they were generally referred to as messages programs, not requests programs). Messages, as read out by Macpherson, but particularly when delivered by the correspondents themselves, had been an early innovation on *Sandy's Half-Hour*, and they carried through in the overseas spin-offs. As the *Radio Times* promised at the start of *Sandy Calling*: "Mothers, wives, and sweethearts are again invited to co-operate.... Sandy's cheery, sympathetic little comments will again run through the programmes, and some of the womenfolk will come to the microphone in person for a word to their men."[63]

The cozy description of *Sandy Calling* echoed an image that the *Radio Times* had published on its cover the preceding week: Macpherson sits at the Compton organ, his face half turned to the camera while his fingers depress the keys, while seven smiling (and singing?) Canadian servicemen stand behind the organ, leaning toward the camera and the microphone, which hangs in the foreground (see fig. 1.3).[64] With the organ at the center, the studio was a site of friendly intimacy, projected outward to include a listening nation and, even, empire.

Although the intimate public fostered by Macpherson's broadcasts was real, the reassuring picture of ordinary people grouped around the Compton at the BBC's headquarters in London would soon become illusory. In September 1940, the same month that the photo was published, a bomb fell on St. George's Hall, destroying the Compton and "much" of Macpherson's own "music and records." "I need hardly say that our arrangements were considerably upset," he wrote after the war. Macpherson moved to the emergency theater organ site—a Hammond electric organ in Evesham, about a hundred miles from London—which had to remain secret for security reasons.[65] Only in April 1941 did the *Radio Times* acknowledge the loss.[66] The announcement of the Compton's demise coincided with Macpherson's move to a more suitable organ, Foort's state-of-the-art portable Moller, which Foort agreed to rent to the BBC and which was installed at the Grand Theatre

Fig. 1.3. Sandy Macpherson and members of the Canadian Forces gather around the BBC Compton organ in August 1940. Getty images.

Llandudno, a seaside resort town in northern Wales.[67] Llandudno remained the center for theater broadcasting until late 1943, when Macpherson and the Moller organ moved to nearby Bangor, where they stayed for the rest of the war.[68]

## "AS INSIDIOUS AS OPIUM": THE THEATER ORGAN AS THREAT

During 1941, the main problem with which Macpherson had to contend, both in his messages programs and in his work administering theater organ programming at the BBC, was that of keeping more than a dozen weekly broadcasts running smoothly under wartime conditions. But throughout 1942, his challenges increasingly came from within the BBC as, under new leadership, questions arose about whether theater organs aligned with the Corporation's musical mission and whether Macpherson's messages programs truly benefited wartime morale. The questions grew out of longstanding critiques of theater organs and their repertoire as embodying poor musical taste—not out of worries about their popularity, which was high, particularly when compared to classical music. BBC Listener Research had found that in August 1941, 34 percent of listeners were enthusiastic about theater organs, while only 7 percent were "violently antipathetic"; in contrast, in September 1941, 40 percent of listeners were "hostile" to symphony concerts, while 10 percent were "enthusiastic."[69] Meanwhile, Macpherson and his messages programs continued to receive support from both the War Office and the press.[70] Nonetheless, theater organs became imbricated in the BBC's internal debates about popular music, musical uplift, and morale, which led in July 1942 to an official ban on male crooners, "over-sentimental ... women singers," and sentimental songs, and, by the fall, to the removal of Macpherson's messages programs from the BBC's domestic wavelengths.[71]

During fall 1941, the *Radio Times* featured a protracted debate about the musical value of theater organs, which foreshadowed the discussions soon to take place within the BBC. The inciting incident was an all-Chaikovsky recital on a Sunday morning in September by the former resident theater organist Reginald Foort (who had negotiated a small performance contract with the BBC as part of the Moller organ agreement). On one side, C. Gordon Glover, the variety columnist, offered his qualified support for theater organists playing certain classical arrangements, concluding that they could "spread the symphonic gospel" to those who might resist "musical emancipation ... by direct assault."[72] On the other side, Ralph Hill, the *Radio Times* music critic, denounced the practice, drawing on language that went back to the 1920s: "What musicians would object to is a cinema organist playing, say, the slow movement of Tchaikovsky's Fifth Symphony with the original harmony and rhythm jazzed up, and all the slimily vulgar mechanical 'effects,' that distinguish a 'theatre' organ from a church organ, substituted for the original orchestration."[73] (No musician worthy of the name, he implied.) *Radio Times* readers piled on, and even Macpherson chimed in to question Hill's "scorn" for the practice.[74]

During 1942, the notion that there was something harmful in a theater organist performing the *1812 Overture* transformed from overwrought critical stance to guiding principle in the BBC's new music policy, which took a hard line on classical adaptations and sentimentality in popular music. The shift reflected the war's grim turn for the British in early 1942: Rommel's Afrika Korps retook most of Libya in January; the Japanese captured Hong Kong, Rangoon, and Singapore (where a record 80,000 British and Empire troops surrendered); the Battle of the Atlantic intensified; and bad news came from the Eastern Front. These events raised fresh concerns about morale among the forces and civilians, and sentimental songs and singers on the radio became a scapegoat. Although sentimental repertoires and performance styles remained popular with the majority of the population, military, government, and cultural leaders cast them as depressing, debilitated, and degenerate—in other words, as actually harmful to morale. Their language drew, often pungently, on discourses about the threat that effeminate men, sexually loose women, and feminine domestic preoccupations posed to the masculine terrains of public life and warfare. This gendered critique of sentimental popular music as bad for morale was all the more potent because it grew out of longstanding concerns in Britain—and at the BBC—about mass culture, commercialism, and Americanization (which were themselves articulated in gendered and racialized terms). Thus, the BBC's response focused on program quality, a perennial concern for the public broadcaster, with staff members expressing their views about "good" and "bad" music through the oppositional discourses of high and low culture, health and degeneracy, masculinity and effeminacy.

The BBC response was led by new Co-Director General Cecil Graves, who was committed to improving program quality, as well as by Controller of Programmes Basil Nicolls and the new Music Department director, Arthur Bliss. Bliss's efforts to raise musical standards encompassed not only the Music Department's output of serious and light music but also the theater organ and dance band music administered by the Variety Department. At issue was not simply technical execution but also more subjective matters of repertoire, style, and interpretation. Popular song was thus a key focus of the new policy, which resulted in the July 1942 "crooner ban" and the formation the Dance Band Policy Committee that was charged with enforcing it.[75] Theater organs also drew the ire of reformers, as reflected in an April 1942 Music Department report, which began, "Are they necessary? ... Are they instruments capable of producing music? ... Is the present standard vile?" Although "musician organist[s]," exemplified by Foort, might be acceptable, the report took issue with "entertainer organist[s]"—exemplified by Macpherson. Entertainer organists were "'stunt' men" uninterested in being "seriously regarded as musicians" but too popular to "be banned from the air."[76]

Banning Macpherson was never considered, but the Music Department did challenge his status as the BBC's primary authority on theater organs. The challenge to Macpherson's authority had begun two months earlier when Music and Variety staff (including Macpherson) began discussing the standard of theater organ performance, which had declined during the war—in large part because many leading organists had been called up for national service. Everyone, including Macpherson, agreed that more vetting was needed. But who was best qualified to make the assessments—a church organist or an "entertainer" theater organist? Nicolls advocated for George Thalben-Ball, the religious broadcasting music advisor and an RCM-trained organ virtuoso, but the director of Variety, John Watt, asserted the theater organs should be evaluated on their own terms and defended Macpherson's expertise.[77]

The compromise was a joint Theatre Organ Committee composed of both Variety and Music Department members, including Macpherson and Thalben-Ball. Its members quickly agreed on a new policy, covering technical execution, style, and repertoire; in May 1942 they informed all broadcasting organists that they would be evaluated according to the new terms. For the limited range of classical works that had entered the theater organ repertoire (further incursions were prohibited), such as Rachmaninoff's Prelude in C-sharp Minor and Robert Schumann's *Traümerei*, the committee insisted on "complete faithfulness" to the original and "recommend[ed] the controlled use of the tremulant and the discouragement of the Jessie Crawford [a prominent US organist] type of 'glissando.'" In the case of popular repertoire, they drew on gendered codes to emphasize the importance of good taste and "virility and artistry" in performance—or, as Bliss explained to the *Radio Times*, "strong rhythmic music with a fine swinging tune [rather than] cloying or over-sentimentalised music." Ultimately, the committee recognized that any further restrictions, such as limiting percussion, the Tibia Clausa, or Vox humana stops, or mellowtone (all of which had been floated by Bliss and Nicolls), would alter "the whole character of the instrument and thereby destroy[] its programme value."[78] The upshot was that guest organists were put on notice, while theater organ broadcasting was preserved as a fixture at the BBC.

As the new policy rolled out, Macpherson's messages programs also became subject to scrutiny at the BBC's highest levels. Although his repertoire included a healthy dose of sentimental musical numbers, the main problem was the quantity and tone of the messages. As an entertainer organist, Macpherson's "stunts" involved bringing ordinary people to the microphone. In particular, Macpherson wanted his guests to be diverse geographically—a challenge with wartime travel restrictions. Therefore, with Watt's enthusiastic support, Macpherson began bringing the microphone *to* his guests in a series of special outside broadcasts of *Sandy Calling* from cities around Britain. In October 1941, he reported on the "great success" of the first semi-experimental broadcast from Glasgow, where he sold two hundred autographed copies of the script to benefit the local War Relief Fund, met Glasgow's lord provost, and had strong coverage in the local press, "after the broadcast of course."[79] Although the plan was to represent every district in the country, the monthly visits ended less than a year later. Meanwhile, by early 1942, Watt cautioned Macpherson to limit live guests in *Sandy's Half-Hour* to a maximum of four, writing "please be careful to avoid overdoing it and making it a completely live message programme."[80] Macpherson was amenable, turning to the military training centers near Llandudno for his guests; their "constantly changing" personnel would enable geographical diversity, including the North Country and Cockney representation requested by Watt.[81]

Achieving the right balance of music and messages remained a challenge for Macpherson, not least because there was no consensus about what the correct balance actually was. The War Office, which followed Macpherson's messages programs closely, wanted them to include a significant number of messages, whereas BBC staff—including Director-General Sir Graves—favored more music.[82] Although grounded in a sense that talk should be limited in music programs, their larger concern involved what people actually said in their messages, particularly in *Sandy's Half-Hour*, which aired only domestically. As G. D. Adams, the director of Programme Planning, wrote in July 1942 (around the time that the BBC was announcing its ban on crooners and sentimental songs): "The messages are of the rather embarrassing, personal and domestic type. There is nothing disgraceful about them, but I think this is the kind of thing best kept off the air."[83] If the bridging of public and private address rendered the voices on *Sandy's Half-Hour* "thrilling" (to quote Loviglio) for listeners, their presence also challenged the lines between public and private in a way deeply discomfiting for the BBC's leadership while the institution was revisiting what should be expressed on the air at a difficult point in the war.

Adams finally gained the leverage he needed to change the popular program when the War Office complained a month later (in August 1942) about a "revoltingly sentimental" broadcast: Macpherson's playing was "sickly and treacley," his repertoire was "contrary" to the BBC's ban on sentiment, and the final message was "in appallingly bad taste." What was the offending message? A "mother-in-law" had requested "I'll See You Again" from Noel Coward's *Bitter Sweet* for a soldier on the anniversary of his wife's death, "an anniversary which must make you feel very, very sad."[84] In August, *Sandy Calling* was taken off the Forces Programme (although it continued to be broadcast overseas), and, in September, *Sandy's Half-Hour* jettisoned the messages and became a music-only program, with musicians as Macpherson's only guests.[85] By February 1943 Macpherson also discontinued live guests on his overseas *Sandy Calling* broadcasts, replacing the extended personal messages with simple dedications.[86]

Although Macpherson's repertoire, instrument, and performance style did nothing to help *Sandy's Half-Hour* survive the 1942 crackdown on sentimentality at the BBC, the program's "embarrassing, personal and domestic" messages inspired the greatest ambivalence within the BBC. In this context, the mother-in-law's message—the description of which was relayed and repeated with a high degree of detail—represented a curious breaking point. What was so appalling about acknowledging this woman's death? Was it the fact that a soldier was sad? That the death was a woman's and not explicitly connected to the war? That the message came from the dead woman's mother (not just the recipient's "mother-in-law")? Perhaps the problem was that the dedication widened the frame of public longing too far beyond the scope of the war into the realm of the feminine, the domestic, the private sphere—and that the reunion the song promised would take place only for the soldier and his wife in the afterlife. Whereas Berlant located her intimate public within the framework of women's entertainment culture—film melodramas and romance novels—Macpherson's intimate public crossed gender lines and encountered him on the BBC, a public broadcaster ambivalent not only about sentimentality but about the public representation of intimate, everyday, and often feminized emotion. For the BBC's leadership, publicizing these emotions was especially problematic when good wartime citizenship involved setting aside personal concerns and embracing the values of resilience, common cause, and sacrifice. But could these private and public concerns actually coexist? For many of Macpherson's listeners, they could. After all, *Sandy's Half-Hour* was popular: its popularity was just not enough to preserve it as a messages program in the fall of 1942.

## CONCLUSION

A much tamer version of Macpherson's messages programs, without the guests, returned briefly to home front listeners in March 1944 when the General Forces Programme replaced the popular domestic Forces Programme. The BBC promoted the cost-saving measure as a way to unite home front listeners with the forces overseas; they would all hear the same programming, much of it drawn from the overseas service.[87] Although listeners could now hear *Sandy Calling the Middle East* and *Sandy Calling India*, they heard fewer theater organs overall because the BBC's overseas music leadership had decided that they reproduced poorly on shortwave. In 1946, the critic Collie Knox reflected back on this "highly peculiar phase": "[The BBC] decided—without any real grounds for such a supposition—that the theater organ was not suitable for broadcasting, that it blasted the microphone, and that the troops overseas did not enjoy it.... The 'someone' at the BBC who had blundered was made aware of his blunder by some amongst us. Then, like a flash, the BBC decided that the cinema organ was, after all, most suitable for broadcasting, that it did not blast the microphone, and that the Troops overseas enjoyed it."[88]

The root of the problem, according to Knox, was the strong emotions that the theater organ inspired. "Either you absolutely adore them or you hate them to death. There is no middle way," he wrote.[89] Indeed, this ambivalence had shaped the reception of the instrument back to the 1920s as well as the debates about Macpherson's marathon sessions in the first weeks of the war, when his ubiquity at the BBC microphone was reviled by some and celebrated by others.

Like his instrument, Macpherson inspired strong emotions with his messages programs. *Sandy's Half-Hour* and *Sandy Calling* discomfited many in the BBC leadership with the sentimentality of music and the personal nature of the messages, but these qualities made the shows popular with listeners and meaningful to Macpherson. As he recalled after the war, "I never hope to do a more interesting or satisfying programme than those in which I sent messages and greetings to the boys serving overseas."[90] Like Gunner Smith listening in the desert, Macpherson's listeners welcomed the expressions of longing and care that he brought to the microphone. The messages may have been personal and domestic, but they also embodied the inclusive, democratic values of the People's War. Going further, the program's affective, intimate public formed part of what Claire Langhamer has called the "emotional watershed" of World War II, in which romantic and familial connections were valued not only at the personal level but as foundational to national life.[91]

These values, along with questions of physical reconstruction, continued to inform postwar British society, in which "the emotional intimacies of private life were explicitly drawn into public policy discussion." The "blurring of boundaries between public and private" that had begun during the war continued in the emerging postwar welfare state.[92] Meanwhile, under the National Service Act, which remained in force until 1960, young men continued to be separated from their families for military service, serving as part of the Allied occupation of Germany, in the Korean Conflict, and in Britain's colonies, many of which were going through the complex and sometimes turbulent process of decolonization. Thus, messages programs remained relevant, continuing in the form of gramophone record requests shows—most notably, the highly popular *Family Favourites* (renamed *Two-Way Family Favourites* in 1955), a weekly show hosted by Jean Metcalfe in London with a series of male cohosts based in Germany.[93]

Given postwar "needletime" restrictions (i.e., the strict limits on how many hours the BBC could devote to gramophone records), there was still plenty of room for the familiar sound of the theater organ on the Light Programme, which succeeded the wartime Forces Programme and became a popular companion to domestic life.[94] Macpherson remained the BBC's resident organist until 1963, playing the Moller organ, which the BBC purchased from Foort in 1945. As Watt explained to his superiors, "Organ programmes are extremely popular and are extremely cheap to produce."[95] Their utility as radio entertainment remained strong for years after the war.

The theater organ, Sandy Macpherson, and his messages programs played a critical role in wartime broadcasting at the BBC. Throughout the war, they weathered numerous attacks, from the bomb that destroyed the BBC Compton in September 1940 to the policies that led to the cancellation of *Sandy's Half-Hour* in fall 1942. Nonetheless, Macpherson used voice and music to forge an intimate wartime public, ensounding the values of community, inclusivity, and care in the face of uncertainty and fear—values that remained relevant for his listeners well beyond 1945.

## NOTES

My thanks to the BBC Written Archives Centre staff, especially Louise North and Els Boonen, for their insight and assistance. BBC copyright content reproduced courtesy of the British Broadcasting Corporation. All rights reserved. My thanks, also, to the Arts Research Board at McMaster University for a SSHRC Exchange—Scholarly Publications Grant, which included funds for image licensing fees. Finally, many thanks to my co-editors, Pam Potter and Roberta Marvin, as well as the anonymous peer reviewers, for their generous and incisive feedback on this chapter.

1. Lawson, "'I Have a Request for Mrs. Smith,'" *Sunday Pictorial*, December 28, 1941, British Broadcasting Corporation Written Archives Centre [BBC WAC]: Press Cuttings.
2. Ibid.
3. Loviglio, *Radio's Intimate Public*, xvi–xvii.
4. See Ben Anderson's discussion of morale as a way to mediate this breakdown of boundaries, which threatened "civilian bodies": "Morale promise[d] . . . to enable bodies to keep going *despite the present*." Anderson, "Modulating the Excess of Affect," 173.
5. Berlant, *The Female Complaint*, 5, 10.
6. Bliss, *As I Remember*, 150.
7. *Ariel* is also the name of the BBC's internal staff publication.
8. "Theatre Organ for the B.B.C." *Times* (London), February 12, 1936.
9. Kendra Preston Leonard is doing important work to address the role of theater organs and organists in her scholarship and curation of the *Silent Film Sound & Music Archive*. See Leonard, "Using Resources for Silent Film Music"; and *Silent Film Sound & Music Archive*, accessed April 30, 2019.
10. Fox, "Cinema Organ."
11. Foort, *The Cinema Organ*, 3.
12. Reginald Foort, "The Modern Cinema Organ. A Remarkable Instrument," *Times* (London), March 19, 1929.
13. Foort, "The Modern Cinema Organ." Foort demonstrated the Compton's range (from a symphony orchestra and church organ to a dog fight) in a 1936 newsreel: British Pathé, "Reginald Foort—Organist (1936)."
14. "A Maida Vale Cinema Organ. LCC Committee and Complaints," *Times* (London), June 27, 1929.
15. Foort, *The Cinema Organ*, 2, 89.
16. Stacey, *Star Gazing*, 83–84.
17. Foort, Preface, x.

18. "BBC Theatre Organ—Staff Organist," British Broadcasting Corporation Internal Circulating Memorandum [BBC ICM], from Variety Ex[ecutive]. to DSA [Director of Staff Administration], October 8, 1936, BBC WAC R94/1, 667/1.

19. Foort, "You *Can* Take It with You!," 25. See British Pathé, "Reginald Foort with His New Wonder Organ" (1939).

20. Foort, Preface, x.

21. In a typical week, July 9–15, 1939, there were thirteen theater organ broadcasts on the National and London Regional wavelengths (not including other regional wavelengths). *BBC Genome*.

22. "Sandy Macpherson," BBC ICM from DV [Director of Variety] to C(P) [Controller (Programmes)], November 3, 1938, BBC WAC R19/686.

23. "What the Wartime Listener Thinks," *Radio Times*, September 15, 1939, 11.

24. Finding a precise tally of Macpherson's broadcasts is difficult. The number here is drawn from Macpherson's response when the BBC director of Programme Administration inquired about his working hours: "As you know I have been on duty more or less continuously since the outbreak of War and have been available whenever I have been needed. During this period I have broadcast fifty times and the work entailed in making up the programmes, practising, and the necessary office work has kept me busy at all hours of the day and night and so far I have not been able to take a day off. This is not intended as a complaint, but is merely to point out the difficulty of making an accurate return of the number of hours I have been working per day." "Emergency Organisation," BBC ICM from Mr. Macpherson to DPA [Director of Programme Administration], September 30, 1939, BBC WAC R94/2, 53/1.

25. Baade, *Victory through Harmony*, 35.

26. Ibid., 36.

27. Collie Knox, "I Call This a Scandal...," *Daily Mail*, September 22, 1939, BBC WAC Press Cuttings; W. R. Anderson, "A Wireless Note."

28. "He Held the BBC Fort with 200 Broadcasts," *The Star*, March 19, 1940, BBC WAC Press Cuttings.

29. "'Round and about This Week's Programmes," *Radio Times*, September 8, 1939, 13.

30. "What the Wartime Listener Thinks," *Radio Times*, October 20, 1939, 9.

31. Carroll, *Popular Modernity in America*, 39.

32. Razlogova, *The Listener's Voice*, 3.

33. "Gardening Programmes on the BBC."

34. Frost, "Dance Band Announcers," 56.

35. Foort, "Organising the Organ," 50.

36. "Sandy Macpherson," BBC ICM from DV to C(P), November 3, 1938, BBC WAC R19/686.

37. Foort, *The Cinema Organ*, 90; "'Round and about This Week's Programmes," *Radio Times*, September 8, 1939, 13.

38. Dyer, *Heavenly Bodies*, 43.

39. "Platoon's Request to Sandy, Pioneer at the Organ," *Empire News*, April 5, 1942, BBC WAC Press Cuttings; Lawson, "'I Have a Request for Mrs. Smith.'"

40. Although profiles emphasized Macpherson's Canadian origins in terms of biography, I have found no discussion of a Canadian accent, in either the press or BBC internal documents. Indeed, in the few recordings I have heard, Macpherson's accent does not strike me as markedly "Canadian" (whatever that means for a multilingual, multicultural nation), an unsurprising situation, given that he grew up in southern Ontario, with its large population of immigrants from the British Isles, and that he had been working in London for more than a decade.

41. "Kinema Music and BBC Broadcasts," *Kinematograph Weekly*, March 14, 1940, BBC WAC Press Cuttings.

42. "What the Wartime Listener Thinks," *Radio Times*, September 15, 1939, 11.

43. Ibid., 7.

44. "'Round and about This Week's Programmes," *Radio Times*, September 8, 1939, 13.

45. "What the Wartime Listener Thinks," *Radio Times*, September 22, 1939, 7.

46. Macpherson, "Sandy Macpherson Thinks You Marvellous," *Radio Times*, December 22, 1939, 20.

47. For example, "Christmas Gifts: 1942," BBC ICM from Mr. Sandy Macpherson to Variety Ex., December 28, 1942, BBC WAC R94/2, 53/1. It is worth noting that food rationing did not begin until 1940; clothing rationing did not begin until 1941.

48. BBC, "Sandy's Half-Hour," February 28, 1940, *BBC Genome*.

49. Guy Fletcher, "This Week's Radio Miscellany," *Radio Times*, February 23, 1940, 7.

50. BBC, "Sandy's Half-Hour," March 26, 1940, *BBC Genome*.

51. See Baade, *Victory through Harmony*, 155–157.

52. "Life-Line between the People at Home and the Men Overseas: BBC Brings Comfort with Its Broadcasts of Messages," *Clip-Sheet* [issued by the MoI for the *Exclusive* Us of Editors of Weekly Newspapers], January 21, 1942, BBC WAC Special Collections S24/54/13. See Baade, *Victory through Harmony*, 55.

53. Hillmer, Hatch, and Myers. "British Commonwealth Air Training Plan."

54. The Broadcasters, "Both Sides of the Microphone," *Radio Times*, October 2, 1942, 3; "PA Sandy's Half-Hour," BBC ICM from Controller (Programmes) to DG [Director General], June 16, 1942, BBC WAC R19/686.

55. Mukerjee, *Churchill's Secret War*, xxx–xxxi, 72. About a third of the multiethnic Indian Army, which had around 900,000 troops, were serving in the Middle East. The British were afraid of adequately equipping the units remaining in India in case they turned against the British colonial authorities.

56. Mukerjee, *Churchill's Secret War*, xxx.

57. Ibid., 77.

58. Baade, *Victory through Harmony*, 6.
59. Lawson, "'I Have a Request for Mrs. Smith.'"
60. Forces Programme: May 30, 1941, BBC Programmes as Broadcast Log.
61. Lawson, "'I Have a Request for Mrs. Smith.'"
62. Lynn, *Vocal Refrain*, 81.
63. The Broadcasters, "Both Sides of the Microphone," September 20, 1940, 4.
64. Cover, *Radio Times*, September 13, 1940, 1.
65. Macpherson, "Broadcasting during the War," 11.
66. The Broadcasters, "Both Sides of the Microphone," April 18, 1941, 2.
67. "Reginald Foort's Organ," BBC ICM from PC.Ex [Programme Contracts Executive] to Mr. Turnell, April 5, 1941, BBC WAC R27/154. Foort, who had become increasing concerned about the safety of his organ (as well as the difficulties of touring with travel restrictions and petrol rationing), had offered to rent his organ to the BBC in November 1940. Negotiations began in earnest in December, with a safe location a paramount consideration. "Interview with Mr. Reginald Foort: Sunday the 1st December at 10:30 a.m.," BBC ICM from DPP [Director of Programme Planning] to DV, December 1, 1940, BBC WAC R27/154; "Reginald Foort and his Organ," BBC ICM from DPP to DPA, December 13, 1940, BBC WAC R27/154.
68. "Transfer of Theatre Organ to Bangor," BBC ICM from Mr. Sandy Macpherson to ADV [Assistant Director of Variety], August 13, 1943, BBC WAC R27/154.
69. Taking more moderate opinions into consideration, 60 percent of listeners liked theater organs, 23 percent were neutral, and 17 percent disliked them, while 23 percent liked symphony concerts, 17 percent were neutral, and 60 percent were negative. It is worth noting that a year later, after the BBC had cracked down on theater organs, Listener Research recorded "a significant decrease in the popularity of Theatre and Cinema Organs": to 27 percent enthusiasts and 10 percent opponents and to 50 percent positive and 23 percent negative. Meanwhile, it celebrated the fact that the percentage of listeners hostile to symphony concerts fell to 28 percent in August 1942, although the enthusiasts rose to only 11 percent, positive numbers rose to 25 percent, and negative fell to 56 percent. BBC Listener Research, "Listener Research Bulletin No. 103," [1942], BBC WAC R27/411/2; "Paper on Listener Research for Royal Statistical Society," BBC ICM from Listener Research Director (RJE Silvey) to C(P), May 23, 1944, BBC WAC R9/15/1. For a fuller discussion of classical music and its audiences, see Baade, "Radio Symphonies," 49–71.
70. "Sandy's Half-Hour," BBC ICM from Director of Programme Planning to C(P), July 9, 1942, BBC WAC R19/686.
71. For a full discussion of the "crooner ban," see Baade, *Victory through Harmony*, 131–152.
72. C. Gordon Glover, "This Week's Miscellany," *Radio Times*, September 19, 1941, 5.

73. Ralph Hill, "This Week's Radio Music," *Radio Times*, September 26, 1941, 5.
74. Sandy Macpherson, "What the Other Listener Thinks," *Radio Times*, October 10, 1941, 8.
75. Baade, *Victory through Harmony*, 131–152.
76. "Cinema Organs," [c. April 1942], BBC WAC R27/411/2.
77. "Cinema Organists: Standard of Playing," BBC ICM from Controller (Programmes) to DV, February 3, 1942, BBC WAC R27/411/2; "Cinema Organists: Standard of Playing," BBC ICM from Director of Variety to Controller (Programmes), February 16, 1942, BBC WAC R27/411/2.
78. "Cinema Organs," BBC ICM from Assistant Controller (Programmes) to C(P), May 12, 1942, BBC WAC R27/411/2; "Cinema Organs," BBC ICM from Assistant Controller (Programmes) to DM [Director of Music] et al., May 14, 1942, BBC WAC R27/411/2; [letter to organists], May 20, 1942; "Leading Questions Put to Arthur Bliss," *Radio Times*, May 15, 1942, 5; "Cinema Organs," BBC ICM from Controller (Programmes) to AC(P) [Assistant Controller (Programmes)], April 9, 1942, BBC WAC R27/411/2; "Cinema Organs," BBC ICM from DM to AC(P), April 21, 1942, BBC WAC R27/411/2.
79. "'Sandy Calling' Friday 17th October from Glasgow," BBC ICM from Sandy Macpherson to DV, October 22, 1941, BBC WAC R19/686. If an outside broadcast was announced in advance, it might become a Luftwaffe target.
80. "Sandy's Half-Hour," BBC ICM from DV to Sandy Macpherson, March 18, 1942, BBC WAC R19/686.
81. "Sandy's Half-Hour," BBC ICM from Sandy Macpherson to DV, March 24, 1942, BBC WAC R19/686.
82. BBC ICM from DG to C(P), June 9, 1942, BBC WAC R19/686.
83. "Sandy's Half-Hour," BBC ICM from Director of Programme Planning to C(P), July 9, 1942, BBC WAC R19/686.
84. "Sandy Macpherson," BBC ICM from Mr. Norman Marshall to DPP, August 6, 1942, BBC WAC R19/686; "Sandy Macpherson," BBC ICM from Director of Programme Planning to DV, August 7, 1942, BBC WAC R19/686.
85. "Sandy's Half-Hour," BBC ICM from Assistant Director of Programme Planning to ADV, September 6, 1942, BBC WAC R19/686. The all-music version of *Sandy's Half-Hour* was replaced in 1943 by *I'll Play to You*, which ran until 1948. BBC Genome.
86. "Sandy Calling the Middle East," BBC ICM from Mr. Sandy Macpherson to GOSM [General Overseas Service Manager], April 14, 1944, BBC WAC R19/686.
87. Baade, *Victory through Harmony*, 166.
88. Knox, "A Little Console-ation," 2–3.
89. Ibid., 2.
90. Macpherson, "Broadcasting during the War," 13.
91. Langhamer, *The English in Love*, 9–10.
92. Ibid., 28.

93. Metcalfe had become popular during World War II as a "radio girl-friend"—i.e., a female host for an overseas forces audience. Baade, *Victory through Harmony*, 153–166.

94. The result of negotiations between the Musicians Union and Phonographic Performance Limited, the recording association, strict needletime restrictions were in force for the BBC from 1946 until the 1960s. Williamson and Cloonan, *Players' Work Time*, 20, 122–124.

95. "Purchase of Theatre Organ," BBC ICM from Director of Variety to C(P), June 7, 1945, BBC WAC R27/154.

## BIBLIOGRAPHY

**Historical Newspapers and Magazines**
*Radio Times*, 1936–1942
*Sunday Pictorial*, 1941
*Times* (London), 1929–1936

**Books and Articles**
Anderson, Ben. "Modulating the Excess of Affect: Morale in a State of 'Total War.'" In *The Affect Theory Reader*, edited by Melissa Gregg and Gregory J. Seigworth, 161–185. Durham: Duke University Press, 2010.

Anderson, W. R. "A Wireless Note." *Musical Times* (October 1939): 712.

Baade, Christina. "Radio Symphonies: Everyday Listening and the Popular Classics Debate during the People's War." In *Ubiquitous Musics: The Everyday Sounds That We Don't Always Notice*, edited by Anahid Kassabian, Marta Garcia Quiñones, and Elena Boschi, 49–71. Aldershot: Ashgate, 2013.

———. *Victory through Harmony: The BBC and Popular Music in World War II*. New York: Oxford University Press, 2012.

*BBC Genome: Radio Times 1923–2009*. Accessed April 30, 2019. https://genome.ch.bbc.co.uk.

BBC Programmes as Broadcast: Forces Programme (May 1941). British Broadcasting Corporation Written Archives Centre. Caversham.

Berlant, Lauren. *The Female Complaint: The Unfinished Business of Sentimentality in American Culture*. Durham, NC: Duke University Press, 2008.

Bliss, Arthur. *As I Remember*. London: Faber & Faber, 1970.

British Pathé. "Reginald Foort—Organist (1936)." *YouTube*. Accessed April 30, 2019. https://www.youtube.com/watch?v=qsq1UFH0AbQ.

British Pathé. "Reginald Foort with His New Wonder Organ (1939)." *YouTube*. Accessed April 30, 2019. https://www.youtube.com/watch?v=P8orjMvVtGU.

Carroll, Michael Thomas. *Popular Modernity in America: Experience, Technology, Mythohistory*. Albany: State University of New York Press, 2000.

Dyer, Richard. *Heavenly Bodies: Film Stars and Society*, 2nd ed. New York: Routledge, 2004.

Foort, Reginald. *The Cinema Organ: A Description in Non-Technical Language of a Fascinating Instrument and How It Is Played*. London: Sir Isaac Pitman & Sons, 1932.
———. Preface to *Behold the Mighty Wurlitzer: The History of the Theatre Pipe Organ*, by John W. Landon. Westport, CT: Greenwood, 1983.
———. "Organising the Organ." *Rhythm*, March 1939.
———. "You *Can* Take It with You!" In *Theatre Organ World*, edited by Jack Courtnay, 25–26. London: Tucker & Oxley, 1946.
Fox, David H. "Cinema Organ." In *Grove Music Online, Oxford Music Online*. Oxford University Press, 2001. Accessed April 30, 2019. https://doi-org.libaccess.lib.mcmaster.ca/10.1093/gmo/9781561592630.article.05796.
Frost, Phyllis. "Dance Band Announcers." *Rhythm* (March 1939), 56–59.
"Gardening Programmes on the BBC." *History of the BBC*, http://www.bbc.co.uk/historyofthebbc/research/programming/gardening.
Hillmer, Norman, Fred J. Hatch, and Patricia Myers (updated by Daniel Panneton). "British Commonwealth Air Training Plan." In *The Canadian Encyclopedia*, February 6, 2006 (last edited April 20, 2016). Accessed April 29, 2019. https://www.thecanadianencyclopedia.ca/en/article/british-commonwealth-air-training-plan.
Knox, Collie. "A Little Console-ation." In *Theatre Organ World*, edited by Jack Courtnay, 2–3. London: Tucker & Oxley, 1946.
Langhamer, Claire. *The English in Love: The Intimate Story of an Emotional Revolution*. New York: Oxford University Press, 2013.
Leonard, Kendra Preston. "Using Resources for Silent Film Music." *Fontes Artis Musicae* 63, no. 4 (2016): 259–276.
Loviglio, Jason. *Radio's Intimate Public: Network Broadcasting and Mass-Mediated Democracy*. Minneapolis: University of Minnesota Press, 2005.
Lynn, Vera. *Vocal Refrain*. London: WH Allen, 1975.
Macpherson, Sandy. "Broadcasting during the War." In *Theatre Organ World*, edited by Jack Courtnay, 11, 13. London: Tucker & Oxley, 1946.
Mukerjee, Madhusree. *Churchill's Secret War: The British Empire and the Ravaging of India during World War II*. New York: Basic Books, 2010.
Press Cuttings. British Broadcasting Corporation Written Archives Centre. Caversham.
Radio Files. Audience Research, Head of Audience Research Department, Wartime Listener Research Policy. R9/15/1. British Broadcasting Corporation Written Archives Centre. Caversham.
———. Entertainment: Macpherson, Sandy Programmes, 1941–1953. R19/686. British Broadcasting Corporation Written Archives Centre. Caversham.
———. Foort, Reginald, January 1, 1936, to December 31, 1942. R94/1, 667/1. British Broadcasting Corporation Written Archives Centre. Caversham.
———. Macpherson, Roderick Hal (Sandy), January 1, 1938, to December 31, 1963. R94/2, 53/1. British Broadcasting Corporation Written Archives Centre. Caversham.

———. Music General: Instruments, Theatre Organ, 1940–1947. R27/154. British Broadcasting Corporation Written Archives Centre. Caversham.
———. Music General: Organs, Cinema and Theatre, 1942–44. R27/411/2. British Broadcasting Corporation Written Archives Centre. Caversham.
Razlogova, Elena. *The Listener's Voice: Early Radio and the American Public.* Philadelphia: University of Pennsylvania Press, 2011.
*Silent Film Sound & Music Archive.* http://www.sfsma.org.
Special collections. Madden: Wartime Radio Diary. S24/54/13. British Broadcasting Corporation Written Archives Centre. Caversham.
Stacey, Jackie. *Star Gazing: Hollywood Cinema and Female Spectatorship.* London: Routledge, 1994.
Williamson, John and Martin Cloonan. *Players' Work Time: A History of the British Musicians' Union, 1893–2013.* Manchester: Manchester University Press, 2016.

CHRISTINA L. BAADE is Professor and Chair in the Department of Communication Studies and Multimedia at McMaster University. She is author of the award-winning *Victory through Harmony: The BBC and Popular Music in World War II* and editor (with James Deaville) of *Music and the Broadcast Experience: Performance, Production, and Audiences.*

TWO

# "ALIEN" CLASSICAL MUSICIANS AND THE BBC, 1939–1945

TONY STOLLER

> The value of a piece of music has nothing whatsoever to do with the character of the composer or with the moral characteristics of his country. The final appeal of music is universal... nevertheless, I think there is quite a lot to say for the banning during wartime of some products of enemy countries. Nobody but an unmusical imbecile could possibly find any connection between Madame Butterfly and Mussolini, but Heldenleben and Hitler might tempt more astute and impressionable minds.
>
> Ralph Hill, "This Week's Radio Music," *Radio Times,* November 1, 1940, 7

WHEN WE THINK NOW ABOUT cultural resonances of the First World War, we think essentially of literature: the contemporary poetry of Wilfred Owen, Siegfried Sassoon, and Isaac Rosenberg; the later novels of Erich Remarque; and the dramas of R. C. Sherriff. For the Second World War, equivalent cultural signifiers can be found in music, both popular and classical, mediated through sound broadcasting. These were already the years of electronic entertainment, with movies widespread and sound broadcasting everywhere, from the home to the canteen, in the factory and in the barracks. High culture in music reached out more widely than it had done before or has done since, and the war between the Allied and Axis powers therefore brought into question the place of German and Italian composers and performers who were so central to that art form.

Radio, or "the wireless" as it was usually called at the time, reached its apogee during the Second World War. As Christina Baade has written, "Music was regarded widely as a key component of the BBC's morale-boosting programming; however, there was significant disagreement over which music would best accomplish this task, especially given the lack of choice imposed by the single wavelength."[1] After a good deal of to-ing and fro-ing, popular music claimed radio in Britain from the limitations of a prewar BBC, which had tended to take itself rather too seriously, and from dance bands to Vera Lynn, it spoke to mass audiences as never before. Nevertheless, classical music also occupied a position of high significance between 1939 and 1945, beyond anything it had enjoyed before or was to enjoy after. The technologies of sound broadcasting and of music recording came together in those years to create and define public perception of what their national culture comprised. Thus, in the clash of ideas between representative democracy and fascism, which at the deepest level was what the war was about, this central element of European culture was paradigmatic.

It is unsurprising therefore that, in many ways, classical music provided the cultural soundtrack for the Second World War: the obligatory performance of the overture to Richard Wagner's *Die Meistersinger* at all Nazi rallies; Dmitry Shostakovich's Seventh Symphony being broadcast over the front lines of besieged Leningrad; Olivier Messiaen's ushering in the second age of musical modernism with his *Quartet for the End of Time*, written and first performed in prisoner-of-war camp Stalag VIIIA; and William Walton's *Agincourt Suite*, composed for Laurence Olivier's propagandist wartime filming of Shakespeare's *Henry V*. For the mass of the wartime public in Britain, especially, music mostly came to them through the radio, and therefore from the BBC.

The significance of classical music in the United Kingdom was enhanced by the role that it played within a society at war, symbolized by Myra Hess's lunchtime concerts at the National Gallery in London and live performances by amateur and professional orchestras and choirs throughout the provinces. The wartime government created the Council for the Encouragement of Music and the Arts (CEMA) in 1940 to promote musical activity on the home front, while the Entertainments National Service Association was not just about comedians and variety but also brought concerts and live music to the troops at home and overseas. Many people speak about a "cultural renaissance" during the later years of the war, which carried forward into peacetime.[2] Among its fruits were the Arts Council, the successor to CEMA, and in broadcasting, the introduction of the Third Programme in September 1946.

There were from the very start of the war challenges about playing music composed or performed by those whom the BBC called "alien" musicians, meaning "enemy aliens," who were nationals or residents of countries with which Britain was at war. Those who compiled popular music radio programs had their own difficulties with such "alien" musicians, although rather more after the war than during it. Several so-called collaborators were excluded from British airwaves, including Maurice Chevalier, who was banned in 1945.[3]

For popular music, this was a reasonably peripheral issue; the majority of wartime popular music was British or American in origin and could be played without concern. For classical music, however, the position was much more challenging. Much of the classical music broadcast on radio was centered on the tradition of Austro-German compositions from the eighteenth century right up until the middle of the twentieth century. That applied to what we may describe as radio's "classical music canonic repertoire," as much as to the slightly different concert-hall and academic canons.

There are those who argue that the BBC followed a policy of "racial exclusion" in respect of programming works by such alien composers and performers.[4] However, as this chapter will demonstrate, whatever seemingly restrictive written policies might have been compiled, the reality in practice was that, by and large, the canonic repertoire did not greatly change during the war years or in its immediate aftermath, albeit with some hotly debated exclusions. This chapter will therefore consider the place of classical music on the BBC at the start of the war; the evolving policy toward works written and/or performed by nationals of enemy countries, especially alien composers; the extent to which actual broadcasts reflected (or more usually did not reflect) the stricter requirements of those policies; how the policy impacted "new" music broadcasts; and the situation at the end of the war. It will primarily be concerned with domestic broadcasting. There are, of course, transnational considerations based on international broadcasting, such as the BBC's Empire Service and then the Overseas Service. However, this is a substantial topic on its own, well researched by Claire Launchbury among others, and it is separate from the examination of the relationship between British domestic broadcasting and non-British composers or performers.[5]

The term *classical music* may in itself seem problematic. The BBC very largely avoided using it, preferring instead *serious music*. Still, whatever debates there may be around the margins, the term is well understood in common usage. The German cultural theorist Theodor Adorno, one of the most notable of the cultural refugees from Germany into the United States, wrote of "the music we are accustomed to call classical."[6] Taking that cue, it is appropriate to work on the basis that if those programming works of music and those listening to them accepted them as part of the classical music canonic repertoire, then that is what they were and are.

In organizational terms, the distinction between serious and popular music was significant for the BBC because they were looked after by separate departments, with the Gramophone Department adding an extra bureaucratic complication. That raises interesting issues about where to place works that are by common consent "light classical," including the operas of Gilbert and Sullivan, which were so popular during these years. The discourse about popular classics is a fascinating one, not least in the way it is revealing about class-based attitudes toward cultural and musical taste. Baade has written revealingly about the debate over the popularizing of classical music on BBC airwaves during the war years.[7] However, for the purposes of this chapter, the reflexive definition sketched in the previous paragraph will serve perfectly well.

There are two ways of examining how the BBC approached this question: contemporary written material, largely from the BBC written archives and relevant journalism; and the actual program content, which is examined in the next section. Some existing scholarship gives extensive prominence to the BBC's internal politics and its reflection in contemporary journalism.[8] That is characteristic of a good deal of broadcasting history because the programs themselves are mostly evanescent, and their analysis is challenging. In that approach, the lists of "banned composers" seem to stand out. However, in this chapter, actual and proxy analysis is used to show the extent to which what was broadcast differed markedly from the supposed policy and its restrictions.

The radio historian would like to be an auditory time traveler, in order to evaluate the actual output and to absorb the sense and style of programming. In place of that delicious implausibility, it is possible to adopt three interlocking methodologies to examine past programming output, drawing on the listings information published in the *Radio Times* (while accepting that those listings are broadly but not universally accurate), a process now made much more practicable by the BBC's Genome project, which as discussed later allows for online searching of the newly digitized *Radio Times* archive.[9] The first method is a quantitative analysis of the number of works of representative composers included in BBC programming during the war. The second is qualitative, looking through those program listings and associated information to gain a sense of what was broadcast. The third method, sampling, is both quantitative and qualitative. It stands as a proxy for complete immersion and involves taking sample weeks from the output, examining the *Radio Times* listings in detail, and checking those against the Programmes as Broadcast logs.[10] Sampling is axiomatically incomplete; however, so long as the analysis of sample weeks is not left to stand on its own, it is a valuable complement to the other more comprehensive but less in-depth methodologies. In this chapter, original analysis of week nineteen (usually the first full week of May) for each year of the war (1940–1945) adds to our understanding of the BBC's policy on alien classical music.

### WHEN WAR BROKE OUT

At the outbreak of war, the BBC got it completely wrong. As Asa Briggs relates, radio output, restricted to a single channel, "consisted of 10 daily news bulletins—there had been five before war broke out—and scores of official announcements, lasting for at least one hour a day, hundreds of gramophone records, pep talks by ministers ... and by civil servants, and large doses of Sandy MacPherson [*sic*]

(23 in the first week and 22 in the second), unruffled and inviolate at the theatre organ."[11]

It was only at the end of 1939 that a sensible pattern of wartime home broadcasting was agreed on. Baade has described the BBC's struggles with popular music, jazz, and light music, but serious music was, from the start, a central part of the output.[12] From 1940 onward, the BBC broadcast two radio channels: the Home Service, for domestic consumption, and the Forces Programme, which was intended, as its name implies, for the fighting troops overseas as much as for those back in the United Kingdom but in practice serving for all listeners as a lighter and more popular alternative to the relative formality of the Home Service. The Forces Programme was to be succeeded by the General Forces Programme, from February 1944. In terms of classical music, the aims and volume of classical music output on the two services were very different, but taken together they represent a substantial and perhaps surprising corpus of programming.

Once programs began to settle down, my own sample week analysis indicates that such music occupied typically twenty-six hours of the weekly output, compared with twenty-one hours of light music.[13] Once two radio channels were operating, classical music initially represented nearly one-fifth of the Home Service output, but just 2.5 percent of the Forces Programme output. Rob Greenway has discussed the debate within the BBC over how much classical music should be included in the Forces Programme.[14] While recognizing an educational dimension to featuring classical music on the Forces Programme, there was some hesitation about overdoing it. Nevertheless, sample week analysis indicates that from the end of 1940 until the end of 1943 classical music typically accounted for around 15 percent of the Home Service output and nearly 4 percent of the Forces Programme, with Home Service output slipping to 10 percent only in the last year of the war (when the percentage in the new General Forces Programme exceeded that of its predecessor).

Such high-level representation and impact for classical music broadcasts was to continue throughout the war. Two programs stand out: *Orchestral Half Hour* from February 1940 and *Forces Music Club*, which was introduced in September 1941. The first broadcast of *Forces Music Club* featured compositions by Bach, Mozart, and Edward Elgar, but also Jean Sibelius (who, as will be discussed, was regarded as an alien composer because of Finland's position as an enemy of the Soviet Union, Britain's ally). Most remarkably, it included the *Ride of the Valkyries* from Wagner's *Die Walküre*, which could hardly have been more central to the musical iconography of the Nazi regime.[15]

The audiences for classical music programs also reached levels that were never to be achieved in peacetime. On the sampled Friday in May 1945, a lunchtime performance of Beethoven's Fifth Symphony was listened to by one and a quarter million adults, while an evening concert of music by Gilbert and Sullivan reached a remarkable three and a half million listeners.[16] The nature of the musical and cultural renaissance in Britain in the immediate postwar years suggests that this was not default listening in the absence of other diversions but a genuine increase in the appetite for this type of output. Postwar analysis indicates a potential audience of between five and six million listeners to classical music radio programs throughout the second half of the century.[17]

These striking listener statistics invite questions about how they were produced and the place of audience research within the Corporation. The BBC had come rather late to the measuring of audience numbers. Sean Street relates how it chose initially to rely on its own judgment in deciding what should be broadcast rather than, as it saw it, pandering to mass taste.[18] It had no audience research function at all until 1936, but by 1939 it was compiling information from a combination of face-to-face interviews and self-completion diaries to produce a Continuous Survey of Listening, which for postwar radio would come to be known as the Daily Listening Barometer.[19] By contemporary standards, the research methodology seems rather antiquated and imprecise, but when a more rigorous industry-wide methodology was introduced in 1974, and then refined in 1993, it confirmed the relative accuracy of the earlier data.[20]

### ALIEN COMPOSERS IN BBC PROGRAMS

When contemplating how to approach classical music programming from 1940 onward, BBC programmers would have been well aware of the strength of anti-German feeling during the First World War, when anti-German riots were not uncommon in British cities.[21] The piano maker Carl Bechstein had opened his Bechstein Hall in 1902, but in 1916 his business was closed down by order of the president of the Board of Trade, and the hall was shut down.[22] It reopened the following January as the Wigmore Hall, but the works of composers such as Richard Strauss disappeared from concert programs there and elsewhere.

Such events were not replicated in the Second World War, although that was an even grimmer existential struggle. Perhaps the most significant action taken by the British government in respect to classical musicians in 1939–1940 was the internment of "enemy aliens," many of them Jewish refugees. Like so much about this period, the history seems two-edged. Indiscriminate internment now appears a gross overreaction, and there is no doubt that internees suffered considerable hardships, and there was some loss of life. For internees such as Hans Keller, whom Alison Garnham describes as the "musical conscience of British broadcasting" through the 1960s and 1970s, it seemed a bitter reward for escaping the Gestapo in Vienna.[23] Yet, as Andrew Marr has noted, the internment camp on the Isle of Man "became a bubbling centre of culture unmatched almost anywhere in wartime Europe, with lectures, string quartets, theoretical science and art all flourishing. So many major musical and cultural figures found themselves in the internment camps that it was said that for two years the centre of European cultural life was in the town of Ramsey on the Isle of Man where the largest camps were situated."[24]

It was here that three émigré musicians—Norbert Brainin, Siegmund Nissel, and Peter Schidlof—first met, forming the Amadeus Quartet after the war with Martin Lovett, and here that Hans Keller was able to develop his musical and critical philosophy, which was to shine within the BBC's postwar classical music radio services. There is a sense that, almost despite itself, Britain was harnessing the best output of those enemy nationals who came to its shores; they may well have been interned amid some privations, but they were laying the foundations for a dominant cultural element in British society for the decade following the conflict.

The prominence of Jewish classical music composers and performers in the mid-century made things difficult for some people within the BBC. Jean Seaton has written that "the BBC displayed, both before and during the war, views and decisions that were quite simply anti-Semitic."[25] If so, then the actions of the successive directors of Music at the BBC, Adrian Boult and Arthur Bliss, in gaining release for Keller and others represent a significant counterbalance. They were also going against much common prejudice.[26] Jenny Doctor notes the evidence given to the Ullswater Committee in 1935 by the Incorporated Society for Musicians (ISM) that the BBC showed an anti-British bias in its selection of music and musicians, "probably due to the predominant influence of London, and to the superficially cosmopolitan perceptions of some of its more active cliques."[27] As contemporary observers would immediately have understood, "cosmopolitan" was a frequent euphemism for "Jewish."

In its own evidence to Ullswater, the BBC strenuously refuted the ISM's claims, even though it was to an extent reflecting the views of its own Music Advisory Committee. For the BBC, Henry Walford Davies "emphatically affirmed the extraordinary opportunities that broadcasting had provided for the entire country."[28] The Ullswater report firmly endorsed his assertion of the validity of the BBC's approach to music broadcasting.[29] Nevertheless, at the outbreak of war three years later, much of the resentment at the BBC's unwillingness to bend to the domestic music lobby would have persisted.

## THE DEVELOPMENT OF PROGRAM POLICY

For those building BBC music programs, a central question in the early years of the Second World War was whether the works of alien composers should be included. The category at the start included composers who were citizens of Axis powers, later joined by Finland, given that Britain was at war with the post-1940 ally of the USSR, and also Vichy France from July 1940. Three elements ran through music policy making in respect to alien composers and musicians throughout the war. The first was the issue of copyright, because playing works that attracted royalty payments to the Axis countries might be seen as trading with the enemy. Second was the deeper matter of morality in either playing works that encapsulated the spirit of Britain's enemies or, alternatively, not playing them and thereby standing aside from mainstream musical culture. The third consideration was how to treat collaborators with the administrations in occupied nations, particularly France, although there the impact was mainly—though not exclusively—on postwar output.[30]

In September 1939, the BBC's deputy director of Music, R. S. Thatcher, set out the initial policy, which was to develop through the war years: "There is no change of policy regarding the broadcasting of music by foreign composers. We are not, I mean, banning German music. It is, however, desirable that music by British composers should be fully exploited and that—within the convenience of programme planning—the broadcasting of music by foreign composers to PRS [Performing Rights Society] payments are due, should be limited."[31]

Perhaps unsure of their moral ground, copyright obligation was to be the BBC's most often cited justification in the early years of the war for limiting the appearance of works composed or performed by alien musicians. It also fitted well with the interests of the ISM, which pressed the Corporation repeatedly to include more works by living British composers. In July 1940, after the British Expeditionary Forces were evacuated from Dunkirk and when Britain began to realize the extent to which it stood alone against the Axis powers, the BBC moved to a fairly rigid exclusion of "copyright works by composers of enemy nationality . . . not only for psychological reasons but because of the increase in performing rights which are thereby made available for British, Allied and friendly composers."[32]

In the event, the extent of this "ban"—although it caused controversy and resentment within the BBC—was relatively limited.[33] The Austro-German-based canon remained at the heart of BBC classical music broadcasting, certainly in terms of the First Viennese School, together with the major Italian operatic composers. Even when the BBC Symphony Orchestra had been evacuated from London to Bristol to avoid the bombing of the capital city, the first concert in its 1940 series had a second part—which was broadcast—entirely devoted to extracts from Wagner's operas. When this was challenged by a letter of complaint to the local newspaper, the *Bristol Evening Post*, its critic Ralph Hill expressed the majority and also the BBC view that "by their unstinted applause, the audience gave the lie to the fantastic myth that the music of Wagner cannot or should not be appreciated by civilised people at war with Germany."[34]

The difficulty of the moral consideration is best exemplified by the treatment of Wagner's compositions. His works had been championed by British musicologists throughout the twentieth century, even when their close identification with the Nazi regime was understood, and were broadcast by the BBC throughout the war years, with little excluded. Wagner—a dead composer, with no copyright entitlement—therefore fared better in terms of stated policy than did the living Richard Strauss.

Much difficulty surrounded the work of Richard Strauss, who was considered to have been "notoriously anti-British during the last war."[35] From the documents alone, it might appear that this composer was to be the chief exception to a relatively flexible policy, partly as consequence of his willingness to accept musical posts in the Third Reich. The BBC's rationale at the time for saying that it would exclude his music was that "he has never hesitated to assume the official leadership of the Nazi Reichskammer, and this is widely known and resented by musicians everywhere."[36] The accuracy of this claim, and the rights and wrongs of Strauss's actions, have been debated ever since, including in a fine 2014 BBC radio drama by Martyn Wade, *Hide the Moon*. Yet, as will be discussed later, any nominal exclusion was honored as much in the breach as the observance, at least after the very early years of the war.

The BBC's developing policy acknowledged by mid-1940 that at least a few alien composers needed to continue to be broadcast "by reason of the firm hold they have obtained on the affection to the public, and because certain of their works are so individual and characteristic as to be irreplaceable any extensive programme scheme [but wished] to limit the performance of the works concerned to a minimum far below their appearance in peacetime."[37]

The composers listed were Max Bruch (who seemed to be picked on by both sides), Ferruccio Busoni, Engelbert Humperdinck, Fritz Kreisler, Adalgiso Ferraris, Giacomo Puccini, Ruggero Leoncavallo, Pietro Mascagni, and Giuseppe Verdi. However, the BBC's music practice was much more flexible even than this slightly modified written policy would suggest. Genome analysis of the *Radio Times* listings shows that works by all of these composers—apart from Leoncavallo and the doubly unfortunate Bruch—were performed during 1941 and more extensively throughout the rest of the war. Perhaps it was unsurprising that the BBC's overseas director of Music, K. A. Wright, wrote about the current list of excluded composers to his producers in December 1941: "I might add that you should not take this list too seriously now, as a good many exceptions have been allowed for various reasons."[38]

Such a flexible approach received critical approval. Notably, in November 1940 Ralph Hill wrote in the *Radio Times* offering an analysis of the issues as those in the clubbable atmosphere of the BBC saw them.[39] He recalled the First World War, when UK newspapers had demanded the complete banning of Beethoven's music, and asked why, "because we are at war with Mozart's country should we wish to deprive ourselves of the many inspired qualities of Mozart music? . . . I feel very deeply that by withholding performances of music by men who themselves are anti-Nazi or even died before 1933, we are using the enemy's own technique to our own moral disadvantage. . . . The matter embraces both money and ethics and I submit that the economic aspect of the question should be subservient to the ethical one."

Hill went on to make an almost postmodernist point, before qualifying it with the pragmatic: "The value of a piece of music has nothing whatsoever to do with the character of the composer or with the moral characteristics of his country. The final appeal of music is universal . . . nevertheless, I think there is quite a lot to say for the banning during wartime of some products of enemy countries. Nobody but an unmusical imbecile could possibly find any connection between *Madame Butterfly* and Mussolini, but *Heldenleben* and Hitler might tempt more astute and impressionable minds."[40] This nuanced attitude very much caught the tone of the BBC's own policy approach, which was to be modified even further in practice.

Some academics, however, have suggested that the BBC operated a much more jingoistic process of exclusion, especially of German composers. It has been asserted that the BBC in its music programming had a policy of "being beastly to the Germans," and operated a "racial filter . . . within days of the start of the war."[41] The dominating presence of Beethoven and Bach in the actual program schedules confounds any suggestion of a policy of racial exclusion. Indeed, Beethoven's music was everywhere, notably in the audio symbol of wartime resistance, the opening notes from his Fifth Symphony.

Still, BBC policy had some bizarre early consequences, not least because the relative isolation of the BBC from prewar contemporary European music meant that it got quite a lot of things wrong. The work of Oscar Straus was initially excluded on the grounds that he was an Austrian composer, despite the fact that he had been "presented, a year [before], with French citizenship by the president of the French Republic."[42] From June 1941 onward, once Hitler had invaded Russia, Sibelius's *Finlandia* was to be excluded because of its nationalistic tone relating to a country at war with the Soviet Union. Bruch had the unwelcome distinction of being banned by the BBC as an alien composer and by the Nazis as a Jew (although he wasn't). Even though he had died in 1920 and therefore had no entitlement to royalties, he remained on the list of composers where "the Corporation wishes to limit the performance of [their] works . . . to a minimum far below their appearance in peace time" because the royalties payable for performances of their works would mean less available for "British, Allied and friendly composers."[43]

## PROGRAM CONTENT

The BBC's *Radio Times* Genome project has been discussed. However, it is important to enter a note of caution here. Material actually broadcast may have differed to a degree from the *Radio Times* listings, and the Genome itself is not yet flawless and is far from complete in its program content listings. With those reservations, searching a series of composer names in different date spans suggests that the most preeminent of what might be supposed alien composers were by no means excluded from the BBC's airwaves. Counting up those programs in which works of their music were actually performed, broadcasts of Wagner's compositions began as low as ten throughout 1940 but had risen to as high as fifty-eight by 1944. Richard Strauss was more obviously excluded in the early years of the war, going unperformed in 1941 and 1942, but, after a small revival in 1943, his works were featured in as many as twenty-five programs in 1944 and nineteen in 1945.

These data can be benchmarked against the most outstanding English composers. Works by Elgar were included in twenty-five programs in 1940, rising to fifty-two in 1942, and then, after a further surge, fell back to forty-two in 1945. Compositions by Ralph Vaughan Williams (excluding hymns broadcast as part of liturgical church services) were in the teens in 1940 and 1941, the twenties in 1942 and 1943, and rose to forty-one in 1944. Thus, while the works of the quintessential English composer Elgar were heard roughly twice as often as those of the German *Ikone* Wagner, the deficit was no more than that, still leaving a substantial Wagnerian offering.

For the other Axis nations, the position was much the same. Programs containing works by Verdi were played throughout the war years, rising from single figures in 1940 and 1941 to thirty separate performances in 1944. Live relays of *La Traviata* were broadcast from Sadler's Wells Theatre as early as April 1940 and then again in January and November 1941. Puccini's oeuvre also enjoyed plenty of performances, appearing in radio schedules on ten occasions in 1940, rising to twenty-six in 1944.[44] Whatever concerns there might have been about the position of Sibelius once the USSR had entered the war against Germany in June 1941, his works were heavily featured. In both 1944 and 1945, there were forty-five performances of his compositions, exceeding the number of times that Vaughan Williams was heard, for all his personal prominence in BBC musical circles.

The details of the program listings themselves are also revealing. As early as spring 1941, the Home Service was broadcasting a talk by Walter Legge to mark the birthday of Wagner.[45] During 1944, both Wagner and Richard Strauss were given the accolade of being "This Week's Composer." The same status was awarded to Sibelius in November 1943 and again in November 1944, and his birthday was celebrated in broadcasts during December 1942. To provide a benchmark once more, through all the war years Vaughan Williams was "This Week's Composer" only once, in April 1944, although he shared the status with John Ireland earlier that year. The clear conclusion is that, whatever policy papers might be written on memoranda exchanged, there was no systematic exclusion of alien composers in BBC radio broadcasts during the war years.

Systematic analysis of program listings in *Radio Times* for the sample week also reveals a more relaxed approach to the works of deceased alien composers than the policy documents suggest. BBC programming before the outbreak of war had relied heavily on works by nineteenth-century Austro-German composers. Analysis of the sample weeks for 1938 and 1939 shows that Bach, Beethoven, Brahms, Mozart, Schubert, Robert Schumann, and Mendelssohn were the most often featured composers. Those who compiled BBC radio programs in May 1939 seemed to have shared the view that, at root, "classical music was German music."[46]

That changed only slightly after 1939. Despite their different approaches, the two BBC wartime radio channels of the Home Service and the Forces Programme were notable in the sampled week in May 1940 for the inclusion of several works by Wagner among the mostly nineteenth-century masters. The most frequently played composer was Mozart, with Beethoven, Elgar, and Wagner all prominent. Whatever the discussions behind the scenes, what the listeners continued to hear was the standard classical canon and very little contemporary music, indeed, of any nationality. During the sampled week in May 1942, for example, the Home Service and Forces Programme included compositions by Bach, Beethoven, Haydn, Mozart, Mendelssohn, Schubert, Johann Strauss (son), plus a talk on "the essence of Brahms," yet still found space for the march from Wagner's *Tannhäuser* in the Forces Programme, striking a German martial note.

BBC Senior Controller Basil Nicolls and Director of Music Bliss had debated in 1941 what the latter called "coaxing Caliban"—getting a maximum audience for classical music radio. Whereas Nicolls was inclusive in his approach to attracting listeners, Bliss tended toward the "blatantly elitist."[47] Yet when he was appointed as BBC director of Music in April 1942, he was greeted by a document prepared by Nicolls that "for the first time formulated the professional broadcaster's point of view about the dissemination of serious music; that it was the size of audience that was primarily important, not what in a later decade was to be called the 'quality of listening.'"[48] This idea, that it was the number of people attracted to the programs that should be the primary concern, rather than the artistic essence of their content, was to be roughly set aside in the 1950s by an increase in the elitism within the BBC.[49] Yet it must be acknowledged that in the 1940s it was a much more significant motivation for the program planners than concerns about alien music-makers; rather, they saw an opportunity to make full use of the increased interest in and profile of classical music in radio programs.

## IMPACT ON "NEW" MUSIC OUTPUT

The chief impact of the restriction of the works of alien composers was felt on newly composed music, which represented then, before, and since only a small proportion of radio broadcasts. Arthur Bliss, who succeeded Adrian Boult as the BBC's director of Music in 1942, held the view "that in wartime, the BBC ought to give special support and encouragement to British Empire composers."[50] As a result, "the period from 1942 was one in which the new music heard on radio almost exclusively originated from countries allied to, or sympathetic to, the cause of Britain in the war."[51] In the 1943 sample week, there was no non-British new music broadcast at all. This was not true for the entire year, in which, for example, there were four programs including works of Francis Poulenc. Nonetheless, Aaron Copland's music was not heard on the BBC during 1943, although it was heard three times in 1944.

Bliss's diaries, as set out in his autobiography *As I Remember*, give little indication that he was exercised at all about the position of alien composers within the BBC's music output; his was a positive wish to promote British composers. Indeed, the plight of Austria after the war seems to have moved him much more than did concerns about the performance of works by its citizens during the six years of conflict: "In May of [1946] ... I conducted the Vienna Philharmonic.... After so many years absence it was a shock to see post-war Vienna, the proud city, brought so low, and its people looking so impoverished and under-nourished. Watching players in the orchestra I just could not bring myself to make them sustain long rehearsals, though the music was completely strange to them: it was sufficient pleasure for me just to work briefly with this famous orchestra."[52] Later scholarship has identified the Vienna Philharmonic as an arch-collaborator with the Nazi regime.[53] That this might be a problem clearly never crossed Bliss's mind at that time.

Had the works of contemporary German, Austrian, or Italian composers been particularly prominent in the broadcasts of the late 1930s, their exclusion or "discouragement" during the war years might have had more meaning. Yet Doctor has demonstrated that, for example, works by the Second Viennese School in BBC programming in the 1930s were few and far between.[54] There were only eighty-five performances of fifty-nine works by members of the Second Viennese School in the five and a half years up to May 1936, a small percentage of the BBC's overall classical music output.

Concerts were from the start in the 1920s a key element in the BBC's output, "as an essential means by which the BBC could interact with its audience."[55] The maintenance of those through the war years was therefore both a practical source of broadcast output and a symbol of continuity when so much was under threat. The BBC house orchestras and other orchestras played concerts in cities around the nation. Malcolm Sargent, who was to take over as the chief conductor of the Henry Wood Promenade Concerts (Proms) in 1947, at least partly made his popular reputation in this way. Garnham explains that "his blitz tour with the LPO [London Philharmonic Orchestra], bringing orchestral music to the music halls and variety theatres of major provincial cities, then suffering heavily under the bombings, had been a tremendously popular contribution to the war effort."[56]

The Proms themselves were dealt a shattering blow when their traditional home, the Queen's Hall in Langham Place, was destroyed by firebombing during the night of May 10–11, 1941. The photograph of Henry Wood standing amid the ruins of the hall became, in Doctor's words, "a powerful symbol of defiant survival" in Britain during the Blitz.[57] The Proms were relocated to the Royal Albert Hall. Once the BBC resumed running them in 1942, these broadcast concerts—along with the recitals of Myra Hess—gave London some cultural continuity in a time of change and horror. The Proms had to be suspended late in June 1944, after a near miss with a V-1 flying bomb, but resumed in time for the dying Henry Wood to complete his final performance "with a forceful and memorable broadcast of Beethoven's Seventh Symphony" on July 28.[58]

The position in occupied France was particularly challenging. At the invitation of Jacques Rouche, director of the Paris Opéra, Poulenc had been considering as early as 1937 the idea of composing a ballet based on fables by Jean de La Fontaine. It received its premiere at the Opéra Garnier in August 1942 in the middle of the season of German music "mounted at the insistence of the occupying forces."[59] There was sufficient concern that this might be a collaborationist work for Poulenc's name to be added to "the main list of those whose work should be included only after a special application to the Assistant Director of Music (general) at the BBC."[60] Yet, as Launchbury demonstrates, by the end of the war Poulenc was working closely with the BBC, especially with the BBC's French Service, and a production in English of his cantata *Figure Humaine* was given its premiere by the BBC at considerable expense and broadcast on the Home Service in March 1945.

### POSTWAR POLICIES

Three particular considerations affected classical music radio broadcasting in the United Kingdom at the end of the war. The first was a keen awareness, especially among BBC staff either returning from war service or through involvement with the BBC German Service, of the significance of classical music in the reconstruction of postwar Germany and Austria. It was deliberate Allied policy to use classical music, including in radio broadcasts, as part of the process of reestablishing civil society. Toby Thacker notes that "many German people turned to elements of their cultural past in an effort to salvage something from the ruins of their national inheritance. Nothing was better suited to this than the music of the 'great composers.' As a consequence of this, in the Federal Republic, these were the 'golden years' when the great German orchestras and performers resumed their former position of supremacy."[61]

Second, the war itself changed classical music. Although from 1945 Europe was divided politically and militarily between the nations of the West and those within the Soviet sphere of influence in the East, for serious music in both halves of the divided continent, the end of the war and its aftermath released a broadly equivalent second wave of modernism. This was to last as a dominant feature in self-regarding musical circles until the fall of the Berlin Wall in 1989 and challenge radio programmers accordingly.[62]

The third issue was the treatment of those composers who were considered to have collaborated in the enemy war effort or whose music was integral to the Nazi project. While it was straightforward to exclude certain works, such as the "Horst-Wessel-Lied," what about Beethoven, Anton Brucker, Wagner, and, above all, that most frequently performed composer during the Third Reich, Richard Strauss?[63] Wagner remained a staple part of the BBC's musical output, with the BBC going out of its way to broadcast his operas in 1946. The *BBC Handbook* reporting on 1946 output also made a point of noting the Wagner broadcasts: "On 24 and 28 October [1946] there were complete performance of 'Tristan and Isolde,' with... Sir Thomas Beecham conducting the BBCSO. In December Beecham conducted two performances of 'Die Walküre.'"[64]

And what of Richard Strauss? While his works were heard less often than were the quintessentially Austrian waltzes and polkas of Johann Strauss father and son, they had appeared in BBC programs throughout the war. In the very week of V-E Day, which marked the end of the European war and was wildly celebrated in the United Kingdom on May 8, 1945, the BBC broadcast Richard Strauss's tone poem *Don Juan* as its main Saturday concert piece. Along with Brahms's *Requiem* on V-E Day itself, four days earlier, these were the major concerts of that whole highly charged week. Otherwise, the BBC's postwar response was equivocal, especially about Richard Strauss. A list "of those [alien] composers most in demand" whose works might now be broadcast was prepared in 1946, but with the warning to "guard against a flooding with foreign works as a result of this clearance... the actual choice of works also should be made more discreetly: for example, apart from its use in an appropriate feature program, we should not yet perform Strauss' 'Ein Heldenleben.'"[65]

The treatment of Richard Strauss's works illustrates the extent to which the BBC had to look both ways on the question of alien composers. In 1947 a BBC producer was warned that "you will have to watch your step about the Strauss Festival, in view of the Board ruling that ex-Nazis can be employed ad hoc but not glorified by a festival or anything equivalent."[66] Yet a photograph of Richard Strauss alongside BBC stalwart Adrian Boult adorns the *BBC Handbook* of 1949, in resolution perhaps of the shattering discord of the image of the firebombed Queens Hall in 1941.[67]

## CONCLUSION

From its start in the eighteenth and nineteenth centuries, classical music, in its accepted canonic forms, had been very heavily influenced by the works of those composers who had been nationals of the very countries with which Britain was at war between 1939 and 1945. The BBC, therefore, had little option other than to consider to what extent the works of what it dubbed alien composers—and their compatriot performers—should be included in radio program output. It had itself set aside an institutional anti-Semitism to behave pretty decently toward émigré musicians, especially those interned in the United Kingdom, and had resisted the kind of unthinking prejudice toward German musicians that had been a feature of the home front in the First World War. Nevertheless, it adopted policies about the inclusion in radio programs of the works of alien composers—from Germany, Italy (until the fall of the Fascist regime), Finland (once it was at war with the USSR), and Vichy France—that appear at first sight from the documents to represent a conscious and quite wide-ranging set of exclusions.

An analysis of what was actually broadcast, however, indicates a much more nuanced approach. It is reasonable to conclude that, taking all in all, the BBC was quintessentially "British" in its wartime broadcasting of classical music, struggling with side issues while fudging the central ones. In practice, BBC radio broadcast lots of Beethoven and Mozart, some Wagner, plenty of Elgar and Vaughan Williams, and even, in the end, quite a deal of Richard Strauss. The programs enjoyed a remarkably wide appeal, reflecting the uniquely high profile of classical music during the war years. The BBC's pragmatic approach proved to be a recipe for radio programs that played a valuable and valued role in sustaining and uplifting those at home and overseas. As a result, classical music radio kept Britain as close as it had ever been to the heart of the European Enlightenment, even as that was reaching its dreadful apotheosis.

## NOTES

Material quoted from the BBC Written Archive Centre is reproduced with permission and is identified as BBC WAC followed by the relevant file number.

1. Baade, *Victory through Harmony*, 36.
2. Pirie, *The English Musical Renaissance*.
3. Assistant Controller (Programmes) (Howgill) to Miss Reeves, *Collaborators*, January 16, 1945, BBC WAC R27/3/5.
4. Mackay, "Being Beastly to the Germans."
5. Launchbury, *Music, Poetry, Propaganda*.
6. Adorno, "Four-Hands, Once Again" (1933), quoted by Gillespie, "Translator's Note," xiii.
7. Baade, "Radio Symphonies."
8. See, for example, Briggs, *The History of Broadcasting in the United Kingdom*.
9. *BBC Genome*.
10. The contents sheets used for individual programs and may differ from the *Radio Times* listings.
11. Briggs, *The History of Broadcasting in the United Kingdom*, 102.
12. Baade, *Victory through Harmony*; Home Broadcasting Committee minutes, September 20, 1939, quoted in Briggs, *The History of Broadcasting in the United Kingdom*, 102.
13. Memorandum on Music Policy, November 14, 1939, quoted in Briggs, *The History of Broadcasting in the United Kingdom*, 102.
14. Greenway, "A Balance of Music on the Forces Programme," 16.
15. Ibid., 19.
16. *General Listening Barometer*, Week 19, 1945, BBC WAC R9/9.
17. Stoller, *Classical Music Radio in the United Kingdom*.
18. Street, *Crossing the Ether*, 84.
19. Silvey, *Who's Listening*, 89.
20. Stoller, *Sounds of Your Life*, 215.
21. Marwick, *The Deluge: British Society and the First World War*.
22. "History," Wigmore-Hall.org.uk.
23. Garnham, *Hans Keller and Internment*.
24. Marr, *The Making of Modern Britain*, 408.
25. Seaton, "The BBC and the Holocaust," 66.
26. Casual anti-Semitism was a constant presence within Britain, increasing with the flood of Jewish immigration in the wake of the Kishniev pogrom in 1903. That led to the enactment of the Aliens Act in 1905, largely to restrict the flow of "foreign" nationals who brought with them issues of identity and separate culture, which the longer-established Jewish communities had largely managed to resolve. Zipperstein, *Pogrom*.
27. Doctor, *The BBC and Ultra-Modern Music*, 302; Ullswater Committee, Paper 83, 71–90, BBC WAC R4/7/8/5.

28. Doctor, *The BBC and Ultra-Modern Music*, 303.
29. Ibid., 305.
30. Launchbury, *Music, Poetry, Propaganda*, 139–165.
31. BBC Deputy Director of Music (R. S. Thatcher), memorandum, September 11, 1939, WAC R27/3/1.
32. Thatcher, *Copyright Music by Alien Composers*, undated [c. July 1940], BBC WAC R27/3/1.
33. Launchbury, *Music, Poetry, Propaganda*, 40–41.
34. Kenyon, *The BBC Symphony Orchestra*, 163.
35. Hill, "This Week's Radio Music."
36. DDM (Thatcher), memorandum, March 21, 1941, BBC WAC R27/3/2.
37. DDM (Thatcher), memorandum, undated [c. July 1940], BBC WAC R27/3/1.
38. Overseas Service Music Director (K. A. Wright), memorandum, December 15, 1941, BBC WAC R/27/3/2.
39. Hill, "This Week's Radio Music"; also quoted in Launchbury, *Music, Poetry, Propaganda*, 42.
40. *Ein Heldenleben* is Strauss's musical account—composed half a century earlier in 1898—of the "Hero's Life," seen in the UK at least as providing support for Nazi heroic mythology.
41. Mackay, 513. Noel Coward's song "Don't Let's Be Beastly to the Germans" was recorded in July 1943 and provides the title for Mackay's article.
42. Eric Maschwitz, memorandum, July 29, 1940, BBC WAC R27/3/1.
43. Thatcher, *Copyright Music by Alien Composers*.
44. By that time, much of Italy was no longer an enemy nation, having changed sides after the initial fall of Mussolini in October 1943, but with a Fascist state, the Italian Social Republic, continuing in the north of Italy until 1945, amid civil war and retaining control of the city of Milan with the Teatro alla Scala opera house.
45. *Radio Times*, May 17, 1941.
46. David Owen Norris, personal communication, July 24, 2012.
47. Kenyon, *The BBC Symphony Orchestra*, 174.
48. Ibid., 174–175.
49. Stoller, *Classical Music Radio in the United Kingdom*, 67–93.
50. Arthur Bliss, *BBC Policy with Regard to Copyright Music by Composers of Enemy Nationality*, October 21, 1942, BBC WAC R27/3/3. A later draft dated November 23, 1942, allows latitude to producers where particular music is needed to meet "special dramatic needs."
51. Kenyon, *The BBC Symphony Orchestra*, 175.
52. Bliss, *As I Remember*, 169.
53. Trumpi, *The Political Orchestras*.
54. Doctor, *The BBC and Ultra-Modern Music*, 334.
55. Doctor, "Concerts," 65.
56. Garnham, "The BBC in Possession," 151.
57. Doctor, "A New Dimension: The BBC Takes on the Proms," 122.

58. Ibid., 128.
59. Launchbury, *Music, Poetry, Propaganda*, 143.
60. KA Wright, *Copyright Music by Enemy Composers*, June 4, 1943, BBC WAC R27/2/4.
61. Thacker, *Music after Hitler*, 3.
62. Ross, *The Rest Is Noise*, 579.
63. Anderton, "Music among the Ruins," 46 (quoting Levi, *Music in the Third Reich*, 217–219) asserts that Richard Strauss and Hans Pfitzner were the most frequently performed twentieth-century composers of the Third Reich.
64. BBC, *BBC Handbook 1947*, 43.
65. BBC WAC R/27/3/6, February 1946.
66. BBC WAC R27/3/7, June 26, 1947.
67. *BBC Handbook 1949*, between 16 and 17. Strauss died on September 8, 1949.

BIBLIOGRAPHY

Anderton, Abby E. "Music among the Ruins: Classical Music, Propaganda, and the American Cultural Agenda in West Berlin (1945–1949)." Ph.D. diss., University of Michigan, 2012.
Baade, Christina. "Radio Symphonies: Everyday Listening and the Popular Classics Debate during the People's War." In *Ubiquitous Musics: The Everyday Sounds That We Don't Always Notice*, edited by Marta Garcia Quiñones, Anahid Kassabian, and Elena Boschi, 49–71. Aldershot: Ashgate, 2013.
———. *Victory through Harmony: The BBC and Popular Music in World War II*. New York: Oxford University Press, 2012.
*BBC Genome: Radio Times 1923–2009*. Accessed April 30, 2019. https://genome.ch.bbc.co.uk.
*BBC Handbook 1947*. London: BBC, n.d.
*BBC Handbook 1949*. London: BBC, n.d.
Bliss, Arthur. *As I Remember*. London: Faber and Faber, 1970.
Briggs, Asa. *The History of Broadcasting in the United Kingdom*. Vol. 3, *The War of Words*. London: Oxford University Press, 1970.
Doctor, Jennifer Ruth. *The BBC and Ultra-Modern Music, 1922–1936: Shaping a Nation's Tastes*. Cambridge: Cambridge University Press, 1999.
———. "Concerts—Confronting the Obvious." In *Music and the Broadcast Experience: Performance, Production, and Audience*, edited by Christina L. Baade and James Deaville. New York: Oxford University Press, 2016.
———. "A New Dimension: The BBC Takes on the Proms, 1920–44." In *The Proms: A New History*, edited by Jennifer Ruth Doctor, David Wright, and Nicholas Kenyon, 74–129. London: Thames & Hudson, Limited, 2009.
Garnham, Alison M. "The BBC in Possession." In *The Proms: A New History*, edited by Jennifer Ruth Doctor, David Wright, and Nicholas Kenyon, 130–167. London: Thames & Hudson, 2009.

———. *Hans Keller and Internment: The Development of an Emigré Musician, 1938–48.* Edited by Christopher Wintle. London: Plumbago, 2011.

———. *Hans Keller and the BBC: The Musical Conscience of British Broadcasting, 1959–1979.* Aldershot: Ashgate, 2003.

Gillespie, Susan H. "Translator's Note." In Theodor W. Adorno, *Essays on Music*, edited by Richard Leppert, translated by Susan H. Gillespie, xiii–xv. Berkeley: University of California Press, 2012.

Greenway, Rob. "A Balance of Music on the Forces Programme." BA thesis, University of York, 2007.

Hill, Ralph. "This Week's Radio Music." *Radio Times*, November 1, 1940.

"History." *Wigmore-Hall.org.uk*, n.d. http://wigmore-hall.org.uk/about-us/history/41-the-history-of-a-concert-hall/file.

Kenyon, Nicholas. *The BBC Symphony Orchestra: The First Fifty Years, 1930–1980.* London: British Broadcasting Corporation, 1981.

Launchbury, Claire. *Music, Poetry, Propaganda: Constructing French Cultural Landscapes at the BBC during the Second World War.* Vol. 78, *Modern French Identities*, edited by Peter Collier. Oxford: Peter Lang, 2012.

Mackay, Robert. "Being Beastly to the Germans: Music, Censorship and the BBC in World War II." *Historical Journal of Film, Radio and Television* 20, no. 4 (2000): 513–525.

Marr, Andrew. *The Making of Modern Britain.* London: Macmillan, 2009.

Marwick, Arthur. *The Deluge: British Society and the First World War.* London: Macmillan, 1991.

Mitchell, Alastair, and Alan J. Poulton, eds. *A Chronicle of First Broadcast Performances of Musical Works in the United Kingdom.* Aldershot: Ashgate, 2001.

Pirie, Peter J. *The English Musical Renaissance.* London: Gollancz, 1979.

Radio Files. Audience Research: Special Reports, Sound and General, file 9, 1945. British Broadcasting Corporation Written Archives Centre. Caversham.

———. Music General: Alien Composers, 27/3/1–7. British Broadcasting Corporation Written Archives Centre. Caversham.

———. R4/7/8/5. British Broadcasting Corporation Written Archives Centre. Caversham.

Rose, Paul Lawrence. *Wagner: Race and Revolution.* New Haven, CT: Yale University Press, 1992.

Ross, Alex. *The Rest Is Noise: Listening to the Twentieth Century.* New York: Picador, 2007.

Seaton, Jean. "The BBC and the Holocaust." *European Journal of Communication* 2, no. 1 (1987): 53–80.

Silvey, Robert. *Who's Listening: The Story of BBC Audience Research.* London: George Allen and Unwin, 1974.

Stoller, Tony. *Classical Music Radio in the United Kingdom, 1945–1995.* London: Palgrave Macmillan, 2017.

———. *Sounds of Your Life: The History of Independent Radio in the UK.* New Barnet: John Libbey, 2010.

Street, Sean. *Crossing the Ether*. Eastleigh: John Libbey, 2006.
Thacker, Toby. *Music after Hitler, 1945–1955*. Aldershot: Ashgate, 2007.
Trumpi, Fritz. *The Political Orchestras: The Vienna and Berlin Philharmonics During the Third Reich*, translated by Kenneth Kronenberg. Chicago: University of Chicago Press, 2016.
Zipperstein, Stephen J. *Pogrom: Kishniev and the Tilt of History*. New York: Liveright, 2018.

TONY STOLLER is Visiting Professor in the Faculty of Media and Communications at Bournemouth University. He is author of *Sounds of Your Life: A History of Independent Radio in the UK* and *Classical Music Radio in the United Kingdom, 1945–1995*.

THREE

# MUSICAL "DIPLOMACY" IN AMERICAN AND SOVIET WORLD WAR II FILMS OF THE 1940s

PETER KUPFER

ACCORDING TO WINSTON CHURCHILL'S FAMOUS quip from an October 1939 radio address, the Soviet Union was "a riddle wrapped in a mystery, inside an enigma."[1] This was as true for Americans in the late 1930s as it was for Churchill's British listeners. When in late 1941 the United States and Soviet Union suddenly became uneasy allies in the fight against fascism, American propagandists knew they needed to try to unwrap the mystery and unravel the enigma as quickly as possible.[2] One of the primary means for winning the hearts and minds of the people in this period was cinema, which was a hugely popular and widely disseminated medium by the late 1930s.[3] Robert McLaughlin and Sally E. Parry aptly summarize the role that films played in the war effort: "Through the narratives that exist overtly or covertly within their plots, the narratives that lie embedded in their dialogue and speeches, and the narratives that are implied in their images, Hollywood war films offered ways to understand what the war was all about, what America's place in the war was, why America should hate its enemies and support its allies, what each American's role in the war should be, how the war would be resolved, and what the postwar world would be like."[4]

To this end, each major Hollywood studio eventually produced at least one pro-Soviet film as their contribution to the war effort, including *The Boy from Stalingrad* (1943, Columbia, dir. Sidney Salkow, mus. M. W. Stoloff), *Mission to Moscow* (1943, Warner Bros., dir. Michael Curtiz, mus. Max Steiner), *The North Star* (1943, Goldwyn/RKO, dir. Lewis Milestone, mus. Aaron Copland), *Song of Russia* (1944, MGM, dir. Gregory Ratoff, mus. Herbert Stothart), *Days of Glory* (1944, RKO, dir. Jacques Tourneur, mus. Daniele Amfitheatrof), and *Counter-Attack* (1945, Columbia, dir. Zoltan Korda, mus. Louis Gruenberg).

Cinema played very much a similar role in the Soviet Union, where, from the very start, it had served ideological purposes and was also well attended and popular.[5] But, unlike for America, the war was on the Soviet Union's doorstep, which meant the major Soviet film studios had to be relocated to Alma-Ata (present-day Almaty, Kazakhstan), where resources were limited. As a result, only seventy feature-length films were made between 1942 and 1945, of which forty-eight (69 percent) treated war-related topics (as compared with 818 of 1,540, or 53 percent, in Hollywood).[6] Given these circumstances, priority was given to making films that had the most direct bearing on morale—the relationship with the United States ally did not fit the bill.[7]

However, after the war the circumstances flipped: Russians largely disappeared from American screens, while Americans suddenly began appearing prominently in Soviet films.[8] In the United States this had to do with, among other things, the rise of anti-communism, the breakup of the studios in 1948, and the rise of television—Hollywood now had bigger fish to fry.[9] The turn to American topics in the Soviet Union was, paradoxically, a reflection of the intense cultural clampdown in the postwar years against Western tendencies in all areas of cultural production (the so-called *Zhdanovshchina*, after Stalin's culture minister Andrey Zhdanov, who led the campaign). Instead of a postwar boom in filmmaking, this period became known as *malokartin'e* (film hunger), during which the number of total productions dropped even *below* wartime output, from a high of twenty-four in 1947 to a low of nine in 1951.[10] Nevertheless, it was during this period of intense political and cultural scrutiny that the United States and both its wartime and postwar actions suddenly became the subject of a number of films, including *Meeting at the Elbe* (Vstrechna na El'be, 1949, dir. Grigory Aleksandrov, mus. Dmitry Shostakovich), *The Secret Mission* (Sekretnaya Missiya, 1950, dir. Mikhail Romm, mus. Aram Khachaturyan), and *Conspiracy of the Doomed* (Zagovor obrechyonnïkh, 1950, dir. Mikhail Kalatozov, mus. Vissarion Shebalin).[11] Echoing McLaughlin and Parry's comment about the function of Hollywood in wartime America, Evgeny Dobrenko describes the role such films played in postwar Russia. They "brought a 'feeling of deep satisfaction'; they removed the trauma of the new global order ... [in them] the new picture of the world was shaped, which determined the world-view for decades; in these years a new Soviet identity, the image of the superpower, was formed."[12]

The way McLaughlin and Parry and Dobrenko describe the power of film to shape worldviews is fitting. But to McLaughlin and Parry's list of narrative components (plot, dialogue, and images) I would add music, which plays a central role in constructing and communicating cinematic narratives, particularly in guiding the viewer's understanding of, among others, a character's personality, emotions, beliefs, and allegiances. Indeed, music was a central component of the storytelling apparatus in both American and Soviet cinema in this period, even if—or especially because—it was "unheard."[13] For better or worse, cinematic images of the Soviet and American "other" were virtually always accompanied by music—music that could imprint itself powerfully in the subconscious of the viewer and be recalled later. W. Anthony Sheppard underscores this point in his study of music in American anti-Japanese films of this period: "The most effective medium for anti-Japanese propaganda in the United States, and the site of music's most important wartime role, was the cinema."[14]

The purpose of this chapter, then, is to consider the ways in which music functioned to code the "other" in American and Soviet World War II films of the 1940s.[15] To this end, in what follows I first broadly describe some of the main musical techniques deployed in the films mentioned above, and then delve into greater detail with case studies on *The North Star* and *Meeting at the Elbe*. I begin with Hollywood, showing that in order to make friends out of the mysterious Russians, directors more or less turned them into average Americans. This is reflected in the films' scores through continued use of typical classical Hollywood underscoring, with little concerted effort made to code the Russians musically as Russian. Even when Russian music does figure prominently into the score, as in *Song of Russia* or *The North Star*, we see that these differences ultimately serve to reinforce a sense of sameness. In postwar Soviet films, we find precisely the opposite: composers use music to clearly differentiate Americans from Soviet heroes, typically relying on tropes of exoticism, mechanization, and excess to paint the United States as corrupt and imperialistic even when the action nominally takes place *before* the end of the war. In the end, both of these approaches helped to underline the depictions of the "other" in films of this period as a "non-meeting of two worlds," which is to say that given the historical circumstances, these representations could not but rest on extremes, whether of similarity or difference, enhanced in both cases by strategic uses of music.[16]

### AMERICANIZED RUSSIANS

Russians appeared occasionally in prewar Hollywood films, but usually in the roles of "buffoons" in need of conversion to American values.[17] Michael Shull and David Wilt have shown that even though there were forty-six "topical references" to Russia in Hollywood films in the years from 1937 to 1941 (of the 2,485 total films produced), the nine that dealt distinctly with the Soviet Union portrayed the country in a negative light.[18] In fact, six of these were comedies, suggesting that "to believe in communism implie[d] a degree of insanity."[19]

But after a partnership with the Soviet Union suddenly became necessary, "U.S. propagandists and Hollywood filmmakers ... strained to naturalize the unnatural Soviet-American partnership for the moviegoing public, which remained uncertain that the alliance ... represented anything other than a marriage of convenience."[20] With its strong leftist leanings and pro-business model, Hollywood was somewhat slow to take up this task, but with prodding from the Office of

War Information (OWI), loosening of the Hays Production Code, and loss of revenue from now-occupied Western Europe, it soon jumped on board.[21] The majority of Hollywood films made about the war had to do with vilifying the enemies, glorifying the armed forces, or supporting the war effort on the home front, but praising the allies became a goal as well. This was, however, more difficult to do in the case of the Soviet Union than for, say, the British or the French, in part because of the great ideological divide separating the nations, but also because a great deal of anti-Soviet sentiment had grown since the signing of the Molotov–Ribbentrop Pact.[22] So how did scriptwriters and directors portray Russians (and they suddenly became "Russians" rather than Soviets)? They did so by eliminating virtually all political differences and showing that they were "one hell of a people" who "look like Americans, dress like Americans, and think like Americans."[23] In practice this meant casting Americans for all major Russian characters (usually without even attempting Russian accents), dressing Russians like Americans, and creating settings that only hinted at a Russian locale. More importantly, it meant stressing apolitical themes that citizens of both countries had in common: honor, loyalty, courage, the future of the children, the need to dream, and so on. Film scoring followed suit.

In *Counter-Attack*, for example, it is easy for the viewer to forget that the main character Kulkov (Paul Muni) and his comrades are Russians because they are all played by Americans who speak in normal English, while the Nazis are played by native German-speaking expat actors who all speak with strong, sharp accents.[24] In addition, the extreme darkness of the cinematography—the action takes place largely in a cellar in which Kulkov and several Nazi prisoners are trapped—makes it difficult to recognize their uniforms as Russian. Louis Gruenberg's score supports this conflation of Russians-as-Americans by mirroring the film's darkness and capturing the psychological tension between Kulkov and his Nazi prisoners as they try to outwit each other, doing so via a sparse score consisting primarily of mysterious tremolos in low strings, with the occasional meandering quasi-atonal rising melody or upward chromatic flourish. The most (and only) "Russian" element in the score is a brief orchestral motif reminiscent of kuchkist nationalism à la Modest Musorgsky or Alexander Borodin. It is first heard in the opening credits sequence amid otherwise classical Hollywood overture style, recurring only a handful of times throughout the film, and is not tied leitmotivically to the Russian characters or their actions.

This example from *Counter-Attack* illustrates how Russian flavor often appeared in these films only as a token acknowledgment of a film's ostensible setting, usually in the form of vague folk inflection in a film's credits music. Another site for musical Russianness was diegetic performances, usually of some kind of stylized folk music, but often with "universalized" English texts. For example, in *Days of Glory* the Russian partisans working behind enemy lines entertain themselves by singing. The accordion accompaniment and melody suggest a Russian folk song, but the words are less specific. They concern a woman who sings and dances with the man she loves; he has told her friends that soon she would be his bride. But he leaves their village to run "away and hide," saying nothing, he "only sighs." While the *sound* of this song passes for Russian given the setting and plot of the film—whether it is authentically Russian is beside the point—the *purpose* (escape/entertainment) and *content* (the woes of love) of their singing are "universal"; it is something with which the American moviegoer could easily identify. Likewise, in *The Boy from Stalingrad*, which tells the story of a band of children who—without the aid of a single adult—halt the German army's advance on Stalingrad, "folk" songs are used to code the children as typical kids with typical routines and desires. At one point, the youngest boy, Yuri, has trouble falling asleep, so two older children, Grisha and Nadya, sing him a lullaby. They urge their "little comrade" to go to sleep, where he will always be at peace and nothing can do him harm. As with the example from *Days of Glory*, we are ostensibly to hear the simple guitar accompaniment and modal inflections of the song as Russian folk music, but the English, accent-free pronunciation, and "everyday" quality of the text and the moment make this difficult. These look, sound, and act like "our" own children. Furthermore, music becomes a metaphor for the victory of humanity over violence. In a later scene, after Grisha's guitar has been destroyed by the Nazis (symbolizing their barbarism), he comes across an unsuspecting German soldier who has left his guitar and rifle leaning against a tree. Rather than taking the rifle, with which he could easily shoot the soldier, Grisha opts for the guitar, which he then uses to sing instructions to his friends in order to save them all. Thus, we see that even a Russian (i.e., American) child understands the value of music over violence but has the wherewithal to use music as a "weapon" if need be.

The great equalizer in these films, though, is the non-diegetic underscore, which functions largely as it does in any other classical Hollywood film score from this period: it is narrative driven, leitmotivically organized, and in a late-nineteenth-century romantic symphonic idiom. There are, of course, differences between individual composer's styles, but by and large non-diegetic music is treated in a relatively standard way, capturing (and at times nearly mimicking) the "universal" emotions and actions of the narrative and characters. For example, in the scene in *Days of Glory* immediately following the song quoted above, Nina (the ballerina who has joined the partisans after having been separated from her entertainment unit) begins to recite Tatyana's letter from *Eugene Onegin*. This profession of love is accompanied by a repeatedly rising and falling figure played low on the violins with pulsing accompaniment in the low strings and the occasional portamento slide to accentuate the romanticism of the moment. The purpose of composer Daniele Amfitheatrof's music here is twofold: to underline the budding relationship between Nina and Semyon (inciting jealousy in the group's leader, Vladimir, played by Gregory Peck in his film debut) and to emphasize the value of Alexander Pushkin as a symbol of the culture for which *both* sides were fighting. It does not, in other words, mark Nina, Semyon, and the partisans as distinctly Russian, but rather as human.

The most musical of the pro-Soviet Hollywood war films was *Song of Russia*. It tells the story of the American conductor (and Chaikovsky specialist) John Meredith (Robert Taylor), who, on an orchestra tour to Russia before the war, falls in love with a Russian pianist Nadya (Susan Peters), whom he eventually marries. But with the onset of the war, he is forced to decide whether to return home or stay by her side. He wavers, she leaves, and he must brave a series of obstacles in order to be reunited with her.[25] Given the musical subject, composer Herbert Stothart had wide latitude in the underscoring, which is nearly omnipresent and seamlessly weaves in a number of different Chaikovsky works (in addition to those we see performed diegetically).

But lest we think that Chaikovsky was chosen as the musical locus of this film purely because of his Russianness, several scholars have shown that already by the time of *Song of Russia*, Chaikovsky had been established within American popular culture, especially cinema, as the "spokesman of deep feelings," as a marker of "extreme high-emotion utterance," and as the furnisher of "emotional pathos."[26] As such, in *Song of Russia* his music functions less as an emblem of Russia and more as a catalyst for emotional transference. Indeed, throughout the film, Chaikovsky's music becomes the great unifier: it is, for example, what brings John (i.e., the United States) and Nadya (Russia) together in the first place; it is one of the central symbols around which the entire Russian nation comes together—in the form of a radio broadcast—during the darkest hours of the war; and, most importantly, it brings us, the viewers, "closer" to the characters on screen. Furthermore, after Nadya's village (named Tschaikowskoye) has been destroyed, the town's music director appears in front of John (who has come to find Nadya) with a smashed violin in his hands and laments, "Look what they've done to our music." As a result, as Anna Nisnevich has noted, "the war of the Soviet people against the invaders became a war *for* the music of Chaikovsky, the very music, as we begin to understand in the process of viewing the film, that is able to unite private and public, Russian and universal, USSR and US."[27] In other words, it is a war for the fate of humanity, symbolized visually and narratively by common themes of love, family, and duty, but *felt* most strongly, even if subconsciously, via the emotional immediacy of Chaikovsky's "potent" music.[28]

*Mission to Moscow* is somewhat different from the other films discussed above in that it does not treat a fictionalized plot solely about Russians and their actions in wartime situations. Instead, as a translation into film of the best-selling memoir of the former Soviet ambassador Joseph Davies, it attempted to present and justify Soviet actions leading up to the war, doing so in near-documentary style but with extreme reinterpretation of the historical record.[29] Its goal was "to persuade American viewers and to create a stable popular consensus for foreign policies that, statesmen believed, would enhance American security and strength."[30] Despite these differences in the film's style, Max Steiner's score nevertheless relies on the kind of period- and location-specific tunes he deployed in many of his scores, including *Stagecoach* (1939), *Gone with the Wind* (1939), and *Casablanca* (1942).[31] These melodies or songs help establish locale, differentiate characters representing different places and interests, and offer "a wash of authenticity."[32] Thus, in *Mission to Moscow*, we hear "La Marseillaise," "Yankee Doodle," a variety of Soviet marches, and similar "identifying" musical themes when we see people, places, or events associated with the various political participants in the film. Since the construction of the film relies so heavily on documentary techniques—it begins, for example, with the real Davies introducing the story and its importance—the purpose of the music here is less to create an emotional wash than to directly guide our viewing, making sure we understand each character's origins, motivations, and allegiances. In the end, then, the music urges us to understand, among other things, that the Soviet Union's actions in the late 1930s were completely justified. While the film and its music thus do not attempt to make Americans out of the Russians, as in the other films discussed here, they do help suggest that anyone would have acted as the Russians did, thereby emphasizing a similarity between American and Russian inclination, if not a direct conflation of character and culture.

### RUSSIA IN KANSAS: *THE NORTH STAR*

*The North Star* was Samuel Goldwyn's contribution to the war effort. It was the brainchild of Harry Hopkins, one of FDR's closest advisers, who approached Lillian Hellman with the offer to make a documentary on the subject of the Soviet Union, initially to be shot on location.[33] She quickly began planning, bringing aboard Academy Award-winning director William Wyler and cinematographer Gregg Toland, best known for his work on *Citizen Kane* (1941). This all-star team had immense promise, but that potential was never realized, as delays and disagreements slowed their work and Wyler eventually enlisted in the Army Air Force. Hellman, who had already given in to demands to alter her original script, refused to make a documentary with any other director, and thus distanced herself from the project. She did, though, provide a script subtitled "A Motion Picture about Some Russian People," which she described as a "simple, carefully researched, semi-documentary movie."[34] Goldwyn, however, realized this would not have made a very good Hollywood film, so he brought in veteran screenwriter Edward Chodorov to doctor Hellman's script and replaced Wyler and Toland with Lewis Milestone and James Wong Howe, both seasoned

Hollywood professionals and Academy Award winners.[35] Goldwyn also engaged Aaron Copland to score the film (but only after Igor Stravinsky had turned him down).[36] Additional changes to the script by Chodorov and Milestone angered Hellman further, which eventually led to a falling-out with Goldwyn.[37] Undeterred and confident in the project, Goldwyn forged ahead, assembling an all-star cast and sparing no expenses: at $3 million, the film was the most expensive of his career. The final production mixed Hellman's desire for documentary realism with a healthy dose of Hollywood fantasy. Though many critics panned the film for its blatant political undertones and melodramatic excess, others were more receptive, understanding the political, social, and moral importance of such propaganda at the time.[38] In the end, *The North Star* was nominated for six Academy Awards, including best dramatic score, but did not win in any category.

The film tells the story of a Ukrainian village, the eponymous North Star, in the days just before and after the Nazi invasion of the Soviet Union in June 1941. Having just finished the school year, a group of children set out on a hike to Kiev, fatefully departing on the day before the German invasion. The next day they are attacked by Nazi warplanes and witness the death of a little boy. Meanwhile, their village is also attacked and occupied, but not before some villagers manage to escape and organize a guerrilla force. A truck that is to supply them with munitions is ambushed before it reaches them, but conveniently this occurs right near the hiking children, who take on the noble task of delivering the weapons. In the process one of them is killed and another is blinded. Their sacrifice pays off, though, as the weapons make it to the guerrillas, who storm the village and drive the Nazis out. The film ends with the remaining villagers leaving the destroyed North Star in a moment that is both "somber and optimistic."[39]

After he had completed the music for the film, Copland reported to his friend Carlos Chávez that "it was a difficult job because of the Russian atmosphere that had to be in the score."[40] He created this Russian atmosphere in two ways: first, by using or arranging actual Russian/Soviet music, including the "Internationale," the "Song of the Motherland"—the hit theme song from the 1936 Soviet musical comedy *The Circus* (with a new text by Ira Gershwin)—and the popular 1937 march "Moscow in May."[41] Copland's second method for imbuing the film with a Russian atmosphere was to write several original "folk songs" based to varying degrees on actual Russian folk melodies he had found in Russian folk song collections.[42] This is especially evident in the first part of the film, which approaches the level of a musical or operetta in the amount of diegetic singing and dancing.[43] The purpose of this is to paint an "authentic" (and utopian) image of village life, an image that will soon be destroyed by war. To further help establish a "Russian" sound, Copland wrote prominently for accordion, balalaika, and harmonica. One such song is "Younger Generation," which the children sing as they set out on their hike (example 3.1).[44] Copland drew the melody for this song from a Russian folk

Example 3.1. Copland, "Younger Generation," mm. 5–33. Transcribed, reduced, and transposed to D major for ease of comparison from version published as: "The Younger Generation" by Aaron Copland. © 1964 By The Aaron Copland Fund For Music, Inc. International Copyright Secured. All Rights Reserved. Used With Permission. Music by Aaron Copland lyrics by Ira Gershwin. Copyright © 1943 (Renewed) Ira Gershwin Music and Boosey & Hawkes. All Rights on behalf of Ira Gershwin Music. Administered by WC Music Corp. All Rights Reserved. Used By Permission of Alfred Music.

Fig. 3.1. "Umorilas'" (I Exhausted Myself), in *50 Russische Volkslieder für Gesang und Klavier* [50 Russian Folksongs for Voice and Piano], E. L. Sverkov, ed. (Berlin: Jul. Heinr. Zimmerman, 1921), 48. Score contained in Box 25, Folder 53 misc, Copland Collection, Library of Congress, Washington, DC.

song entitled "Umorilas" (I Exhausted Myself), which he found in a collection of folk songs he had consulted in preparing the music for the film (fig. 3.1). The basic harmonic structure, modal inflection, simple text, and repetitive, syllabic four-bar melody clearly marks this as folk music, while the balalaika accompaniment, the dress, and the rural setting additionally help lend it an ostensible Russian flavor. And while the original subject matter of the source

Fig. 3.1. *(continued).* Translation: "I walked up a hill, up a hill, / I exhausted myself, exhausted myself, exhausted myself. / For sure, I exhausted myself, exhausted myself."

folk song may have been applicable to this moment in the film, like the songs in *The Boy from Stalingrad* and *Days of Glory*, Ira Gershwin's new text makes it clear that we are to understand that these Ukrainian children are just like American kids—they also eat too much jam and don't wipe their noses, either.

We are thus reminded that the purpose of the pro-Soviet propaganda films of this period was not to depict Russian life per se, but to depict it in a manner with which Americans audiences could easily identify and sympathize. "The best way to allay xenophobia and rehabilitate formerly threatening aliens," writes film historian Thomas Doherty, "was to transform the rest of the planet's inhabitants into proto-Americans holding democratic values. . . . The godless and enslaved Soviet Union under Joseph Stalin was transformed to expose a tolerant and affluent side not at all unlike the Kansas heartland."[45]

In the case of *The North Star*, this feat of reinterpretation had begun already in Hellman's initial screenplay, in which she put "the reason for fighting in terms of day-to-day desires" and "by diminishing the differences between the two cultures, she shows that, despite the antithetical nature of capitalism and communism, both nations are actually fighting for the same goals."[46] Indeed, the film's main themes—self-sacrifice for the greater good, the bravery of the ordinary citizen, and defiance against Nazi barbarism—were common to both Soviets and Americans during the war. Significantly, at no point does the film deal explicitly with Soviet politics or ideology. Thus, as much as the characters and the world of *The North Star* are Russian or Soviet, they are just as American as those who are watching the movie. The setting and décor are also only vaguely Russian, and even less Soviet, which was noticed by reviewers at the time. Writing in the *Los Angeles Times*, Edwin Schallert explained, for example, that "there is a certain lack of atmosphere we like to associate with Russia" and "that one has the impression that the [scenes in the village] might have occurred rather closer to home."[47] More recently, Clayton Koppes and Gregory Black go so far as to suggest that "except for [an] icon in the dining room and the picturesque rooflines this could be Iowa or Oklahoma" (figs. 3.2 and 3.3).[48] Copland thus had to strike a balance in the score. As he later wrote about the experience: 'There were decisions to make, principally questions of [musical] style. Since the picture took place in Russia, how authentically "Russian" ought the music to be? . . . When I saw that the actors were Americans performing without even attempting Russian accents, I decided to use a musical style that would suggest, rather than emphasize, the Russian flavor.'"[49] He explained that the process was similar to what he had done with Mexican and cowboy songs in earlier works such as *El Salón México* (1936), *Billy the Kid* (1938), and *Rodeo* (1942): "By using the same technique with Russian folk songs, I developed fragments of a few carefully chosen tunes until they became very much my own, while still retaining a sense of their Russian derivation."[50]

This process is most evident in his treatment of the continuation of the "Younger Generation" cue. After the children have finished singing, we see them in the next scene settling in for the night. Copland stealthily connects the music for these scenes by transferring the "diegetic" folk instrument accompaniment to the non-diegetic underscoring: the balalaika strumming is picked up by pizzicato strings and a clarinet takes up the vocal melody. As the children prepare to sleep, the music slows and becomes more lullaby-like, yet continues to develop on the melody of "Younger Generation"/"Umorilas" (example 3.2, compare to example 3.1 and fig. 3.2).

Fig. 3.2. Domestic life in *The North Star*.

Fig. 3.3. Exterior shots of the village in *The North Star*.

Example 3.2. Copland, "Night Sequence Part II," mm. 1–33. (Transcribed by the author with permission from conductor's score in Box 25, Folder 53.3, Reel 4, M-50, Copland Collection, Library of Congress, Washington, DC.)

We can see in example 3.2 how Copland appropriates this Russian folk song fragment directly into his own unique sound, with its spacious textures, contrast of wind and string timbres, and contrarily moving melodic and bass lines.[51] This new "pastoral" mode, as well as the jump to the non-diegetic track, indicates that we have moved away from the (nominal) world of these Soviet villagers into a more utopian place. This is echoed by the girl Clavdia, who asks her companion Kolya to "make a fire. We must have a fire. A fire is so romantic. We must have a fire. Otherwise, we can't sit around and dream." It is during these words that Copland first noticeably departs from the more direct quotation of "Umorilas." While he maintains its basic quarter-eighth-eighth rhythmic pattern, the rocking accompaniment dissolves into floating half-note chords, and he expands the melodic range and chromatic palette, leading to a brief "dreamy" climax on G minor before the horn resumes the song quotation (see example 3.2, mm. 10–21).

From this point on, in fact, it is primarily this distinctly Coplandesque pastoral sound that marks the world of the children, and the film as a whole. For every important emotional turning point in the second half of the film, Copland deploys this "American" style: we hear it, for example, when the children are attacked by German warplanes and witness the death of a young boy; when two of the teenagers have their first kiss; when one of the girls asks for strength before the attack on the German line; when she is then killed and her companion blinded; and especially when the villagers leave North Star. Like the desire to dream, these are all "human" rather than political moments that deal in some way with the wish for or loss of an idealized, utopian past.

As Neil Lerner has demonstrated, these types of associations are a key component of Copland's pastoral idiom, which his film scores in particular helped to ground. This style, he writes, "is most often used as the music of nostalgia, a longing for the place that is no more, perhaps the music of Utopian desire. This particular Coplandesque trope carries the poignancy of nostalgic longing, the bittersweet or melancholic desire to return home. . . . It speaks to a collective, inclusive longing."[52] And Sally Bick has shown that this style, especially Copland's use of it in his score for the film adaptation of Steinbeck's *Of Mice and Men* (1939)—also directed by Milestone—was instrumental in establishing his specifically "American" sound: "The intertextual medium of commercial film proved to be a far more powerful instrument [than concert music alone] to establish an Americanist musical trope. For Copland, the striking visual and narrative images in *Of Mice and Men*, those of the American West and the pastoral scenes of nature, could now be married to Copland's contemporary musical style, therefore establishing what would eventually become identified as an American nondiegetic style."[53]

*The North Star* participated centrally in this process. Indeed, one of the few contemporary reviewers even to mention the film's music specifically describes Copland as a "talented *American* composer," as if to distinguish him from the sea of European film composers working in Hollywood at the time and to emphasize the fundamental Americanness of the film's music.[54] In appropriating his Russian sources into this style, and then shifting solely to that style for the latter part of *The North Star*, Copland subtly underscores the film's message; namely, that the plight and dreams of the "average" Soviet and American citizen are one and the same. This is underlined by the fact that while nearly all of the "Russian" music is heard diegetically, the "American" music is almost exclusively non-diegetic. It is on this plane—where it functions as the voice of subjectivity and sympathy—that the music can most powerfully communicate the film's message of similarity.[55]

### AMERICANS VILIFIED

As mentioned, the situation with the American "other" in Soviet film during the war was virtually the exact opposite from that in the United States: neither Americans nor America appeared prominently in any Soviet war films. This had to do with a number of factors, including the simple fact that any war-related films that were even able to be produced had to directly support the war effort, which in practice meant vilification of the enemy or glorification of the partisan. After the war, though, under the pressure of Zhdanov and his repressive attacks against anything deemed too Western, the Ministry for Cinematography changed gears dramatically. To respond to reports of Red Army brutalities in occupied territories and other anti-Soviet propaganda, filmmakers were tasked with creating an "offensive" propaganda campaign.[56] In the face of supposed US "imperialism," exemplified most clearly by the Marshall Plan, Americans were to be portrayed as aggressors, instigators, and underminers. The result was that "45.6 percent of screen villains in Soviet films from 1946 to 1950 were American or British, compared with just 13 percent British from 1923 to 1945."[57] Not all of these films dealt directly with US actions in the war, but as Peter Kenez has noted: "In spite of the widely different topics, the message is always the same: Russian ways are superior, the Soviet people courageous, patriotic and handsome, foreigners treacherous and infinitely mean and cruel."[58]

Though many fewer films were produced in this period, those that did get made were generally lavish productions, often approved by Stalin directly, with large budgets (several films, including *Conspiracy of the Doomed*, were even shot on captured German color stock). Unsurprisingly, many of these films, including the ones discussed here, won Stalin Prizes in the first or second degree. But because the USSR was a closed country by this time, all actors were Russian, and thus directors had to differentiate (Soviet) heroes from (foreign) enemies through various other means, including costumes, lighting, and, of course, music.

In Mikhail Kalatozov's *Conspiracy of the Doomed*, which tells the story of the fate of an unnamed Eastern Europe country in the immediate postwar years, the main means by which the Americans are coded as corrupt "imperialists" is through jazz. Jazz had a checkered history in the Soviet Union, with waves of support and repression in the 1930s. During the war, contact with Western allies and the distraction of the war meant that jazz once again flourished. As Frederick Starr notes, "The war . . . gave Soviet jazz greater freedom than it had enjoyed in years . . . For all its Americanisms, jazz was more nearly acceptable to the ultranationalists in wartime than at any other time in the decades preceding and following the fighting."[59] But in part because of this popularity and its association with America, in the immediate postwar years jazz, like any type of Western cultural import, was deemed unacceptable, a supposed tool of Western capitalist imperialism.[60] But the jazz heard in films of this period is not "real" American jazz—that would be too dangerous. Rather, it was typically far more symphonic (the saxophone having been effectively banned), chromatic, and erratically syncopated than anything Soviet listeners would have heard during the war or in the little amount of state-sanctioned jazz performed in the postwar years. What was most important, of course, was not the actual sound of the music, but what it was used to represent.

In *Conspiracy of the Doomed*, we first encounter composer Vissarion Shebalin's "jazz" at a ball at the American embassy. The music resembles Paul Whiteman's symphonic jazz of the 1920 and 1930s: it is heavy on the strings, but the rhythm is rather square and march-like, with particularly heavy emphasis on the downbeats. The melody, heard most prominently in the piccolo, unwinds chromatically above this, but its arrival points are often misaligned with the beat, creating a sense of jerkiness rather than true syncopation. This is mimicked by the dancers, who sway back and forth only to then lurch unnaturally, as if to catch up with the beat. While this music approaches jazz in some ways—one reviewer called it a "clever parody of American jazz"—it is clearly to be understood as something perverse, thus underscoring the suspicious activities of the Americans in this unnamed country.[61] In a later scene, we see an American "peace train," ostensibly delivering goods as part of the Marshall Plan, though instead of useful provisions such as bread, it carries cigarettes. Standing on the locomotive is a jazz band, performing another chromatic and awkwardly syncopated jazz tune, complete with a very out-of-tune trombone solo (fig. 3.4). Not only is jazz once again used to depict the Americans as corrupt, but the placement of the band on a train

Fig. 3.4. The American "Peace" Train (a) with jazz band atop its locomotive (b).

highlights another feature of supposed American imperialism in this period: its inevitable, mechanized progress (which must be halted).

In *The Secret Mission*, it is this association that composer Aram Khachaturyan most centrally employs to code the American spies in the film who are on a secret mission to make deals with the Nazis before the end of the war. While the glorious feats of the Red Army on the Eastern Front are accompanied by grandiose, full orchestral fanfares, the other recurring leitmotif in the film is associated with the Americans and their nefarious plot to undermine relations with their Soviet allies. This cue is first heard when Marta (actually Masha, a Soviet agent working undercover in the Gestapo) picks up the American agents from the airport and whisks them quickly through Berlin. We do not yet know who they are or what their plans are, but the music tells us as much. Nami Mikoyan describes Khachaturyan's music: "The restless ostinato figure sounding continuously throughout this symphonic episode in the eighth notes of the basses, cellos, and harps is perceived like the swift spinning of wheels. Over this mysterious rustling ostinato short motifs in the upper orchestral voices start to peel off, creating the impression of alarms and beeps."[62]

Indeed, the quickly moving, chromatically rising and falling ostinato figure in the low strings (reminiscent today of the original American *Batman* television series theme) creates a sense of urgency, mystery, and anxiety. We know these gentlemen are up to no good and hope they can be stopped before it's too late. The woodwinds chords that "peel off" from the ostinato do indeed resemble car horns, thus almost Mickey-Mousing their driving, but they also underscore the sense of mechanization already present in the ostinato figure. Furthermore, the same music comes back every time the American conspirators travel to meet with their coconspirators (i.e., when the "wheels" of conspiracy are in motion). Thus, this music takes on heightened significance; it mostly certainly, in the words of one reviewer, "never assumes a random, 'plugged-in' character."[63] In contrast to the triumphant music associated with Soviet victories, this is Khachaturyan's way of telling the viewer that the Americans are now the inhuman force on the march toward imperialistic takeover, a reversal of wartime musical depictions of Nazis as mechanized barbarians.[64] Because of this cue's ability to function on several symbolic levels simultaneously, I agree with Nami Mikoyan that we might "rightfully call this musical episode one of Khachaturyan's best discoveries in the area of film music."[65]

### DISTINCTIVE INTONATIONS: *MEETING AT THE ELBE*

The purpose of *Meeting at the Elbe* was, as Tony Shaw and Denise Youngblood suggest, to "dramatically demonstrate that the [Soviet Union's] Second World War ally had now become the enemy" and to justify "the emergence of the new 'empire' in east-central Europe."[66] With film production at an all-time low, Stalinist art criticism at a new apex of repression, and the emergence of the Cold War, films like this one played a central role in transmitting the official Soviet position on world politics and history.

The film, for which, like *The North Star*, no expense was spared, tells the story of the meeting of Soviet and American troops in the fictional German city of Altenstadt at the end of the war. Though the plot has many loose ends and unconnected elements, it is nominally a spy thriller concerning the efforts of Janet Sherwood (played by Lyubov' Orlova), an undercover American "Federal Intelligence Service" officer, to usher her "father" (in reality a Nazi war criminal named Schrank who has been tasked with stealing a set of patents from a local scientist) to the United States. In opposition to this evil plot, the Soviets, led by the wise and noble Major Kuzmin, work hard to restore order and normalcy in their sector: they hold elections, denazify the town's children, and are generally concerned with the physical and spiritual well-being of the Germans. The Americans, by contrast, are corrupt, materialistic, decadent, and racist. Their main goal is to exploit the Germans by selling off wood from their forests, stealing their valuables, and harassing their women.

Shostakovich described his task in scoring the film as follows:

> Writing the music for the film *Encounter at the Elbe* was ... a responsible task for me. The themes I had to treat in the music were weighty ones: the victory of the Soviet Union, the tragedy of the German people and the construction of a new, democratic Germany with the friendly, sensitive aid of our country. The spectrum to be covered by the music ranged from these extensive themes to individual episodes and characters: such work requires great shrewdness and versatility. The film was a good example of something I mentioned earlier—that for the composer the cinema is not only an artistic school, but often also a political seminar.[67]

Though Shostakovich's work on the film has been denigrated, largely due to the implications of this latter comment, the score is nevertheless revealing from the perspective of film-music coding in this period.

To achieve this, Shostakovich (and the director Grigory Aleksandrov) resorted to clear musical markers, as demonstrated by the film's opening scene, in which the Soviet and American troops first meet.[68] This encounter is underlined by a meeting of musics: march versions of "Yankee Doodle Dandy" and the "Battle Hymn of the Republic" are juxtaposed with two Soviet marches, including the aforementioned "Song of the Motherland," each coming on the heels of the other without a chance for a full musical presentation.[69] Shostakovich and Aleksandrov are careful not to let the marches overlap; they are clearly set *against* each other, despite the initial camaraderie of the soldiers. While this was done most likely to ensure that audiences would hear and understand the juxtaposition, it is symbolic of the role music will play in the film: the two sides are depicted throughout with their own easily distinguishable musics that never intersect and that clearly instruct the viewer on how to interpret the people the music represents. The director Mikhail Chiaureli noted as much in his review of the film, writing that Shostakovich's music is successful because he "found distinctive intonations for the musical characterization of each of the worlds shown in the film."[70]

Indeed, the Americans are represented primarily by the two aforementioned marches, as well as by a recurring jazz tune of Shostakovich's own creation, heard whenever we see images of the (constant) debauchery that takes place in the American occupation sector. Regardless of its authenticity (or lack thereof), this music is, through its pairing with drunk, philandering, and racist American soldiers, clearly to be heard as the music of decadence and corruption (fig. 3.5).[71] The danger that the Americans represent is transmitted in one final cue near the end of the film. In this scene, in which Sherwood tries to seduce Kuzmin into letting her smuggle Schrank into the United States without any resistance, her true intentions are eventually unmasked. Her lavish outfit, flirtatious manner, and the vodka she offers Kuzmin tell us in part what she is up to, but music drives this point home. Accompanying the scene is a slithering, repetitive, chromatically inflected, and syncopated melody played at first in the strings (replete with glissandi) and later in the celeste and upper woodwinds, all above a drum-like, "throbbing" accompaniment in the bass. These are, of course, the traditional markers of the musical exotic—in particular, of the dangerous, seductive, femme fatale.[72] The music reveals Sherwood's true identity to us before it actually happens narratively.

In contrast, the music of the Soviets, and by extension the music of the Germans, defines them as noble, sensitive, and human. For example, when the new German mayor of Altenstadt accepts his candidacy for mayor, underlining the purported democracy that the Soviets foster in their occupation (or rather "partnership") zone, the ensuing campaign montage is accompanied by the finale of Beethoven's Fifth Symphony. Yet again Beethoven is co-opted in the name of freedom.[73]

## CONCLUSION

"Propaganda films," Peter Kenez tells us, "by definition, distort reality."[74] This much is clear, as this chapter's plot descriptions alone reveal. What has been less studied, though, is how cinematic elements beyond plot contribute to this distorting, which, as the preceding discussion has attempted to demonstrate, was especially

Fig. 3.5a. Rules of the American Nightclub: "Women of all nationalities are permitted into the American Club. We require proof of: political trustworthiness [and] absence of venereal diseases."

Fig. 3.5b. White American soldiers remove a black soldier from the club and beat him.

evident in depictions of World War II and its aftermath in American and Soviet films of the 1940s. As we have seen, music participated centrally in constructing the messages in many of these films. For better or worse, these sonic markers filled the minds of millions of moviegoers at a time when understanding one's friends and foes could be a complex and quickly changing process. Cinema simplified this, and music helped do so, even if in the case of the United States and the Soviet Union in the 1940s "the main thing [was] the cultural incompatibility of the two countries."[75] Nevertheless, whether this incompatibility took the form of the Americanization of Russians in Hollywood films or the vilification of Americans in Soviet films, it speaks to the semantic plasticity and communicative efficacy of music that it could be used just as effectively to underscore such differing messages.

## NOTES

1. Quoted in McLaughlin and Parry, *We'll Always Have the Movies*, 148.
2. This subject has been treated extensively in, among others, Biskupski, "The Roosevelt Adminstration and Film during the War"; McLaughlin and Parry, *We'll Always Have the Movies*; Doherty, *Projections of War*; Shull and Wilt, *Hollywood War Films*; Koppes and Black, *Hollywood Goes to War*. On the Office of War Information, which played a central role in this process, see Winkler, *The Politics of Propaganda*.
3. Small, "Buffoons and Brave Hearts," 326.
4. McLaughlin and Parry, *We'll Always Have the Movies*, 14.
5. See Kenez, *Cinema and Soviet Society*.
6. Kenez, "Film Propaganda in the Soviet Union," 115; Shull and Wilt, *Hollywood War Films*, 291.
7. Youngblood, *Russian War Films*, 55–81.
8. This is not to say Russians disappeared entirely from American screens, but there was a precipitous drop off. One film that did treat a Russian topic, and used music in a provocative way, was William Wellman's *The Iron Curtain* (1948, 20th Century Fox). On the music in this film, see Platte, "Fighting for the Enemy?"
9. Strada and Troper, *Friend or Foe?*, 60–72. Of course, many of the pro-Soviet films made during the war suddenly became liabilities for their makers. On this, see Sbardellati, *J. Edgar Hoover Goes to the Movies*; Mayhew, *Ayn Rand and Song of Russia*; Radosh and Radosh, *Red Star over Hollywood*, 109–233.
10. Beumers, *A History of Russian Cinema*, 109.
11. Though *Russkiy Vopros* (*The Russian Question*, dir. Mikhail Romm, 1948) also treats an American topic—a journalist who refuses to denounce the Soviet Union—the film does not directly relate to wartime events or decisions, so I do not include it in my discussion here.
12. Dobrenko, "Late Stalinist Cinema," 944.

13. Egorova, *Soviet Film Music*; Kalinak, *Settling the Score*; Gorbman, *Unheard Melodies*.

14. Sheppard, "An Exotic Enemy," 307.

15. Though documentaries, such as the *Why We Fight* series, were hugely influential in this period, I am interested here only in feature films. Furthermore, I focus on films that thematize the war itself or its immediate aftermath and aftereffects.

16. Dobrenko, "Late Stalinist Cinema," 935.

17. Small, "Buffoons and Brave Hearts." See also Robinson, *Russians in Hollywood*, 95–114.

18. Shull and Wilt, *Hollywood War Films*, 52, 84.

19. Ibid., 52. On prewar depictions of Russians, see Robinson, *Russians in Hollywood*, 95–114.

20. Bennett, *One World, Big Screen*, 170.

21. Koppes and Black, *Hollywood Goes to War*, 17–141.

22. Shull and Wilt, *Hollywood War Films*, 201.

23. "The Peoples of the U.S.S.R.: The Fighting Great Russians Brought Them All Together," *Life*, March 29, 1943, 23, quoted in Koppes and Black, *Hollywood Goes to War*, 219.

24. Full cast list and further details available at https://catalog.afi.com/Catalog/moviedetails/24371 (accessed May 18, 2018).

25. On the creation, reception, and dubious afterlife of the film during the postwar communist witch hunt, see Mayhew, *Ayn Rand and Song of Russia*.

26. Quotations come from, respectively, Nisnevich, "Chaykovskiy, *Song of Russia* i sovetsko–amerikanskie otnosheniya," 13 ("Vïrazitel' glubokikh chuvstv"); Long, *Beautiful Monsters*, 53; Robinson, *Russians in Hollywood*, 127. A similar (if more hotly contested) romanticization and popularization of Chaikovsky occurred in the Great Britain during the war. On this, see Baade, "Radio Symphonies." All translations from the Russian are my own.

27. "Voyna sovetskogo naroda protiv zakhvatchikov stanovilas' voynoy *za muzïku Chaykovskogo*, tu samuyu muzïku, kotoraya, kak mï nachinayem ponimat' v protsesse prosmotra fil'ma, sposobna soyedinit' chastnoye i obshchestvennoye, russkoye i vsemirnoye, SSSR i SShA," Nisnevich, "Chaykovskiy, *Song of Russia* i sovetsko-amerikanskie otnosheniya," 19.

28. "Reviews of the New Films: *Song of Russia*," *The Film Daily*, December 29, 1943, 8.

29. The development, propaganda content, and reception of the film—including accusations after the war by the House Committee on Un-American Activities of communist infiltration in the making of the film—have been treated extensively: Radosh and Radosh, "A Great Historic Mistake"; Bennett, "Culture, Power, and *Mission to Moscow*"; Koppes and Black, *Hollywood Goes to War*, 189–209; Culbert, *Mission to Moscow*.

30. Bennett, "Culture, Power, and *Mission to Moscow*," 492.

31. On the scores for these films, see Kalinak, *How the West Was Sung*, 49–75; Platte, *Making Music in Selznick's Hollywood*, 149–195 (on the use of period tunes specifically, see 184–189); Wegele, *Max Steiner*; Marks, "Music, Drama, Warner Brothers."

32. Kalinak, *How the West Was Sung*, 60.

33. The following background is based on Koppes and Black, *Hollywood Goes to War*, 209–210.

34. Koppes and Black, *Hollywood Goes to War*, 209.

35. Born as Leib Milstein in Odessa in 1895 and raised in Kishinev, Bessarabia (now Moldova), Lewis Milestone was himself of Russian heritage.

36. Pollack, *Aaron Copland*, 379.

37. Hellman was so furious that she eventually bought herself out of her contract with Goldwyn. See Berg, *Goldwyn: A Biography*, 374–379. And, as if to prove the worth of her original script, she had it published separately, with an introduction by Louis Kronenberger, before the film was released. See Hellman, *The North Star*.

38. On the critical reception of *The North Star*, see Berg, *Goldwyn: A Biography*, 377–378; Koppes and Black, *Hollywood Goes to War*, 213–215; Millichap, *Lewis Milestone*, 115–117.

39. Westbrook, "Fighting for What's Good," 177.

40. Letter of March 28, 1944, in Copland, *Selected Correspondence*, 158.

41. "The Song of the Motherland" (mus. Isaak Dunayevsky, text Vasiliy Lebedyev-Kumach); "Moscow in May" (*Moskva mayskaya*, 1937, mus. Pokrass Brothers, text Vasiliy Lebedyev-Kumach), erroneously re-titled as "My Moscow" (*Moya Moskva*) in the collection of Russian folk songs from which Copland took the song (see Box 25, Folder 53 misc., Copland Collection, Library of Congress, Washington, DC). The former song was hugely popular, becoming the call sign for Moscow Radio and an unofficial Soviet anthem until 1943. On *The Circus* and the role that music plays in the film, see Kupfer, "Music, Ideology, and Entertainment," 135–181.

42. The collections he consulted include *Songs of the Red Army Song and Dance Ensemble of the USSR* (Moscow: Muzgiz, 1939); *Russian Folksongs from the Voronezh Region* (Moscow: Muzgiz, 1939); *20 Russian Folksongs*, Vladimir Zakharov and Pyotr Kazmin, eds. (Moscow: Muzgiz, 1936); *50 Russian Folksongs*, E. L. Sverkov, ed. (Berlin: Jul. Heinr. Zimmerman, 1921). Title pages and selected songs from these collections can be found in Library of Congress, Copland Collection, Box 25, Folder 53 misc. Copland composed five "original" folk tunes based on songs from these collections, though only four made it into the film.

43. Bosley Crowther, "*The North Star* (1943): 'The North Star,' Invasion Drama, with Walter Huston, Opens in Two Theatres Here—'Claudia' at Music Hall," *New York Times*, November 5, 1943.

44. *The North Star* is available to view online at https://archive.org/details/TheNorthStar (accessed April 29, 2019).

45. Doherty, *Projections of War*, 144.

46. Westbrook, "Fighting for What's Good," 172.
47. Edwin Schallert, "*North Star* Sensational War Medical Revelation," *Los Angeles Times*, December 26, 1943, B3.
48. Koppes and Black, *Hollywood Goes to War*, 211. Telling, also, is that the "icon" on the wall is *not* a portrait of Stalin or Lenin, but Orest Kiprensky's famous portrait of Alexander Pushkin, underscoring the humanistic rather than specifically political nature of the villagers' world (see Fig. 3a).
49. Copland and Perlis, *Copland: Since 1943*, 15.
50. Ibid., 15.
51. The music toward the end of the clip—with its gently rocking scalar bass line, offbeat accompaniment, grace note accents, and folk song-inspired melody—is strongly reminiscent of Copland's "Saturday Night Waltz" from *Rodeo*.
52. Lerner, "Copland's Music of Wide Open Spaces," 483. See also Lerner's "Aaron Copland, Norman Rockwell, and the 'Four Freedoms.'"
53. Bick, "Of Mice and Men," 438.
54. "*The North Star* (RKO-Goldwyn): Peace and War," *Motion Picture Herald*, October 16, 1943, 1585.
55. Gorbman, *Unheard Melodies*, 67.
56. Shaw and Youngblood, *Cinematic Cold War*, 41.
57. Ibid., 41–42.
58. Kenez, *Cinema and Soviet Society*, 212. This anti-American attitude is somewhat ironic given that Soviet filmmakers were very strongly impressed with and influenced by Hollywood techniques in this period due to a large number of Hollywood films that were shown on Soviet screens during the war and ones that had been acquired by Mikhail Kalatozov, the Committee for Cinema Affairs's representative in the United States from the summer of 1943 until the end of the war (and director of *Conspiracy of the Doomed*). See Kapterev, "Illusionary Spoils"; Shcherbenok, "Asymmetric Warfare."
59. Starr, *Red and Hot*, 202–203. See also Batashev, *Sovetskiy Dzhaz*, 88–98.
60. Starr, *Red and Hot*, 204–234. Unsurprisingly, a Soviet history of jazz in this period fails to mention any of the backlash or American influence, describing the jazz scene as a flourishing of new ensembles, large and small, in cities all throughout the Soviet Union. Batashev, *Sovetskiy Dzhaz*, 99–116.
61. "Umno sparodiroval amerikanskiy dzhaz." R. Yurenev, "*Zagovor obrechyonnïkh*," *Sovetskoye iskusstvo*, June 27, 1950, 2. Yurenev, like all other reviewers who mentioned Shebalin's music, noted also how it connected deeply to the content of the film. See G. Mdivani, "*Zagovor obrechyonnïkh*," *Komsomol'skaya pravda*, June 28, 1950, 3; M. Chiaureli, "Narod Pobezhdayet: O fil'me *Zagovor obrechyonnïkh*," *Pravda*, June 27, 1950, 5.
62. "Slovno stremitel'nïy beg koles vosprinimayetsya nepreriïvno zvuchashchaya na portyazhenii vsego simfonicheskogo epizoda bespokoynaya ostinatnaya figura vos'mïmi u kontrabasov, violoncheley i arfï. Na tainstvenno shurshashchee

dvizhenie ostinato nachinayut naslaivat'sya korotkie popevki v verkhnikh orkestrovïkh golosakh, sozdavaya vpechatlenie trevozhnïkh signalov, gudkov." Mikoyan, *Kinomuzïka Arama Khachaturyana*, 43.

63. "Nigde ni priobretaya sluchaynogo, 'vstavnogo' kharaktera." A. Yevseyev, "Ideynost' i masterstvo," *Sovetskoye isskustvo*, August 19, 1950, 2.

64. Depicted famously, for example, in the "invasion" theme in the first movement of Shostakovich's Seventh Symphony ("The Leningrad," 1941), which Richard Taruskin has described as a "brutish" image of "invaders ... assaulting Russia with a mind-numbing march." See Taruskin, Review of Symphony No. 7 "Leningrad," *Notes* 50, no. 2 (1993): 757.

65. "Mozhno po pravu nazvat' etot muzïkal'nïy epizod odnoy iz luchshikh nakhodok Khachaturyana v oblasti kinomuzïki," Mikoyan, *Kinomuzïka Arama Khachaturyana*, 42.

66. Shaw and Youngblood, *Cinematic Cold War*, 66–67. On the politics and history of the film's depictions, see also Keghel, "Meeting on the Elbe"; Kenez, "The Picture of the Enemy in Stalinist Films"; Turovskaya, "Soviet Films of the Cold War." The film is available for viewing online at Mosfilm's website: http://cinema.mosfilm.ru/films/film/1940-1949/vstrecha-na-elbe/ (accessed April 20, 2019).

67. Grigoryev and Platek, *About Himself and His Times*, 135.

68. According to Shaw and Youngblood, Aleksandrov noted specifically that he wanted to contrast the music of the two nations. See Grigory Aleksandrov, "Dva mira," *Ogonek*, no. 12 (1949), cited in Shaw and Youngblood, *Cinematic Cold War*, 240, n. 16. On Shostakovich's work on the film, see also Riley, *Dmitri Shostakovich*, 66–68.

69. "The Song of the Motherland," we recall, was the theme song for *The Circus*, which is about an American circus performer who, having had a child with a black man and having thus been run out of the racist United States, finds refuge in the Moscow circus, where both she and her son are welcomed with open arms. We might thus also read the use of "The Song of the Motherland" in *Meeting at the Elbe* as a foreshadowing of the film's political message, i.e., that Soviet values must supersede American ones.

70. "Nashedshego svoyeobraznïe intonatsii dlya muzïkal'noy kharakteristiki kazhdogo iz pokazannïkh v fil'me mirov," M. Chiaureli, "Dva Mira," *Literaturnaya gazeta*, March 9, 1949, 3. Other reviewers who mention Shostakovich's music described its close relationship to the ideological meaning and content of the film. See V. Pudovkin, "Vstrecha na El'be," *Pravda*, March 10, 1949, 3; Dm. Shcheglov, "Vstrecha na El'be," *Leningradskaya Pravda*, March 10, 1949, 3; and B. D'yakov, "Vstrecha na El'be," Sovetskoye iskusstvo, March 12, 1949, 3.

71. Shostakovich was actually rather proud of this tune, as he later recalled: "I have written some jazz music, and though I cannot claim to have been outstandingly successful, I do take some pride in the jazz numbers I wrote for the film *Encounter at the Elbe*." Cited in Grigoryev and Platek, *About Himself and His Times*, 183.

72. See, for example, Locke, "Constructing the Oriental 'Other.'"
73. See Buch, *Beethoven's Ninth*; Dennis, *Beethoven in German Politics*.
74. Kenez, "Film Propaganda in the Soviet Union," 122.
75. Dobrenko, "Late Stalinist Cinema," 935.

BIBLIOGRAPHY

Baade, Christina. "Radio Symphonies: The BBC, Everyday Listening and the Popular Classics Debate during the People's War." In *Ubiquitous Musics: The Everyday Sounds That We Don't Always Notice*, edited by Marta García Quiñones, Anahid Kassabian, and Elena Boschi, 49–71. London: Routledge, 2013.

Batashev, Aleksey. *Sovetskiy Dzhaz: Istoricheskiy ocherk* [Soviet Jazz: An Historical Essay]. Moscow: Muzïka, 1972.

Bennett, M. Todd. *One World, Big Screen: Hollywood, the Allies, and World War II*. Chapel Hill: University of North Carolina Press, 2012.

———. "Culture, Power, and *Mission to Moscow*: Film and Soviet-American Relations during World War II." *Journal of American History* 88, no. 2 (2001): 489–518.

Berg, A. Scott. *Goldwyn: A Biography*. New York: Knopf, 1989.

Beumers, Birgit. *A History of Russian Cinema*. Oxford: Berg, 2009.

Bick, Sally. "'Of Mice and Men': Copland, Hollywood, and American Musical Modernism." *American Music* 23, no. 4 (2005): 426–472.

Biskupski, Mieczyslaw B. "The Roosevelt Administration and Film during the War." In *Hollywood's War with Poland, 1939–1945*, 67–81. Lexington: University Press of Kentucky, 2010.

Buch, Esteban. *Beethoven's Ninth: A Political History*. Translated by Richard Miller. Chicago: University of Chicago Press, 2003.

Copland, Aaron. *The Selected Correspondence of Aaron Copland*. Edited by Elizabeth B. Crist and Wayne Shirley. New Haven, CT: Yale University Press, 2006.

Copland, Aaron, and Vivian Perlis. *Copland: Since 1943*. New York: St. Martin's, 1989.

Culbert, David Holbrook, ed. *Mission to Moscow*. Madison: University of Wisconsin Press, 1980.

Dennis, David B. *Beethoven in German Politics, 1870–1989*. New Haven, CT: Yale University Press, 1996.

Dobrenko, Evgeny. "Late Stalinist Cinema and the Cold War: An Equation without Unknowns." *The Modern Language Review* 98, no. 4 (2003): 929–944.

Doherty, Thomas. *Projections of War: Hollywood, American Culture, and World War II*. New York: Columbia University Press, 1999.

Egorova, Tatiana. *Soviet Film Music: An Historical Survey*. Translated by Tatiana A. Ganf and Natalia A. Egunova. Amsterdam: Harwood, 1997.

Gorbman, Claudia. *Unheard Melodies: Narrative Film Music*. Bloomington: Indiana University Press, 1987.

Grigoryev, Lev, and Yakov Platek, eds. *Dmitry Shostakovich, about Himself and His Times*. Translated by Angus and Neilian Roxburgh. Moscow: Progress, 1981.

Hellman, Lillian. *The North Star: A Motion Picture about Some Russian People*. New York: Viking, 1943.

Kalinak, Kathryn. *How the West Was Sung: Music in the Westerns of John Ford*. Berkeley: University of California Press, 2007.

———. *Settling the Score: Music and the Classical Hollywood Film*. Madison: University of Wisconsin Press, 1992.

Kapterev, Sergei. "Illusionary Spoils: Soviet Attitudes toward American Cinema during the Early Cold War." *Kritika: Explorations in Russian and Eurasian History* 10, no. 4 (2009): 779–807.

Keghel, Isabelle de. "*Meeting on the Elbe* (*Vstrecha Na El'be*): A Visual Representation of the Incipient Cold War from a Soviet Perspective." *Cold War History* 9, no. 4 (2009): 455–467.

Kenez, Peter. *Cinema and Soviet Society from the Revolution to the Death of Stalin*. New ed. London: I. B. Tauris, 2001.

———. "Film Propaganda in the Soviet Union, 1941–1945: Two Views." In *Film & Radio Propaganda in World War II*, edited by K.R.M. Short, 108–123. Knoxville: University of Tennessee Press, 1983.

———. "The Picture of the Enemy in Stalinist Films." In *Insiders and Outsiders in Russian Cinema*, edited by Stephen M. Norris and Zara M. Torlone, 96–112. Bloomington: Indiana University Press, 2008.

Koppes, Clayton R., and Gregory D. Black. *Hollywood Goes to War: How Politics, Profits, and Propaganda Shaped World War II Movies*. New York: Free Press, 1987.

Kupfer, Peter. "Music, Ideology, and Entertainment in the Soviet Musical Comedies of Grigory Aleksandrov and Isaak Dunayevsky." Ph.D. diss., University of Chicago, 2010.

Lerner, Neil. "Aaron Copland, Norman Rockwell, and the 'Four Freedoms': The Office of War Information's Vision and Sound in *The Cummington Story* (1945)." In *Aaron Copland and His World*, edited by Carol J. Oja and Judith Tick, 351–377. Princeton, NJ: Princeton University Press, 2005.

———. "Copland's Music of Wide-Open Spaces: Surveying the Pastoral Trope in Hollywood." *The Musical Quarterly* 85, no. 3 (2001): 477–515.

Locke, Ralph P. "Constructing the Oriental 'Other': Saint-Saëns's 'Samson et Dalila.'" *Cambridge Opera Journal* 3, no. 3 (1991): 261–302.

Long, Michael. *Beautiful Monsters: Imagining the Classic in Musical Media*. Berkeley: University of California Press, 2008.

Marks, Martin. "Music, Drama, Warner Brothers: The Cases of *Casablanca* and the *Maltese Falcon*." In *Music and Cinema*, edited by James Buhler, Caryl Flinn, and David Neumeyer, 161–186. Hanover, NH: University Press of New England, 2000.

Mayhew, Robert. *Ayn Rand and Song of Russia: Communism and Anti-Communism in 1940s Hollywood*. Lanham, MD: Scarecrow, 2005.

McLaughlin, Robert L., and Sally E. Parry. *We'll Always Have the Movies: American Cinema during World War II*. Lexington: University Press of Kentucky, 2006.

Mikoyan, Nami. *Kinomuzïka Arama Khachaturyana*. Moscow: Sovetskiy kompozitor, 1983.

Millichap, Joseph R. *Lewis Milestone*. Boston: Twayne, 1981.

Nisnevich, Anna. "Chaykovskiy, *Song of Russia* i sovetsko–amerikanskie otnosheniya [Chaikovsky, *Song of Russia* and Soviet–American Relations]." Moscow Conservatory, Moscow, Russia, 2014.

Platte, Nathan. "Fighting for the Enemy? Musical Duplicity as Propaganda in *The Iron Curtain*." Paper delivered at the Annual Conference of the American Musicological Society, New Orleans, LA, 2012.

———. *Making Music in Selznick's Hollywood*. New York: Oxford University Press, 2018.

Pollack, Howard. *Aaron Copland: The Life and Work of an Uncommon Man*. New York: Henry Holt, 1999.

Radosh, Ronald, and Allis Radosh. "A Great Historic Mistake." In *Red Star over Hollywood: The Film Colony's Long Romance with the Left*, 93–108. San Francisco: Encounter Books, 2005.

———. *Red Star over Hollywood: The Film Colony's Long Romance with the Left*. San Francisco: Encounter Books, 2005.

Riley, John. *Dmitri Shostakovich: A Life in Film*. London: I. B. Tauris, 2005.

Robinson, Harlow. *Russians in Hollywood, Hollywood's Russians: Biography of an Image*. Boston, MA: Northeastern University Press, 2007.

Sbardellati, John. *J. Edgar Hoover Goes to the Movies: The FBI and the Origins of Hollywood's Cold War*. Ithaca, NY: Cornell University Press, 2012.

Shaw, Tony, and Denise J. Youngblood. *Cinematic Cold War: The American and Soviet Struggle for Hearts and Minds*. Lawrence: University Press of Kansas, 2010.

Shcherbenok, Andrey. "Asymmetric Warfare: The Vision of the Enemy in American and Soviet Cold War Cinemas." *KinoKultura*, no. 28 (2010). www.kinokultura.com/2010/28-shcherbenok.shtml (accessed February 1, 2016).

Sheppard, W. Anthony. "An Exotic Enemy: Anti–Japanese Musical Propaganda in World War II Hollywood." *Journal of the American Musicological Society* 54, no. 2 (2001): 303–357.

Shull, Michael S., and David E. Wilt. *Hollywood War Films, 1937–1945: An Exhaustive Filmography of American Feature-Length Motion Pictures Relating to World War II*. Jefferson, NC: McFarland, 1996.

Small, Melvin. "Buffoons and Brave Hearts: Hollywood Portrays the Russians, 1939–1944." *California Historical Quarterly* 52, no. 4 (1973): 326–337.

Starr, S. Frederick. *Red and Hot: The Fate of Jazz in the Soviet Union, 1917–1991*. 2nd ed. New York: Limelight, 1994.

Strada, Michael J., and Harold R. Troper. *Friend or Foe? Russians in American Film and Foreign Policy, 1933–1991*. Lanham, MD: Scarecrow, 1997.

Taruskin, Richard. Review of Symphony No. 7 "Leningrad" op. 60 (1941) by Dmitri Shostakovich; Manashir Yakubov. *Notes* 50, no. 2 (1993): 756–761.

Turovskaya, Maya. "Soviet Films of the Cold War." In *Stalinism and Soviet Cinema*, edited by Derek Spring and Richard Taylor, 131–141. New York: Routledge, 1993.

Wegele, Peter. *Max Steiner: Composing,* Casablanca, *and the Golden Age of Film Music*. Lanham, MD: Rowman & Littlefield, 2014.

Westbrook, Brett. "Fighting for What's Good: Strategies of Propaganda in Lillian Hellman's 'Negro Picture' and 'The North Star.'" *Film History* 4, no. 2 (1990): 165–178.

Winkler, Allan M. *The Politics of Propaganda: The Office of War Information, 1942–1945*. New Haven, CT: Yale University Press, 1978.

Youngblood, Denise J. *Russian War Films: On the Cinema Front, 1914–2005*. Lawrence: University Press of Kansas, 2007.

PETER KUPFER is Associate Professor of Musicology in the Meadows School of the Arts at Southern Methodist University.

PART II

## OPERA, THEATER STAGE, AND CONCERTS

FOUR

# THE METROPOLITAN OPERA HOUSE AND THE "WAR OF IDEOLOGIES"

The Politics of Opera Publicity in Wartime

CHRISTOPHER LYNCH

ON DECEMBER 11, 1941—JUST FOUR days after the Japanese attack on Pearl Harbor—the Board of Directors of the Metropolitan Opera House asked general manager Edward Johnson if he believed the company should adjust its plans for the season in response to the new geopolitical situation. The question was certainly warranted. The memory of the First World War was not too distant, and board chairman Cornelius N. Bliss was surely thinking of the decision to expunge German-language opera from the repertoire between 1917 and 1921.[1] Johnson, however, did not believe canceling scheduled performances to be a feasible option for the company in the 1940s. The minutes from the board meeting read: "Mr. Johnson spoke briefly on the repertoire and the problems inherent in any change of policy as to the performance of foreign opera in foreign languages. He pointed out that Italian and German operas represented the bulk of the repertoire and that artists had been engaged and plans laid for what such artists should sing long before the war situation had developed. It was felt that until the public served by the Association indicated its dissatisfaction with the present management policy with respect to opera that no change should be made."[2]

Perhaps canceling the performances of only German operas would have been possible, as it had been during World War I. But sacrificing both German and Italian operas was believed to be too disruptive. Had all German and Italian works been cut, Johnson would have had great difficulty identifying enough viable alternatives and hiring performers on such short notice, and canceling contracts and mounting new productions would have been too costly for the company. As this chapter demonstrates, rather than significantly changing the Metropolitan's repertoire, the management embarked on a publicity campaign to situate their current plans within the American war effort. This is not to say that there were no significant changes that occurred at the Metropolitan during the war. Lack of resources—financial and material—led to the cancellation of national tours and a downturn in the number of new productions. In fact, the 1943/44 and 1944/45 seasons had no new productions (see Appendix). Moreover, the perennial favorite *Madama Butterfly*—a sympathetic portrayal of the Japanese as victims of Western imperialism—was withheld from the stage.[3] Nevertheless, the Metropolitan campaigned to ensure that the public would not grow dissatisfied with the overall "present management policy."

Before turning to an examination of the publicity tactics employed during the war, it may be useful to account for and contextualize significant wartime developments that reshaped the organization in other ways, many of them already underway for a decade or more. Most notably, the war sped up the development of gradual changes specifically in the engagement of foreign conductors, in the "democratization" of the opera, and in the promotion of American artists. Beginning under Johnson's predecessor, Giulio Gatti-Casazza, the company had engaged internationally renowned conductors such as Artur Bodanzky and Ettore Panizza throughout the 1930s. During the war several additional esteemed conductors, including Bruno Walter, Thomas Beecham, George Szell, Emil Cooper, Fritz Busch, and Fritz Reiner, fled Europe and joined the Metropolitan, turning the 1940s into what Charles and Mirella Jona Affron refer to as "a conductor's decade."[4]

Gatti also spearheaded an initiative that aimed to "democratize" the opera house. The year 1931 witnessed the inauguration of weekly live radio broadcasts, which Gatti claimed were aimed at "a multitude of listeners." The broadcasts, he added, would encourage opera to "grow rapidly in the estimation of the people."[5] Johnson extended such endeavors. He oversaw the company's effort to raise funds from the public to purchase the opera house from its owners, which, according to chairman of the board Bliss, made the company a "public enterprise."[6] During the war Johnson transformed the makeup of the audience by reducing ticket prices (fig. 4.1) and reserving seats at every performance for members of the armed services. The press often remarked on the new composition of the audience. For example, reflecting on the 1942/43 season, Olin Downes commented: "The Metropolitan has made opera popular.... The audiences are not those of earlier seasons. They now involve a cross section of the general public of the city, rather than of the socially or even musically elect. The man on the street, the Broadway denizen, the visitor from out of town, large numbers of the armed forces quartered in and about the city, and plain people in every walk of life, frequent the performances."[7]

Perhaps the most striking development of the 1930s and 1940s was the increased presence of American singers on the Metropolitan's rosters. In 1933 Gatti negotiated an agreement with the Juilliard Foundation in which the foundation pledged significant financial support in exchange for the Metropolitan's

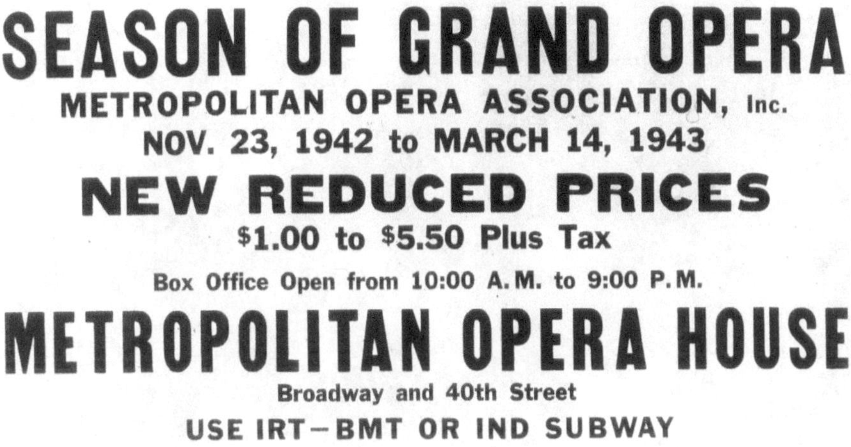

# SEASON OF GRAND OPERA
## METROPOLITAN OPERA ASSOCIATION, Inc.
### NOV. 23, 1942 to MARCH 14, 1943
## NEW REDUCED PRICES
### $1.00 to $5.50 Plus Tax
Box Office Open from 10:00 A.M. to 9:00 P.M.
# METROPOLITAN OPERA HOUSE
Broadway and 40th Street
## USE IRT—BMT OR IND SUBWAY

Fig. 4.1. Poster for the Metropolitan's 1942–43 season. (Courtesy of the Metropolitan Opera Archives.)

assurance that it would produce opera in English, which would provide the Juilliard School's American singers with performance opportunities. This agreement led to a number of English-language productions before the war, including *The Bartered Bride* in 1936 and *Amelia Goes to the Ball* in 1938. Furthermore, in 1935 Johnson introduced the "Metropolitan Auditions of the Air," a radio program in which American singers competed for a place in the company. Performers such as Risë Stevens, Eleanor Steber, and Richard Tucker, all of whom rose to prominence in the 1940s, were among the first winners (fig. 4.2). During the war, the company's roster of artists changed significantly as travel restrictions, politics, and warfare prevented many European singers—most notably Kirsten Flagstad, Jussi Bjoerling, and Zinka Milanov—from making the journey across the Atlantic. As American singers flooded the company's ranks, the Metropolitan performed additional operas in English, including *Die Zauberflöte* in 1941 and *Phoebus and Pan*, adapted from J. S. Bach's cantata *Der Streit zwischen Phoebus und Pan*, in 1942.[8]

Even more profoundly, however, the war accelerated one additional trend at the opera house: the company's use of new forms of publicity. In 1936 the Metropolitan Opera Guild launched the weekly magazine *Opera News*, which featured informational articles about the history of the operas the company produced as well as the manner in which the Metropolitan produced them. An internal memo from 1942 indicates that these new promotional strategies acquired increased urgency in the war years. It reads: "A Press Department organized merely to jolly the critics along and feed them pictures and notes on artists with well-known names is a survival of days gone by." Of course, the Metropolitan continued to

Fig. 4.2. Eleanor Steber and Arthur Kent at the Winners Reception of the Metropolitan Auditions of the Air in 1940. (Courtesy of the Metropolitan Opera Archives.)

boast about its stars, but the publicity department decided it would also "prepare articles and give information on the operas we present" to "reach [a] larger public."[9] Indeed, after Pearl Harbor the Metropolitan's publicity department worked tirelessly in the pages of *Opera News* and other periodicals to align its operations with the war effort and give the impression that its plans were made with national service and politics in mind.

The remainder of this chapter analyzes this new publicity to illuminate the management's strategies for situating its artists, operas, and repertoire within international debates regarding opera and politics during the war. This case study exhibits the parameters of the wartime discussions that involved many American classical music institutions and provides an example of how some things—in this case, the Metropolitan's international repertoire—were marketed in new ways so that they could remain largely unchanged at a time of dramatic instability and uncertainty.

Aligning the Metropolitan's practices with notions of American strength and leadership was an undertaking of national scope. Johnson wrote an article titled "Opera in War Time" that appeared in newspapers in many US cities in December 1942. In the article, the manager provided numerous examples of American singers who had replaced Europeans at the Metropolitan, and he praised this Americanization of the company. Although this process had begun in the previous decade, in his opening sentence Johnson claimed that it extended from complications caused by the war: "The exigencies of war have brought to an end the tradition of presenting famous European artists at the Metropolitan Opera House—a tradition generally in practice since 1883." By emphasizing his artists' ability to rise to the occasion, Johnson played into the patriotic sentiment that America was strong enough to triumph in the face of the adversity caused by the war. The manager, in fact, claimed that American opera houses not only would triumph but would emerge as international leaders in cultural activities. He posited that in the aftermath of the war the world would look to America for help rebuilding the operatic tradition: "European countries, drained and exhausted in worldly goods and cultural riches, will turn to the United States as they never have before for aid in restoring the musical heritage they once possessed."[10] Thus Johnson announced across the country that opera was an important component of American leadership. This was the linchpin of the Metropolitan's publicity, for it advertised operas in ways that portrayed the opera house as championing American values throughout the war.

Whereas the rise of homegrown artists enabled the Metropolitan to assert its global prowess, the influx of Jewish artists who had escaped Nazi persecution allowed the company to portray itself as a defender of values that were contrary to those of the Nazis. In the case of conductor Bruno Walter, who arrived in the United States and made his Metropolitan debut conducting Beethoven's *Fidelio* in 1941, his personal story of fleeing the Nazis from Czechoslovakia to Paris, and then once again to the United States, was linked to the plot of the opera he was to conduct (fig. 4.3). Ahead of the *Fidelio* premiere, *Opera News* ran an interview in which the conductor pronounced: "The principal issue of our time is the theme of Beethoven's *Fidelio*. Should we live

Fig. 4.3. Kirsten Flagstad and René Maison rehearsing *Fidelio* in 1941. (Courtesy of the Metropolitan Opera Archives.)

as slaves, or should every possible sacrifice be made in order to secure our liberty?" In response, the author of the article established a firm connection between the opera and Walter's experience, writing, "Such is the question to which . . . the distinguished German conductor, exiled in turn from Germany, Austria, and France, has answered in his own tragic escape from tyranny." Walter helped the Metropolitan align itself with the victims of the Germans and, therefore, against German aggression. The conductor also demonstrated that the opera house served as a kind of refuge for exiled artists. He indicated the personal significance of this in the interview, stating: "I can rejoice to find myself among the Metropolitan artists with whom I have worked abroad: Pinza and Kullman, Thorborg and Rethberg, Herbert Graf—it is like coming home again to the world into which I lived as a child in Berlin, the world where I have labored since I was seventeen as a coach in Cologne—the world of opera."[11] For Walter, the Metropolitan represented the ideals of international cooperation that he had come to define as home, a home that, in Europe, had been destroyed by the National Socialists.

The parallels between *Fidelio*'s triumph of liberty and the struggle against Nazi oppression were relatively self-evident, but the Metropolitan's publicity department also worked to draw parallels between current geopolitical circumstances and operas whose themes were not so obviously relatable to the war. To open the 1943/44 season, Johnson selected a forty-year-old production of the Russian opera *Boris Godunov*, which *Opera News* publicized as a celebration of America's new alliance with the Soviet Union (fig. 4.4). Despite being clumsily written, the opening of the article linked the production to recent news from the Russian front: "The triumphant news of the Soviet advance blazoning forth to the world the invincible spirit of the Russian people bestows a special significance on the choice of *Boris Godunoff* [sic] to open the jubilee season of Metropolitan Opera."[12] There was an obstacle, however, to featuring this work as a tribute to Russia: the opera, which centers on the self-destruction and demise of the oppressive titular tsar, features a harsh portrayal of a Russian ruler—a portrayal that could have inspired comparisons to the well-publicized atrocities of Lenin and Stalin. To address this, the Metropolitan took a new approach to publicizing the work. *Opera News* downplayed the opera's emphasis on Godunov's terror and demise to play up the work as "a tribute to the resilience of the people."[13] This publicity did not go unnoticed. For example, critic Louis Biancolli echoed the publicity department, writing, "Many critics regard the brave, long-suffering Russian people as the hero of Moussorgsky's tense score, not the remorse-haunted Tsar."[14] Significantly, those critics to whom Biancolli referred were Soviets who had reinterpreted the opera to demonstrate that it was in agreement with Bolshevism. Russian critic Anatoly Lunacharsky, for example, argued in 1920 that the real heroes of the work were the Russian people, and he compared the chorus of the opera to the people who had participated in the Revolution of 1917.[15] Therefore, while the Metropolitan's *Boris Godunov* celebrated America's ally, journalistic commentaries actually absorbed contemporaneous Soviet rhetoric that minimized the opera's potential for political agitation, reflecting the new spirit of cooperation between the two countries.

Fig. 4.4. Ezio Pinza in the title role of *Boris Godunov* in 1943. (Courtesy of the Metropolitan Opera Archives.)

To advertise Pergolesi's *La serva padrona*, the Metropolitan's press department drew parallels between the historical context of the work's composition and the current context of the war. In the January 11, 1943, issue of *Opera News*, Czech-born musicologist Paul Nettl, who had immigrated to America after the German invasion of Czechoslovakia, wrote an article that positioned the opera as reflective of anti-imperialist sentiments.[16] The article was surely intended to stir up interest in the upcoming performance starring Salvatore Baccaloni and Bidu Sayao on January 14 (fig. 4.5). Since *opera buffa* was rarely produced at the Metropolitan in these years, Nettl used his description of the plot, which revolves around the servants Serpina and the mute Vespone as they manipulate their employer Uberto into marrying Serpina, to introduce readers to the conventions of the genre. Nettl pointed out that disguise was "a time-honored device" in *opera buffa*, thereby clarifying the scene in which Vespone is disguised as a Croatian soldier named Scapin. Nettl then expounded on the scene's politics. When it was written in 1733, "Naples . . . was under the rule of Austria . . . [and] a regiment of three thousand Croats were [*sic*] stationed in Naples to uphold the hated rule of the Hapsburgs [*sic*]. . . . The Croats were especially despised because they didn't know any Italian. This last fact explains Vespone-Scapin as mute and brandishing his sword all about him."

He pointed out, "When [Serpina], after attaining her goal, called mockingly to him: 'Scapin, out with thee! We can now dispense with thee,' there was always resounding applause. The Austrians alone were unaware that the applause expressed the hope that they, too, soon would be gone." Nettl then articulated the importance of protesting occupation in 1943: "Thus it is the mute figure in an *opera buffa* which gives testimony to the military occupation of another century when, as today, silence could be eloquent with meaning."[17] Put another way, Nettl—whose homeland was currently occupied—suggested that operagoers identify the actions surrounding the character Vespone with protest against the Nazi occupation of Europe.

Both Walter and Nettl made important contributions to the political positioning of the "Mozart revival," which commenced at the Metropolitan in 1941, the year of the 150th anniversary of Mozart's death. For the first time in the Metropolitan's history, the 1941/42 season featured three of Mozart's operas (*Don Giovanni, Le nozze di Figaro,* and *Die Zauberflöte*), and two more (*Die Entführung aus dem Serail* and *Così fan tutte*) were added over the following decade.[18] Taking to the pages of *Opera News*, Walter and Nettl responded to Nazi propaganda that situated the Austrian Mozart as a symbol of German purity and greatness. As Erik Levi demonstrated, after the *Anschluss* in 1938, Nazi officials and German musicologists and artists worked to minimize the influence of Italian music and Freemasonry on Mozart, who was initiated into the Masonic lodge *Zur Wohltätigkeit* (Beneficence) in 1784. The Nazis opposed Freemasonry's commitment to

Fig. 4.5. Salvatore Baccaloni, Bidú Sayao, and Paul Breisach in rehearsal for *La serva padrona*, 1942. (Courtesy of the Metropolitan Opera Archives.)

universal rather than German brotherhood, and Hitler believed that it was a tool used by the Jew to "tear down the racial and civil barriers which for a time continue to restrain him at every step."[19] In the face of such comments, Walter reaffirmed Mozart's Austrian (rather than German) identity and asserted that *Die Zauberflöte* was "blood and fibre of the Austrian soul" and that it "represents the composer's nationality as perhaps no other of his works," thus refuting the Germans' claims that Mozart was German (fig. 4.6). Walter also asserted that, beyond its Austrian character, *Die Zauberflöte*'s allure exceeded national boundaries. "Its deep human content was not meant for the Austrian public alone," he wrote. "Its appeal is universal."[20] This claim not only further refuted the Nazi position that Mozart represented German purity, but it also suggested that the opera possessed elements that American audiences would find pleasing. Nettl took Walter's claims further, writing that the overall message of the opera was one of universality and cooperation across boundaries. He identified the opera's message—that "the life of man is bound up with the life of his fellow man"—as a particularly Masonic theme, and he thoroughly explained the Masonic symbolism of the work. He pointed out that in Austria the Masonic lodges were closed

Fig. 4.6. The Temple of the Sun in *Die Zauberflöte* at the Metropolitan Opera in 1941. (Courtesy of the Metropolitan Opera Archives.)

shortly after Mozart's death, and he subtly indicated that the Nazis once again suppressed them: "Not until after the [First] World War did Freemasonry rise again for a short time in Austria."[21] As his wording suggested, the "short time" that had seen the resurgence of Freemasonry had come to an end. Nettl's emphasis of the Masonic elements of the opera, therefore, was a political act, a gesture of dissent aimed at the oppressive German regime.[22]

The Metropolitan extended the rhetoric of universalism to the justification of its entire repertoire. Johnson had begun defending the company's international repertoire prior to the entry of the United States into the war. For example, in the October 6, 1941, issue of *Opera News*, the manager wrote optimistically about the coming season, proudly proclaiming that "the repertory will be as varied as is our custom, that we will continue to present opera in its original language, that Wagner will still be produced, and that our company, while offering hospitality to young Americans of talent, will not base either its choice of personnel or its repertory on national lines."

At this time, two months prior to America's entrance into the war, Johnson rationalized the company's international repertoire by claiming allegiance to art, not to any particular nation. He wrote: "We are proud to have earned the title of a national institution but as an artistic organization our first loyalty is to the art we serve."[23] This attitude of nonalignment would dramatically shift in the following months. After the attack on Pearl Harbor, Johnson no longer claimed fidelity to art, arguing instead that the Metropolitan embodied uniquely American ideals. He wrote in *Opera News*: "We at home must fight to maintain those concepts and institutions which are symbolic of our democracy and which we believe are worth preserving. For in this global war of ideologies and not nationalities we are fighting to preserve our cultural as well as our political institutions."[24]

Johnson emphasized the way in which the Metropolitan was "symbolic of our democracy" in the last line of the article, asserting that the Metropolitan's goal is the production of art that "in its essence is international." In other words, Johnson contended that the Metropolitan's international repertoire was an embodiment of the democratic ideals that American soldiers were defending against German jingoism and totalitarianism. Conductor Erich Leinsdorf further elucidated this notion when he stated that one of the "guiding principles" that the Metropolitan embraced during the war was "to keep the Opera international" because "every day we realize how dangerously exaggerated nationalism can become." That exaggerated nationalism, of course, was exhibited daily by the Nazis. Turning away from internationalism, Leinsdorf implied, would align the Metropolitan with Nazi ideology. "Where would we find ourselves," he asked, "if we denied the world-embracing language of music the right to speak freely, uncurbed and uncensored to the hearts of all men? All music, all opera, must therefore remain international."[25]

---

In July 1942, the Metropolitan published a fiscal report detailing the expenses and income of the season that had just concluded. The report indicated that in the 1941/42 season the company had incurred a deficit of $214,374. By the 1943/44 season, the deficit had been reduced to $110,506, and at the conclusion of the following season the opera reported a profit of $5,872.[26] The management credited the profit to tax relief and increased ticket sales, suggesting that the Metropolitan's wartime publicity was effective and contributed to the company's improved finances. Of course, the Metropolitan was just one of many American arts institutions that situated their activities within wartime ideals. Annegret Fauser has brought to light many instances of Americans and institutions employing the rhetoric of internationalism and universality to justify the international character of their work. For example, on his radio show Deems Taylor featured the music of foreign-born composers exiled in the United States as "a reminder of... American tolerance and individual liberty"; conductor Serge Koussevitzky proclaimed that "we give [music] joyfully to serve the cause of freedom"; and first lady Eleanor Roosevelt urged the continuation of all musical practices in America because music is "one of the finest flowerings of... free civilization."[27] Thus, the effectiveness of the Metropolitan's publicity is owed in part to the fact that it was one voice in a growing chorus that positioned internationalism as emblematic of American tolerance, freedom, and democracy.

When victory was achieved, Johnson again took to the pages of *Opera News*. His words suggest that he envisioned continuing into the postwar period the types of publicity that had effectively aligned the Metropolitan with patriotic ideals during the war, but his campaign would not persist for long. He stated that the company had "the support of the representatives of government, press, and radio who are insisting that the leaders in education and culture raise a strong voice in the remaking of a new world." When he wrote these words, Johnson had reason to be optimistic that he could continue to position the company as playing an important political role. In the glow of victory, he could point to the "demonstration of teamwork throughout the ranks of our great organization."[28] But that spirit of cooperation would soon dissipate as the manager became mired in two lengthy labor disputes. Disappearing with that spirit was the abundance of patriotic publicity, and then Johnson himself. He retired in 1950 after five challenging postwar seasons. The war years therefore stand out as a unique period in the Metropolitan's history. Perhaps Johnson's greatest achievement as manager was having the foresight to see that rather than making drastic changes to the company's practices during the war, the best way forward was to market current practices in a manner that portrayed the opera house as a champion of American values. By repackaging the company's existing practices, Johnson was able to proceed with predetermined plans and avoid costly changes in repertoire and personnel that might have put the company's future in jeopardy.

APPENDIX. THE REPERTOIRE OF THE
METROPOLITAN OPERA, 1935–45

\* Denotes new production
† Denotes revised production

**1935/36**
Aida
The Bartered Bride
La bohème
Carmen
Cavalleria rusticana
Faust

Fidelio
Gianni Schicchi
Götterdämmerung
Hänsel und Gretel
La juive
Lakmé
Lohengrin

Lucia di Lammermoor
Madama Butterfly
Manon
Die Meistersinger von Nürnberg
Mignon
*Orfeo ed Euridice
Pagliacci
Parsifal
Das Rheingold
Rigoletto
La rondine
Siegfried
Tannhäuser
Tosca
*La traviata
Tristan und Isolde
Il trovatore
*Die Walküre

**1936/37**
Aida
The Bartered Bride
La bohème
Carmen
Cavalleria rusticana
Les contes d'Hoffmann
†Le coq d'or
Faust
Der fliegende Holländer
La gioconda
Götterdämmerung
Hänsel und Gretel
Lakmé
Lohengrin
Lucia di Lammermoor
Madama Butterfly
*The Man without a Country
Manon
Mârouf
*Il matrimonio segreto

Die Meistersinger von Nürnberg
Mignon
Norma
Pagliacci
Parsifal
Das Rheingold
Rigoletto
*Samson et Dalila
Siegfried
Tannhäuser
La traviata
Tristan und Isolde
Il trovatore
Die Walküre

**1937/38**
Aida
*Amelia Goes to the Ball
Il barbiere di Siviglia
The Bartered Bride
La bohème
Carmen
Cavalleria rusticana
Le coq d'or
Don Giovanni
Elektra
Faust
Gianni Schicchi
Götterdämmerung
Hänsel und Gretel
Lohengrin
Lucia di Lammermoor
The Man without a Country
Manon
Die Meistersinger von Nürnberg
Norma
*Otello
Pagliacci
Parsifal
Das Rheingold

Rigoletto
Roméo et Juliette
Der Rosenkavalier
Salome
Samson et Dalila
Siegfried
Tannhäuser
La traviata
Tristan und Isolde
Il trovatore
Die Walküre

**1938/39**
Aida
Amelia Goes to the Ball
Il barbiere di Siviglia
La bohème
Boris Godunov
Carmen
Cavalleria rusticana
Don Giovanni
Elektra
Falstaff
Fidelio
Götterdämmerung
Hänsel und Gretel
Lakmé
Lohengrin
Louise
Lucia di Lammermoor
Manon
Die Meistersinger von Nürnberg
Mignon
*Orfeo ed Euridice
Otello
Pagliacci
Parsifal
Das Rheingold
Rigoletto
Der Rosenkavalier

Salome
Siegfried
Simon Boccanegra
Tannhäuser
Thaïs
Tosca
La traviata
Tristan und Isolde
Il trovatore
Die Walküre

**1939/40**
Aida
L'amore dei tre re
Il barbiere di Siviglia
La bohème
Boris Godunov
Carmen
Faust
Der fliegende Holländer
La gioconda
Götterdämmerung
Lakmé
Lohengrin
Louise
Lucia di Lammermoor
Madama Butterfly
Manon
Die Meistersinger von Nürnberg
Mignon
*Le nozze di Figaro
Orfeo ed Euridice
Otello
Parsifal
Pelléas et Mélisande
Das Rheingold
Rigoletto
Der Rosenkavalier
Siegfried
Simon Boccanegra

*Tannhäuser*
*Tosca*
*La traviata*
*Tristan und Isolde*
*Die Walküre*

**1940/41**
*Aida*
*\*Alceste*
*L'amore dei tre re*
*\*Un ballo in maschera*
*Il barbiere di Siviglia*
*The Bartered Bride*
*La bohème*
*Carmen*
*Cavalleria rusticana*
*Don Giovanni*
*Don Pasquale*
*Faust*
*Fidelio*
*\*La fille du régiment*
*Götterdämmerung*
*Lohengrin*
*Louise*
*Lucia di Lammermoor*
*Madama Butterfly*
*Manon*
*Le nozze di Figaro*
*Otello*
*Pagliacci*
*Parsifal*
*Pelléas et Mélisande*
*Das Rheingold*
*Rigoletto*
*Der Rosenkavalier*
*Samson et Dalila*
*Siegfried*
*Tannhäuser*
*Tristan und Isolde*
*\*Il trovatore*
*Die Walküre*

**1941/42**
*Aida*
*Un ballo in maschera*
*Il barbiere di Siviglia*
*The Bartered Bride*
*La bohème*
*Carmen*
*Le coq d'or*
*Don Giovanni*
*L'elisir d'amore*
*Faust*
*La fille du régiment*
*Götterdämmerung*
*\*The Island God*
*Lakmé*
*Lohengrin*
*Lucia di Lammermoor*
*Madama Butterfly*
*Le nozze di Figaro*
*Orfeo ed Euridice*
*Otello*
*Pagliacci*
*Parsifal*
*\*Phoebus and Pan*
*Das Rheingold*
*Rigoletto*
*Der Rosenkavalier*
*Samson et Dalila*
*Siegfried*
*Tannhäuser*
*Tosca*
*La traviata*
*Die Walküre*
*\*Die Zauberflöte*

**1942/43**
*Aida*
*Il barbiere di Siviglia*
*La bohème*
*Boris Godunov*
*Carmen*

Cavalleria rusticana
Don Giovanni
Faust
La fille du régiment
La forza del destino
Götterdämmerung
Lakmé
Lohengrin
Louise
*Lucia di Lammermoor
Manon
Le nozze di Figaro
Pagliacci
Parsifal
Das Rheingold
Der Rosenkavalier
Salome
*La serva padrona
Siegfried
Tannhäuser
Tosca
La traviata
Tristan und Isolde
Il trovatore
Die Walküre
Die Zauberflöte

**1943/44**
Aida
Il barbiere di Siviglia
Un ballo in maschera
La bohème
Boris Godunov
Carmen
Cavalleria rusticana
Les contes d'Hoffmann
Falstaff
Faust
La forza del destino
Gianni Schicchi
Götterdämmerung

Lucia di Lammermoor
Mignon
Norma
Le nozze di Figaro
Pagliacci
Parsifal
Pelléas et Mélisande
Das Rheingold
Rigoletto
Der Rosenkavalier
Salome
Siegfried
Tannhäuser
Tosca
La traviata
Tristan und Isolde
Il trovatore
Die Walküre
Die Zauberflöte

**1944/45**
Aida
Il barbiere di Siviglia
La bohème
Carmen
Cavalleria rusticana
Le coq d'or
Don Giovanni
Faust
Fidelio
La gioconda
Götterdämmerung
Lohengrin
Lucia di Lammermoor
Die Meistersinger von Nürnberg
Mignon
Norma
Le nozze di Figaro
Pagliacci
Parsifal
Pelléas et Mélisande

| | |
|---|---|
| Das Rheingold | Tristan und Isolde |
| Rigoletto | Il trovatore |
| Der Rosenkavalier | Die Walküre |
| Siegfried | Die Zauberflöte |
| La traviata | |

NOTES

I would like to thank John Pennino and John Tomasicchio, archivists at the Metropolitan Opera House, for their assistance with the research for this chapter.

1. The ban on the German language lasted until the 1921/22 season, but Wagner's operas were reintroduced in English in the 1919/20 season. Davide Ceriani ("Italianizing the Metropolitan Opera House") has argued that the First World War helped general manager Giulio Gatti-Casazza steer the repertoire away from German works and toward Italian opera. Some American opera composers attempted to capitalize on this shift away from German opera as well. See Ziegel, "National Service and Operatic Ambitions."

2. Metropolitan Opera Association, Inc., Board Minutes, 1941–45, Metropolitan Opera Archives, New York City.

3. *Butterfly* was not performed at all during US involvement in the war. After November 29, 1941, it was not seen on the stage again until January 14, 1946.

4. Affron and Affron, *Grand Opera*, 172.

5. "Electrified Opera: Gatti-Casazza Tells of Radio's March into the Golden Horseshoe," *New York Times*, December 31, 1933.

6. "Metropolitan's Historic Home Changes Hands," *New York Herald Tribune*, June 29, 1940. Even though the company did not technically become a public enterprise in the sense that the public could purchase stock in the company, such rhetoric was common. For example, when the fundraising plan was first announced, Eleanor Robson Belmont, founder of the Metropolitan Opera Guild, said that the opera house was to shift from "private to public ownership." "Announcing a Campaign to Raise a Million for the Opera," *New York Herald Tribune*, January 26, 1940.

7. Olin Downes, "Season in Review," *New York Times*, March 21, 1943.

8. The premiere of *Phoebus and Pan* on January 15, 1942, was Thomas Beecham's debut at the Metropolitan. The production featured orchestrations by Eugene Goossens. For more on the Americanization of opera during the war, see Fauser, *Sounds of War*, 161–177. Fauser details performances of operas in English and American operas on Broadway and at the Metropolitan, New York City Center, Philadelphia Opera, Chicago Civic Opera, and National Negro Opera.

9. Memo dated January 13, 1942, Edward Johnson Correspondence, 1941–42, Box A–J, Folder C, Metropolitan Opera Archives, New York City.

10. Edward Johnson, "Opera in War Time." I have found this article reproduced in several sources, including *Fort Wayne Journal-Gazette* (Indiana), December 21, 1942; *Indianapolis Star*, December 20, 1942; *St. Petersburg Times* (Florida), December 21, 1942; and *The Daily Times* (Burlington, North Carolina), December 21, 1942.

11. "Bruno Walter Talks of Liberty," *Opera News*, February 17, 1942, 21, 23. For more on the events that caused Walter and other artists to flee Germany, see Potter, "The Nazi 'Seizure' of the Berlin Philharmonic."

12. "Russian Opera Goes to War," *Opera News*, November 15, 1943, 4.

13. Ibid.

14. Louis Biancolli, "Choice of Opening Night Opera Proves Met is Intent on Serving Art Alone," *New York World Telegram*, November 20, 1943.

15. Emerson and Oldani, *Modest Musorgsky and "Boris Godunov,"* 160.

16. For more on the politics of musicology during the rise of the Nazis and the Second World War, see Potter, *Most German of the Arts*; see also Levi, *Music in the Third Reich*, 220–242.

17. Paul Nettl, "Mute Evidence of Enemy Occupation: The Story of *La serva padrona*," *Opera News*, January 11, 1943, 22–25.

18. The revival of Mozart's operas was another wartime development that was first envisioned prior to the war. The Metropolitan Opera Archives contains many lists of works that Johnson considered for production. *Così fan tutte* appears on a list of operas that the general manager made in his first season with the company for the planning of an opera-in-English series for spring 1936. That same season, Johnson included *Le nozze di Figaro* and *Don Giovanni* on a list of potential Italian and French operas. Edward Johnson Correspondence, Box 1935–36, Folder "Repertoire (Opera)," Metropolitan Opera Archives, New York City.

19. Levi, *Mozart and the Nazis*, 33.

20. Bruno Walter, "The Flute's Magic Today," *Opera News*, November 17, 1941, 7.

21. Paul Nettl, "Pamina and Freemasonry," *Opera News*, November 17, 1941, 28.

22. For more on the politics of the Mozart revival during the war years, see Lynch, "*Die Zauberflöte* at the Metropolitan Opera House in 1941."

23. Edward Johnson, "A Glad Hand for Opera," *Opera News*, October 6, 1941, 7.

24. Edward Johnson, "Opera on the Home Front," *Opera News*, October 5, 1942, 6.

25. Erich Leinsdorf, "The Challenge of Opera in Wartime," *Opera News*, January 8, 1945, 30.

26. "Opera Submits First Detailed Fiscal Report," *New York Herald Tribune*, August 3, 1942; "Sloan Predicts Opera's Deficit Days are Over," *New York Herald Tribune*, July 17, 1944; "Metropolitan's Profit is $5,872 for the Season," *New York Herald Tribune*, July 20, 1945.

27. Taylor, radio script for *America Preferred*, September 6, 1941, Deems Taylor Papers, Yale University, Irving S. Gilmore Music Library, series V, "Scripts";

Roosevelt, "Music Should Go On!," *Musical America*, February 10, 1942, 3; and Koussevitzky, "Musicians as Soldiers," typescript, Serge Koussevitzky Collection, Library of Congress, Music Division; all quoted in Fauser, *Sounds of War*, 69, 35, and 15, respectively.

28. Edward Johnson, "Opera Faces the Peace," *Opera News*, October 15, 1945, 5.

BIBLIOGRAPHY

**Historical Newspapers and Magazines**
*Indianapolis Star*, 1942
*New York Herald Tribune*, 1940–1945
*New York Times*, 1933, 1943
*New York World Telegram*, 1943
*Opera News*, 1941–1945

**Books and Articles**
Affron, Charles, and Mirella Jona Affron. *Grand Opera: The Story of the Met*. Berkeley: University of California Press, 2014.
Ceriani, Davide. "Italianizing the Metropolitan Opera House: Giulio Gatti-Casazza's Era and the Politics of Opera in New York City, 1908–1935." Ph.D. diss., Harvard University, 2011.
Emerson, Caryl, and Robert William Oldani. *Modest Musorgsky and "Boris Godunov."* New York: Cambridge University Press, 1994.
Fauser, Annegret. *Sounds of War: Music in the United States during World War II*. New York: Oxford University Press, 2013.
Levi, Erik. *Mozart and the Nazis: How the Third Reich Abused a Cultural Icon*. New Haven, CT: Yale University Press, 2010.
———. *Music in the Third Reich*. New York: St. Martin's, 1994.
Lynch, Christopher. "*Die Zauberflöte* at the Metropolitan Opera House in 1941: The Mozart Revival, Broadway, and Exile." *The Musical Quarterly* 100, no. 1 (Spring 2017): 33–84.
Potter, Pamela M. *Most German of the Arts: Musicology and Society from the Weimar Republic to the End of Hitler's Reich*. New Haven, CT: Yale University Press, 1998.
———. "The Nazi 'Seizure' of the Berlin Philharmonic, or the Decline of a Bourgeois Institution." In *National Socialist Cultural Policy*, edited by Glenn R. Cuomo, 39–66. New York: St. Martin's, 1995.
Ziegel, Aaron. "National Service and Operatic Ambitions: Arthur Nevin's Musical Activities during World War I." *American Music* 34, no. 4 (Winter 2016): 414–46.

CHRISTOPHER LYNCH is Artist Lecturer at Carnegie Mellon University and Project Coordinator at the Center for American Music at the University of Pittsburgh.

# FIVE

## BROADWAY GOES TO WAR

TIM CARTER

NEW YORK CITY, FRIDAY, OCTOBER 16, 1942. You are dismayed at the front-page headlines in the *New York Times*: "Japanese Press Heavy Solomons Drive... Russians Fall Back in North Stalingrad: Nazis Crash Ahead." But perhaps the paper's "Amusements" section will offer a brief escape from all this bad news of the battles currently being lost in Europe and in the Pacific. You scan the entertainments listed for the day. Toscanini conducting Shostakovich's famous wartime Symphony No. 7 (*Leningrad*) at Carnegie Hall seems a bit too highbrow, and anyway, like so many Americans, you heard it on the radio just three months before. Guy Lombardo and his orchestra at the Roosevelt Grill would probably be best for a late supper after an 8:30 or 8:40 p.m. show lets out. Noël Coward's *Blithe Spirit* with Clifton Webb?—not your cup of English tea. Maxwell Anderson's new play about war in the South Pacific, *The Eve of St. Mark*?—too serious, it seems, even though it has previously been billed as "Heroic! Hilarious! Overwhelming!" John Kesselring's *Arsenic and Old Lace*?—you know that Frank Capra has already made the film with Cary Grant and are annoyed that the playwright is deliberately delaying its release. Maybe Howard Lindsay and Russel Crouse's *Strip for Action*?—the title has a promising pun. But if it's something risqué you're after, then Michael Todd's revue, *Star and Garter*, has already cornered that market, with Gypsy Rose Lee strutting her classic number, "I Can't Strip to Brahms," not to mention the show's great finale, "Brazilian Nuts." Your thoughts turn to a musical: Johnny Green's new *Beat the Band*, Rodgers and Hart's *By Jupiter*, Danny Kaye in Cole Porter's *Let's Face It!*—but probably not Ann Ronell's new show, which last week got a terrible first-night review from the venerable *Times* drama critic Brooks Atkinson ("Probably a deaf man would enjoy *Count Me In* better than a man whose faculties are unfortunately unimpaired"). Nor are you quite up for Molly Picon in the Yiddish musical comedy *Oy Is Dus a Leben!* even though it is "a sensational success."[1]

You think again about *Strip for Action* (a "whale of a show") but check your wallet: $3.85 each for the best seats is a bit steep given your salary of $200 per month—the average for the period unless you're a typical stenographer (a predominantly female occupation) earning $20–25 per week—but the $1.10 ones will be too far up in the back. *Beat the Band* costs even more ($4.40), though *Star and Garter* is cheaper ($2.75). Then your eye is caught by an ad at the top of the list: Sol Hurok's "Season of Ballet" at the Metropolitan Opera House (1,500 seats at 85¢ to $1.65 for all performances). This seems just the thing: ballet is classy but more approachable than long-haired opera. That ad only gives the titles of the works to be performed by the Ballet Russe de Monte Carlo, but they seem artistic enough: *Rouge et noir* and *Gaîté parisienne,* sandwiching something that looks more homely, *Rodeo* (a "premiere," even). You wonder who wrote the music for them (or maybe you don't care) but decide to cough up for orchestra seats and hope for the best.

As the curtain goes up on *Rouge et noir,* you realize that you've been lured into hearing Shostakovich after all (his First Symphony), but Henri Matisse's sets and costumes are interesting enough, and Léonid Massine's choreography is always thrilling. *Gaîté parisienne* (Offenbach) seems more of a potboiler, though everyone loves how Massine handles it. But it reminds you of the last time you saw Paris: those photographs of the German army marching under the Arc de Triomphe in June 1940 marked the passing of an age. Aaron Copland's new score for *Rodeo,* however, captures the frontier spirit in ways that make you proud to be an American, and the choreographer (and lead dancer in that performance), Agnes de Mille, seems to be a rising star. During the intermission, you spot in the crowd Richard Rodgers, Oscar Hammerstein II, and Theresa Helburn of the Theatre Guild. You remember the gossip: they are here to check out de Mille as a potential choreographer for their new musical, currently called *Green Grow the Lilacs* (remember that old play by Lynn Riggs?).[2] But you do not know that the title will switch to *Away We Go!* and then to *Oklahoma!*

This fictional "you" created in my preamble is, of course, troublesome, not least because it presumes someone of a demographic likely to read the *New York Times* in the first place, or who would prefer a balletic rodeo over the real-life one currently playing at Madison Square Garden, with Roy Rogers in the saddle. For example, none of these Broadway entertainments was advertised in the relevant weekly edition of the *New York Amsterdam Star-News* (October 10, 1942), one of the leading African American newspapers, though it did plug Earl "Fatha" Hines's new revue, which ran for a week (until October 16) at the Apollo Theatre in Harlem. While New York theaters were officially desegregated, marketing departments made clear assumptions about who would be able or willing to travel where for a night out: thus, Carnegie Hall thought it worth putting a small display ad in that October 10 issue for the performance of Orelio and Pedro, "Afro Cuban dancers," and their "Native Bongo Orchestra" on Sunday, October 11 (with seats from $1.10 to $2.20), but nothing else that week. Likewise, while the *Brooklyn Daily Eagle* (October 16, 1942), catering to another different demographic, included the standard block-listing of "Stage Plays—Manhattan," its larger display ads were for local venues; nor did it contain any publicity for Hurok's "Season of Ballet," although the paper had earlier noted the upcoming premiere of *Rodeo*, and Miles Kastendieck issued a very favorable review the next day.[3]

Issues of race, class, income, and locale all had a bearing on which audiences Broadway theaters variously sought to reach. No less striking in scanning these newspapers is the far greater publicity (in terms of column inches and of graphics) granted to what the *New York Times* somewhat pompously insisted on calling "photoplays" but which others labeled "motion pictures." Cinemas offered bigger stars, greater variety, more convenient showtimes and locations, and far cheaper seats. Here lay Broadway's greatest competition, and anything other than a hit was unlikely to beat it. Thus, Ann Ronell certainly misjudged her *Count Me In*—panned by Brooks Atkinson—with its terrible book by Walter Kerr and Leo Brady. It opened on October 8 and closed on November 21 after desperately trying to fill the Barrymore Theatre by giving away free passes to the troops passing through New York en route to Europe.[4] The show aimed for a humorous depiction of a fighting nation, with songs such as "On Leave for Love" and "Who is General Staff?" But as Richard Cooke pointed out in the *Wall Street Journal*, not even a song-and-dance routine for Japanese prisoners of war was going to rescue matters in the ninth inning.[5] *Count Me In* revealed a problem, as did that prior billing for *The Eve of St. Mark* ("Heroic! Hilarious! Overwhelming!"). If Broadway was to engage with World War II while still entertaining its paying customers, how could it be done?

Catering to the troops was one thing: the American Theatre Wing mobilized its forces for the war effort almost immediately after the declaration following Pearl Harbor, and the Stage Door Canteen—where stars of stage and screen entertained soldiers, sailors, and airmen for free—opened its doors in the basement of the 44th Street Theatre on March 2, 1942.[6] But Cooke raised the broader issues in his piece on the front page of the *Wall Street Journal* on July 7, 1942, headlined "People Want Fun in Theatre, Broadway Proves Since Dec. 7": "Since Pearl Harbor, Broadway has seen the opening of about 47 plays and the closing of 39 of them. Of the 'plays' which remain of this group, two are vaudeville shows, one a gold-plated burlesque, one a musical comedy, and one an Army show. Only two are anything with a plot.... This gives a rough but quite comprehensible picture of what wartime America wants by way of stage entertainment."

Cooke wondered whether current playwrights were being too overwhelmed by the immensity of daily events to be able to create moving and inspiring drama; he even hoped optimistically that "art will arise afresh from the scrap pile of the first winter of America at war." But he admitted that people mostly wanted fun at the moment: "To ask audiences to absorb still more facts through the medium of the stage may be asking too much." Likewise, on December 13, 1942, *New York Times* drama critic Lewis Nichols noted that of the twenty-nine current offerings on Broadway, only two dealt directly with the war, which he thought "curiously bad, but also curiously normal." The situation had changed by spring 1943, when the *Times* reported that more than thirty plays dealing with war themes had been mounted on Broadway since Pearl Harbor but admitted that most of them had not lasted very long.[7]

Theresa Helburn and Lawrence Langner, executive directors of the Theatre Guild, and the distinguished American playwright Eugene O'Neill had already worried about the problem in summer 1940. They exchanged letters on how the theater might best respond to wartime necessity. Helburn argued in favor of "greatness and beauty and emotional lift." O'Neill, however, was more realistic:

> Later on, after the victory in the war which must be won is won, and the reaction to the realities behind the surface of the peace sinks in, there will again be an audience able to feel the inner meaning of plays dealing with the everlasting mystery and irony and tragedy of men's lives and dreams; plays which are propaganda only for life as the artist attempts to illuminate it and transmute it into Art. People are too damned preoccupied with the tragedy of war now—as they should be—to want to face such plays. And I don't blame them. I'd rather spend an escapist evening with legs and music myself—or with pipe dreams that were treated as truth.[8]

By the time of Cooke's July 1942 article, Helburn already had her mind set on a compromise: the show that was to become Rodgers and Hammerstein's *Oklahoma!*, which did indeed—so history has viewed it—show art arising afresh. But *Oklahoma!* was an exception that many at its New Haven tryout thought was a loser: "No legs, no jokes, no chance," the feared columnist Walter Winchell was told (perhaps apocryphally). And even as it then took Broadway by storm, most saw the show as escapist fun, albeit with a higher-class artistic twist. It took Olin Downes, music critic for the *New York Times*, to see *Oklahoma!* as something more: a step on the way to that elusive form, a genuine American opera.[9]

The war was good for Broadway business. The marquees outside theaters may have been dark due to periodic brownouts, while restrictions on private motor traffic from January 7, 1943, by the Office of Price Administration, the federal agency dealing with rationing, produced the remarkable sight of horse-drawn hansom cabs bringing patrons to the door.[10] But metropolitan New York had the largest urban population in the United States, and one swelled by defense workers newly recruited to factories and agencies located in the area, as well as large numbers of troops and their support in transit to and from Europe. Broad statistics suggest that Broadway offerings held up well: indeed, one could be forgiven for thinking that not much had changed, as contemporary comments also noted. On December 7, 1941, the day of the attack on Pearl Harbor, audiences had eight musical entertainments from which to choose (see the appendix); on the same day in subsequent years, one could see nine in 1942, eleven in 1943, ten in 1944, and twelve in 1945; these typically made up around a third of Broadway offerings on any given night. The same composers keep reappearing: Richard Rodgers, Sigmund Romberg, and Kurt Weill, with Cole Porter leading the field—he could be relied upon for a new musical each season and clearly was ahead of the game.[11] Among the other musical names, we find Vernon Duke (i.e., Vladimir Dukelsky) trying but failing to stay in the running, though another 1920s immigrant, Frederick Loewe, was gradually starting to make a name for himself. Further digging would reveal the consistent presence of lyricists, "book"-writers, directors, and choreographers, save where they were drafted (as with Joshua Logan) or where new arrivals rose to prominence (Agnes de Mille).

There was the customary mix of musicals, operettas, and revues or vaudeville shows. But some shifts are noticeable during this five-year period. Richard Cooke predicted in July 1942 that vaudevilles and revues would become the standard Broadway fare, which seems to be true for December 1942 but not subsequently: vaudeville never recovered in the postwar years. Indeed, 1942 was not a great year for musicals, presumably because producers were still adjusting to new circumstances. It is striking, however, that as the war progressed, shows save for the duds tended to stay on stage for longer: *Hellzapoppin'* (1938), still running in 1941, and *Oklahoma!* (1943–1948) were clearly exceptions, but excluding them, the average run of musicals showing on December 7, 1941, was 410 performances, which increased to 480 for 1944 and 490 for 1945. The shows from 1941 counting as successes on Broadway ran for between 326 and 721 performances; those of 1944 ran for between 481 and 888. Two musicals playing on December 7, 1941, were still there a year later; three 1943 musicals were on the stage in December 1944, and one of them plus four 1944 musicals were still filling the theaters in December 1945. One can read this in three ways: Broadway producers became cannier in spotting a good thing, audiences were becoming less critical of what they paid to see, and New York now had vast numbers of people passing through who provided an ever-changing pool of customers. But not even *Oklahoma!* managed to match Howard Lindsay and Russel Crouse's comedy *Life with Father*, which had 3,224 performances in a continuous run from November 8, 1939, to July 12, 1947.

Most of these shows were whiter than white. All-black (or nearly so) productions certainly had a niche on Broadway: Vernon Duke's *Cabin in the Sky* had a decent run from October 1940 to early March 1941 with 156 performances, and Cheryl Crawford's revised version of the Gershwins' *Porgy and Bess* gained a total of 374 in separate runs in 1942, 1943, and 1944 and provided the impetus for Oscar Hammerstein II's reworking of Bizet's *Carmen* as an African American *Carmen Jones* (503 performances from December 2, 1943, to February 10, 1945). However, their singers and dancers could also be relegated to exotic productions, such as the brief revival of Hall Johnson's *Run, Little Chillun* in August 1943 and Katherine Dunham's *Tropical Revue* (on Broadway from September to November 1943 prior to a successful tour, returning for the Christmas season spanning 1944–1945), or just to novelty spots in otherwise all-white shows, as with the unfortunately named "Whitey's Steppers" in *Hellzapoppin'*. The economics of the Broadway industry probably worked against any greater representation: Hammerstein struggled for almost two years to get the funding for *Carmen Jones*, and his repeated efforts from 1942 on to revive his mixed-race *Show Boat* on Broadway did not bear fruit until 1946.[12]

Certainly, the huge financial investment required of a musical—some $90,000 up front—required careful thought.[13] Much depended on the calculation of start-up and running costs versus likely profits, the latter being strongly determined by the size of the theater. The 44th Street Theatre was one of the larger ones owned by the Shubert brothers, with a capacity of just under 1,500. It was a gold mine if one could fill it, and a sinkhole if not. Its offerings from the 1940/41 season to the 1944/45 season are revealing (table 5.1). The Shuberts had difficulties finding shows for it in 1940/41, relying on vaudeville for the second half of the season. The first half of the 1941/42 season was devoted to the New Opera Company, and the second to a disastrous musical flop, Vernon Duke's *The Lady Comes Across*—which closed after three performances, $80,000 in the red—before turning once more to vaudeville.[14] The Shuberts then hit gold in the 1942/43 season with the New Opera Company's production of *Rosalinda* (a reworking of Strauss's *Die Fledermaus* of 1874), brought back in the first half of 1943 after a short run of *Porgy and Bess*. From then through July 1945, the 44th Street Theatre was booked solid with the Army Air Forces show *Winged Victory*, then two musicals, one of the latter a transfer of Leonard Bernstein's *On the Town*. These were big productions, which is what was needed to fill a very large stage: *Winged Victory* had a company of some three hundred airmen and forty-two women, plus a large orchestra of servicemen directed by Sergeant David Rose.[15]

*Winged Victory* followed Irving Berlin's *This Is the Army*, which ran on Broadway in summer 1942 before going on a hugely successful tour: in both cases,

Table 5.1. Playlist for the 44th Street Theatre, 1940/41 season to 1944/45 season

| | |
|---|---|
| 9/30–10/19/40 | *The Pirates of Penzance/Trial by Jury*; *The Mikado*; *The Gondoliers* (Gilbert and Sullivan) |
| 1/14–4/19/41 | *Crazy with the Heat* (revue) |
| 10/21–11/11/41 | The New Opera Company (conducted by Antal Dorati): works by Mozart, Verdi, and Tchaikovsky, then *La vie parisienne* (Offenbach) |
| 11/12–12/14/41 | The New Opera Company: ballets |
| 1/9–1/10/42 | *The Lady Comes Across* (musical; Vernon Duke) |
| 4/24–6/20/42 | *Keep 'Em Laughing*, then revised as *Top-Notchers* (vaudeville) |
| 10/28/42–5/22/43 | The New Opera Company: *Rosalinda* (operetta; Johann Strauss, Jr. [= *Die Fledermaus*]); transferred to Imperial Theatre, 5/24–10/2/43 |
| 9/13–10/2/43 | *Porgy and Bess* (musical; George Gershwin [adapted by Cheryl Crawford]) |
| 10/4–11/13/43 | *Rosalinda* (operetta): see above; transferred to 46th Street Theatre, 11/15/43–1/22/44 |
| 11/20/43–5/20/44 | *Winged Victory* (musical; various) |
| 6/12/44–6/2/45 | *Follow the Girls* (musical; Dan Shapiro, Milton Pascal, Phil Charig); transferred from New Century Theatre (opened 4/8/44); transferred to Broadhurst Theatre, 6/4/45–5/18/46 |
| 6/4–7/28/45 | *On the Town* (musical; Leonard Bernstein): transferred from Adelphi Theatre (opened 12/28/44); transferred to Martin Beck Theatre, 7/30/45–2/2/46 |

Source: www.ibdb.com (with some alterations). Dates are given in month/day/year format.

profits went to the Army Emergency Relief Fund. Berlin's patriotic contribution, reworking his World War I *Yip Yip Yaphank* (1918), certainly was a propaganda coup, but for *Winged Victory*, its creator, Moss Hart, claimed greater authenticity by virtue of having spent eight weeks touring US Army Air Forces bases from which he garnered sufficient experiences to represent the progress of six cadets through training and flight school to their first tour of duty.[16] The gender imbalance of its cast, however, reveals one of the problems of war-specific shows on Broadway. Reviewers of *Winged Victory* noted the touching quality of one female scene in the show: as airmen's wives sat in a hotel hearing their husbands fly off to battle. But fighting the enemy was mostly a male affair, and not one likely to provide much opportunity for dancing chorines.

Revues and vaudeville referred to the war through comic skits or patriotic sequences. The revue *Top-Notchers* at the 44th Street Theatre had both: it gave the comedian Zero Mostel his first break, and it had as its Act I finale the number "The Yanks Are Coming Again" by Lew Pollock and Tony Stern that in turn was taken up in a well-known war film (*The Yanks Are Coming*; Producers Releasing Corporation, 1942); inevitably, the song was reprised in Act II. Another revue, *New Priorities of 1943* (opened September 15, 1942), featured the striptease artiste Dorothy Parkington covered in sprays of US war stamps that she auctioned off to the audience every night until left standing just in a G-string bearing the legend "Buy War Bonds": critics, and for that matter the US Treasury, did not know whether to be scandalized or delighted.[17]

Operetta revivals, on the other hand, were popular precisely because they involved sugar-coated nostalgia for an old Europe (or was it a new one?). In the second half of 1943, one could see *Rosalinda* representing a Vienna of happier times, or revivals of Rudolf Friml's *The Vagabond King* (1925) and of Sigmund Romberg's *The Student Prince* (1924), the latter set in a glorious Heidelberg that even as the war came to a close stayed protected from American bombs. However, the New Opera Company's spectacular production of Franz Lehár's *The Merry Widow* (1904) that same season, starring Marta Eggerth, caused at least one critic some concern, given Lehár's well-known connections to Goebbels and Hitler.[18] Somewhat safer ground was provided by operettas based on music by classical composers: the obvious precedent was the 1921 *Blossom Time*, based on Schubert, although *Song of Norway* (brought over from the West Coast and running on Broadway from 1944 to 1946), on the life and music of Grieg, and *Polonaise* (1945–1946), with the eighteenth-century Polish American patriot Tadeusz Kościuszko singing Chopin, played on wartime sentimentalities for the occupied countries, a feeling that may also have motivated the periodic revivals of Offenbach's *La vie parisienne*.[19]

Bringing "classical" music to the Broadway stage was part of a wider strategy of targeting "middlebrow" audiences that were as ecumenical in the United States as anywhere else: Billy Rose's *Seven Lively Arts* (1944), with songs by Cole Porter, Benny Goodman on stage, and ballet music by Igor Stravinsky, is another good example. The reverse was also true. Robert Russell Bennett, who orchestrated *Oklahoma!*, missed the opening night of the show because his "symphonic picture" of *Porgy and Bess* was receiving its first performance by the New York Philharmonic under Fritz Reiner that same evening (March 31, 1943). However, his "symphonic suite" based on *Oklahoma!* soon became an orchestra favorite at "pops" concerts at New York's Lewisohn Stadium and elsewhere, and it was recorded by the Los Angeles Philharmonic under Alfred Wallenstein in 1944. There was also a further agenda in play here. Already in 1941, the music critic of the *New York Times*, Olin Downes, had labeled Jerome Kern a "symphonist" when previewing the upcoming premiere of the "symphonic scenario" on themes from *Show Boat* (in fact, arranged by Charles Miller), praising him for presenting "a national as well as individual voice in the music." The search for an American vernacular style in the concert hall, which was such a preoccupation in World War II, could take many different forms.[20]

Back on the stage, however, matters were trickier for musical comedies with a war-based theme, given that one had to find dramatic reasons to get men and women in close proximity with the raunchy titillation required of a Broadway unfettered by the cinema's censorship codes. Members of the Women's Army Corps (the WACs) or the Rosie the Riveters working in the factories might be shown singing and dancing on film, but it was harder to bring them into play on the stage.[21] Subjects therefore turned to another service industry for the nation's military: the bar, canteen, or whorehouse next to a military base where servicemen could find entertainment and relief. This reflected the fact that the typical gender trap, defining women as "good" or "bad" according to the patriarchal rules, was now being further inflected, and even nuanced, by way of what Marilyn Hegarty has called "a comprehensive notion of patriotic sexuality as a female wartime obligation."[22] Congress had passed the so-called May Act (approved on July 11, 1941) prohibiting prostitution near military and naval establishments, but the dangers of representing such dens of iniquity onstage could be mitigated by some creative misunderstanding or if the outcome involved finding true love in the end. The trope also allowed for "putting on a show" production numbers that would meet vague canons of verisimilitude—which still mattered for some in the musical theater—as well as space for the comedians that were standard in the genre. The model was Cole Porter's prewar *Panama Hattie* (1940–1942), where Ethel Merman had her first big role as the eponymous burlesque queen—the tart with the heart of gold—running a bar for sailors south of the border. *Early to Bed* (1943–1944) was set in a spurious girl's finishing school in Martinique; *Follow the Girls* (1944–1946) came closer to home with a servicemen's canteen in Great Neck, Long Island, where another burlesque queen, Bubbles LaMarr (played by Gertrude Niesen), had as her sidekick the comic character Goofy Gale (Jackie Gleason). The best example, however, is another successful Cole Porter musical, *Something for the Boys* (1943–1944), which originally had the working title *Jenny, Get Your Gun*: here two sisters and a brother inherit equal shares of a Texas ranch next to Kelly Field and its Advanced Flying School. The sisters are a defense worker, Blossom (Ethel Merman), and, inevitably, a burlesque queen named Chiquita (Paula Laurence); the base commander, Lt. Col. Grubbs, is convinced that theirs is a house of ill repute, but Blossom manages to clear the family name. Chiquita and her associates are there, it seems, simply to provide an excuse for exotic Mexican dance numbers.[23]

*Something for the Boys* opened as Rodgers, Hammerstein, and the Theatre Guild were getting ready to put *Oklahoma!* into rehearsal, and they, too, planned to introduce a burlesque Mexican number in the second act until it was dropped.[24] This reflects a degree of uncertainty about *Oklahoma!* from its outset. Theresa Helburn, one of the show's producers, was torn: she knew the commercial advantages of a simple cowboy show, but her search for what she described to Eugene O'Neill as "greatness and beauty and emotional lift" eventually headed in the different direction of a more sophisticated "musical play." The fact that *Oklahoma!* was set in an Arcadian Southwest around 1900 did not make it any less a wartime musical: plenty of patriotic hearts swelled to the idea of Curly and Laurey united in working the beneficent soil of the land that is grand. The power of American history to serve present purposes was clear also in a show that was in many ways a counterpart to *Oklahoma!* and included a number of those involved in its creation: Harold Arlen's *Bloomer Girl*, opening in late 1944.[25] Here the setting is the American Civil War, as a rebellious Evalina Bloomer refuses to wear hooped skirts, preferring more modern dress. It, too, covered all the wartime bases: women's emancipation, men in battle and its consequences on the home front, and even the liberation of African American slaves.

The Theatre Guild certainly saw *Oklahoma!* as part of the war effort: it made the case forcefully when trying to secure for its male cast members exemptions from the draft, and as was common, it provided subsidized performances for servicemen. Like a number of Broadway shows, it was selected for recording on V-disc and for short-wave radio transmission to troops in the field. It probably also did the show no harm that *Oklahoma!* later became embroiled in a surprisingly fierce debate between dance critic George Beiswanger and the Marxist theorist Eric Bentley. Beiswanger enthusiastically embraced the idea of the "integrated musical," unifying music and drama within an almost Wagnerian Gesamtkunstwerk; he also argued (as did others) that here lay the roots of a nascent American "opera." For Bentley, however, this was like a red flag to a bull: not only was such popularized Wagnerism specious—it also had strong fascist overtones. Not everyone was willing to submit to the triumphalist rhetoric.[26]

As the tide demonstrably turned in the war in Europe (after D-Day on June 6, 1944) and in the Pacific (after the victory in Guam in August 1944), Broadway musicals needed to put a softer edge on a military that would eventually be coming home. Instead of bars and brothels, we find roguish-but-brave sailors on shore leave finding love in the big city, as in Bernstein's *On the Town*, set in New York (opened December 28, 1944)—developing Jerome Robbins's April 1944 ballet *Fancy Free*—and in its contemporary cinematic counterpart, *Anchors Aweigh* (in production from June to November 1944 and released in July 1945), where Gene Kelly and Frank Sinatra woo Kathryn Grayson in Los Angeles.[27] Bernstein's horny taxi driver, Hildy Esterhazy, may have echoes of the burlesque queen, but she focuses more on the domestic front in her bump-and-grind up-tempo number, "I Can Cook, Too," if with the obvious innuendos: "I'm a pot of joy for a hungry boy, / Baby, I'm cookin' with gas." When *On the Town* moved to the 44th Street Theatre, however, many in the audience would have appreciated the connection with the Stage Door Canteen right beneath their feet. Meanwhile, the day before *On the Town* first opened, the Theatre Guild tried its next foray into musical theater after *Oklahoma!* with *Sing Out, Sweet Land*, a "salute" to American folk and popular music from the time of the Puritans to the present day held together by a loose narrative linked by a time-traveling Alfred Drake (the first Curly in *Oklahoma!*) as the minstrel Barnaby Goodchild, who ends up as a sailor on deck singing "Praise the Lord, and pass the ammunition." Other musicals, however, dealt with impending postwar readjustments. Rodgers and Hammerstein's surprisingly dark—even "operatic"—*Carousel* (opened April 19, 1945) engaged with the problems of reintegrating into society men inured to violence, of widows left to bring up children on miserable pensions who, despite all, will "never walk alone," and of the massive increase in the divorce rate. Irving Berlin's slightly later *Annie Get Your Gun* (a Rodgers and Hammerstein production that opened on May 16, 1946) instead focused on putting aggressive, independent women back in the home, given that "You Can't Get a Man with a Gun," and also on how two Wild West shows that formerly were bitter rivals now needed to merge so as to secure their future.[28]

On May 16, 1943, the *New York Times* published Martha Dreiblatt's report on interviews with a number of Broadway luminaries for their "Words on the Theatre and War." Many did not know what to say, and those who did favored a softly-softly approach: as the veteran producer Max Gordon claimed, "All we know is that people want entertainment in larger doses than ever before." Playwright Elmer Rice had a bigger ax to grind: "The theatre is flourishing today because people have more money to spend. But the war hasn't developed anything of significance. What should the theatre in wartime be? I would like this flourishing public to see good plays, good plays on many themes. The trouble is there are very few good young playwrights to turn them out."[29]

Broadway may not have been as wholly committed to the war effort as some government officials and others would have liked, and it never succumbed to the pressures facing the contemporary film industry to serve in effect as the propaganda arm of the wartime administration: on October 16, 1942, one could have gone instead to see the anti-Japanese spy thriller *Across the Pacific* (starring Humphrey Bogart), the celebration of the American baseball hero Lou Gehrig in *Pride of the Yankees* (Gary Cooper)—with *Manila Calling* as the B-movie in some cinemas—or even the Soviet-made *In the Rear of the Enemy* (with a new English-language soundtrack). However, in the case of *Oklahoma!* and some other musicals, Broadway's wartime products eventually established significant grounds for a debate that, like the war itself, raised profound questions about what it might mean to be American in a brave, new postwar world. Not for nothing did the United Service Organizations (USO) include *Oklahoma!* and *Porgy and Bess* in their repertory of cut-down musicals touring military bases at home and overseas in 1944 and 1945: the others included the very old *Irene* (music by Harry Tierney), *Mexican Hayride* (Cole Porter), and the revues *Hellzapoppin'* and *Star and Garter*. Likewise, in the early 1950s the US State Department supported European productions of both shows as part of its new wave of cultural diplomacy (*Oklahoma!* in Berlin in September 1951; *Porgy and Bess* on quite extensive tours in 1952–1953 and 1954–1956, the latter also including Latin America).[30] Whatever the realities of life in the United States, the messages they delivered were clear enough: the American Way was now a force to be reckoned with on the international stage.

### APPENDIX: MUSICALS PLAYING ON BROADWAY, 1941–1945 (ON DECEMBER 7 EACH YEAR)

*Source:* www.ibdb.com (with some changes). Dates are given in month/day/year format; the number of performances is indicated in parentheses.

For obvious reasons, this does not capture all the musicals done in the period, but most of the longer-running ones appear here. My labeling of these shows ("musical," "revue," etc.) avoids the nuances ("musical comedy," "musical play") but serves the present purpose. For reasons of space, I identify only the composers involved, which does a severe injustice to all others involved in a given show's creation.

December 7, 1941 (30 productions onstage: 6 musicals, 2 revues)
- *Hellzapoppin'* (revue): 9/22/38–12/17/41 (1404)
- *Panama Hattie* (musical; Cole Porter): 10/30/40–1/3/1942 (501)
- *Lady in the Dark* (musical; Kurt Weill): 1/21–6/15/41, 9/2–5/30/42, 2/27–5/15/43 (550 in total)
- *Best Foot Forward* (musical; Hugh Martin, Ralph Blane): 10/1/41–7/4/42 (326)
- *Let's Face It!* (musical; Cole Porter): 10/29/41–3/20/1943 (547)
- *High Kickers* (musical; Bert Kalmar, Harry Ruby): 10/31/41–3/28/42 (171)
- *Sons o' Fun* (revue): 12/1/41–8/29/43 (742)
- *Sunny River* (musical; Sigmund Romberg): 12/4/41–1/3/42 (36)

December 7, 1942 (30 productions onstage; 4 revues/vaudeville, 3 musicals, 2 operettas)
- *Let's Face It!* (musical): see 1941
- *Sons o' Fun* (revue): see 1941
- *By Jupiter* (musical; Richard Rodgers): 6/3/42–6/12/43 (427)

*Star and Garter* (revue): 6/24/42–12/4/43 (609)
*Show Time* (vaudeville): 9/16/42–4/3/43 (342)
*Oy Is Dus a Leben!* (revue): 10/12/42–2/6/43 (139)
*Beat the Band* (musical; Johnny Green): 10/14–12/12/42 (67)
*Rosalinda* (operetta; Johann Strauss, Jr. [= *Die Fledermaus*]): 10/28/42–5/22/44 (611)
*La vie parisienne* (operetta; Jacques Offenbach): 11/5–11/11/41, 11/10–12/7/42, 1/12/45–? (61 in total)

December 7, 1943 (31 productions onstage; 8 musicals, 2 operettas, 1 revue)
*Rosalinda* (operetta): see 1942
*Something for the Boys* (musical; Cole Porter): 1/7/43–1/8/44 (422)
*Oklahoma!* (musical; Richard Rodgers): 3/31/43–5/29/48 (2212)
*Ziegfeld Follies of 1943* (revue): 4/1/43–7/2/44 (553)
*Early to Bed* (musical; Thomas "Fats" Waller): 6/17/43–5/13/44 (380)
*The Merry Widow* (operetta; Franz Lehár): 8/4/43–5/6/44 (322)
*One Touch of Venus* (musical; Kurt Weill): 10/7/43–2/10/45 (567)
*What's Up?* (musical; Frederick Loewe): 11/11/43–1/4/44 (63)
*A Connecticut Yankee* (musical; Richard Rodgers): 11/17/43–3/11/44 (135)
*Winged Victory* (musical; various): 11/20/43–5/20/44 (212)
*Carmen Jones* (musical; Georges Bizet): 12/2/43–2/10/45 (503)

December 7, 1944 (36 productions onstage; 8 musicals, 2 revues/vaudeville)
*Oklahoma!* (musical): see 1943
*One Touch of Venus* (musical): see 1943
*Carmen Jones* (musical): see 1943
*Mexican Hayride* (musical; Cole Porter): 1/28/44–3/17/45 (481)
*Follow the Girls* (musical; Dan Shapiro, Milton Pascal, Phil Charig): 4/8/44–5/18/46 (888)
*Song of Norway* (musical; Edvard Grieg): 8/21/44–9/7/46 (860)
*Star Time* (vaudeville): 9/12–12/9/44 (120)
*Bloomer Girl* (musical; Harold Arlen): 10/5/44–4/27/46 (654)
*Sadie Thompson* (musical; Vernon Duke): 11/16/44–1/6/45 (60)
*Seven Lively Arts* (revue; Cole Porter, Igor Stravinsky): 12/7/44–5/12/45 (183)

December 7, 1945 (33 productions onstage; 12 musicals)
*Oklahoma!* (musical): see 1943
*Follow the Girls* (musical): see 1944
*Song of Norway* (musical): see 1944
*Bloomer Girl* (musical): see 1944

*On the Town* (musical; Leonard Bernstein): 12/28/44–2/2/46 (462)
*Up in Central Park* (musical; Sigmund Romberg): 1/27/45–4/13/46 (504)
*Carousel* (musical; Richard Rodgers): 4/19/45–7/24/47 (890)
*Marinka* (musical; Emmerich Kálmán): 7/18–12/8/45 (165)
*Polonaise* (musical; Frédéric Chopin): 10/6/45–1/12/46 (113)
*The Red Mill* (musical; Victor Herbert): 10/16/45–1/18/47 (531)
*Are You With It?* (musical; Harry Revel): 11/10/45–6/29/46 (264)
*The Day Before Spring* (musical; Frederick Loewe): 11/22/45–4/13/46 (167)

NOTES

1. I draw on the display ads and listings in the *New York Times* (henceforth *NYT*), October 16, 1942, 22. Atkinson's review of Ronell's *Count Me In* is in "The Play," *NYT*, October 9, 1942, 24, which also contains a display ad for *The Eve of St. Mark*. For Shostakovich's Seventh Symphony and its arrival in the United States, see Fauser, *Sounds of War*, 257.

2. Carter, "*Oklahoma!*," 50.

3. "Ballet Russe Begins Engagement at Met," *Brooklyn Daily Eagle*, October 11, 1942, 5; "Agnes de Mille Wins Ovation for 'Rodeo,'" *Brooklyn Daily Eagle*, October 17, 1942, 14.

4. "For Service Men," *NYT*, October 18, 1942, 51. Free passes were available for *Count Me In*, *Stars on Ice* at the Center Theatre, and the ballet at the Met, as well as several films, two football games (including the Brooklyn Dodgers versus the Washington Redskins) and other sports, a visit to the top of the Empire State Building, and several college parties.

5. "The Theatre: *Include Me Out*," *Wall Street Journal*, October 10, 1942, 10. The four prisoners of war were played by the Rhythmaires, an all-white vocal ensemble (but no direct relation to the backing group associated with Bing Crosby in the later 1940s) that came together in *High Kickers* (1941) and also appeared in the *Ziegfeld Follies of 1943* (including the Bizet pastiche, *Carmen in Zoot*, as the Act I finale that, in turn, sought to preempt Oscar Hammerstein II's *Carmen Jones*).

6. "Gossip of the Rialto: The American Theatre Wing Sets Forth its Plans," *NYT*, December 21, 1941, X1; Brooks Atkinson, "Curtain's Up at the Stage Door Canteen," *NYT*, March 3, 1942, 26. The basement was donated by theater owner Lee Shubert.

7. Lewis Nichols, "Of War Plays," *NYT*, December 13, 1942, X1; Martha Dreiblatt, "Words on the Theatre and War," *NYT*, May 16, 1943, X1–2 (more than thirty plays).

8. Carter, "*Oklahoma!*," 173–174 (Helburn to O'Neill, May 1940; O'Neill to Langner, August 11, 1940)

9. Ibid., 79 (Winchell), 208–209 (Downes). Downes's "Broadway's Gift to Opera," *NYT*, June 6, 1943, X5, argued that *Oklahoma!* "shows one of the ways to an integrated and indigenous form of American lyric theatre."

10. Theodore Strauss, "Broadway Sees a Gold Rush," *NYT*, September 6, 1942, SM10 (good for business); "War Comes to Broadway," *NYT*, May 1, 1942, 18; and Meyer Berger, "The Not-So-Gay White Way," *NYT*, May 24, 1942, SM10–11 (reduced lighting on Broadway); Ellis T. Baker III, "Hansom Cab Era on Broadway Revived as Result of Ban on Pleasure Driving," *Baltimore Sun*, January 9, 1943, 1.

11. Richard Rodgers rather wickedly explained Porter's preeminence by the fact that despite his being an Episcopalian millionaire from Peru, Indiana, he wrote the best "Jewish" music of all; Rodgers, *Musical Stages*, 88. It is a revealing comment given the prominent role of Jewish luminaries in the entertainment industry, which, in turn, provoked some wartime sympathy; compare Carter, *"Oklahoma!,"* 197–200.

12. For *Carmen Jones* and other "race" musicals, see Fauser, "'Dixie *Carmen*.'" Hammerstein's attempts to revive *Show Boat* are discussed in Carter, *"Oklahoma!,"* 25–26. He had mixed feelings about *Porgy and Bess*, but clearly sought some response to it via *Carmen Jones* as well as in his first collaborations with Richard Rodgers; see Carter, *Rodgers and Hammerstein's "Carousel,"* 28.

13. Carter, *"Oklahoma!,"* 70. The final cost of *Oklahoma!* up to its opening night was around $82,000, which was about ten times the typical capitalization needed for a spoken play. The start-up budget for Cole Porter's *Something for the Boys* was $125,000.

14. "Costly Show Ends," *NYT*, January 12, 1942, 23. *The Lady Comes Across* took over the scenery and costumes of *She Had to Say Yes* that had flopped at its tryout in Philadelphia the previous year, and it had a sorry history thereafter: not even George Balanchine's choreography could save the show.

15. E. F. Melvin, "Air Forces Show Greeted in Boston," *NYT*, November 3, 1943, 22, reporting on the Boston tryout, counted 158 soldiers, some sixty civilian actresses, an orchestra of forty-five, and a choir of fifty. The higher estimate for the men (and lower for the women) comes from John Chapman, "*Winged Victory* Lives Up to Advanced Notices," *Chicago Daily Tribune*, November 28, 1943, D4.

16. *This Is the Army* opened on July 4, 1942, and played on Broadway through the summer before going on tour. The *New York Times* reported on February 21, 1943 ("Gossip of the Rialto," X1; in anticipation of a radio broadcast the next day), that it had raised almost $2M for the Army Emergency Relief Fund. Moss Hart described his tour of Army Air Forces bases in "A Winged Victory," *NYT*, November 14, 1943, X1–2.

17. See the editorial "Question of Taste," *Washington Post*, October 14, 1942, 6.

18. Lewis Nichols, "Singing Some Old Songs," *NYT*, August 15, 1943, X1: "It is a beautiful score which never grows old, which has withstood time, the radio, repetition and the fact that its composer, as a friend of Hitler, has chosen to depart a state of good will." See also Curt L. Heymann's letter to the Drama Editor, *NYT*, August 23, 1942, X2, asking about the freezing of Lehár's royalties, given that he

is "next to Wagner, not only A. Hitler's most favorite composer but likewise very proud of the honors that nazism has bestowed upon him." For similar arguments over Richard Strauss, see Fauser, *Sounds of War*, 70–71.

19. The Russians fared less well, however: the revue *Chauve-Souris*, which had a very brief run on August 12–21, 1943, was a mixed-language presentation that bombed. Lewis Nichols's review (*NYT*, August 13, 1943, 13) noted "a dreadful song about an American WAC and a Russian sniper, which while it will not ruin Soviet–American relations will not cement them either."

20. Carter, "*Oklahoma!*," 213 (Bennett); O'Leary, "Keeping Faith with John Q. Public" (*Seven Lively Arts*); Olin Downes, "Kern: Symphonist," *NYT*, July 20, 1941, X5. For the broader issues, see Fauser, *Sounds of War*, chap. 5.

21. For films, compare *Star Spangled Rhythm* (Paramount Pictures, 1942) with its big production number, "On the Swing Shift," set in an aircraft factory.

22. Hegarty, *Victory Girls, Khaki-Wackies, and Patriotutes*, 112.

23. Lewis Nichols was ecstatic in his review (*NYT*, January 8, 1943, 24), not just about the show but also about Ethel Merman in her greatest role thus far: "She is 'the missing link between Lily Pons and Mae West.' And a credit, of course, to the pair of them." He returned to her in "Merman for the Boys," *NYT*, January 17, 1943, X1. As Nichols also noted in his January 8 review, "Anita Alvarez is present to lead the Spanish dance without which no musical show set in Texas would be considered legal."

24. Carter, "*Oklahoma!*," 99. *Something for the Boys* also had a square dance, as does *Oklahoma!* at the beginning of Act II ("The Farmer and the Cowman").

25. *Bloomer Girl* starred Celeste Holm (Ado Annie in *Oklahoma!*) and featured Joan McCracken (a lead dancer in the former show). Also shared were Agnes de Mille (choreography), Lemuel Ayers (stage design), Miles White (costumes), and Robert Russell Bennett (orchestrations), though save for de Mille, that was not unusual.

26. Carter, "*Oklahoma!*," 148–149 (draft exemption and special performances), 208–212 (Beiswanger and Bentley). For the broader argument over musical theater as American opera, see Carter, *Rodgers and Hammerstein's "Carousel,"* 98–106.

27. *Anchors Aweigh* included an *Oklahoma!* alumna, Pamela Britton (she played Ado Annie in the touring company), as the unnamed "Girl from Brooklyn" who falls for the Frank Sinatra character. Britton ignored the warnings of the company manager against leaving *Oklahoma!* in Chicago to pursue a career in Hollywood; Carter, "*Oklahoma!*," 238. Her plan failed, and she returned to Broadway in 1947 to play in Lerner and Loewe's *Brigadoon*.

28. Oja, *Bernstein Meets Broadway* (*On the Town*); Fauser, *Sounds of War*, 151–155 (*Sing Out, Sweet Land*; see also the photospread in "Cavalcade of American Song," *NYT*, December 24, 1944, 70–71); Carter, *Rodgers and Hammerstein's "Carousel,"* 89–95; Magee, *Irving Berlin's American Musical Theater*, chap. 7 (*Annie Get Your Gun*).

29. Martha Dreiblatt, "Words on the Theatre and War," *NYT*, May 16, 1943, X1.

30. Sam Zolotow, "USO Ready to Send 16 Shows Overseas," *NYT*, August 9, 1944, 14 (which also notes that the USO is looking to recruit dancing chorus girls

for top salaries, traveling uniforms, transportation, and room and board); Carter, *"Oklahoma!,"* 232 (USO), 235 (Berlin); Pollack, *George Gershwin*, 611–612 (USO), 614–623 (the Breen/Davis production of *Porgy and Bess* on tour).

BIBLIOGRAPHY

**Historical Newspapers**
*Baltimore Sun*, 1943
*Brooklyn Daily Eagle*, 1942
*Chicago Daily Tribune*, 1943
*New York Amsterdam Star-News*, 1942
*New York Times*, 1941–1944
*Wall Street Journal*, 1942
*Washington Post*, 1942

**Books and Articles**
Carter, Tim. *"Oklahoma!": The Making of an American Musical (Revised Edition)*. New York: Oxford University Press, 2020.
———. *Rodgers and Hammerstein's "Carousel."* New York: Oxford University Press, 2017.
Fauser, Annegret. "'Dixie *Carmen*': War, Race, and Identity in Oscar Hammerstein's *Carmen Jones* (1943)." *Journal of the Society for American Music* 4 (2010): 127–174.
———. *Sounds of War: Music in the United States During World War II*. New York: Oxford University Press, 2013.
Hegarty, Marilyn E. *Victory Girls, Khaki-Wackies, and Patriotutes: The Regulation of Female Sexuality during World War II*. New York: New York University Press, 2008.
Magee, Jeffrey. *Irving Berlin's American Musical Theater*. New York: Oxford University Press, 2012.
Oja, Carol J. *Bernstein Meets Broadway: Collaborative Art in a Time of War*. New York: Oxford University Press, 2014.
O'Leary, James. "Keeping Faith with John Q. Public: Cole Porter, Billy Rose, and *Seven Lively Arts*." In *A Cole Porter Companion*, edited by Don M. Randel, Matthew Shaftel, and Susan Forscher Weiss, 165–181. Champaign: University of Illinois Press, 2016.
Pollack, Howard. *George Gershwin: His Life and Work*. Berkeley: University of California Press, 2006.
Rodgers, Richard. *Musical Stages: An Autobiography*. 2nd ed. Cambridge, MA: Da Capo, 2002.

TIM CARTER is David G. Frey Distinguished Professor of Music at the University of North Carolina at Chapel Hill. He is author of many books, including *"Oklahoma!": The Making of an American Musical* and *Rodgers and Hammerstein's "Carousel."*

## SIX

## THROWING SOME LIGHT ON THE *DUNKELKONZERTE*

Toward a New Image of Concert Life in Vienna, 1939–1944

NICHOLAS ATTFIELD

"'THE NAZIS DUG HIM, TOO,' Evelyn finally said. 'His monumental scale, grandiose, lavish, spiritual . . . They'd play him in *Dunkelkonzerte*—lights all out, sacred space. Nazis listening to Bruckner was like going to church.' She snuggled in under the quilt."[1] In Marc Estrin's coming-of-age novel *The Education of Arnold Hitler* (2005), the eponymous protagonist is an American Harvard graduate finding his way in the New York City of the early 1970s. Unsurprisingly, many of his struggles involve his last name and the meaning it holds for those around him. He is approached, for example, by the beautiful and enigmatic Evelyn Brown, an artist and part-time stripper fascinated by Nazism and drawn to him simply on the basis of the name that she finds "attractive and exceptional."[2] They begin a relationship. Evelyn has a home built for Arnold underneath an on-ramp of the Bruckner Expressway in the Bronx. Together, in the bedroom scene quoted above, they pour some champagne, switch out the lights, and listen to the Adagio of Anton Bruckner's Seventh Symphony, the greatest work of (Adolf) Hitler's "favorite composer after Wagner."[3]

As Estrin's book demonstrates, the so-called *Dunkelkonzerte* (literally, "darkness concerts") have become a stereotype of Nazi-era concert practice and an object of fascination, even fetishization. Originally staged in Vienna between November 1939 and March 1944, these events first captured scholarly attention in an institutional history of the early 1980s. Friedrich C. Heller's work on the Vienna Konzerthaus during the Second World War revealed the existence of these programs; noting that they apparently featured a succession of German masterworks—most obviously Bruckner's symphonies—performed in a "darkened hall," Heller remarked that they were best understood in terms of the "romanticizing philosophy of National Socialist art-dreams."[4] Similarly, Benjamin Korstvedt's 1995 doctoral dissertation pointed toward them as evidence of the "ideological baggage" attached to an ostensibly "nonpolitical" concert under the Nazi regime, while in 2000, Manfred Permoser's wartime history of the Wiener Symphoniker (the Vienna Symphony Orchestra)—the presiding orchestra for the concerts—added a brief account of their genesis and speculated on their underlying aesthetics.[5]

It is surely from Bryan Gilliam's account, however, that most readers will be familiar with the term. (Judging by the vocabulary he uses, this is certainly where Marc Estrin took the idea from). According to Gilliam, the Dunkelkonzerte audiences flocked to a Konzerthaus that, through the simple means of the "fully darkened hall," had been transformed into a "sacred space where listening to Bruckner became tantamount to attending church," and where "only those who shared the same blood and soil could comprehend the message."[6] The broader point of his essay, moreover, is to relate this practice to the contemporary appropriation of Bruckner as a cultural symbol of the *Anschluss*, Nazi Germany's annexation of Austrian territory in early 1938. Bruckner's statue had taken its place in the hallowed pantheon of the Regensburg Valhalla, hall of German heroes; now the congregation at this Viennese "Bruckner Church" came to worship the deified pan-Germanness channeled by the composer and ultimately embodied by Hitler, allegedly one of Bruckner's most fervent admirers.[7]

On the basis of this account, Brian Kane has recently gone even further, with the claim that the Dunkelkonzerte darkness enforced a separation of eye and ear that served as a deliberate technology of control. Thus, the organizers of these events had far surpassed concert-hall reformers of the earlier twentieth century who had hidden their orchestras in order to reinforce the commonplace belief in music's powers of transcendence.[8] Rather, they aimed for the creation of a "new social body," something to be knitted together within the darkened room from those listening blind to the music's "transcendental sonic message of spiritual destiny and fate" and called to the "spiritual mission" it propounded.[9] Kane's clear implication is that this "social body" and this "mission" were the sharply exclusive ones of National Socialism. Accordingly, there is only one fitting word for the Dunkelkonzerte: he finds them simply "frightful."[10]

This chapter begins by proposing that such perspectives on the Dunkelkonzerte are in need of thoroughgoing revision. Pamela Potter has warned of the dangers of the "heavy reliance on totalitarian and intentionalist models" commonly found in historical accounts of music during the Third Reich; she has drawn our attention, too, to the stereotypes attendant on prevalent turns of phrase such as "Nazi music."[11] The current image of these Dunkelkonzerte, it seems, is narrowly guided and constrained by the now long-outdated vision of Hitler, Goebbels, and their Viennese henchmen enforcing social control and cohesion by means of a nefarious concert practice inspired by their favorite symphonist. At once as radical as it is conservative, as resonant with the twentieth century as it is with the nineteenth, the idea of switching out the concert-hall lights to create a romantic experience of communal worship powerfully recalls the Nazi tactics of harnessing technology to promote a tribal sense of belonging to the people's community (*Volksgemeinschaft*).

Yet, if we allow the loosening of the grip of this totalitarian model, it soon becomes clear that there is much more at play. As this chapter suggests, we might begin by taking heed of the gains of recent research into the two relevant institutions—Konzerthaus (venue) and Symphoniker (orchestra)—in order to pose some pertinent questions about the Dunkelkonzerte. What difference does it make, for example, that these concerts were performed not in Berlin or Munich but in Vienna, a city with its own prominent musical traditions and its own recent fascist history? And how might that difference, in turn, inflect our view of the ideology of concert programming for Viennese concertgoers during the Second World War?

Toward the same end, the chapter also poses a series of practical questions that sound as flippant as they are important: what did a "fully darkened hall" really mean anyway, and how could a program of concerts in such an environment function effectively? Are a "new social body" or a sense of "spiritual destiny" likely outcomes of so simple a conceit as dimming the concert hall lights, or are other outcomes—perhaps those of a less exalted nature—rather more likely? Looking at contemporary descriptions and responses from organizers, performers, critics, and audience members provides new insights into pragmatic considerations that may have inspired the technique. These resources have been overlooked up to now, leading scholars instead to speculate on the practice as a totalitarian tactic of mind control.

## "VIENNA—A REFUGE FOR THE GERMAN SOUL"

To a certain extent, it makes sense to trace the roots of the Dunkelkonzerte back to the Anschluss of March 1938. It was then, after all, that money began to flow into the coffers of the Konzerthaus and Symphoniker, bringing both institutions back from the brink of the insolvency that had plagued them for much of the prior decade.[12] Restorative funds arrived from newly founded city and state bodies established to oversee cultural and educational affairs in the expanded Reich, including the Ministerium für innere und kulturelle Angelegenheiten (Ministry for Internal and Cultural Affairs), the office of the Reichsstatthalter (Reich Governor) for Austria, and the Gemeinde Wien (City of Vienna).[13] No less significantly, the expansion to Austria of Kraft durch Freude (Strength through Joy), the German state leisure organization for workers, resolved the long-standing problem of dwindling rental contracts for the hall: beginning in October 1938, its broad program of concerts and other events called for the regular engagement of both venue and orchestra.[14] At the Konzerthaus, these extra funds allowed vital and long-postponed repairs to the building and its organ to take place.[15] They also resulted in a sharp increase in the number of concerts offered over the next few years: in spite of the onset of war, the 132 concerts of the 1938/39 season grew to 460 four years later, an expansion that cemented the long-standing connection between the concert hall and the Symphoniker.[16] The orchestra was additionally supported by its close association with Austrian radio and by its engagements to provide music for official state and party functions. It now became rebranded, indeed, as a Viennese Stadtorchester (city orchestra).[17]

Both institutions had, however, been marked out for such favor well before 1938. Under Oswald Kabasta, the chief conductor from 1934, the Symphoniker took part in the gradual introduction of Nazi policies into key Austrian cultural organizations: in 1938, Kabasta referred to his "systematic repression of Jewish influence" on the orchestra and boasted that, for the prior five years, he had admitted "not a single Jew" to the ranks of its players.[18] The Konzerthaus became similarly embroiled. In spite of its management's repeated assurances of political neutrality, the venue had hosted numerous local National Socialist rallies until the party was officially banned in Austria in June 1933.[19] After the ban was relaxed some three years later, the German propaganda ministry took an active interest in the institution, permitting the Austrian-born Karl Böhm to conduct there in 1936 as a means of galvanizing local National Socialist support.[20] Thus the Konzerthaus came to be named specifically in the so-called *kulturelles Sofortprogramm* (emergency cultural program) that Hitler's ambassador to Austria, Franz von Papen, prepared in anticipation of the annexation.[21] A "working relationship" with the German Reich, according to von Papen, ought readily to be forged: indeed, it was in the Great Hall of the Konzerthaus that the result of the plebiscite on the union of Austria and Germany was announced on the evening of April 10, 1938.[22]

At the time of the Anschluss, then, the Nazi grip seems to have tightened—not least because, in addition to the changes noted above, Jewish management figures at both institutions were swiftly replaced by those acceptable to the new regime.[23] At this point, scholars have generally looked no further, assuming instead that a complete takeover of the institutions had been carried out. In his sociological study of the Symphoniker, for example, Ernst Kobau turned away from the post-1938 period with the remark that the Stadtorchester had now become a *Reichsorchester*, that is, a "Viennese" organization in name only, actually managed from Berlin by Goebbels and his Reichskulturkammer (Reich Culture Chamber).[24] With a long-standing plan having come to fruition, as it were, and the coveted cultural institutions fully aligned, there was little more that needed to be said.

Yet if we shift our attention to consider the records of performed repertory from 1938 to 1945, we observe some striking trends. Changes did not reflect a sudden move toward excluding the music of composers now considered unacceptable to the regime on racial or political grounds as one would expect, for this was already a noticeable trend in Viennese concert life for much of the 1930s, under the two prior Austrian regimes. There had been a decline in performances of Gustav Mahler, Felix Mendelssohn, and Arnold Schoenberg at the Konzerthaus from 1930, particularly after the implementation of the fascist *Ständestaat* (corporate state) in 1934, as well as a marginalizing of social-democratic cultural influences from the same time onward.[25] Rather, what is more surprising across both "light" entertainment repertories and those of the "serious" art canon is the overwhelming emphasis on certain *Austrian* composers, particularly those originating from the capital city. As Erwin Barta's statistical analysis of post-1938 repertory suggests, this was unusual even for Vienna: it seems that local concert planners now filled the halls of the Konzerthaus with the waltzes of Carl Michael Ziehrer, Joseph Lanner, and the Strausses father and son, as well as with the songs of Heinrich Strecker, Johann Schrammel, and Ludwig Gruber (to cite only a few prominent examples). Schubert's *Unfinished*, meanwhile, was the most frequently performed symphonic work.[26] Likewise, Manfred Permoser's list of post-annexation Symphoniker programs presents numerous *volkstümlich* (popular) symphony concerts, musical memorials, and operetta-excerpt evenings with a comparably strong Austrian or Viennese profile.[27]

How might we interpret this swerve toward the Austrian? We might initially suspect an official attempt at *Ablenkung* (diversion), in tune with the September 1939 propaganda ministry directive that concert programs across the Reich should delight their audiences and distract them from the realities of the new war.[28] In this view, the likes of Ziehrer's "O Wien, mein liebes Wien" (O Vienna, My Dear Vienna) or Schrammel's "Wien bleibt Wien" (Vienna Will Always Be Vienna) might be heard to give audiences a temporary escape from the present by means of a firm footing in the luxurious melodies of the past. In this case, however, it should be noted that the same trend also encompassed numerous concerts of new and contemporary "serious" Austrian music, much of which would hardly fit the mold of the "good old Vienna" emphasis elsewhere. Indeed, a Konzerthaus–Symphoniker collaboration expressly for the "promotion of contemporary music" was launched in December 1940 and, in spite of the non-specificity of its title, focused largely on the instrumental works of living Austrian composers: the premieres of Franz Hasenöhrl's Piano Concerto and Otto Siegl's *Concerto grosso antico* in G minor, for example, and a performance of (the recently deceased) Franz Schmidt's Organ Toccata in C major; or Alfred Uhl's Double Fugue for Orchestra, Viktor Hruby's *Phantastisches Scherzo*, and a movement from Oskar Wagner's Symphony in C minor. Ernst Geutebrück, a board member of both concert hall and orchestra, also used this series to have his music performed.[29]

It may be better, then, to talk of a sudden exaggeration of local cultural identity around the time of the Anschluss—a forceful foregrounding of Viennese and

Austrian musical traditions that in turn hints at local anxieties over their elision within the new regime. To dub this a cultural expression of "resistance" or "defiance" would surely be too strong: such rhetoric, after all, seems to presume the existence of a specific prohibition; more importantly, it risks feeding into the typical post-1945 mythology of Austria as "Hitler's first victim," and encourages us to forget the narrow conception of Austrian identity presented here. Rather, always remembering the racial, social, and political confines in which it operated, we might consider this foregrounding an attempt to put forward a resilient image of "Austrianness" as exemplified through one of the region's chief commodities, its musical heritage. A legacy of the specifically Austrian fascism of the preceding four years, this would serve as a means of projecting an image of cultural supremacy against Berlin, even as Vienna ceded its former political importance to the German capital. With the onset of war, it would also dovetail with the invocation of local patriotism toward a defense of the home front.[30]

Certainly, the new control structure allowed for these possibilities. With the Anschluss, attempts had been made to streamline the chain of command and minimize infighting among governing bodies in the cultural sector, typically by installing the same person into several different positions at once across party and city administrative divisions. Around the time of the annexation, for example, Hanns Blaschke—a Viennese councilor, vice mayor, and member of the Schutzstaffel (SS)—became head of the cultural wing of the party Propagandaamt (Propaganda Office) and the leader of the city's newly formed Kulturamt (Culture Office); he was also appointed to the directorial boards of the Konzerthaus and Symphoniker.[31] Armin Caspar Hochstetter, general secretary of the Konzerthaus board, became a representative of the Reich Music Chamber in Vienna and held the role of the city's *Musikbeauftragte*, an honorary position with limited oversight of music programming.[32] Yet, whatever the intended effect of such streamlining, its results could be unpredictable.[33] While in theory this structure was to serve as a direct and efficient conduit for reporting back to the Culture Chamber in Berlin, in practice the investment of so much cultural authority in single figures led to something more like a Viennese "bloc"—within which those suspicious of Berlin and simultaneously protective of their own local cultural influence and career ambitions could rally.[34]

These effects became most obvious under Baldur von Schirach, the *Gauleiter* (regional party leader) of Austria from 1940, who entered into numerous open spats with the Culture Chamber over his support for Austrian cultural hegemony, not least as demonstrated through its music.[35] But similar tensions were already palpable from 1938 onward. Soon after the annexation, Anton Haasbauer—a special commissioner for "cultural issues" in Austria—attempted to quell fears of a "Prussianizing of Austrian culture" by promising that, for all that German "forms of organization" would now be adopted, "indigenous cultural values and their unique character" would be "protected unconditionally," allowing Vienna to remain a "cultural bastion" of the region.[36] Similarly, in a speech of June 1938 at the Hofburg, the first Austrian Gauleiter, Odilo Globocnik, told the Viennese artistic community that "this old city must maintain its characteristic tone" within the new Reich, specifying that the "sense for good music" should be expressed not only through "high art" but through "entertainment music" as well, so that "even in cafés and restaurants the foreigner will form an opinion of our musical city of Vienna."[37]

Far less diplomatic was the account of Aurel Wolfram, a "cultural consultant" for the Reich Propaganda Office in Vienna. Wolfram's long September 1940 article for the *Neues Wiener Tagblatt* may begin with official Anschluss rhetoric, depicting Berlin and Vienna as erstwhile "rivals" that, through the "people's destiny," had become complementary poles of a "greater unity."[38] But this argument quickly transforms into an open attack on the German capital, presenting it as a modern dystopia that changed little since the nightmare of the Weimar Republic. A center for "Americanism," sobriety, realism, and the machine, Berlin showed no interest for preserving tradition, for true inwardness, or for the growth of genuine culture.

Vienna, conversely, was always where the heart was, a "refuge for the German soul." Berlin may "astound one like an athlete," but it was only Vienna that one could "love as one loves a mother."[39] Moreover, it was the place where "the bloodstream of new youth" pulsed under the skin of the old; a place where "silhouettes of old churches and palaces speak eloquently against the silent night's sky," where "muted music sounds across peaceful streets," and thus where an "atmosphere woven from subtle shades of feeling" could still persist in art and culture.[40] Though it may have lost its political primacy, that very loss had brought Vienna's cultural "mission" more prominently to the fore: the day must soon come when the German soul would break from the "yoke of the machine" and migrate back from the virile body of German fascism toward the eternal mother, the "capital of the inward Reich."[41]

Here, then, is the backdrop against which we might place the inception of the Dunkelkonzerte in November 1939. On this matter, Ernst Kobau writes that they were "introduced by the Nazis," but clearly, bearing in mind the internal tensions outlined above, this explanation does not suffice.[42] Making use of the archival documentary record, we can specify that they were a proud initiative of the Symphoniker alone, coinciding not with the Anschluss but rather with the arrival of a new artistic director, Friedrich Dürauer, and a new principal conductor, Hans Weisbach; and with the beginning of the war.[43] A memorandum written by Dürauer just before the first concert urges orchestra members to advertise this event "organized under our own direction" in local coffee houses and restaurants, while a personal invitation to Schirach in November 1940 emphasizes "our newly introduced concerts."[44] An interview with Dürauer in the *Österreichische Volks-Zeitung*, moreover, states his intention to deliver both the music of the "Viennese classics" and a series of "city concerts"—a creation that, on account of its "unique tone," would assume a "special place" in local concert life.[45]

Leaving aside the issue of the darkened performance conditions just for a moment and looking across the five seasons from November 1939 to March 1944, we might first consider the Dunkelkonzerte simply as a concert series.[46] As has been much discussed, Bruckner's symphonies featured prominently in these concerts and seemingly became the chief draw. Except for the Second and the Sixth Symphonies, each of these works was performed at least once in the Dunkelkonzerte, expressly in the recently prepared "original versions," a collaboration between the Austrian National Library and the Leipzig-centered Bruckner-Gesellschaft. Again, however, the local identity stamp was often placed foremost in their advertising. In 1940/41, the fortieth anniversary season of the Symphoniker's founding, the run of six Friday night darkness concerts began with a performance of Bruckner's unfinished Ninth, preceded by a lecture–recital to present the Viennese premiere of fragments of its finale.[47] As an unpublished text—most likely the draft of a press release—recounts, this was the work of "our Austrian Master" premiered and made famous by this orchestra, the origins of which ensemble could be traced back to a "purely Viennese idealism."[48] The front cover for the season's concert schedule underlines the point: here the illuminated conductor stands with baton raised not above the swastika, but rather above the double-headed eagle of Austria–Hungary and, beneath that, the incipit of the first theme of Bruckner's Fourth (*Romantic*) Symphony, the principal work of the season's fourth concert. Were the reproduction in color, indeed, it could be seen that the shield at the eagle's heart is that of Vienna, a white cross on a red background (fig. 6.1).

In the same season, moreover, Mozart ("another genius inextricably bound to the musical history of Vienna") was added to complement Bruckner and was again represented both by canonic favorites (the *Jupiter* Symphony and the Violin Concerto in D major, K. 218) and by rarities and premieres.[49] An early setting of the *Regina Coeli*, for example, preceded the performance of Bruckner's Ninth in the first Dunkelkonzert of the season.[50] A hymn scored for soprano solo, choir, orchestra, and organ, this work might easily be heard to flow directly into Bruckner's symphony famously "dedicated to Almighty God." But it is harder to see how such programming might pander to the National Socialist anti-Catholic *Gottgläubigkeit* (lit. God-belief) with which these Dunkelkonzerte have been connected.[51] On the contrary, one suspects that the inclusion of Mozart foreshadowed a showdown between Schirach and Goebbels in 1941 that centered on

Fig. 6.1. Front cover of Symphoniker concert schedule, 1940/41 season. Archiv der Wiener Konzerthausgesellschaft / Programmarchiv / Vortragsfolge Wiener Symphoniker (1940/41).

a lavishly state-funded but locally organized Viennese "Mozart-Week."[52] Characteristically, Schirach's inaugural speech declared the city to be the "capital of German music"; Goebbels would object furiously to what he saw as the one goal sought during the week, namely to give Vienna "a monopoly on the arts." Moreover, he banned the broadcast of a Vienna Philharmonic performance of Mozart's *Requiem*, apparently for fear of how it might fuel local religious propaganda.[53]

Despite Bruckner's obvious prominence on the Dunkelkonzerte programs, however, it would be quite wrong to assume that *every* darkness concert featured Bruckner, as scholars have suggested.[54] Over the five such concerts of the 1941/42 season, in fact, only one symphony by Bruckner—the Seventh—was performed. The Symphoniker programmers instead branched out, echoing the tendencies of the other concert series at the Konzerthaus to feature instrumental works by contemporary Austrians—Wilhelm Kienzl, Theodor Streicher—as well as Schubert's *Great* and, with a broader Austro-Hungarian stamp, Antonín Dvořák's Piano Concerto. The November 1941 performance of Max Reger's choral setting of Friedrich Hebbel's poem "Requiem," meanwhile, seems deliberately placed not only to commemorate the war dead, but also to align with the local appropriation of Hebbel—a German who had spent much of his creative maturity in the city—that would be fully exploited in the following year by a Viennese festival week in his honor.[55]

An obvious exception here is the repeated presence of J. S. Bach, whose *Art of Fugue* was performed in an experimental setting for large orchestra, organ, and two harpsichords across four of the five Dunkelkonzerte seasons. This was a heavily pathos-laden concert that concluded with Bach's "deathbed" chorale, "Vor Deinen Thron tret' ich hiermit" (Before Your Throne I Now Appear), and the polite request that the audience refrain from showing its appreciation through applause.[56] But even this showcased Viennese talent: one of the returning soloists, Bruno Seidlhofer, was an early keyboard music specialist who had prepared his own four-hands edition of the work and, from 1942, would preside over the "Konzert alter Meister" series at the Konzerthaus.[57] Walter Pach, conservatory professor and organist at the city's Votivkirche, was another.

## "IM GÄNZLICH VERDUNKELTEN SAAL . . ."

But what of the chief fascination of these concerts, their darkness? Where did the idea originate, and what purposes did it serve? Gilliam points to the "obvious Bayreuth-*Parsifal* parallel" as well as to "various Nazi ceremonies where focused light cut through the night: evening book burnings, torch processions, nighttime political rallies with a spotlight on the Führer, and the like."[58] Others, thinking along more pragmatic lines, have suggested that air raid blackout practices or wartime fuel shortages must have necessitated these drastic performance conditions.[59]

Each of these explanations has merit, yet there are also other forces at play. With Wagner and Nazi-era ceremony, darkness, as Gilliam states, is used to focus the spectator's attention on the figure in the spotlight, perhaps, or on the "blinding ray of light" that falls upon the *Parsifal* Grail from above, whereas the instructions "im gänzlich verdunkelten Saal" (in the completely darkened hall) at first blush seems to suggest a complete absence of light. Fuel restrictions and shortages may have played a role, not least because there are examples from the First World War of German venues taking exactly these measures in response to such problems.[60] Air raids on Vienna, however, did not take place with any regularity until September 1944; while widespread anxieties and defensive measures were certainly in evidence across the city long before that, there is no particular evidence that the Konzerthaus—host venue for myriad lit concerts in the same period—ever had to implement the practice.[61]

We might approach the problem by asking a more preliminary question. What exactly did "im gänzlich verdunkelten Saal" (in the completely darkened hall) mean? Some of the extant documents suggest that the description should be taken at its word: a January 1940 note from Dürauer to the head usher, for example, forbids him from leaving the doors of the hall even slightly ajar, since "any chink of light will destroy the effect of the Dunkelkonzert."[62] This may serve to reinforce the view that the darkness was primarily a means of hiding the distracting bodies of performers, conductor, and fellow audience members, thus encouraging greater concentration on the "purely" musical experience—a conceit with a decades-long history in European concert practice. In fact, it is in this context of early twentieth-century conservative concert practices of hiding the orchestral body that Kane brings up the example of the Dunkelkonzerte.[63]

Even so, we surely cannot conclude that the Konzerthaus auditorium was plunged into abject darkness. This would, after all, hardly have suited the orchestral performers, who, seated on a dais in front of the audience, needed desk lights to see their parts—particularly when, as in the case of the Bruckner symphonies, they were newly revised. Nor did it suit the choir of the Wiener Schubertbund, for whom lights were requested in October 1941 so that they might be able to read their music. Nor did it suit Roland Raupenstrauch, the soloist for Dvořák's Piano Concerto, who required illumination for the keyboard in front of him; nor did it suit the conductor, Hans Weisbach, who, standing beyond the grand piano's lid, needed to be seen by every member of the orchestra. Nor, finally, did it suit the inevitable latecomers among the audience, for whom the hall's main chandelier needed to be relit so that they might find their seats.[64]

There is some evidence that all this necessary illumination was minimized where possible. Various memoranda mention, for example, the importance of orienting desk lights carefully so as to reduce the chance of blinding the audience with a streak of bright light. For the same reason, the organ's mirror, too, had to be reversed.[65] But there is also evidence—and here the most surprising point—that minimal lights were utilized for their effect. When Georg Kulenkampff played Brahms's Violin Concerto in January 1940, Dürauer's sketch for a program note is highly suggestive: "This event is anticipated with great excitement because, for the very first time, we will experience the German master-violinist raised up as a silhouette—through the dusk that shimmers magically from the desk lights of the musicians until it reaches the mighty pillars of the hall's front wall."[66] This promised to provide, indeed, a "completely new impression" for the listener, one matched to the "pure sound of the solo violin as it floats through the darkness of the hall."[67]

These words might bring to mind Aurel Wolfram's talk of Vienna as the home of "silhouettes that speak eloquently against the silent night's sky," of its "muted music" and its "atmosphere woven from subtle shades of feeling." But more than that, they may make us think of a kind of theater. If so, it is hardly Wagnerian theater, but rather something far more rudimentary and far less exalted and focused, a "phantasmagoria," perhaps, not in the Marx–Adorno sense but in the sense from which those thinkers took the term—the early nineteenth-century "phantasmagoric" magic lantern show that projected "extraordinarily realistic images of approaching skeletons, apparitions, and specters, to frightening effect."[68]

When Dürauer claimed to Schirach in November 1940 that these events would "transform the virtuoso's pose of technical brilliance" into "a gesture of devoted interpretation of the musical content," he might have hoped to downplay the fact that his concerts had become something of a lowly mass entertainment masquerading as a high Viennese cultural experience.[69] In this connection, it is worth recalling that the Konzerthaus had long reveled in and relied on such popular events. In contrast to its more pompous rival, the Musikverein, its management had attempted to augment an already wide variety of musical performances by hosting conferences, conventions, and sporting events, such that boxing, handball, and the European fencing championships now found a home there.[70]

From this viewpoint, the Dunkelkonzerte became another instance of simply produced, easily managed, and entertaining novelty—one akin, perhaps, to the cinema housed in the same hall that had been restored in mid-1938.[71] Indeed, records of audience reaction tend to reinforce that some light was present in the hall, but also that pure entertainment was the goal. At the first concert in November 1939, the reviewer for the *Österreichische Volks-Zeitung* states irritably that a "consecrated atmosphere" would hardly visit upon those without the "good will" to create it; he complains that some performers were unaccustomed to playing in such a "theatrical" environment, and that some audience members yielded to the temptation to stare at the "scarce sources of light" remaining in the room.[72] Others in the audience, according to a memory of the Symphoniker flautist Camillo Wanausek, fell asleep "the moment the lights were switched off."[73] Still others apparently had more amorous reasons for attending: "As a visitor to the Dunkelkonzerte, I always found it very pleasing that it was dark, because I was always there with one sweetheart or another. If you went to a concert, your parents couldn't say anything against you. If you went to the cinema, it was obvious what you were up to."[74] This recollection, made by the young Heinrich Haerdtl (later a leading figure in the Konzerthaus management), gestures again toward the masquerade of these concerts: the idea that they gave an appearance of salutary esotericism—something approved by the patriarchs of Viennese culture—even as they descended into regions rather lower.[75]

It may simply be the case, ultimately, that very few Dunkelkonzerte audience members sat "breathless and unutterably moved, as if possessed by God" (in the characterization of one recent commentator).[76] It may be, too, that audience behavior at these events formed far less of a "glaring contrast" with that of the raucous audiences at the Konzerthaus events sponsored by Kraft durch Freude than has previously been suspected.[77] Most of all, it seems unlikely that these concerts communicated a direct sense of threat or oppression, of spiritual destiny, or of being overpowered by the "authoritative strength of German music."[78] Further testimony on this point comes from the young Viennese political activist Karl Mark. A Social Democrat and Jewish on his father's side, Mark was certainly no friend of fascism: in his memoirs he recalls singing Eisler's "Solidarity Song" at a Konzerthaus Workers' Symphony concert the night before all such political activities were banned in February 1934. He also tells of his arrest, beating, and imprisonment during the subsequent purges and the persecution and terror he experienced throughout the war years.[79] Yet even Mark fondly and cheerfully recalls the Dunkelkonzerte, chiefly because it was one of these events (with their "focused podium illumination," in his account) to which he took Gretl Afritsch, his future wife, on their first date. "While chatting I ascertained that she, like me, was very interested in music. I asked whether she would like to go to a concert with me. 'Yes,' she said. 'Wonderful,' I replied."[80]

These kinds of fond accounts underline the conclusion that, in a public concert environment continually threatened by the ever-growing popularity of the domestic radio, these Dunkelkonzerte remained a wildly successful enterprise.[81] Some concerts were apparently sold out or standing room only in advance, while for the 1941/42 season, an all-Dunkelkonzert subscription was introduced in order to take advantage of the pressures of demand.[82]

Thus, they undoubtedly helped to shore up dwindling institutional finances and quickly became, to use a term prevalent in surrounding discussions, fully "*eingebürgert*"—that is, vernacularized, a part of the Viennese concert landscape of the war years. Shortly after their inception, indeed, the term "Dunkelkonzert" became a prominent brand across all these concerts' advertising, replacing the rather more descriptive "Konzert im verdunkelten Saal" of the early programs.[83] By late 1942, Hans Weisbach had also taken the idea on the road to the nearby spa town of Baden bei Wien, where, according to one report, he led "Beethoven-Dunkelkonzerte" with the newly formed symphony orchestra for the Niederdonau region.[84]

In this regard, most revealing of all is a small advertisement that can be found in the last pages of the *Wiener Neueste Nachrichten* for June 6, 1940. Amid announcements for variety shows, nightclubs with dancing girls, and an insalubrious-sounding tavern named the Crooked Lantern, we once again light upon the word "Dunkelkonzert."[85] But this is not a concert of Bruckner or Bach or Mozart. Rather, it is a twice-weekly performance on the terrace of the café-restaurant "Johann Strauss," delivered by Gustav Macho, a local violinist and bandleader and a well-known figure in Viennese entertainment circles on account of songs such as "Wien, ich bin in dich verliebt" (Vienna, I Am so in Love with You).[86] One wonders how, in the open air, the darkened performance conditions were managed and maintained, and what exactly Macho and his band played; what seems clear is that, apparently hitching itself to the great success at the nearby Konzerthaus, this café series exploited its potentially frivolous aspect to the full, and it cast off all pretensions to high culture as it did so.

Studies of early twentieth-century Viennese culture have tended to gravitate toward the vibrancy, color, and chaos of the fin de siècle, or the decadence of the Habsburgs' last days. As a result, the city's interwar years and the Anschluss period have tended to remain somewhat untreated and have thus been left to sometimes rigid assumptions about the nature of their public cultural lives.[87]

Particularly in the latter case, this is an understandable reaction: we should not forget or overlook that in Vienna and wider Austria, as in other places in the expanding German Reich, citizens were subjected daily to persecution, oppression, and acts of terror, and that the cultural landscape was in many cases restricted by racist ideologies that joined almost seamlessly with those of the fascist Austrian Ständestaat from 1934. The memoirs of Karl Mark, to cite only one voice of many, attest to this; his singing of Eisler's "Solidarity Song" on February 11, 1934, was a simple and communal form of expression that, the next day, was banned, ushering in a decade of punishment and censure.

Even so, for Mark, as for many commentators, the Dunkelkonzerte have formed something of an exception within this landscape. They have remained an object of fascination, and scholars have gravitated toward two versions of a reading that, though apparently approaching from opposite directions, end up at the same place. On the one hand, Hitler, in his devotion to his fellow Austrian Anton Bruckner, permitted a concert series symbolic of the Anschluss and generative of a Nazi high church; on the other, Hitler, who hated Vienna for its condescending treatment of Bruckner and all "true" artists, punished the city with a carefully restricted and tightly controlled cultural diet, not least the frightful specter of a darkened concert life.[88]

By loosening the hold of such intentionalist readings, however, we can begin to see how, even in this cultural and political climate, greater nuance might come to light. What has never been in doubt is the enormous popularity of the Dunkelkonzerte across their five wartime seasons, a fact in all probability conferred by the entertainment aspects discussed above: the sheer novelty of the darkened public environment, or the impromptu silhouette show against the wall of the hall. In turn, this suggests that these concerts should not simply be abstracted as examples of Nazi terror and control, but rather considered as a public musical practice instigated and shaped by the threats and realities of the Anschluss and the war—in which both Konzerthaus and Symphoniker, with their rich histories of diverse musical offerings catering to all strata of Viennese society, had a part to play. Though official records (and thus histories) may show this practice as unilaterally "aligned" with and funded by the German authorities, we might consider it the result of a far more complex dialogue shifting between Viennese institutional voices beloved of their autonomy and influence, interpretations of state ideology in a local context, the ongoing need for financial gain, and strong musical-cultural traditions that shuttled fluidly from the "high" to the "low" and back again.

Thus, we might say that there was scope still in wartime Vienna for mass public appeal, entertainment as diversion from conflict, and even something that might resemble entrepreneurship—particularly once, as in the case of Gustav Macho and his band, the idea left the concert hall and went out on to the streets and terraces of the city. Moreover, we might look onward from the Dunkelkonzerte toward the popular varieties, concerts for welfare, charity, and military support, and events for women and for youth that accounts of the period mention in passing, and ask if similar dialogues can be reconstructed in these cases.[89] In so doing, the old image of post-Anschluss Vienna as a kind of cultural backwater—one deliberately restricted by Hitler's personal grudge—might be replaced by one that sets it alongside other major cities also adapting to the privations and possibilities of the ongoing war.

## NOTES

1. Marc Estrin, *The Education of Arnold Hitler*, 405.
2. Ibid., 376.
3. Ibid., 401. In the interest of balance, it should be pointed out that this is only a brief phase of Arnold Hitler's *Bildung*. True to Evelyn's motto of "paradox and ambiguity," the couple back away from the committed neo-Nazi extremism of their associates and explore their own Judaic roots instead—culminating at the end of the novel in their quasi-Jewish wedding ceremony (for which music is provided by Arnold's old Harvard friend Leonard Bernstein). The New York Bruckner Expressway is, of course, named after the Bronx borough president Henry Bruckner.
4. Heller, "Von der Arbeiterkultur zur Theatersperre," 101: " die romantisierende Gedankenwelt nationalsozialistischer Kunstträume." All translations are my own unless otherwise indicated.
5. See Korstvedt, "The First Edition of Anton Bruckner's Fourth Symphony," 60; and Permoser, *Die Wiener Symphoniker im NS-Staat*, 35–39.
6. Gilliam, "The Annexation of Anton Bruckner," 596.
7. On the Regensburg Bruckner ceremony in June 1937, see Brüstle, *Anton Bruckner und die Nachwelt*, 107–122; and Gilliam, "The Annexation of Anton Bruckner," esp. 584–587 and 591–593. Gilliam's reading of the Dunkelkonzerte is followed in Painter, *Symphonic Aspirations*, 250; and Rehding, *Music and Monumentality*, 181.
8. See Kane, *Sound Unseen*, 103–108.
9. Ibid., 118.
10. Ibid., 117.
11. See Potter, "Dismantling a Dystopia," 624; also Potter, "What Is Nazi Music?," 428–455.
12. On the financial problems of the Konzerthaus during the early 1930s, see Stein, "Das Wiener Konzerthaus 1930–1945," in particular 8–54. On those of the *Symphoniker*, see Permoser, "Die Wiener Symphoniker im NS-Staat," 187–190; also, Kobau, *Die Wiener Symphoniker*, 43–52.
13. See Stein, "Das Wiener Konzerthaus 1930–1945," 78 and 87–89; Barta, "Kunst, Kommerz und Politik," 295–296; and Permoser, "Die Wiener Symphoniker im NS-Staat," 73–74.
14. See Barta, "Kunst, Kommerz und Politik," 296–297; and Stein, "Das Wiener Konzerthaus 1930–1945," 123–127.
15. See Stein, "Das Wiener Konzerthaus 1930–1945," 78–79 and 89–90.
16. See ibid., 99–100.
17. See Kobau, *Die Wiener Symphoniker*, 67–68. The closing of a contract between the Symphoniker and Radio-Verkehrs AG (the Austrian radio corporation otherwise known as RAVAG) had saved the orchestra from bankruptcy in 1933; this was also the point at which its name had become firmly established (having previously been known variously as the "Tonkünstlerorchester,"

"Konzertvereinorchester," or "Sinfonieorchester") and the beginning of its politicization as a potential tool of the state. On these matters, see Kobau, *Die Wiener Symphoniker*, 51–57; and Permoser, "Die Wiener Symphoniker im NS-Staat," 188. On the early links of the Konzerthaus and Symphoniker, mediated by the Wiener Konzertverein, see Stein, "Das Wiener Konzerthaus 1930–1945," 8–13.

18. See Permoser, "Die Wiener Symphoniker im NS-Staat," 189–190.

19. See Stein, "Das Wiener Konzerthaus 1930–1945," 17 and 27: on April 18–19, 1933, for example, the local National Socialists organized a "festival concert" at the Konzerthaus in honor of Hitler's birthday.

20. See Stein, "Das Wiener Konzerthaus 1930–1945," 55–62. Until 1936, a similar role had been undertaken by the conductor (and committed party member) Leopold Reichwein.

21. See Barta, "Kunst, Kommerz und Politik," 293–295.

22. "Working relationship [*Arbeitsverbindung*]" is quoted from Stein, "Das Wiener Konzerthaus 1930–1945," 72, which reproduces some of von Papen's program. On the plebiscite announcement, see Heller, "Von der Arbeiterkultur zur Theatersperre," 98–99.

23. For example, on account of their Jewish heritage, Hugo Botstiber (general secretary of the Konzerthausgesellschaft), Felix Stransky (its vice president and financial advisor), and Gustav Bloch-Bauer (a delegate of the Wiener Konzertverein, the parent organization of the Symphoniker) were forced to stand down from the Konzerthaus management; they were replaced by Armin Caspar Hochstetter, Otto Winger, and numerous new "general members." See Stein, "Das Wiener Konzerthaus 1930–1945," 77–78, 92, and the short biographies at 151–169.

24. Kobau, *Die Wiener Symphoniker*, 67.

25. Stein, "Das Wiener Konzerthaus 1930–1945," 40–41 and 105–107.

26. See Barta, "Kunst, Kommerz und Politik," 298–303.

27. See Permoser's concert listings in *Die Wiener Symphoniker im NS-Staat*, 111–212. A good example of a "popular" symphony concert is February 4, 1940, which placed Schubert's Third Symphony alongside instrumental works by Alfred Uhl, Karel Komzák, and Carl Ziehrer; December 8, 1940, was dedicated entirely to Schubert, and March 14, 1940, to Hugo Wolf. Examples of Viennese operetta concerts are those held on October 14, 1938, and December 2, 1938 (organized in conjunction with Kraft durch Freude). January 29, 1939, is entitled "Composers of the *Ostmark*," i.e., the Nazi name for Austria, and includes instrumental music by Paul Königer, Guido Binkau, Schubert, and—typically treated as an honorary Viennese Austrian—Beethoven.

28. On this directive, see Christoph Schmidt, *Nationalsozialistische Kulturpolitik im Gau Westfalen-Nord*, 185.

29. See, for example, Permoser, *Die Wiener Symphoniker im NS-Staat*, 148 and 159–160 for the full programs of these concerts "Zur Förderung zeitgenössischer Musik"; see also the report on the "Week for Contemporary Composers" in the *Neues Wiener Tagblatt*, May 15, 1942, 8, which makes the Viennese identity of such

events clear. On the inception of this series and the role of Geutebrück, see Stein, "Das Wiener Konzerthaus 1930–1945," 71 and 92–95.

30. See also the discussions of this point in Barta, "Kunst, Kommerz und Politik," 301–302, and Rathkolb, *Führertreu und gottbegnadet*, 52–53.

31. See Permoser, *Die Wiener Symphoniker im NS-Staat*, 30–1; also, Stein, "Das Wiener Konzerthaus 1930–1945," 118; and Luža, *Austro-German Relations in the Anschluss Era*, 286.

32. See Stein, "Das Wiener Konzerthaus 1930–1945," 164–166.

33. See ibid., 117–119.

34. On this point, see also Luža, *Austro-German Relations in the Anschluss Era*, 278–279.

35. On Schirach's cultural stance and his disputes with Goebbels, see Rathkolb, *Führertreu und gottbegnadet*, 68–78; Heller, "Von der Arbeiterkultur zur Theatersperre," 100–101; Permoser, "Die Wiener Symphoniker im NS-Staat," 192–193; and Fred K. Prieberg, *Musik im NS-Staat*, 332–334.

36. As reported in the *Neues Wiener Tagblatt*, May 19, 1938, 4: "Wien wird nach wie vor das Kulturbollwerk im Südosten sein.... Mit Nachdruck betont Dr. Haasbauer, daß die vielfach geäußerten Befürchtungen einer 'Verpreußung der Ostmarkkultur' hinfällig sind. An Organisationsformen wird vieles übernommen werden, aber die bodenständigen Kulturwerte und ihre Eigenarten sollen unbedingt geschützt werden." Haasbauer is here identified as a "Beauftragte für die kulturelle Fragen in Österreich." On this source, see also Rathkolb, *Führertreu und gottbegnadet*, 50–51.

37. According to the report in the *Neues Wiener Tagblatt*, June 24, 1938, 12: "Diese alte Stadt soll ihre Note beibehalten ... der Sinn für gute Musik dürfe sich nicht auf die hohe Kunst beschränken, er müsse auch in der Unterhaltungsmusik zum Ausdruck kommen. Denn schon im Café und Restaurant werde sich der Fremde über die Musikstadt Wien ein Urteil bilden."

38. Aurel Wolfram, "Wien—Refugium der deutschen Seele," *Neues Wiener Tagblatt*, September 29, 1940: 13: "Hat man sie oft als Rivalinnen betrachtet.... Mehr und mehr aber beginnt sich die Erkenntnis einzustellen, daß sie im Schicksal unsres Volkes zu polarer Ergänzung, als Gegensatzpunkte größerer Einheit vorgesehen sind." Wolfram is identified as "Kulturreferent" in Rathkolb, *Führertreu und gottbegnadet*, 51. On this Wolfram source, see also Luža, *Austro-German Relations in the Anschluss Era*, 288–289; and Rathkolb, *Führertreu und gottbegnadet*, 68–69.

39. Wolfram, "Wien—Refugium der deutschen Seele," 13: "Berlin wird man bestaunen wie einen Athleten—Wien kann man lieben wie eine Mutter."

40. Wolfram, "Wien—Refugium der deutschen Seele," 13: "Unter der Patina alter Bewährung pulst der Blutstrom neuer Jugend," "wenn nachts Silhouetten alter Kirchen und Paläste beredsam in den Himmel schweigen, wenn in stillen Gassen gedämpft von irgendwo Musik herklingt," "Stimmung, gewoben aus allen Zwischenschattierungen ... aus der nicht zuletzt der Nuancenreichtum quillt in Ton, Wort und Bild, der Wiens Kunst und Kultur so einzigartig macht."

41. Wolfram, "Wien—Refugium der deutschen Seele," 14: "vom Joch der Maschine ... zur Hauptstadt des inneren Reiches." See also Rathkolb, *Führertreu und gottbegnadet*, 69, for a brief reading of this source.

42. Kobau, "Geschichte der Wiener Symphoniker," 35: "der von den Nazis 1939 eingeführten, äußerst beliebten 'Dunkelkonzerte.'"

43. On Dürauer (appointed December 1938) and Weisbach (the former director of the radio orchestra for Leipzig, appointed April 1939), see Permoser, *Die Wiener Symphoniker in NS-Staat*, 35–37.

44. Memorandum to "all members of the Symphoniker Orchestra," signed by Dürauer and dated November 11, 1939: "Für das von uns in eigener Regie veranstaltete 1. Konzert im verdunkelten Saal"; also letter from Dürauer to Schirach, November 14, 1940: "Die von uns neu eingeführten Konzerte im verdunkelten Saal[.]" Both these sources are found in the Archiv der Wiener Symphoniker, housed in the Konzerthaus on the Lothringerstraße, and both are currently uncatalogued. I am very grateful to Ulrike Grandke for assisting me in consulting these and other similar sources cited in the following.

45. See the article "Treuhänder deutscher Musik" in the *Österreichische Musik-Zeitung*, March 8, 1939, 10: "Die klassische Wiener Musik bildet denn auch die Grundlage unsrer Arbeit ... Für die weitere Zukunft sind vor allem einige, wahrscheinlich fünf, Stadtkonzerte geplant, die durch ihre eigene Note einen besonderen Platz im Wiener Musikleben einnehmen können."

46. In this paragraph and the following ones, I draw on the original concert bills, as found in the Archiv der Wiener Konzerthausgesellschaft / Programmarchiv. My thanks to Barbara Alhuter for assisting me in consulting these sources.

47. This event is advertised in the *Wiener Neueste Nachrichten*, November 2, 1940, 8.

48. These quotations are taken from an uncatalogued text entitled "40 Jahre Wiener Konzert-Kultur-Orchester. Die Dunkelkonzerte der Wiener Symphoniker" in the Archiv der Wiener Symphoniker: "eine der grossen Symphonien unseres Ostmärkischen Meisters Bruckner," "Der Anfang liegt in echt Wienerische Weise im Idealismus."

49. Quoted passage from the text "40 Jahre Wiener Konzert-Kultur-Orchester. Die Dunkelkonzerte der Wiener Symphoniker" (Archiv der Wiener Symphoniker): "Der andere Teil der Programme ... wird dem ebenfalls mit der Musikgeschichte Wiens unzertrennlich verbundenen Genius W. A. Mozart gewidmet."

50. This setting was K. 127, composed in Salzburg in 1772. The report in the poetry journal *Der Augarten* 5 (1940), 43, confirms that this performance was a Viennese premiere.

51. See, for example, Gilliam, "The Annexation of Anton Bruckner," 593–596.

52. On this festival week, held in honor of the 150th anniversary of Mozart's death, see in particular Levi, *Mozart and the Nazis*, 168–184. The week was split into a "Reich-Program" and a "Vienna-Program," the latter combining opera and chamber music performances with popular events ("Our Mozart—A Slideshow Presentation with Music and Dance"). See the program reproduced in Levi, *Mozart and the Nazis*, 173.

53. For Schirach's speech, see Levi, *Mozart and the Nazis*, 251–256, quotation at 252. On the ensuing fight with Goebbels, see Weyr, *The Setting of the Pearl*, 200–202 (quotation at 202) and Stein, "Das Wiener Konzerthaus 1930–1945," 127–131.

54. See Gilliam, "The Annexation of Anton Bruckner," 596 ("the highlight was always a symphony by Bruckner"); and the echo of the same claim in Kane, *Sound Unseen*, 118; and Painter, *Symphonic Aspirations*, 250.

55. On the terms of this appropriation, see the article "Hebbel und Wien" in the *Neues Wiener Tagblatt*, May 29, 1942, 8; or the article "Wien wurde Schicksal für Friedrich Hebbel" ("Vienna became Friedrich Hebbel's destiny") in the *Wiener Montagblatt*, June 1, 1942, 2.

56. See, for example, the program for March 6, 1942, and its closing line: "Es wird gebeten, nach dem Schluß von Beifallsbezeugungen Abstand zu nehmen" (Archiv der Wiener Konzerthausgesellschaft / Programmarchiv / Abendprogramm, März 6, 1942, 19:30 Uhr, Großer Saal, Wiener Symphoniker / Weisbach); compare Permoser, *Die Wiener Symphoniker im NS-Staat*, 39: "Beifallskundgebungen waren bei diesem Konzert untersagt!"

57. See the short review of Seidlhofer's edition in the *Zeitschrift für Musik* 105/6 (1938), 626; and Stein, "Das Wiener Konzerthaus 1930–1945," 96.

58. Gilliam, "The Annexation of Anton Bruckner," 603n29.

59. See Heller, "Von der Arbeiterkultur zur Theatersperre," 102; and the discussion in Ottner, ed., *Musik in Wien*, 207. Also Painter, *Symphonic Aspirations*, 250.

60. See, for example, Richard Möbius, "Konzerte im Dunkeln," *Neue Musik-Zeitung* 39/23 (1918): 310–311. See also the report in the *Österreichische Volks-Zeitung* of May 15, 1943, which recommends more "concerts in the dark" (of chamber music as well as orchestral music) as a means of saving coal and electricity.

61. On air raids in Vienna, see Healy, "Local Space and Total War: Enemies in Vienna in the Two World Wars," 119–120. See also, as one contemporary example, the fireman's journal *Der Brandschutz* 59/6 (1939), which gives details of recent air raid rehearsals and electric siren systems.

62. From an uncatalogued note to "Oberbilleteur Schödl," dated January 4, 1940, and found in the Archiv der Wiener Symphoniker: "Spaltenweises Öffnen der Türen ist verboten! Jeder Lichtspalt zerstört die Wirkung des Dunkelk[on]z[er]tes."

63. See Kane, *Sound Unseen*, 102–108.

64. I draw here on numerous archival memoranda from January 1940 to January 1942. These are uncatalogued and found in the Archiv der Wiener Symphoniker.

65. From an uncatalogued note to "Saalmeister Bernhard," dated January 4, 1940, and found in the Archiv der Wiener Symphoniker: "Den Spiegel bei der Orgel bitte umdrehen zu lassen! . . . Bei der Aufsetzung der Pultlampen sind die Lichtschlitze möglichst klein zu stellen und so zu richten, dass in den Sitzraum des Publikums kein blendender Lichtstrahl fallen kann."

66. As cited in Permoser, *Die Wiener Symphoniker im NS-Staat*, 38: "Nun wird zum ersten Male ein Solist mit dem Orchester auftreten, und zwar der Violinvirtuose Prof. Georg Kulenkampff. [. . .] Diesem Ereignis wird mit großer Spannung entgegengesehen,

weil man zum ersten Mal erleben wird, daß der deutsche Meistergeiger sich als Silhouette von dem Dämmerschein abheben wird, der von den Pultlampen der Musiker magisch hinschimmert bis zu den mächtigen Säulen der Stirnwand des Saales."

67. As cited in Permoser, *Die Wiener Symphoniker im NS-Staat*, 38: "Es verspricht ein ganz neuartiger Eindruck für den Zuhörer zu werden, wenn der schlackenreine Klang der Sologeige in das Dunkel des Saales hineinschwebt."

68. Kane, *Sound Unseen*, 97.

69. Letter from Dürauer to Schirach, November 14, 1940, Archiv der Wiener Symphoniker: "Die virtuose [sic] Pose technischer Brillanz umformen in die Geste hingebungsvoller Interpretation des musikalischen Inhaltes meisterlicher Werke."

70. On these sporting events, see Revers, "Geschichte des Konzerthauses während der ersten Republik," 84; and Stein, "Das Wiener Konzerthaus 1930–1945," 18–19. Revers, 78–82, identifies operetta, cabarets, jazz concerts, and dance evenings as among these entertainment events, many of them originating in the aftermath of the First World War.

71. On the renovation of the Konzerthaus projection booth in 1938, see Stein, "Das Wiener Konzerthaus 1930–1945," 79.

72. Hanns Salaschek, "Vom Hellen ins Dunkle," *Österreichische Volks-Zeitung*, November 19, 1939, 10: "Rein technisch genommen, waren für Zuhörer und Orchester Hemmungen zu überwinden. Theaterspiel (Musik bei verdunkeltem Raum) ist für gewisse Instrumente nicht das gleiche wie Spiel bei hellem Saal; andererseits müssen die Zuhörer das Dunkel nicht als Versuchung auffassen, erst recht nach den spärlichen Lichtquellen zu starren.... Weihevolle Stimmung stellt sich nicht von vornherein ein, wer nicht guten Willens ist... der muss getäuscht werden."

73. See Permoser's comment in the discussion in Ottner, ed., *Musik in Wien*, 207.

74. Heinrich Haerdtl's comment in the discussion in Ottner, ed., *Musik in Wien*, 207–208: "Als Besucher der Dunkelkonzerte empfand ich es als sehr angenehm, dass es finster war, weil ich immer mit einem Flirt dort war. Wenn man ins Konzert ging, konnten die Eltern nichts dagegen sagen. Ging man ins Kino, war das auffällig."

75. Haerdtl was first the leader of the artistic office of the Konzerthaus (1950–1960), and then president of its management board (1981–1997). This information is from http://austria-forum.org/af/AEIOU/Haerdtl,_Heinrich, accessed April 9, 2019.

76. This description of the Dunkelkonzerte audience quoted from Marvick, *Waking the Face That No-One Is*, 54–55.

77. Heller, "Von der Arbeiterkultur zur Theatersperre," 103: "In krassem Gegensatz dazu stand offenbar das Betragen vieler Besucher des Konzerthauses, die zu den KdF-Unterhaltungen kamen."

78. Kobau, "Geschichte der Wiener Symphoniker," 35: "'Überbewältigung' durch die autoritative Kraft deutscher Musik[.]"

79. See Mark, *75 Jahre Roter Hund*, particularly 84 and 236 (on the last Workers' Concert), and 87–91 on his subsequent treatment under the fascist regime.

80. Mark, *75 Jahre Roter Hund*, 123: "Beim Plaudern stellte ich fest, daß sie, wie ich, musikalisch sehr interessiert war. Ich fragte, ob sie gerne in ein Konzert gehen

würde. Sie sagte 'Ja.' Ich sagte: 'Wunderbar.' Wir besuchten einige der damals üblichen, von Hans Weisbach dirigierten, Dunkelkonzerte, bei denen, abgesehen von einer gezielten Podiumsbeleuchtung, der Saal im Dunkeln lag, was die Konzentration auf die Musik steigerte."

81. On the long-standing connection between RAVAG (Radio-Verkehrs AG) and the Konzerthaus since the former's founding in 1924, see Revers, "Geschichte des Konzerthauses während der ersten Republik," 70. On the important role of radio broadcasting in the financial maintenance of the Symphoniker, as well as the threat posed by domestic radio to concert life, see Kobau, *Die Wiener Symphoniker*, 48–62. As Stein points out ("Das Wiener Konzerthaus 1930–1945," 35–36), RAVAG withdrew to its own premises in the 1936/7 season, negating its need to hire the Konzerthaus as a broadcast venue and thus heightening financial strain upon the concert venue.

82. On the concert subscription (which carried a 10 percent reduction in ticket price), see the advertisement in the *Österreichische Volks-Zeitung*, October 1, 1941, 6. A similar advertisement in the same newspaper, November 7, 1941, 4, announces that all seats for that evening's concert are sold out.

83. This change is evident from the third program of the first season (January 26, 1940): the formerly small-font parenthetic term "Dunkelkonzert" is now trumpeted as the principal label for these concerts and seemingly needs no further gloss (Archiv der Wiener Konzerthausgesellschaft / Programmarchiv / Abendprogramm, January 26, 1940, 20:00 Uhr, Großer Saal, Wiener Symphoniker / Weisbach).

84. See Karl Gutkas, *Kunst, Kultur und Wissenschaft in Niederösterreich im 20. Jahrhundert*, 95–96.

85. *Wiener Neueste Nachrichten*, June 6, 1940, 7.

86. See, for example, the write-up on Macho on the occasion of his sixtieth birthday, in the *Neues Wiener Tagblatt*, October 26, 1942, 3. This article lists several more of his best-known compositions.

87. On typical scholarly attitudes toward interwar Vienna, see Deborah Holmes and Lisa Silverman, "Introduction: Beyond the Coffeehouse: Vienna as a Cultural Center between the World Wars," in Holmes and Silverman, eds. *Interwar Vienna: Culture between Tradition and Modernity*, 1–3.

88. See, for example, Gilliam, "The Annexation of Anton Bruckner," 587–588.

89. See, for example, the many references in Heller, "Von der Arbeiterkultur zur Theatersperre," 96–106.

BIBLIOGRAPHY

**Historical Newspapers and Magazines**
*Neue Musik-Zeitung*, 1918
*Neues Wiener Tagblatt*, 1938–42
*Österreichische Musik-Zeitung*, 1939
*Österreichische Volks-Zeitung*, 1939–43
*Wiener Neueste Nachrichten*, 1940

## Books and Articles

Barta, Erwin. "Kunst, Kommerz und Politik. Das Wiener Konzerthaus 1938–1945." In *Musik in Wien 1938–1945: Symposion 2004*, edited by Carmen Ottner, 291–309. Vienna: Döblinger, 2006.

Brüstle, Christa. *Anton Bruckner und die Nachwelt. Zur Rezeptionsgeschichte des Komponisten in der ersten Hälfte des 20. Jahrhunderts*. Stuttgart: J. B. Metzler, 1998.

Estrin, Marc. *The Education of Arnold Hitler*. Denver, CO: Unbridled, 2005.

Gilliam, Bryan. "The Annexation of Anton Bruckner: Nazi Revisionism and the Politics of Appropriation." *The Musical Quarterly* 78 (1994): 584–604.

Gutkas, Karl. *Kunst, Kultur und Wissenschaft in Niederösterreich im 20. Jahrhundert*. Horn: Berger, 2006.

Healy, Maureen. "Local Space and Total War: Enemies in Vienna in the Two World Wars." In *Cities into Battlefields: Metropolitan Scenarios, Experiences and Commemorations of Total War*, edited by Stefan Goebel and Derek Keene, 119–132. Farnham: Ashgate, 2011.

Heller, Friedrich C. "Von der Arbeiterkultur zur Theatersperre." In *Das Wiener Konzerthaus: Geschichte und Bedeutung, 1918–1983*, edited by Friedrich C. Heller and Peter Revers, 87–109. Vienna: Wiener Konzerthausgesellschaft, 1983.

Holmes, Deborah, and Lisa Silverman, eds. *Interwar Vienna: Culture between Tradition and Modernity*. Rochester, NY: Camden House, 2009.

Kane, Brian. *Sound Unseen: Acousmatic Sound in Theory and Practice*. Oxford: Oxford University Press, 2014.

Kobau, Ernst. *Die Wiener Symphoniker. Eine sozialgeschichtliche Studie*. Vienna: Böhlau, 1991.

———. "Geschichte der Wiener Symphoniker." In *Ein Jahrhundert Wiener Symphoniker*, edited by Rainer Bischof, 21–53. Vienna: Holzhausen, 2000.

Korstvedt, Benjamin M. "The First Edition of Anton Bruckner's Fourth Symphony: Authorship, Production, and Reception." Ph.D. diss., University of Pennsylvania, 1995.

Levi, Erik. *Mozart and the Nazis: How the Third Reich Abused a Cultural Icon*. New Haven, CT: Yale University Press, 2010.

Luža, Radomír. *Austro-German Relations in the Anschluss Era*. Princeton, NJ: Princeton University Press, 1975.

Mark, Karl. *75 Jahre Roter Hund. Lebenserinnerungen*. Vienna: Böhlau, 1990.

Marvick, Louis Wirth. *Waking the Face That No-One Is: A Study in the Musical Context of Symbolist Aesthetics*. Amsterdam: Rodopi, 2004.

Ottner, Carmen, ed. *Musik in Wien 1938–1945: Symposion 2004*. Vienna: Döblinger, 2006.

Painter, Karen. *Symphonic Aspirations: German Music and Politics, 1900–1945*. Cambridge, MA: Harvard University Press, 2007.

Permoser, Manfred. *Die Wiener Symphoniker im NS-Staat*. Frankfurt: Peter Lang, 2000.

———. "Die Wiener Symphoniker im NS-Staat." In *Musik in Wien 1938–1945: Symposion 2004*, edited by Carmen Ottner, 187–197. Vienna: Döblinger, 2006.
Potter, Pamela. "What Is Nazi Music?" *The Musical Quarterly* 88 (2005): 428–455.
———. "Dismantling a Dystopia: On the Historiography of Music in the Third Reich." *Central European History* 40 (2007): 623–651.
Prieberg, Fred K. *Musik im NS-Staat*. Frankfurt: Fischer, 1982.
Rathkolb, Oliver. *Führertreu und gottbegnadet. Künstlereliten im Dritten Reich.* Vienna: Österreichischer Bundesverlag, 1991.
Rehding, Alexander. *Music and Monumentality: Commemoration and Wonderment in Nineteenth-Century Germany*. Oxford: Oxford University Press, 2009.
Revers, Peter. "Geschichte des Konzerthauses während der ersten Republik." In *Das Wiener Konzerthaus: Geschichte und Bedeutung, 1918–1983*, edited by Friedrich C. Heller and Peter Revers, 69–86. Vienna: Wiener Konzerthausgesellschaft, 1983.
Schmidt, Christoph. *Nationalsozialistische Kulturpolitik im Gau Westfalen-Nord. Regionale Strukturen und lokale Milieus*. Paderborn: Schöningh, 2006.
Stein, Philipp, "Das Wiener Konzerthaus 1930–1945." Ph.D. diss., Universität Wien, 2013.
Weyr, Thomas. *The Setting of the Pearl: Vienna under Hitler*. Oxford: Oxford University Press, 2005.

NICHOLAS ATTFIELD is Lecturer in Music at the University of Birmingham. He is author of *Challenging the Modern: Conservative Revolution in German Music, 1918–1933* and editor (with Ben Winters) of *Music, Modern Culture, and the Critical Ear*.

SEVEN

# BEFORE THE END OF TIME

General Huntziger's Centre Musical et Théâtral

CHRISTOPHER BRENT MURRAY

FOLLOWING THE DEPLOYMENT THAT CAME with the declaration of war in September 1939, France's armies fell into a waiting game. The tedium and uncertainty of what became familiarly known as the *drôle de guerre* led to a decline in troop morale as the autumn and winter wore on, causing disciplinary problems that concerned the hierarchy of the French army. In response, initiatives to entertain soldiers and officers sprang up in many different forms. This chapter discusses the historic significance of one such initiative, a nearly forgotten orchestra and theater troupe based in Verdun and composed of drafted soldiers from the French Second Army.

The Centre musical et théâtral de la II<sup>e</sup> armée (hereafter CMT) was conceived by General Charles Huntziger and the officers of his staff, or *état-major*, in January 1940. Political reactionaries, many of them devout Catholics, Huntziger and his men envisaged the CMT as a remedy to the moral and intellectual dissolution of more popular forms of soldier entertainment. Through classical music and classic French theater, they hoped to offer what they felt would be appropriately dignified, uplifting, and patriotic diversion to the Second Army's troops.

According to different sources, the CMT counted between sixty and seventy professional actors and musicians selected from among the approximately 250,000 soldiers of the Second Army.[1] One of several armies stationed on France's northern and eastern fronts, the Second Army was based in a strategic zone situated between Sedan and the end of the Maginot Line. The CMT's members came from varied walks of life and did not necessarily share the political views and artistic tastes of Huntziger and his officers. They included Olivier Messiaen and the future musicians of the celebrated *Quatuor pour la fin du Temps* (*Quartet for the End of Time*), along with other French musicians, actors, lyric artists, and music-hall entertainers. To these drafted men whose developing careers had been put on hold by their new military duties, the CMT offered an unexpected opportunity to practice their craft as part of a privileged artistic community while continuing to serve their country.

Planned in January and February and then progressively formed in March and April, the CMT only existed for about two months before Germany invaded the Low Countries on May 10, 1940. In retreat from Verdun, the CMT was broken up into small groups that were taken prisoner just before the Armistice of June 22. Staying together and continuing their creative activity in holding camps (*Frontstalags*) that summer and in German prisoner of war camps (*Stalags*) during the fall and winter allowed many former members of the CMT to benefit from special treatment as artists. Like the French officers of the Second Army, the German officers running POW camps felt that professional musicians and actors might be better occupied entertaining their colleagues than laboring in work details (*Arbeitskommandos*).

When negotiations between Vichy and Germany began to lead to the conditional release of certain categories of POWs in late 1940 and early 1941, some former CMT members became eligible for release through policies written to repatriate medical workers and the infirm. Many were sent home in February and March 1941, a time when it was still professionally advantageous to be a former soldier and prisoner of war. Moreover, the artistic activity of former CMT members was integrated into Vichy propaganda, which used stories of artist–prisoners to project a positive image of life in POW camps during a period when Vichy was struggling to convince Germany to release the 1.6 million French POWs who were providing cheap labor to farms, mines, and factories across the Third Reich.

Although the CMT played a central role in the careers of many prominent French artists, its ephemeral, controversial existence has translated to its near erasure from studies of wartime cultural life. Sources concerning the CMT are rare (its records were likely lost in the Battle of France), its creator, Huntziger, later became Philippe Pétain's minister of war, and its former members were freed from captivity much earlier than other French POWs, a reality that has received little attention, likely in part due to their own silence on the matter. Conceived by a general turned Vichy minister, blanketed in military secrecy during its short existence, and overshadowed by the greater military disaster of the Battle of France in which it played a role, Huntziger's CMT slipped into obscurity after the war.

Building upon Yannick Simon and Leslie Sprout's studies of soldier musicians and composers, this chapter uses isolated documents from a range of musical and military archives to reconstruct the forgotten history of the CMT.[2] The first section explores the political sympathies and aesthetic views of Huntziger and two of the CMT's primary cofounders; the second describes how the CMT was created and shows how the constraints of an all-male ensemble working in a military context interacted with the politics and taste of Huntziger and his officers to shape the CMT's repertoire. The third and final section investigates how the interpersonal networks created by the CMT survived the institution's demise in the flight, captivity, and liberation of its former members. Throughout, I remark on the special status accorded to classical musicians by both the French and German military hierarchy and consider how military service and captivity affected the artistic and professional development of particular musicians.

## THE FOUNDERS OF THE CMT AND THEIR POLITICAL AND SOCIAL ORIGINS

Three men with similar political views and artistic tastes were instrumental in the creation of the CMT and the definition of its aesthetics: the leader of the French Second Army, General Charles Huntziger; his press officer, the political and literary critic Henri Massis; and the CMT's theatrical director, Xavier de Courville. Understanding the prewar careers and projects of these men is essential to interpreting the repertoire and goals of the CMT.

Charles Huntziger (1881–1941) was the son of Léon Jacques Huntziger, an organist trained at the Strasbourg Conservatory who left Alsace as a young man to avoid being conscripted in the German army after the Franco–Prussian War.[3] Huntziger's father resettled in Lesneven, Brittany, where he worked as the parish organist, taught music and German in the local Catholic school, and led the municipal band.[4] Charles Huntziger's upbringing shaped him into a devout Catholic, a patriot, and an avid and sensitive amateur violinist.[5] After strategically building a military career in postings across the French colonial empire, Huntziger received his fifth star in 1938. He was subsequently placed at the head of France's Second Army when war broke out the following year.[6] A central figure in the French defeat at the Second Battle of Sedan, Huntziger is perhaps best known as a signatory of the Armistice in 1940. Rising as quickly as France had fallen, he subsequently led the French delegation at the Armistice negotiations in Wiesbaden and was placed at the head of the French Army as Maréchal Pétain's war minister in September 1940. He died in a plane crash en route from Algiers to Vichy in November 1941.

A sense of Huntziger's political leanings can be gained by studying the men with whom he chose to surround himself. When Huntziger took the head of the Second Army in 1939, he selected Henri Massis (1886–1970) to become his press officer, subsequently appointing Massis as director of the CMT.[7] Massis, who was later elected to the Académie française in 1960, was a longtime disciple of Charles Maurras, a contributor to the *Revue critique* and an editor of the *Revue universelle*. The *Revue critique* and *Revue universelle* were Maurrasian literary and political reviews that grew out of the far-right, anti-Dreyfusard political movement called Action Française.[8] Jane Fulcher has described the importance of Massis's widely read polemical essays in defining reactionary political and cultural positions during the interwar period, notably his 1935 *Manifeste des intellectuels français pour la défense de l'Occident et la paix en Europe*, a racist pro-colonialist tract that called for entente with Italy following Mussolini's invasion of Ethiopia.[9] In his capacities as a member of Huntziger's staff, Massis was officially responsible for accompanying journalists visiting the front, publishing a newspaper to boost officer morale (*Les documents du combattant*), and organizing entertainment and measures for improving troop comfort (such as touring trucks offering showers and reading materials).[10]

After the war, Massis decried what he felt had been the degenerate conduct and complacent attitude of the French during the drôle de guerre and explained that he had felt a moral responsibility toward the troops.[11] In a decision that can be considered an extension of what Sandrine Sanos calls an "enduring motive" of Massis's political essays, "the possible and dangerous demise of Western civilisation—an essence he understood in cultural, aesthetic, ethical and racial terms," Massis and Huntziger decided it was urgent to provide spiritually nourishing entertainment to the troops in the form of classical music and classic French theater as an alternative to slapstick amateur theater and the American-influenced popular music of the Théâtre aux Armées.[12]

To do so, they turned to Xavier de Courville (1894–1984), an aristocratic amateur pianist and theater director particularly interested in seventeenth- and eighteenth-century music and stagecraft.[13] His father Maurice, the Comte de Courville, was a military engineer who later became director of the Schneider-Creusot steelworks and arms factory.[14] A friend of Vincent d'Indy, Maurice de Courville sat on the board of the Schola Cantorum (a private institution of music education that offered a Catholic-oriented alternative to the Republican Conservatory) and was president of the Société de Musique d'Autrefois, the same group that later published the influential bilingual musicological journal *Annales musicologiques*.[15] Xavier's mother, Louise, née Rondel, was a royalist activist who ran an influential political and literary salon closely tied to the Action Française movement from its earliest days.[16] Courville neatly summed up his parent's tastes by recalling that "my mother was happiest when [Maurice] Barrès [debated with] Maurras in the sitting room, whereas my father preferred to open the piano in the parlor and accompany Marie-Ange in a melody by [Henri] Duparc or [Ernest] Chausson."[17]

Marie-Ange, Xavier's sister, married Jean Rivain, an important second-generation Action Française militant and defender of a nationalist, classicist vision of art in his capacity as a cofounder of the *Revue critique*.[18] In 1912, the couple created La Petite Scène, an amateur theater group intended to "revive neglected monuments of French genius and taste" and to "provide living examples of the humanism defended by the *Revue critique*." Their productions of ancien régime repertoire (music by Christoph Willibald Gluck and Jean-Baptiste Lully; dramatic works by Pierre Marivaux, Molière, and Michel-Jean Sedaine) sought to revive the spirit of court theater and were performed by aristocratic casts to audiences invited from the readership of the *Revue critique*.

Following the First World War, La Petite Scène called upon nonaristocratic professionals to assure that it properly performed the repertoire it had selected. Xavier de Courville took an increasingly active role in the theater during this period, directing productions that included Francophone revivals of Claudio Monteverdi conducted by Vincent d'Indy, as well as d'Indy's comédie lyrique, *Le Rêve de Cinyras*, based on a libretto that Courville had published in the *Revue critique*.[19] In 1932, Courville married Jacqueline Casadesus, a soprano and former piano student of Alfred Cortot. (The Courville and Casadesus families may have been connected through a common interest in early music—Henri Casadesus, Jacqueline's father, was the founder of the Société des Instruments Anciens.) Over the course of the 1930s, Xavier and Jacqueline created their own independent theater, one of the projects of which was a varied collection of staged musical numbers based on traditional French songs and little-known classical works that they called *Arlequinades*.[20] Courville's spring 1940 revival of the *Arlequinades* and theater by Molière for the CMT was approved by Huntziger and Massis. This underlines the CMT's connections to Courville's earlier projects with their political and artistic origins in the orbit of the *Revue critique* and La Petite Scène. Indeed, one knowing journalist simply referred to Courville's new project for Huntziger as a "drafted" reincarnation of La Petite Scène.[21]

### PURPOSES, ACTIVITY, AND MEMBERS OF THE CMT

After the declaration of war in September 1939, the calling-up and stationing of French reserve forces soon gave way to waiting for an eventual German attack. As time passed, maintaining troop morale became a major challenge. Among other initiatives, recreational centers in which soldiers could spend their free time, *Foyers du soldat*, were created through a government office directed by Alfred Cortot and created at his request in November 1939, the Service Lecture, Arts, Sports et Loisirs aux Armées.[22] Cortot was also charged with overseeing the rebirth of the Théâtre aux Armées, a program he had helped to create during the First World War.[23] In 1939 and 1940, the Théâtre aux Armées featured popular stars such as Josephine Baker and Maurice Chevalier playing to huge military audiences.[24] This was the most visible form of entertainment provided to the French

Army, the sort that Huntziger felt was not sufficiently serious, morally uplifting, or particularly French.[25]

The few surviving documents dating to the period of the CMT's creation reassure soldiers that it intended to replace neither the inside jokes and slapstick of amateur theater nor the star-studded tours of the Théâtre aux Armées. Instead, it would offer alternative "quality" entertainment to the Second Army at more regular intervals.[26] The CMT's organizers believed that its repertoire should be composed of short numbers that would be accessible to the ordinary soldier, but avoided explicitly naming the classic repertoire that they intended to present. Instead, they implied that the Théâtre aux Armées, with its American-influenced acts, had failed to remind soldiers that they were defending France's cultural specificity.[27] Massis's March 1, 1940, announcement of the coming CMT both patronized and flattered troops, calling them an "elite" that deserved "an elite form of entertainment."[28] Massis held that soldiers would be better equipped to fight if they had a certain image of their country in mind: "Created by soldier artists for soldier spectators, a young theater of war must differ from the old theater of peace ... When the French are defending France against Germany, it is important that they know and feel what France is."[29] An article profiling Huntziger indicated that planning for the CMT had begun in late January and noted that the general had called for "programs, specialists for putting those programs in place, ... troops for the dramatic arts, and an orchestra of quality for classical music [*musique savante*]."[30]

One might counterbalance Massis's claims that the CMT was created for the edification of the common soldier with the observation that the Second Army's senior officers wanted to be entertained with a repertoire that corresponded to their personal tastes, and that, frequently amateur artists themselves, they sympathized with the plight of drafted professional actors and musicians. Fragments of tour schedules show that, for every free matinee presented to ordinary soldiers, there was an evening production with paid entry reserved for officers.[31] Indeed, framing the theater and orchestra in terms of a patriotic project of nationalist cultural proselytism targeting the ordinary soldier may have been an excuse to justify creating a structure destined primarily for the entertainment of officers.

At present, it has been possible to identify a little more than thirty of the sixty-some artists who made up the CMT's troupe and orchestra.[32] Selected from the men under Huntziger's command, the professional musicians in the CMT orchestra were often recommended by prominent figures, such as Alfred Cortot and Nadia Boulanger, with social connections to the CMT's directors.[33] The CMT orchestra, for example, was conducted by Henri Challan, who had been recommended by his former composition teacher Henri Büsser.[34] Olivier Messiaen may have been recommended by composer Marcel Dupré; he became a rehearsal pianist for the CMT, where he met the future musicians of his *Quatuor pour la fin du Temps*, the clarinetist Henri Akoka and cellist Etienne Pasquier, as well as his future companion in captivity, the singer and music-hall artist René Charle.[35]

Other well-known members of the CMT included André Dassary, the actor and singer who later became known for recording Vichy's unofficial anthem "Maréchal, nous voilà!"; Henri Echourin, a member of the Comédie-Française; Emile Rousseau, a baritone with the Opéra-Comique; the violinist Jean Fournier; and the composers Raymond Gallois-Montbrun, Jean Martinon, and Maurice Thiriet. The CMT's members were an artistic elite of diverse origins, largely trained in music and theater at the Paris Conservatory, a Republican institution. They seem to have been recruited principally for their talent and not their politics. Many already knew each other from their studies or professional life.[36]

The CMT's administration was based in Huntziger's headquarters at the Château de Senuc, whereas the artists themselves lived in Verdun in barracks (the Caserne Niel) that had been specially renovated before their arrival in March 1940.[37] Military records show that the members of the CMT were officially transferred to the 412th Pioneer Regiment (*régiment de pionniers*), but they did not take part in the regiment's manual labor.[38] Apart from a 5 a.m. roll call, CMT artists were exempt from ordinary soldier's duties. Their days were devoted to rehearsals in their barracks or at the Hôtel des Sociétés and Théâtre de Verdun, which had been offered with the blessings of Verdun's mayor.[39]

Few traces remain of the CMT's musical programs. It is known, however, that Alfred Cortot, cited in one source as a friend of Huntziger, played the Schumann Concerto, a veritable calling card for Cortot, with the CMT orchestra in Sedan and Montmédy on May 3 and 4, 1940.[40] In a book written after the war, largely with the aim of defending Huntziger's honor, Edmond Ruby, then a colonel on Huntziger's staff, claimed the concert had been successful: "The audience, by no means prepared for a concert of serious music, gave the artists a veritable ovation, proving that man can be sensitive to something other than the vulgarity of a cinema clown. Cortot vowed that he had never been so moved in all his career."[41]

The best documented CMT concert was a visit by Nadia Boulanger and her vocal ensemble, which, in early April 1940, was touring military installations across northern France. Following an invitation from Huntziger himself, Boulanger and her singers performed with the CMT orchestra on April 12. Boulanger's connections to Huntziger dated to at least the beginning of the war when she and Huntziger's wife, Anne, organized benefit concerts for the Foyers militaires de l'armée, and it also seems likely that she knew Xavier de Courville through his interwar projects involving early music and opera.[42] One of Huntziger's officers, Jean Labusquière (who continued serving under Huntziger after the Armistice, dying in the same 1941 plane crash), had long worked for the couturier Jeanne

Lanvin and was close to Lanvin's daughter, Marie-Blanche de Polignac, who sang in Boulanger's ensemble.[43] Boulanger later recalled that Huntziger requested a program of her "very best" music, and that she dutifully complied, still fearing her carefully crafted program of short masterworks was "too severe." In spite of an enthusiastic reception with several encores, Boulanger remained skeptical, betraying her assumptions about ordinary soldiers by wondering years later whether they wouldn't have really preferred something noisy and popular ("*du bastringue*").[44] The program with Boulanger and her singers was framed by Henri Challan directing the orchestra in Debussy's *Petite suite* and Chabrier's *Marche joyeuse*. Between these works, Nathalie and Irène Kédroff, Marie-Blanche de Polignac, and Paul Derenne sang a typically (for Boulanger) eclectic assortment of popular song, motets, and arias, ranging from the fifteenth-century rondeau *Par un regart des deux biaulx yeux riant* by Franchois de Gemblaco to recent works by Jean Françaix and Stravinsky. The program's center of gravity, however, was composed of traditional, accessible works: arias by Mozart and Charles Gounod and instrumental pieces featuring soloists from the CMT. Violinist Jean Fournier played Lili Boulanger's *Nocturne* and *Cortège*, and flutist Henri Lebon performed the *Nocturne* from Gabriel Fauré's *Shylock*. No individual number lasted more than about three minutes, and the overall tone of Boulanger's choices was poignant and sentimental. Letters to Boulanger from both Huntziger and Labusquière indicate that her stay with the Second Army was cut short two days later by a false alarm of German troop movements. Huntziger subsequently invited Boulanger to return and direct the orchestra in mid-May, but this plan was interrupted by the real German invasion.[45]

During its two-month existence, the CMT also created two mixed programs of theater and music. These were given at the theater in Verdun, at Huntziger's headquarters in the Château de Senuc, and in cinemas, theaters, and community centers across the region where the Second Army was stationed. The CMT's "test program," as Courville called it, was premiered in the second half of March, and was performed about twenty times. It featured Offenbach's 1855 one-act operetta *Les deux aveugles* sung by Henri Echourin and Messiaen's future companion in captivity, René Charle, and also included Georges Courteline's 1896 one-act play *Un client sérieux*.[46] Both the Offenbach and Courteline works were farcical nineteenth-century Parisian slices of life that dispensed with the need for female actors. Although entertaining, neither harked back to the mythical France called for by Massis's founding manifesto; they were probably chosen for the ease with which they might be staged on short notice with a still-forming troupe. Around these theatrical numbers, CMT musicians played an hour's worth of music that Courville vaguely recalled as a "prudent" selection ranging from Schubert to Debussy. A journalist who attended a performance on March 23 heard Challan direct works by Mozart, César Franck, Fauré, and Debussy, but did not indicate any specific titles.[47]

Huntziger was not satisfied with this test run, and a second program was subsequently developed using feedback from superior officers. The new program clearly retreated into the classic seventeenth- and eighteenth-century repertoire of La Petite Scène. Whereas in late March Henri Echourin had indicated his intentions to find another two-character operetta and direct a production of *Le médecin malgré lui*, the latter was rejected in favor of *Le mariage forcé*, a shorter work with music by Lully that still featured Echourin in his signature role (and that of Molière before him), Sganarelle.[48] Instead of a second operetta, Courville revived twenty of the *Arlequinades* he had developed with his wife. These included Mozart's comic dialect trio "Das Bandel" in translation as "Le ruban égaré," Amadée de Beauplan's "Le secret," and old popular songs such as "Les cloches de Nantes," "Malbrough," "Le retour du marin," and "La belle fille et le petit bossu."[49] These numbers referenced both their ancien régime origins and Yvette Guilbert's pre-1914 revivals of the *chanson ancienne*, which were an important influence on Courville and Casadesus.[50] Maurice Thiriet composed musical interludes to connect these numbers, but this music is not described in any of the sources.

This second program was met with approval following premieres in Verdun and Senuc in early May and was set to tour through the various encampments of the Second Army, with a special performance in Sedan, to which Massis had invited a number of Parisian critics.[51] A critical difference in the second program, and a likely factor in its success, was its exceptional inclusion of three actresses, all wives of the CMT's leading members: Xavier de Courville's wife, Jacqueline Casadesus; Henri Echourin's wife, Simone Chatelain; and Etienne Pasquier's wife, Suzanne Gouts.[52] The unorthodox request to bring in three officers' wives initially met with administrative resistance but was forced through with Huntziger's insistence.[53]

After a gala performance at the Stella Cinema in Vouziers on the evening of May 9, the tour was cut short: later that same night, German armies invaded the Low Countries. The CMT's last performance and its role in the ensuing Battle of France is recounted differently by different sources, all of them invested in the politically charged task of accounting for the unpreparedness of France's armies, including Huntziger's, particularly in the episode of the Battle of Sedan.[54] Some sources claim that Huntziger was oblivious to the threat and present in the audience at the cinema in Vouziers, others confirm that officers from the general's staff had gone to Vouziers but that Huntziger had not, whereas an unreliable account written Bernard Faÿ omits mention of the CMT and gives the impression that Huntziger foresaw the German attack. Courville's somewhat vague account of that evening also places the first sound of enemy fire much earlier in the evening than it was likely to have been heard.

The first version, recorded by Claude Paillat after interviews with General Michel de Lombarès, was later developed by Jean-Pierre Richardot using sources from Lombarès's archives. Lombarès, then a captain of Operations in the Second Army, received intelligence from a reliable Belgian informant about German troop movements and passed them on to Colonel Paquin, who, busy preparing to leave for Vouziers with Huntziger and the other staff officers, asked simply that a report be written up for later reading.[55] (It may be that Paquin was hesitant to take Lombarès's intelligence seriously after the false alarm that had sent Boulanger and Marie-Blanche de Polignac back to Paris so disappointingly early.) Paillat also cites the recollections of Paul Troller, mayor of Sedan from 1935 to 1940, who claimed Huntziger told him on the occasion of Cortot's concert in Sedan, "I don't believe that the Germans would ever dream of attacking this region."[56] For Paillat, Huntziger's insouciance was emblematic of a general attitude among the French high command of the period.

In a second account of that evening—according to Alphonse Goutard citing documents from the colonel Henri Lacaille who was also a member of Huntziger's staff—a convoy of officers went from Senuc to the theater in Vouziers while Huntziger was occupied with the opening of a Foyer du soldat in Mouzay (but was no more alert to the warnings of German movements than was Colonel Paquin in the first version). Claude Gounelle indicates that Huntziger only learned of the German invasion by telephone around five in the morning after returning to his headquarters in Senuc. Edmond Ruby recalls that news of the attack reached Senuc by telephone at 5:20 a.m.[57]

Finally, there is Bernard Faÿ's version of the story. A familiar of Virgil Thomson and the composers of Les Six, one of France's leading scholars on the United States during the interwar period, and later a signatory of Massis's *Manifeste d'intellectuels français pour la défense de l'Occident*, Faÿ is now perhaps best known for his role as the head of Vichy's anti-Masonic propaganda and as the wartime director of the Bibliothèque nationale.[58] On a tour of the French armies like Boulanger and Cortot before him, Faÿ was in Senuc visiting Huntziger and his officers and scheduled to present a lecture on American politics to them on the evening of May 10.[59] He portrayed Huntziger as a lucid man, aware of the events to come and the shortcomings of his position, who, hearing enemy fire in the distance, advised Faÿ to return to Paris the evening of May 9. Streicher underlines that there was no fire to be heard that evening and that Faÿ's account is a fabrication.[60] But Faÿ's friendliness with Huntziger and his officers offers a broader picture of Huntziger's social circles and further evidence of the entertainment and reactionary political atmosphere at the Second Army's headquarters.

Xavier de Courville recalls that a "false rumor" of an invasion of the Low Countries had spread backstage in Vouziers just before the curtain went up on the evening of May 9 (perhaps an echo of the warnings received by Paquin), but that the successful performance was later "crowned by champagne." As the artists left the theater, Courville claimed they could hear antiaircraft fire.[61] Again, this recollection of gunfire also conflicts with accounts in which Huntziger only received news of German troop movements at five the following morning. Even with the news of the German attack in hand, Huntziger did not imagine the rapidity of German troop movements. Although the officer's wives, like Faÿ, were sent back to Paris upon news of the attack, the CMT was not disbanded. Thinking the front might stabilize, Huntziger simply ordered CMT artists back to Verdun.[62]

## THE LEGACY OF THE CMT AFTER ITS DISSOLUTION

The conditions in which the CMT was finally dissolved are not clear, nor is it known what the actors and musicians did in the citadel of Verdun between May 10 and the beginning of their retreat on June 14. Once it was clear that they would not perform again soon, they probably participated in efforts to slow the arrival of the German armies. A few accounts from this period refer to Olivier Messiaen and his request to be assigned the early morning watch, aligning with Rebecca Rischin's revelation that the *Quatuor pour la fin du Temps*'s movement for solo clarinet, "Abîme des oiseaux," was inspired by the birdsong of Verdun in May 1940.[63] On June 14, when shells began to fall on the Verdun citadel, the CMT and the other reserve forces stationed there, deemed unprepared and ill-equipped to fight, were instructed to retreat. They headed south and east along the Meuse river, only to be surrounded by the German armies a week later. Many were taken prisoner in the forests near the village of Germiny, south of Toul.[64]

German prisoner-of-war archives allow us to follow the paths of two distinct groups of former CMT artists who were taken prisoner together and sent to two different holding camps in France. Thiriet later recalled how he and fifteen other men from the CMT entertained themselves with music as they waited in the limbo of the Frontstalag between the end of June and the end of July, with Thiriet, Martinon, and Gallois-Montbrun even writing choral pieces for their companions to sing.[65] In a different Frontstalag, but in similarly tenuous, tedious circumstances, Messiaen and three of his comrades passed the time making music and reading.[66]

After about a month, the soldiers in Frontstalags were sent to two different prisoner-of-war camps: Stalag VIIIA in Görlitz (Akoka, Charle, Messiaen, Pasquier) and Stalag IXA in Zieghenhain (Echourin, Gallois-Montbrun, Martinon, Thiriet, and others).[67] Like Messiaen and his companions in Stalag VIIIA, Thiriet and fellow prisoners from the CMT were eventually able to set up a theater and orchestra in Stalag IXA in the autumn of 1940. These centers of cultural activity in the Stalags likely resulted from earlier French requests for permission to send books, clothing, and other supplies to POWs that were accepted by German authorities following Hitler's meetings with Vichy officials at Montoire in late October.[68] Spared from the heavy labor of the Arbeitskommando, composers wrote music, actors prepared plays, and musicians rehearsed for orchestra and chamber music concerts. The special treatment received by these two groups of artists was in large part due to the fact that the CMT had brought them together and that they managed to remain together in visible and active groups during their captivity.

That visibility also likely played a role in their early liberation. Three out of four of the men in Messiaen's group (Messiaen, Pasquier, and René Charle) would return to France in February 1941, shortly after the first performance of the *Quatuor pour la fin du Temps* in the Stalag VIIIA. Among the prisoners in Stalag IXA, Thiriet and Martinon were also released in February 1941, shortly after the performance of Thiriet's *Œdipe-Roi*, whereas Gallois-Montbrun, Henri Echourin, and several others were returned home just a month later.[69] Overall, most of the former members of the CMT fared far better than the more than 1.6 million French soldiers taken prisoner in 1940, the majority of whom remained in captivity until 1945.[70] Yannick Simon's study of French composers during the Second World War identifies twenty composers who were taken prisoner in 1940. Of these, only six were able to return in 1941.[71] All six had ties to Huntziger's CMT: five were former members (Challan, Gallois-Montbrun, Martinon, Messiaen, and Thiriet) and the sixth was the popular jazz violinist Michel Warlop, who met the composers of the CMT and became an active member of the musical center they created in the Stalag IXA.

Although I have found no documentary evidence of his intervention, it seems entirely plausible that Huntziger, who, as Vichy's war minister, oversaw the fate of French POWs and the propaganda concerning them, played a role in the early release of the high-profile members of his former orchestra and theater. Huntziger and his wife were also often featured in Vichy's POW propaganda: from late January 1941 Huntziger was regularly pictured in the press welcoming home former prisoners, and his wife, through her Pétainiste charity La famille du prisonnier de guerre, accompanied Georges Scapini, France's top representative for its prisoners of war, on tours of POW camps.[72] Huntziger's interest in assisting musicians and actors was not only proven by his choice to create the CMT in the first place, but also through admiring letters written to Nadia Boulanger by Huntziger's faithful staff officer Jean Labusquière during the summer of 1940. These reveal that Labusquière and Huntziger were eager to help Boulanger in any way they could, even offering to help her procure a position at the Paris Conservatory (Boulanger preferred exile).[73]

Interpreting the reasons for the return of former CMT members in the spring of 1941 is no easier with prisoner records in hand. The reason given by many artists themselves for their early return was that they were considered "*sanitaires*," a problematic term that was used to refer both to non-arms-bearing medical personnel ("sanitary personnel") and those who were in extremely poor health ("sanitary cases"). As part of a larger agreement signed November 16, 1940, in which Vichy accepted Germany's proposition that France replace the United States as the protective power for the oversight of French prisoners of war, Germany agreed to release certain categories of prisoners, notably fathers of large families and medical personnel (it was not until May 11, 1941, that Hitler agreed to free veterans of the First World War).[74] Many CMT musicians were technically medical personnel at the time of their capture and had been nurses or stretcher-bearers before being sent to the CMT. This was the official reason allowing for the early release of Messiaen and his companions. In Thiriet's group, several men's records show brief hospitalizations for various medical conditions upon their return, and it might be that these medical reasons were also used to allow their return France.[75] Still, not all "sanitaires" were liberated at the same time, and it is worth noting that high-profile prisoners tend to have been liberated the earliest.

Copies of outgoing correspondence in the archives of the Paris Conservatory show that the Service des prisonniers de guerre and the Conservatory were already in touch in late October 1940 concerning the potential liberation of former Conservatory students who were POWs and members of "service sanitaires," several weeks before the official November 16 agreement, but shortly after Pétain's October 24 meeting with Hitler at Montoire. This timing suggests that the wheels of French administration might have begun turning in anticipation of positive results from Pétain's public acceptance of the policy of collaboration at Montoire.[76] As Raffael Scheck has noted, "Montoire raised expectations in France for a return of prisoners, and it provided a diplomatic momentum that Scapini was keen to exploit for further concessions."[77] The Conservatory sent the first of many lists of student and former student POWs to the Service des prisonniers de guerre on October 31, 1940, indicating the names of students, their field of study, their achievements, and the Stalags in which they were held. Gallois-Montbrun and Challan both figure on the first list alongside the CMT violinist Jean Gitton (who was liberated in May, three months later than his composer comrades).[78] Perhaps these requests from the Conservatory played a role in the wave of artist–prisoners liberated beginning in February 1941.

A factor further complicating interpretation of the early return of certain artist–prisoners is their contribution, active or passive, voluntary or involuntary, to propaganda on cultural life in the Stalags: as authors of propaganda; as beneficiaries of jobs, concerts, commissions, and other creative projects; or simply as characters figuring in stories about the camps.[79] One former prisoner's publications in particular demonstrate how propaganda on artistic life in the camps in early 1941 mobilized the stories of former CMT members. Guy Roissard de Bellet, who wrote about the Stalag under the pseudonym Jean Mariat, was a member of the theater in Stalag IXA where he worked with many former CMT composers and actors. Shortly after his early release in early 1941, Roissard de Bellet published a series of articles about life in the camp for the collaborationist newspaper *Les Nouveaux Temps*. These were subsequently compiled in *Prisonnier en Allemagne*, a book dedicated to Maréchal Pétain and published in a series alongside titles such as *De l'Hostilité à la Collaboration* and *Le Juif, cet inconnu*.[80] His text is typical of the Vichy portrayals of life in the Stalags as characterized by Sarah Fishman: a program of self-improvement through the combination of concentrated study and rustic summer-camp physicality.[81] Roissard de Bellet also mentions interactions between Christian and Jewish prisoners of war, defending both anti-Semitism of the former and Pétain's adoption of anti-Semitic legislation.[82] Roissard de Bellet's preface opens with praise for the conditions in which prisoners of war were held and remarks upon the importance of music in the daily life of the Stalag, mentioning a *Requiem* composed by Jean Martinon for an All Saints' Day commemoration in 1940.[83] Later passages detail the positive ambiance in the Stalag's theater, its continuation of projects already begun in the CMT, and creative collaborations with the former CMT musicians and actors.[84] Furthermore, after their liberation, Mariat and the CMT composers continued to work together, as is illustrated by the 1941 publication of Raymond Gallois-Montbrun's *Trois mélodies sur trois poèmes de Jean Mariat* and the 1942 radio play *La nuit des bergers*, adapted by Roissard de Bellet from Giono's *Le Serpent d'étoiles* with music by Maurice Thiriet.

Although the musicians of Messiaen's *Quatuor* gradually fell out of touch after the war, upon their return to Paris, they played the *Quatuor* in a number of public and semipublic events.[85] Early release from captivity allowed Messiaen and Challan (who had been interned in a third camp, the Stalag VIIA, but who was also liberated in February 1941) to be hired for their first teaching jobs, coveted positions leading harmony classes at the Paris Conservatory.[86] Indeed, the impact of early liberations on musical life in Occupied France is strikingly present in the jury minutes of the Paris Conservatory's composition *concours* of June 17, 1941, in which a jury including the recently liberated (and hired) Olivier Messiaen attributed a *premier prix* to the recently liberated Gallois-Montbrun for a string trio played by the Trio Pasquier (including the recently liberated Etienne Pasquier) and the abovementioned song cycle on texts by the recently liberated Jean Mariat (Roissard de Bellet).[87] One of the most prestigious prizes of France's most prestigious institution of musical education was awarded in a setting dominated by the presence of prominent former POWs.

The composers of Stalag IXA also continued working together after their liberation: Thiriet and Martinon collaborated on the music of the 1942 documentary film *Alerte aux champs*, while Thiriet and Gallois-Montbrun cowrote the music of *La rivière enchantée* the same year. Reactivating old networks long after the war, Xavier de Courville even called on Thiriet and Challan to write and conduct music for his theatrical productions: Thiriet composed music for the 1948 *Le chariot d'Arlequin*, and Challan was involved in Courville's 1954 production of Monteverdi's *Il ritorno d'Ulisse in patria*, a long-term project Courville claimed he first mentioned to Challan when they were in Verdun at the beginning of the war.[88]

Although Jean Martinon was the object of minor sanctions for other musical activities during the Occupation, notably his score for an anti-Semitic and anti-Masonic documentary, postwar political purges (*épurations*) did not target individuals like the former members of the CMT for their active or passive roles in creating Vichy POW propaganda.[89] Still, the relative privilege enjoyed by musicians and artists during their military service, captivity, and early liberation was in large part due to attention from Huntziger and Vichy. Messiaen, for example, later preferred to gloss over or distort the events of 1940–41 rather than provide the full account that inevitably would have brought up Huntziger's controversial name.[90] Although music was part of the wartime experience of French soldiers, both in service and in captivity, as entertainment, it was easily opposed with the notion of duty. This meant that making music in the context of war, particularly as part of military service, was a delicate matter. As historical accounts of the CMT's last performance on May 9 show, the CMT had potential to be seen as symbol of the French Army's unpreparedness for the new German warfare and, more specifically, as a fateful distraction to Huntziger and his staff on the eve of the Battle of France. Whether deserved or not, fear of reproach and feelings of guilt likely contributed to silencing the story of Huntziger's CMT and its long-term legacy.

## CONCLUSION

The history of the CMT and its artists concentrates the central themes of French musical and political life during the early twentieth century. Future research might consider the long-term cultural and political consequences of Huntziger's experience as the child of a musician refugee of the Franco–Prussian war, or the way in which his Parisian social connections in Catholic and military circles were steeped in the cultural consequences of the Dreyfus Affair, the Action Française, and the aftermath of the First World War. Further extending those connections, the younger generation of Huntziger's staff officers involved in the creation of the

CMT link with a much broader network of Maurrassian intellectual and cultural figures with strong connections to France's musical elite. Huntziger and his men subsequently materialized their particular vision of what French music and theater ought to be, drawing on young Conservatory-trained men for officer entertainment, and may have later extended that pattern of exception in negotiating the internment and conditional liberation of French POWs.

From a broader point of view, study of the CMT brings to the fore the near-universal experience of the military service and captivity in the lives of male French musicians during this period. During the interwar years, obligatory military service was a universal rite of masculinity, and in September 1939 nearly all men under the age of forty were called back into service. This shared, direct experience of military authority cannot have failed to affect musicians' vision of the French state and their relationship with the world at large. It should not be neglected in studies of their lives and works and of the larger trends and institutions to which they contributed.

Just as the CMT was one of many army theaters and orchestras organized during the drôle de guerre, the music and theater activities in Stalags VIIIA and IXA are not exceptional; rather, they are the most prominent examples of what was a widespread phenomenon.[91] Even the dramatic account of the CMT's last performance on the evening of May 9 finds echoes in other sites across the French frontlines. Take, for example, José David's recollection of a performance on May 8 near the border with Luxembourg:

> The first days of May 1940 unfolded, monotonous and tranquil.... The 'théâtre aux armées' had just given a performance of *Ta bouche* in Ottange... and I had been designated to play the piano in a decision that came from the General's staff. This says something of the insouciant euphoria that reigned, even in the most advanced sectors of along the French border! The colonel of the 31st group himself put a car at my disposition so I could return to my station in Rochonvilliers after the concert.... Nothing allowed us to imagine the sudden attack that would come two days later.[92]

It seems likely—were this study extended to follow the trajectories of other army orchestras and soldiers chosen to entertain their peers in service, captivity, and liberation—that variations on the central themes of authority, privilege, and guilt examined here would reveal that the CMT and its members represent individual cases of a broader phenomenon. Studying the trajectories of those army orchestras and the erasure of their musical activity from the larger shared experience of France's armies during the Second World War has the potential to reveal larger patterns of privilege that affected the lives of hundreds of French musicians and likely shaped the direction of French musical life for decades after the conflict's end.

## NOTES

Parts of this research were initially presented at the Annual Meeting of the American Musicological Society in New Orleans (2012). I would like to thank Marie-Hélène Benoit-Otis and Cécile Quesney along with the editors of the present volume for their constructive remarks on this article. I am also extremely grateful to archivists Pascal Hureau and Alain Alexandra at the Bureau des Archives des Victimes des Conflits Contemporains in Caen, as well as to the devoted staff of the Music Department of the Bibliothèque Nationale de France, the Archives Nationales in Saint-Denis, and the Service Historique de la Défense in Vincennes.

1. Streicher indicates sixty artists were chosen from an army of 300,000 men, whereas Le Boterf indicates about seventy from an army of 250,000. Streicher, *Le général Huntziger*, 21; Le Boterf, *Le théâtre en uniforme*, 64.

2. See, in particular, Simon, *Composer sous Vichy*, and Sprout, *The Musical Legacy*. Archives consulted include the Bureau des Archives des Victimes des Conflits Contemporains, Caen; Archives Nationales, Saint-Denis; Département de la Musique, Bibliothèque Nationale de France, Paris; and the Service Historique de la Défense, Vincennes.

3. Streicher, *Le général Huntziger*, 5–8.

4. Ibid., 7–8; Paxton, *L'Armée de Vichy*, 21–22.

5. Streicher, *Le général Huntziger*, 8–15; Haag, "Un grand Saint-Cyrien"; Unattributed, "Les obsèques"; Benoist-Méchin, *De la défaite*, 113; Groussard, *Chemins secrets*, 209.

6. For a complete account of Huntziger's military career, see Delmas, "Huntziger (Charles)." For a succinct analysis of how Huntziger's career may have failed to prepare him for combat at the head of the Second Army, see Rocolle, *La guerre de 1940*, 49–51.

7. Courville, *Soixante ans de théâtre*, 188.

8. Massis, *Maurras et notre temps*, vol. 2 of 2, 22, 124, 134, 139. On Massis's literary influence, see Dard, "Henri Massis," 219–233; Sanos, *The Aesthetics of Hate*, 58–62; Wilson, "The 'Action Française,'" 328–350.

9. Fulcher, *The Composer as Intellectual*, 119–122, 204–205. See also Massis, *Défense de l'Occident*.

10. Streicher, *Le général Huntziger*, 19–20.

11. Massis, *Maurras et notre temps*, 134–139.

12. Sanos, *The Aesthetics of Hate*, 58; Massis, "Le théâtre de l'Armée"; Le Boterf, Hervé, *Le théâtre en uniforme*, 64–66; Courville, *Soixante ans de théâtre*, 188–191.

13. Courville, *Soixante ans de théâtre*, 188.

14. Weber, *Action Française*, 38.

15. Lioncourt, *Un témoignage*; Courville, *Soixante ans de théâtre*. See also Gétreau, "Les archives."

16. Dumons, "Action Française," 230–231; Weber, *Action Française*, 38.

17. Courville, *Soixante ans de théâtre*, 122. "Ma mère se plaisait de voir dans le grand salon Barrès deviser avec Maurras. Mon père préférait ouvrir dans le petit son piano, pour accompagner Marie-Ange dans une mélodie de Duparc ou de Chausson." All translations are my own unless otherwise indicated.

18. On the *Revue critique*, see Joly, "La *Revue critique*," 45–59. See also Wilson, "The 'Action Française,'" 334–335.

19. The information in this paragraph summarizes content found in Courville, *Soixante ans de théâtre*, 119–180. See also Carsalade du Pont, "Une alliance."

20. Courville, *Soixante ans de théâtre*, 181–188.

21. Villier, "La 'Petite Scène.'"

22. Chimènes, "Drôles de concerts," 304.

23. Anselmini, "Alfred Cortot," 147–157; Anselmini and Jacobs, *Alfred Cortot*, 299–310; Gavoty, *Alfred Cortot*, 156–157.

24. Le Boterf, *Le théâtre en uniforme*, 35–52.

25. Carsalade du Pont, "Une alliance," 99; Le Boterf, *Le théâtre en uniforme*, 64; Courville, *Soixante ans de théâtre*, 188.

26. Gaujac, *Sedan 1940*, 85.

27. Villier, "La 'Petite Scène.'"

28. Massis, "Le théâtre de l'armée."

29. Courville, *Soixante ans de théâtre*, 190. "Créé par des artistes combattants pour des spectateurs combattants, un jeune théâtre de guerre doit être autre chose que les vieux théâtres de la paix... Dans une défense de la France contre l'Allemagne, il importe que le Français sache et sente ce que c'est que la France."

30. Bonnardi, "Le général"; cited and corrected in Streicher, *Le général Huntziger*, 20. "Il a dit: divertissez mes soldats. Aussitôt il fallu lui présenter des programmes des spécialistes pour mettre en train ces programmes, des appareils pour les spectateurs [Streicher corrects this to *spectacles*] d'arts mécaniques, des troupes pour l'art dramatique et un orchestre de qualité pour la musique savante."

31. Archives du service historique de l'armée de terre, Vincennes, Box 31 N 86, Folder 9².

32. The names of CMT members are found in sources such as Courville, *Soixante ans de théâtre* and Le Boterf, *Le théâtre en uniforme*. Further members were identified through the consultation of dossiers in the Bureau des Archives des Victimes des Conflits Contemporains in Caen. Copies of German records indicate groups of soldiers taken prisoner together. Often members of the CMT remained grouped together, permitting the identification of CMT members not mentioned in published sources. In March 2018, at the time I was finishing work on this chapter, I was contacted by Virginie Chauffeté, a master's student in musicology at the Sorbonne, whose grandfather was a bassoonist in the CMT orchestra. Her forthcoming master's dissertation draws upon her grandfather's personal papers and will surely add to our knowledge of the CMT orchestra and its activities.

33. Thiriet, "Musique au Stalag," 52; Letter from Jean Vuillermoz to Nadia Boulanger, January 24, 1940 (F-Pn) NLA 115 (200).

34. Courville, *Soixante ans de théâtre*, 189.

35. Rebecca Rischin was the first to establish this link, but her work focuses little on the CMT itself. For previous studies on the genesis of the *Quatuor pour la fin du Temps*, see Balmer and Murray, "Olivier Messiaen"; Murray, "Nouveaux regards"; Rischin, *For the End of Time*; and Sprout, *The Musical Legacy*. Yves Balmer's most recent work on the previously unstudied documents found in the new Messiaen Collection of the Bibliothèque Nationale de France promises to further change our understanding of the *Quatuor's* genesis and Messiaen's creative activity while in captivity. His initial findings were presented at the Annual Meeting of the American Musicological Society, Rochester, November 10, 2017, as "Listening in Görlitz: *The Quartet for the End of Time* in Context."

36. More than half (eighteen) of the CMT members I have identified studied theater or music at the Paris Conservatory during the 1920s or 1930s. See Bongrain, *Le Conservatoire*.

37. Courville, *Soixante ans de théâtre*, 189; Le Boterf, *Le Théâtre en uniforme*, 64.

38. Prisoner of war records, Bureau des Archives des Victimes des Conflits Contemporains, Caen; Service Historique de la Défense, Vincennes, Archives of 412th Company of Pioneers: 34 N 328.

39. Courville, *Soixante ans de théâtre*, 189; Le Boterf, *Le Théâtre en uniforme*, 64–65; Villier, "La 'Petite Scène.'"

40. Gavoty, *Alfred Cortot*, 156–157. Cortot reprised the same work in his controversial May 1942 concert under Furtwängler in Berlin, and he was meant to play it in the project for a 1947 French comeback concert that failed when the musicians of orchestra of the Société des concerts refused to accompany him. Yagil, "Alfred Cortot," 117, 125. Claude Paillat, through an anecdote of the Sedan concert told by the former mayor of Sedan, indicates that Cortot was a friend of Huntziger's. Paillat, *Dossiers secrets*, 44.

41. Ruby, *Sedan*, 61. "L'assistance, nullement préparée à une audition de musique sérieuse, fit une véritable ovation aux artistes, ce qui prouve que l'homme peut être sensible à autre chose qu'à la vulgarité d'un pitre de cinéma. Cortot avoua que jamais, au cours de sa carrière, il n'avait été aussi ému."

42. Numerous traces of this tour are found in Boulanger's papers at the Bibliothèque Nationale de France (F-Pn), Res Vm dossier 195. The April 12, 1940, program is document no. 677 and Boulanger's collaboration with Anne Huntziger is found in document no. 664.

43. See Jean Labusquière's letters to Nadia Boulanger, (F-Pn) NLA 78 (356–361) as well as the unattributed obituary "Jean Labusquière" in *L'Officiel de la Mode* (December 1941), 37.

44. Monsaingeon, *Mademoiselle*, 47–48. "Tout cela a passé magnifiquement, ils étaient enchantés, il n'y avait que du meilleur. Je me demande malgré tout si, ayant mis du bastringue au milieu du meilleur, c'est le bastringue qui aurait eu le succès...."

45. Charles Huntziger, letter to Nadia Boulanger, April 25, 1940 (F-Pn) NLA 76 (286); Jean Labusquière, letters to Nadia Boulanger, 1940–1941 (F-Pn) NLA 78

(356–361). Georges Auric was also scheduled to work with the orchestra in mid-May, but this too was cancelled with the German invasion. Kaldor, "Entretien," 251–251.

46. Although it might seem surprising to see Offenbach on the program of a theater with roots in the notoriously anti-Semitic culture of Action Française, Courville was an Offenbach admirer and had already programmed works by the composer in his own theater during the interwar years.

47. Villier, "La 'Petite Scène.'"

48. Ibid.

49. Courville, *Soixante ans de théâtre*.

50. On the political implications of Guilbert's revivals of popular song (*chanson ancienne*), see Waeber, "Yvette Guilbert."

51. Courville, *Soixante ans de théâtre*, 188–191.

52. My thanks to Michel Baudier, president of the association "Ardennes 1940" for sending me a copy of the theater poster for the canceled Vouziers program of May 10 mentioned in Richardot's *100.000 morts oubliés*. It was this poster that allowed for the identification of the two other officers' wives present in the CMT's productions.

53. Courville, *Soixante ans de théâtre*, 189.

54. Streicher compares most of these sources in his biography of Huntziger, *Le général Huntziger*, 22–29.

55. Paillat, *Dossiers secrets*, 43–44; Richardot, *100.000 morts*, 48–65. (Paillat is also cited in Striecher, *Le général Huntziger*, 28–29.)

56. Paillat, *Dossiers secrets*, 44. "Je ne crois pas que les Allemands songeront jamais à attaquer dans la région."

57. Goutard, "Les Français accueillent," 29; Chauvy, *Le Drame*, 440–441; Gounelle, *Sedan Mai 1940*, 32–33; Ruby, *Sedan*, 77.

58. On Faÿ and his career, see Compagnon, *Le cas Bernard Faÿ*; and Will, *Unlikely Collaboration*. Compagnon indicates Faÿ's signature of Massis's *Manifeste* on p. 148 and reads it as a political gesture marking movement away from his more moderate friends of the 1920s. On Faÿ's influence on musicology in occupied France as director of the Bibliothèque Nationale, see Iglesias, *Musicologie et Occupation*, 255–292.

59. Faÿ, *La guerre*, 89, cited in Compagnon, *Le cas Bernard Faÿ*, 182.

60. Faÿ, *La guerre*, 95–100; Streicher, *Le général Huntziger*, 27–29.

61. Courville, *Soixante ans de théâtre*, 190.

62. Le Boterf, *Le théâtre en uniforme*, 65–66; Courville, *Soixante ans de théâtre*, 190–191.

63. Rischin, *For the End of Time*, 12; Le Boterf, *Le théâtre en uniforme*, 84–85.

64. Service Historique de la Défense, Vincennes, Box 34 N 1, Folder "Verdun," as well as individual dossiers for captured soldiers such as Olivier Messiaen and Maurice Thiriet in the Bureau des Archives des Victimes des Conflits Contemporains, Caen.

65. Thiriet, "Musique au Stalag," 52; Solar, *Maurice Thiriet*, 20.

66. Murray, "Nouveaux regards," 250–251.

67. Bureau des Archives des Victimes des Conflits Contemporains, Caen; Le Boterf, *Le théâtre en uniforme*, 95, 98; Solar, *Maurice Thiriet*, 20, 25.

68. Scheck, "The Prisoner," 373–374.

69. Prisoner of war records, Bureau des Archives des Victimes des Conflits Contemporains, Caen.

70. Simon, *Composer sous Vichy*, 27–28.

71. Ibid., 30–31.

72. Streicher, *Le général Huntziger*, 153–154, 229–238.

73. Jean Labusquière, letters to Nadia Boulanger dated August 21 and September 4, 1940 (F-Pn) NLA 78 (358, 360). On Boulanger's departure for the United States following a stay in Vichy in the late summer and early autumn of 1940, see Brooks, *The Musical Work*, 253.

74. Scheck, "The Prisoner," 376, 381.

75. Prisoner of war records, Bureau des Archives des Victimes des Conflits Contemporains, Caen.

76. These lists are found in the Archives Nationales, Archives of the Paris Conservatory, AJ$^{37}$ 427, Outgoing mail 1939–1941.

77. Scheck, "The Prisoner," 373.

78. Upon return from captivity, Gitton took over the Chorale universitaire formerly directed by Jean Vuillermoz (who had died on the battlefield in 1940) and later directed gala concerts of POW music by Thiriet, Challan, and Goué under the patronage of Scapini in December 1942. See Simon, *Composer sous Vichy*, 146, 153. See similar concerts described in Le Bail, *La musique au pas*, 98, 308.

79. The role of composers and the works they composed in captivity within projects of Vichy propaganda (in the press, but also in commissions and concerts of POW music) has already been explored in work by Sarah Fishman, Yannick Simon, Karine Le Bail, and, in particular, Leslie Sprout. Fishman, "Grand Delusions," 229–254; Sprout, *The Musical Legacy*, 80–119, first published in Sprout, "Messiaen, Jolivet"; Simon, *Composer sous Vichy*, 152–157; Le Bail, *La musique au pas*, 98–99.

80. Mariat, *Prisonnier en Allemagne*.

81. Fishman, "Grand Delusions."

82. Ibid., 89–92.

83. Mariat, *Prisonnier en Allemagne*, i–iii.

84. Ibid., 59–73.

85. A partial listing of Messiaen's wartime concerts is given in Sprout, *The Musical Legacy*, 92–94.

86. For an account of Messiaen's nomination, see Balmer and Murray, "Olivier Messiaen."

87. Archives Nationales, AJ$^{37}$ 558, 157–158. Gallois-Montbrun received the last prix de Rome of the Occupation in 1944 and later directed the Paris Conservatory from 1962 to 1983.

88. Courville, *Soixante ans de théâtre*, 177, 220–223.

89. Le Bail, *La musique au pas*, 260; Simon, *Composer sous Vichy*, 356–364. On the musical *épuration* in France in general, see Le Bail, *La musique au pas*, 211–271.

90. Balmer and Murray, "Olivier Messiaen."

91. See for example Elias and Elias, *Artistes au Stalag*; or Simon, *Composer sous Vichy*, 27–31.

92. David, "Fini le piano..." "Les premiers jours de mai 1940 se déroulaient monotones et tranquilles; les trois batteries du 75 du 1er groupe surveillant la frontière luxembourgeoise à Nondtreil, Roussy-le-Village et Ottange. Le 'théâtre aux armées' venait donner, à Ottange (un kilomètre de Rumelange, en territoire luxembourgeois), une représentation de *Ta bouche* et j'avais été désigné par une décision de l'E.M. [Etat-Major] pour tenir le piano. C'est dire l'insouciante euphorie qui régnait, même dans les secteurs les plus avancés de la frontière française! C'est le colonel lui-même du 31e groupe qui mettait une voiture à ma disposition, à l'issue de la représentation, afin que je regagne mon cantonnement de Rochonvilliers où se trouvait la C.R. de mon régiment. Rien ne laissait prévoir l'attaque soudaine qui allait se déclencher le surlendemain."

## BIBLIOGRAPHY

Anselmini, François. "Alfred Cortot et la mobilisation des musiciens français pendant la Première Guerre mondiale." *Vingtième siècle. Revue d'histoire* 118 (2013): 147–157.

Anselmini, François and Rémi Jacobs. *Alfred Cortot*. Paris: Fayard, 2018.

Archives nationales, Saint-Denis, France. Archives of the Paris Conservatory (AJ[37]).

Balmer, Yves, and Christopher Brent Murray. "Olivier Messiaen et la reconstruction de son parcours sous l'Occupation. Le vide de l'année 1941." In *La musique à Paris sous l'Occupation*, edited by Myriam Chimènes and Yannick Simon, 149–160. Paris: Fayard, 2013.

Benoist-Méchin, Jacques. *De la défaite au désastre*. Paris: Albin Michel, 1984.

Bibliothèque nationale de France, Paris, France. Département de la musique. Nadia Boulanger's correspondence and program collection.

Bongrain, Anne, ed. *Le Conservatoire national de musique et de déclamation 1900–1930*. Paris: Vrin, 2012.

Bonnardi, Pierre. "Le général d'armée Huntziger." *Gringoire*, February 1, 1940.

Brooks, Jeanice. *The Musical Work of Nadia Boulanger: Performing Past and Future between the Wars*. Cambridge: Cambridge University Press, 2013.

Bureau des archives des victimes des conflits contemporains (BAVCC), Caen, France. French prisoner-of-war records for the Second World War.

Carsalade du Pont, Henri de. "Une alliance du théâtre et de la musique: Les Courville." *Études* (October 1960): 97–103.

Chauvy, Gérard. *Le Drame de l'armée française: du Front populaire à Vichy*. Paris: Pygmalion, 2009.

Chimènes, Myriam. "Drôles de concerts. La tournée du duo Bernac-Poulenc en Afrique du Nord au printemps 1940." In *Quatre siècles d'édition musicale. Mélanges offertes à Jean Gribenski*, edited by Joann Élart, Étienne Jardin, and Patrick Taïeb, 325–331. Brussels: Peter Lang, 2014.

Compagnon, Antoine. *Le cas Bernard Faÿ. Du Collège de France à l'indignité nationale*. Paris: Gallimard, 2009.

Courville, Xavier de. *Soixante ans de théâtre en marge des théâtres. Revue de la société d'histoire du théâtre* 31, no. 2 (1979).

Dard, Olivier. "Henri Massis (1886–1970)." In *Le maurrassisme et la culture. L'Action française. Culture, société, politique (III)*, edited by Olivier Dard, Michel Leymarie, and Neil McWilliam, 219–233. Villeneuve d'Ascq: Presses universitaires du Septentrion, 2010.

David, José. "Fini le piano . . ." In *Les français racontent leur guerre*, undated supplement to *Le journal de la France de l'occupation à la libération, les années 40* (1971): 1.

Delmas, Jean. "Huntziger (Charles)." In *Dictionnaire de la Seconde Guerre mondiale*, edited by Philippe Masson, 931–932. Paris: Larousse, 1979.

Dumons, Bruno. "Action Française au féminin: Réseaux et figures militantes au début du XXe siècle." In *L'Action française: culture, société, politique*, edited by Michel Leymarie and Jacques Prévotat, 229–241. Villeneuve d'Ascq: Presses universitaires du Septentrion, 2008.

Elias, Agnès, and Georges Elias. *Artistes au Stalag*. La Crèche: Geste éditions, 2015.

Faÿ, Bernard. *La guerre des trois fous. Hitler-Staline-Roosevelt*. Paris: Perrin, 1968.

Fishman, Sarah. "Grand Delusions: The Unintended Consequences of Vichy France's Prisoner of War Propaganda." *Journal of Contemporary History* 26, no. 2 (1991): 229–254.

Fulcher, Jane F. *The Composer as Intellectual: Music and Ideology in France, 1914–1940*. Oxford: Oxford University Press, 2005.

Gaujac, Paul, et al., eds. *Sedan 1940*. Vincennes: SHAT, 1991.

Gavoty, Bernard. *Alfred Cortot*. Paris: Buchet Chastel, 1995.

Gétreau, Florence. "Les archives de la Société de la musique d'autrefois, 1926–1975." *Fontis Artis Musicae* 54, no. 1 (2007): 38–54.

Gounelle, Claude. *Sedan Mai 1940*. Paris: Presses de la Cité, 1980.

Goutard, Alphonse. "Les Français accueillent l'attaque avec optimisme . . ." *Le journal de la France de l'occupation à la libération, les années 40*, no. 96 (1971): 29.

Groussard, Georges André. *Chemins secrets*. Mulhouse: Bader, 1948.

Haag, Jules. "Un grand Saint-Cyrien blond, à Lesneven un dimanche." *L'Ouest-Éclair* November 14, 1941.

Iglesias, Sara. *Musicologie et Occupation: Science, musique et politique dans la France des années noires*. Paris: Editions de la Maison des sciences de l'homme, 2014.

Joly, Laurent. "La *Revue critique des idées et des livres*. Première dissidence d'Action française ou première génération intellectuelle de maurrassiens indépendents?" In *Le maurrassisme et la culture. L'Action française. Culture, société, politique (III)*, edited by Olivier Dard, Michel Leymarie, and Neil McWilliam, 45–59. Villeneuve d'Ascq: Presses universitaires du Septentrion, 2010.

Kaldor, Pierre. "Entretien avec Maryse Vassvière." *Recherches croisées Aragon/Elsa Triolet* 5 (1994): 237–259.
Le Bail, Karine. *La musique au pas: être musicien sous l'Occupation*. Paris: CNRS, 2016.
Le Boterf, Hervé. *Le théâtre en uniforme: Le spectacle aux armées, de la "drôle de guerre" aux accords d'Evian*. Paris: Editions France-Empire, 1973.
Lioncourt, Guy de. *Un témoignage sur la musique et sur la vie au xx$^e$ siècle*. Paris: L'Arche de Noé, 1956.
Mariat, Jean [pseud. Guy Roissard de Bellet]. *Prisonnier en Allemagne*. Paris: Les Éditions de France, 1941.
Massis, Henri. *Défense de l'Occident*. Paris: Plon, 1927.
———. "Le théâtre de l'Armée." *Les documents du combattant. Bulletin d'information* 5 (March 1, 1940).
———. *Maurras et notre temps*, vol. 2. Paris: La Palatine, 1951.
Monsaingeon, Bruno. *Mademoiselle: Entretiens avec Nadia Boulanger*. Luynes: Van de Velde, 1981.
Murray, Christopher Brent. "Nouveaux regards sur le soldat Messiaen." In *De la guerre dans l'art, de l'art dans la guerre*, edited by David Mastin and Marine Branland, 243–265. Paris: Université Paris 7, 2010.
Paillat, Claude. *Dossiers secrets de la France contemporaine. Le désastre de 1940. La guerre éclair: 10 mai–24 juin 1940*. Paris: Laffont, 1985.
Paxton, Robert O. *L'Armée de Vichy: le corps des officiers français 1940–1944*. Translated by Pierre Longuemar. Paris: Taillandier, 2003.
Richardot, Jean-Pierre. *100.000 morts oubliés: les 47 jours et 47 nuits de la bataille de France: 10 mai–25 juin 1940*. Paris: le Cherche midi, 2009.
Rischin, Rebecca. *For the End of Time: The Story of the Messiaen Quartet*. Ithaca: Cornell University Press, 2006.
Rocolle, Pierre. *La guerre de 1940. La défaite 10 mai-25 juin*. Paris: Armand Colin, 1990.
Ruby, Edmond. *Sedan, terre d'épreuve. Avec la IIe armée Mai-Juin 1940*. Paris: Flammarion, 1948.
Sanos, Sandrine. *The Aesthetics of Hate: Far-Right Intellectuals, Anti-Semitism, and Gender in 1930s France*. Stanford, CA: Stanford University Press, 2013.
Scheck, Raffael. "The Prisoner of War Question and the Beginnings of Collaboration: The Franco-German Agreement of 16 November 1940." *Journal of Contemporary History* 45, no. 2 (2010): 364–388.
Service Historique de la Défense (SHD), Vincennes, France. Conflits et opérations, Seconde Guerre Mondiale, Régions militaires (31 N), Journaux des marches et opérations (34 N).
Simon, Yannick. *Composer sous Vichy*. Lyon: Symétrie, 2009.
Solar, Jean. *Maurice Thiriet*. Paris: Ventadour, 1957.
Sprout, Leslie. "Messiaen, Jolivet, and the Soldier-Composers of Wartime France." *The Musical Quarterly* 87, no. 2 (2004): 259–304.
———. *The Musical Legacy of Wartime France*. Berkeley: University of California Press, 2013.

Streicher, Jean-Claude. *Le général Huntziger: L'"Alsacien" du maréchal Pétain*. Colmar: Do Bentziger, 2014.

Thiriet, Maurice. "Musique au Stalag." In *Art et Connaissance, Le rythme et la vie*, 51–57. Paris: Maurice Mariage, 1942.

Unattributed. "Jean Labusquière." *L'Officiel de la Mode*, December 1941.

———. "Les obsèques du général Huntziger." *L'Ouest-Éclair*, November 17, 1941.

Villier, Claude. "La 'Petite Scène' est mobilisée." *Le Figaro*, March 23, 1940.

Waeber, Jacqueline. "Yvette Guilbert and the Revaluation of the *Chanson Populaire* and *Chanson Ancienne* During the Third Republic, 1889–1914." In *Oxford Handbook of the New Cultural History of Music*, edited by Jane F. Fulcher, 264–306. New York: Oxford University Press, 2014.

Weber, Eugen. *Action Française: Royalism and Reaction in Twentieth-Century France*. Stanford, CA: Stanford University Press, 1962.

Will, Barbara. *Unlikely Collabration: Gertrude Stein, Bernard Faÿ, and the Vichy Dilemma*. New York: Columbia University Press, 2011.

Wilson, Stephen. "The 'Action Française' in French Intellectual Life." *The Historical Journal* 12, no. 2 (1969): 328–350.

Yagil, Limore. "Alfred Cortot, entre mémoire et oubli: le destin d'un grand pianiste." *Guerres mondiales et conflits contemporains* 246, no. 2 (2012): 117–136.

CHRISTOPHER BRENT MURRAY is Maître de conférences in the Department of Musicology at the Université Libre de Bruxelles. He is author (with Y. Balmer and T. Lacôte) of *Le modèle et l'invention: Olivier Messiaen et la technique de l'emprunt*.

PART III

**NATIONAL IMAGINARIES**

EIGHT

# SWING IN THE PROTECTORATE

Czech Popular Music under the
Nazi Occupation, 1938–1945

BRIAN S. LOCKE

IN THE FALL OF 1938, Germany annexed the borderlands of Czechoslovakia—known as the Sudetenland—and within six months the Wehrmacht occupied the rest of the country, which became part of the Third Reich for the duration of the Second World War. Until recently, memoirs and historical accounts of this period have portrayed the seven years of German occupation as a time when everyday Czechs resisted German oppression, be it overtly, covertly, or through some form of (subsequently declared) moral objection. Popular music plays a special role in such narratives, describing how the Czechs defiantly played jazz and swing at the risk of Nazi retribution.[1] Given the Nazis' notorious attacks on "Negro jazz" in the 1938 exhibition *Degenerate Music* and their reputed opposition to American popular culture, conventional wisdom assumes that the German authorities would be especially heavy-handed in enforcing restrictive ideological policies in the lands it occupied. Indeed, one might regard the persistence of Czech jazz and swing music as a potentially powerful and effective vehicle for defying the Germans' attempts to dominate the region and enslave its population, both physically and mentally. Yet popular music during the German occupation of the Czech lands (the so-called Protectorate of Bohemia and Moravia) openly thrived in those years, achieving a high standard of professionalism and attracting a loyal following among Czech listeners. Remarkably, this dedicated listenership even included high-ranking German officials, who treated Bohemia and Moravia as their own "Garden of Eden" where they could indulge hedonistically in the local offerings.[2] Whether by design or happenstance, Czech-language swing in particular was allowed to flourish and was even encouraged by the German authorities, in one form or another, from the initial phase of occupation in October 1938 until the final months of the war.

The remarkable ascendancy of swing during the Protectorate years subverts a number of assumptions about life and culture under the German occupation, undermining accepted historical narratives that the Nazis enforced strict censorship, rooted out all forms of culture deemed "racially inferior," and suppressed the creative impulses of "non-Aryan" Czechs, while privileging the ethnic Germans living in the region. Above all, the phenomenon of its success calls into question postwar accounts that portray the Czechs' cultivation of American-style popular music as an act of resistance.[3] Doubtlessly, for its young listeners and practitioners, the uniquely Czech forms of jazz and swing that flourished during the occupation years played an important role in the formation or preservation of local Czech identity, but much of its implicitly anti-German sentiment had grown out of a long-standing rivalry between neighboring cultures. Significantly, most elements of American-style popular music took root in Prague well before 1938 (some as early as 1919) as an expression of Czech cosmopolitanism in the face of Austro-German cultural hegemony. Nevertheless, the very existence of Czech-language swing under the Protectorate has since acquired an association with anti-Nazi resistance in Czech historiography, whether fully warranted or not.[4] Far from being banned or even marginalized, Czech swing flourished under the Nazi occupation owing to a complex combination of seemingly contradictory forces.

Thus, the precipitous success of swing is consistent with the "Garden of Eden" role assigned to the Protectorate in the years of occupation: the equally sudden decline of swing after the Communist takeover in February 1948, however, marks an even clearer break in Czech cultural history. The Communists' relentless suppression of all vestiges of Western, capitalist culture focused especially on the swing community, and most of its leaders were forced to abandon their careers virtually overnight. This state of affairs prompted many dispossessed musicians and listeners to look back on the years of the Protectorate with a marked degree of nostalgia for the heyday of Czech swing.[5]

In this chapter, I describe the emergence of the Czech jazz community in the early years of the First Czechoslovak Republic (1918–1938) and its development throughout the interwar period under the leadership of the musician and entrepreneur R. A. Dvorský. The second generation of Czech jazz, the practitioners of swing, reached professional status almost exactly at the start of the German occupation. My narrative demonstrates that, even amid social and political upheaval, local artists such as the songwriter Jiří Traxler, the vocalist Inka Zemánková, and their listeners—the Czech variant of zootsuiters known as *potápky*—could rely on a multifaceted music industry established well before the war.[6] To be sure, critical events of the Protectorate years affected the swing generation substantially, such as the Germans' closure of the Czech universities, the assassination of Reinhard Heydrich, and the declaration of Total War throughout the Reich.

Nevertheless, each of these upheavals also witnessed the regeneration of the Czech swing movement, which survived the conflict: it was only the onset of postwar Communism that effectively halted its creative momentum and popular appeal.

### INTERWAR CZECH JAZZ AND THE SWING GENERATION UNDER NAZI OCCUPATION

Before the First World War, as in other European capitals, jazz performance in Prague was limited to a few nightclubs, although urban Czech musicians had little direct contact with other European professionals, let alone Americans. Beginning in 1919, when a new wave of American popular music distribution coincided with the emergence of an independent Czechoslovak state, Czech musicians encountered and embraced almost every form of Western popular culture, from Tin Pan Alley all the way to big band swing.[7] Czechs in the First Republic channeled these cosmopolitan experiences toward defining a new Czech national identity in the modern world after centuries of Austro-German cultural domination. For Czech-speaking citizens of the new nation, kinship with Paris, London, and above all Woodrow Wilson's America took precedence over the cultural subservience to Vienna and Berlin that had prevailed under the Habsburg monarchy.[8]

While English, French, and German sheet music and recordings gradually became available in Prague and other cities, a fledgling industry of Czech jazz rapidly developed into a self-sustaining enterprise. New and/or revamped dance bands modeled themselves diligently on contemporary American combos of the 1920s, fronted by Czech vocalists whose initial repertoire consisted primarily of translated American contrafacts. By 1930, however, homegrown Czech songwriters had begun to flood the local market with new songs exploiting a witty blend of local and imported musical elements, and amalgams such as the "fox-polka" became vehicles for a Czech textual argot that reached near virtuosic complexity in its play with language and meaning. One of the most prolific songwriters of this early period was the talented young tenor and pianist Rudolf Antonín (1899–1967), who moved to Prague in 1919 and began publishing under the pseudonym "R. A. Dvorský."[9] In 1929, R. A. Dvorský and his Melody Boys emerged as the premiere performance group for large-ensemble dance music. Modeled on Paul Whiteman's band, the fifty-piece Melody Boys included sizeable string and woodwind sections and specialized in foxtrots, tangos, and waltzes, genres popular with the older, pre-swing generation.[10] Significantly, Dvorský also expanded the scope of the jazz industry to include newer popular styles and an increasingly large Czech-language repertoire. He thereby sought to open up opportunities for his younger contemporaries, such as the swing-influenced composer and bandleader Jaroslav Ježek (1906–1942) and the journalist Emanuel Uggé (1900–1970).[11] Uggé's Gramoklub Orchestra (Orchestr Gramoklubu), established in 1935, became the first Czech swing group to embrace African American blues and improvisation.[12] Dvorský promoted the younger generation with contracts from local and international recording companies, Czechoslovak Radio, and the Barrandov film studios.[13] In 1932, he purchased the Ultraphon record label and in 1936 founded the publishing company Nakladatelství R. A. Dvorský, which disseminated the vast majority of Czech swing arrangements ranging from commercial dance orchestras to smaller "hot ensembles," instrumental solos, and ubiquitous two-page song sheets (see figs. 8.1 and 8.4).[14] Each of these businesses continued through the Protectorate, ensuring that swing not only survived the arrival of the German occupiers, but grew considerably, despite the upheavals experienced by Czech society.

The first of these upheavals came on September 30, 1938, in Munich, when the British and French prime ministers signed over the Sudetenland—the Czechs' fortified borderlands—to Germany as a final attempt at appeasing Hitler. The Czech president Edvard Beneš went into exile, as the short-lived, collaborationist Second Republic ("Czecho-Slovakia") was formed. This compromise collapsed on March 15, 1939, with the Germans' complete occupation and the creation of the Protectorate. The Wehrmacht troops marched into Prague that same day, unopposed; Hitler arrived on March 16 with his first Reichsprotektor, Konstantin von Neurath.[15] An initial period of martial law gave way on April 15 to a new order for Protectorate inhabitants, including the establishment of the Gruppe für kulturpolitische Angelegenheiten (Group for Cultural Policy Affairs) under the direction of SS-Standartenführer Karl von Gregory, the former print media attaché to the German embassy in Prague.[16] In June, another new agency, the National Professional Employment Center (Národní odborová ústředna zaměstnanecká, or NOÚZ), began a central registry of all professional musicians in the Protectorate, licensing all performances and controlling touring activities for the remainder of the occupation.[17] After August 31, all radio broadcasts were censored, and increasingly restrictive laws reflected patterns throughout Central and Western Europe: initial public resistance was dealt with harshly and decisively, followed by even more limitations on public behavior. By September 1, any anti-German speech was punishable by death. On September 28 and October 28—both dates of Czech nationalist significance—massive demonstrations swept through Prague, and a riot resulted in the shooting death of the student Jan Opletal.[18] His public funeral on November 15 became one of the last open manifestations of Czech resistance, after which several more students were shot, major cultural figures were arrested, and as many as 1,200 young people were imprisoned in Buchenwald. Two days later, the Czech universities were closed. The borders had

Fig. 8.1. *R. A. Dvorský Album 10* (Prague: Nakladatelství R. A. Dvorský, 1939) showing the mixed repertoire of the Melody Boys and iconic cover art designed by Rotterův reklamní ateliér. © OOA-S, Czech Republic 2019. Used by permission.

already been sealed after the Blitzkrieg on Poland, and life in the Protectorate became inescapably grim.

Despite the physical isolation from Western popular culture in the ensuing war years, the Czech swing generation experienced what may be considered its heyday, as artists and listeners succeeded in forming a vibrant swing community. To be sure, the demand for escapism from the growing privations in daily life spurred Dvorský and his younger colleagues to create lighthearted entertainment in their own language: an expression of local identity that was emerging in film and radio, in concert and dance halls, and in recordings and sheet music. But the sudden success of swing in the early Protectorate owes much to the strange array of political, ideological, and demographic shifts that arose out of the conditions of the occupation. That a nominally alien expression of "Judeo-Negroid" culture was allowed to blossom amid an "inferior" subjugated population flies in the face of conventional wisdom surrounding jazz in the Third Reich. Perhaps the result of the Germans' calculated efforts to mollify the Czechs and preserve their "Garden of Eden"—or a reflection of their general inconsistency in applying ideological strictures trumpeted at home—the root causes of the relative tolerance in the Protectorate are amorphous and multifaceted.[19]

The first two years of the war afforded the most liberal atmosphere for cultural expression in Bohemia and Moravia, in both a general sense and more specifically with regard to the cultivation of swing. Indeed, Dvorský's newest enterprise, the Karel Vlach Orchestra (Orchestr Karla Vlacha), began performances in July 1939: together with smaller ensembles led by Karel Slavík (Blue Music) and Emil Ludvík (Hot Kvintet), it became the main conduit for Czech-language swing, employing its major stars. It was in this period that the pianist-songwriter Jiří Traxler (1912–2011), the "hot accordionist" Kamil Běhounek (1916–1983), and the swing vocalist Inka Zemánková (1915–2000) became household names.[20] The first limitations on any performance of swing came with prohibitions on dancing, first temporarily amid the Wehrmacht operations in France and the Low Countries (May 15 to late July 1940), and then definitively from April 6, 1941, in preparation for the push into Yugoslavia and the Soviet Union.[21] After the entrance of the Americans into the war that December, performance of American standards was discouraged, though quite likely continued as an open secret.[22] Yet again, newly written Czech-language swing—now primarily a listener's music, not a dancer's—reaped the benefits. Moreover, the Protectorate capital was a haven for hedonistic pleasures, as documented in Traxler's account of this period: in summer 1940, the hotel where he lived was commandeered as a residence for SS officers on leave (who promptly rendered it unlivable); and the terrace bar at Barrandov was the scene of Wehrmacht carousing during his performances there.[23] Such public displays of German impropriety caused concern with the local Sicherheitsdienst (Security Force), whose report of July 30, 1940, noted uniformed officers dancing at Barrandov, ignoring the initial, temporary ban.[24]

The lax attitude of the German occupiers toward allowing these exuberant expressions of Czech national identity was also a byproduct of the complex relationships among Germans and the various sectors of the population they were now controlling. Obviously the most vulnerable group were the Jews. As of June 21, 1939, von Neurath decreed that the Nuremberg Race Laws would apply in the Protectorate. Non-Jewish Czechs, as members of the Slavic race, were considered inferiors, or *Untermenschen* (though superior to Poles through their supposed racial mixture with Austro-Germans).[25] Despite the Nazi authorities' stated intention to delineate ethnic boundaries in the Protectorate, however, its population continued to be what Bryant refers to as "a hopelessly mixed people": some 22 percent of respondents to the 1930 census declared themselves of German nationality, though a significant proportion of these were Jews, especially in urban areas such as Prague.[26] Moreover, Czechoslovak Jews had begun to shift their allegiance to the Czech community over the previous generation as the latter grew more urban and cosmopolitan.[27] The ethnic Germans, the largest of Czechoslovakia's minorities (which also included significant numbers of Polish, Hungarian, Roma, and Rusyn enclaves), voted overwhelmingly in the 1935 parliamentary elections for Hitler's fifth columnist, Konrad Henlein and his Sudetendeutsche Partei—a victory that supposedly triggered the German annexations of 1938–1939. Contrary to their expectations, however, German Bohemians did not experience a precipitous rise to power after the Munich Agreement (of their number, only Karl Hermann Frank rose to the level of deputy Reichsprotektor), and many complained of their systematic marginalization within the Reich. Neither did the small contingent of Czech fascists (who until recently had been vocally anti-German followers of Mussolini) benefit from the new regime; in fact, von Neurath agreed with the meager request from the near-powerless Czech president, Emil Hácha, that the Czech fascists be kept as far as possible from political power.[28] It is significant that almost all preexistent German Bohemian and Czech fascist newspapers were closed by the first months of the occupation.[29]

This complex array of relationships had correspondingly complex and conflicting effects on the swing community. By the time of the establishment of the Protectorate, all of the Jewish jazz musicians active in interwar Czechoslovakia had either fled or ceased to participate publicly in musical life. Two of Dvorský's colleagues, the bandleaders Harry Osten (born Siegfried Grzyb) and Harry Harden (born David Stoljarovič), emigrated in the spring and autumn of 1938, respectively; Osten signed over his ensemble to Jaroslav Malina, who preserved it intact until the end of the war. Among the younger contingent, the bandleader Milan Halla emigrated in March 1939, although several of his tunes were still performed and even broadcast well into the occupation; Karel Slavík, the (non-Jewish) founder of Blue Music, left for the United States with his Jewish wife around the same time.[30] The brilliant young arranger Fritz (Fricek/Bedřich) Weiss remained in Prague, as did Edith (or Ruth, known as "Duca") Fischerová, one of the first swing vocalists to sing in Czech.[31] Weiss continued his work clandestinely for many bands, who employed him anonymously even after his deportation to Theresienstadt in 1941. Several other Jewish jazz musicians were known to participate in secret jam sessions after curfew in private homes, where louder instruments such as trumpets were avoided for fear of detection by the authorities.[32]

Some ethnic Germans also began to disappear from Czech bands, though not, it would seem, entirely motivated by nationalist or pro-Nazi sympathies.[33] Several were conscripted into the Wehrmacht, as in the case of Gramoklub's top trombonist, Walter Paul, who perished on the Eastern Front in 1941.[34] Indeed, evidence suggests that (non-Jewish) Czech swing musicians experienced greater latitude than did their Sudeten-German counterparts, who as *Volksdeutsche* were held to higher expectations; Czechs, furthermore, were exempt from conscription.[35] One of the tremendous ironies surrounding swing in the Protectorate is that the voices protesting the loudest against Czech jazz were neither the Nazi overlords nor the German Bohemians, but rather the small cadre of ethnically Czech fascist collaborators, seeking to curry favor with Nazi ideologues. Their publications, *Vlajka* (*The Flag*) and especially *Arijský boj* (*Aryan Struggle*), contained page after page of virulent attacks against jazz, its most public representatives (Dvorský, Zemánková, Slavík, and others), and their fan-base, the *potápky*.[36] As the war progressed, intensifying pressure from the contributors of *Arijský boj* had a damaging effect on the public behavior, dress codes, and eventually the musical style of swing.[37]

Another reason why the growing popularity of swing coincided with the years of the Protectorate had to do with the changing situation of Czech youth. Czech swing's core listenership consisted primarily of teenagers and university students: in a strange twist of luck, the Nazis' closure of the Czech universities on October 17, 1939, immediately freed up thousands of young people for musical pursuits. Under any other circumstances, the timing could be considered "perfect": the youths who had played with the Orchestr Gramoklubu had achieved the status of professionals, and their listeners were beginning to find a distinct generational identity—albeit one forged in international humiliation and widespread distrust of their elders. Even as the drama unfolded in Munich the previous September, many of the one million Czechs aged sixteen to twenty-five began strongly identifying as the "saxophone generation" (*saxofonová generace*) or *potápky*.[38] The musical activities of their close contemporaries—Vlach, Běhounek, Traxler, and Zemánková, all employed by Dvorský—shaped the popular experience of swing in the Protectorate.

## JIŘÍ TRAXLER, INKA ZEMÁNKOVÁ, AND THE RISE OF CZECH SWING IN THE PROTECTORATE

In their postwar memoirs, both the composer/performer/arranger Jiří Traxler and the singer Inka Zemánková strived to delineate their roles in Czech swing under the occupation as purveyors of popular entertainment and escapism, as survivors of terrifying experiences, or even (implicitly or explicitly) as figureheads of a form of anti-German cultural resistance. Perhaps most important, however, they offer important glimpses into the ironies of Czech swing's endurance during the Protectorate.

Traxler's autobiography serves as one of the most detailed resources for understanding the swing community. Born in Tábor, Bohemia, in 1912, Traxler had his earliest exposure to popular music from Czechoslovak Radio, which began broadcasting in 1923, and from the BBC, which inspired him in the early 1930s to order sheet music for the latest international titles before they were available in Prague for use by his amateur student jazz ensemble, The Red Ace Players.[39] In 1935, Emanuel Uggé invited Traxler to move to Prague as a pianist for the Orchestr Gramoklubu, and the young musician composed instrumental numbers for the ensemble's inaugural December 1935 concert, attended by Dvorský and Ježek.[40] His role increased to include most of the arranging, and for a brief time he directed the ensemble before its dissolution in 1937. In early 1939, Traxler was performing as the pianist of Blue Music when the Wehrmacht crossed into Czecho-Slovakia to form the Protectorate: the precise moment was marked by the nightclub's owner, a Nazi sympathizer, who donned a swastika at midnight on March 15, 1939, and summarily nullified their contract. "It was unbelievable, but only now did I find out how long our employer, a perfectly accent-free, Czech-speaking Nazi, had waited for this."[41] Nevertheless, Traxler's encounters with Dvorský allowed him to secure his career by signing a five-year publishing contract. At the time, Dvorský's empire was expanding into the realm of swing and promoting the Orchestr Karla Vlacha, which became the premiere representative of Czech swing from 1939 onward under the leadership of Karel Vlach (1911–1986). Vlach's composers, lyricists, and arrangers were contracted through Dvorský, and everything he recorded—on Dvorský's Ultraphon label—was simultaneously published by Nakladatelství R. A. Dvorský (see fig. 8.2).[42]

Traxler's career in the Dvorský–Vlach popular music enterprise continued apace during the first four years of the Protectorate, with increasing success and visibility before the Czech listenership. Each season, as a member of these bands, he took part in one or more extended nightly engagements at major Prague nightclubs or fashionable hotels, a lengthy summer tour throughout the smaller cities of Bohemia and Moravia, and several recording sessions at Ultraphon or live performances on Czech Radio. Dvorský also published a collection of his songs with

Fig. 8.2. Jiří Traxler, Ultraphon recording company publicity photo, ca. 1940. (Traxler estate private ownership, used by permission.)

piano accompaniment for each year.[43] A typical season also featured at least one "monster concert" in Prague, in which multiple bands took part for full-evening performances. In January 1940, these were the "Three Kings' Concerts," named for the participation of Dvorský, Vlach, and Blue Music over several evenings.[44] In November of that same year, Prague's trendy Lucerna Hall hosted its own "Monstre Show" [sic], with performances by no fewer than ten pianists, including Traxler; Dvorský and Vlach's orchestras; a danced swing pantomime; and a grand finale with the entire cast including solos for Běhounek and Zemánková. Privately, the exhausted Dvorský commented, "Never again!"[45]

In his autobiography, Traxler describes a milieu in which freelancing artists could maintain a professional career with relatively little interference from the governing forces of the Protectorate. He lists only a handful of occasions on which he took individual directives from NOÚZ or worked alongside German musicians from the Reich: whether or not (as he later asserted) Traxler himself deliberately kept his distance from contemporary politics, this scenario seems to reflect a degree of latitude afforded Czech-language swing from above. If his music was the locus of overt (or even covert) resistance, this subversion was lost on Germans in more exalted realms who took a keen interest in Traxler's music. His popular foxtrot "Hádej, hádej . . ." (Guess, guess . . .), originally recorded by Dvorský in 1940, attracted the interest of Peter Schaeffers Musikverlag in Berlin, who published it with new German lyrics by Klaus Richter under the suggestive title "Peter, Peter, wo warst du heute nacht?" (Peter, Peter, Where were You Tonight?).[46] In 1941–1942, no less than nine German dance bands recorded it, including Michael Jary's performance of an anonymous arrangement by the Czech Jew Fricek Weiss, who had already been deported to Theresienstadt.[47] Traxler's Protectorate-era success with "Peter, Peter" (as well as occasional requests for German film-score arrangements) was never considered suspect among the Czechs, for whom command performances were part of a passive mode of survival. Decades later, Traxler asserted that active collaboration lay beyond his moral code, citing his refusal of lucrative engagements with German bands; indeed, he subsequently cast aspersions on those who accepted such offers.[48]

Such a precarious balancing act, sustainable for a songwriter, would prove substantially more difficult for the star soloists of Czech swing, who exposed themselves to criticism from the more extreme Czech fascists publishing in *Arijský boj*. The image of Inka Zemánková is indelible in the minds of Czech listeners who lived through the Protectorate era. Born in 1915 as Anna Inéz Koníčková, she worked as a teenager in the cloakroom of Bratislava's Reduta Café, where she began to imitate foreign singers passing through on tour and eventually launched her singing career as "Inka Zemánková" at Zlín only a few weeks before Hitler's annexation of the Sudetenland.[49] As Traxler and his colleagues were writing the hit songs that would define the Protectorate's popular culture, Zemánková reportedly spent hours obsessively poring over the gramophone, trying to capture the nuances of Ella Fitzgerald.[50] To do so, she had to reconcile swing with the Czech language, where the stress patterns are significantly different from those of English, and discovered that Czech's phenomenon of "vowel length"—a double set of long and short vowel durations that produce a noticeable rhythmic pulsation—could be bent toward the new rhythmic style. In the early months of the war, Zemánková performed newly written songs by Běhounek, Traxler, and Alfons Jindra that portrayed her as an ingénue with music befitting a Tin Pan Alley-style character singer, and by 1940–41 she routinely featured songs about the act of singing jazz: Běhounek's "Ráda zpívám hot" (I Like to Sing Hot)

Fig. 8.3. Song sheet cover art with publicity photo of Inka Zemánková. Alfons Jindra, "Dívka k rytmu zrozená" (A Girl Born to Rhythm), Nakladatelství R. A. Dvorský, 1940. © OOA-S, Czech Republic 2019. Used by permission.

and "Má láska je jazz" (Jazz Is My Love), Jindra's "Dívka k rytmu zrozená" (A Girl Born to Rhythm; see fig. 8.3), and Traxler's "Bloudění v rytmu" (Wandering in Rhythm; see fig. 8.4). The novelist Josef Škvorecký (1924–2012) related how Zemánková's innovations in diction appealed to Czech youth, the *potápky*, who modeled an entire system of slang after it.[51] However, her successes also made her a target of print attacks on swing culture in *Arijský boj*, which persisted to

Fig. 8.4. Two-page song sheet with complete melody, chords, and text for Jiří Traxler, "Bloudění v rytmu" (Wandering in Rhythm), Nakladatelství R. A. Dvorský, 1941. Margins include advertisements for swing sheet music by Běhounek, a recent operetta, and Dvorský's recording of Traxler's "Hádej, hádej..." ("Guess, guess..."). Used by permission from the estate of Jiří Traxler.

1944, some of them referencing Zemánková, "the girl born to rhythm," in particular.[52] In response, she retreated by taking an extended engagement with Jaroslav Malina, whose Whiteman-esque jazz orchestra predominantly played slow foxtrots. Her contract with Malina represented not only greater pay and stability, but also the safe harbor of old-fashioned repertoire before a more established listenership. Such were the times that extreme visibility and iconicity could represent personal risk, especially when facing the unwanted scrutiny of *Arijský boj*.[53]

### SWING AMID THE *HEYDRICHIÁDA* AND THE TOTAL WAR, 1941–1945

In early autumn 1941, events unfolded that would result in tragic upheavals for the Protectorate but that testified further to the endurance of Czech swing. Hitler considered von Neurath's relative tolerance and compassion unbefitting his position of Reichsprotektor. For the week of September 14–21, Czech resistance groups ordered a territory-wide boycott of all collaborationist newspapers, provoking a 70 percent drop in urban sales.[54] Two days later, von Neurath was relieved of all duties: his replacement, as so-called "acting" Reichsprotektor, was the SS-Obergruppenführer Reinhard Heydrich, a high-ranking Nazi who had already distinguished himself as co-organizer of *Kristallnacht*, and who would soon engineer the "Final Solution" for Europe's Jews. His work in the Protectorate was swift and vicious. He had already drafted a plan for half of the non-Jewish Czechs to undergo "Germanization" (*Eindeutschung*)—which is to say, reeducation and assimilation based on pseudoscientific racial testing—and the other, less suitable half deported to the East as slaves.[55] Heydrich's attempts to crush the remnants of Czech resistance were much more public. Within days of becoming acting Reichsprotektor, he had the prime minister arrested as a leader of the Resistance and Prague's mayor executed. These events provoked the London-based Czech government-in-exile to take drastic measures: on December 28, 1941, they launched Operation Anthropoid, wherein Czech paratroopers would drop into the Protectorate to assassinate Heydrich.[56] They succeeded: on May 27, 1942, Jozef Gabčík and Jan Kubiš ambushed Heydrich's car, and the Nazi leader died eight days later from his injuries. The assassination, known in Czech as the *Heydrichiáda*, unleashed the full fury of Nazi reprisals on the Czech people: all high-profile prisoners seized by the Gestapo were executed. Most infamously, the villages of Lidice and Ležáky were razed to the ground and all but a few inhabitants put to death. Roughly 13,000 non-Jewish Czechs were arrested and 5,000 killed in retaliation. The Heydrichiáda also propelled the Final Solution that Heydrich himself had initiated. He had previously ordered Adolf Eichmann to register all Jews in the Protectorate on October 1, 1941; the first transports left Prague on October 17 for the Łódź Ghetto in central Poland. On November 24, Jews were sent to convert the historic garrison town of Terezín, once built to house the troops of Empress Maria Theresa, into the concentration camp at Theresienstadt. It would soon become a collection point for all Protectorate Jews (a process accelerated by Heydrich's assassination) and was later infamously exploited to represent a "model ghetto" in an elaborate hoax for the visiting Red Cross in July 1944. Meanwhile, the first Jewish transports had already left Theresienstadt for Auschwitz–Birkenau on October 26, 1942.

The initial phases of Heydrich's new order affected Czech swing in significant ways. Czechs had lived through a relatively benign occupation to this point: theirs had been a nonmilitary annexation, and the sudden disappearance of citizens off their streets caught them unawares. Many Jewish musicians were among the first deportees to Theresienstadt, including the twenty-two-year-old Fricek Weiss on December 4, 1941. Weiss had developed into one of the most promising swing arrangers in the Prague community.[57] He had not performed publicly since 1939 but was employed steadily, albeit clandestinely, as an arranger for both Vlach's and Emil Ludvík's big bands, and many of his tunes were recorded and played, unwittingly, on Nazi-censored radio.[58] Weiss continued to arrange for Vlach and Ludvík even in Theresienstadt. In January 1943 he was among the founding members of the Ghetto Swingers, who performed for the Red Cross prior to the ensemble's deportation to the gas chambers at Auschwitz, where they arrived on September 28, 1944.[59] The new order also emboldened the fanatics writing for *Arijský boj* to intensify their attacks on Czech swing culture. Their public identification of the Jewish painter Robert Guttmann as the "first *potápka*" (*prapotápka*) had already resulted in his deportation; their continued attacks on the community ensured that any behaviors, clothing styles, and speech patterns associated with swing listenership disappeared from public view during 1942.[60]

But the new order also unexpectedly secured the perseverance of Czech swing. In summer 1942, the collaborator Emanuel Moravec established the Kuratorium pro výchovu mládeže v Čechách a na Moravě (Institute for Youth Education in Bohemia and Moravia), ostensibly a replacement for the universities closed three years earlier, but more accurately a means to control young Czechs' free time and prepare them for forced labor.[61] Nevertheless, such restrictions also bore unforeseen benefits to musical activity: the 8 p.m. curfew imposed on Czech youth made exception for attendance at concerts and theaters. Another directive, the *Stilllegungsaktion* of June 9, 1942, officially closed all music cafés and nightclubs in the Protectorate (both Sudeten-German and Czech) as unnecessary for the war effort; but Czech businesses circumvented the rule by reclassifying themselves as variety theaters, much to the dismay of their disenfranchised German-speaking counterparts.[62]

Despite its tightening of control over the Protectorate, the fortunes of the Thousand-Year Reich were about to turn. Autumn and winter 1942/43 witnessed the Battle of Stalingrad and Rommel's defeat in North Africa, followed shortly by Allied gains on all fronts. The Protectorate was dead center within Nazi-conquered Europe, however, and the Czechs could not hope for swift liberation. On 18 February 18, 1943, Joseph Goebbels's "Sportpalast Speech" gave the signal for *Totaleinsatz* (Total War), compelling all able-bodied citizens of the Reich toward Final Victory. As noncitizens, some 400,000 Czech men and women were pressed into a forced-labor contingent for the remainder of the war, and it became the duty of Czech entertainers to boost their morale.[63] Yet again, Czechs played primarily for other Czechs, though now in horrifying conditions imposed by the German authorities via their central employment registry, NOÚZ. These work camps—at industrial construction sites and armament factories—were among the highest-risk targets for Allied bombardment, potentially a death sentence at any moment.[64] Inka Zemánková was among those who performed. As she related: "At that time, the majority of our professional musicians encountered this. It didn't work to protest, but on the other hand there was the feeling that one is playing for people who maybe at such a time, in a hostile environment, needed most to hear Czech songs and their favorite singers. And how proud they were of us too!"[65]

In such times, the lines between collaboration, opportunism, and artistic survival were hard to distinguish. For bandleaders, the decisions were dire, as they held the fates of multiple musician–employees in their hands. Both Dvorský and Vlach disbanded their ensembles in 1944, thereby saving many musicians from this form of Totaleinsatz.[66]

These measures would bring the history of Protectorate swing to its last chapter, for both performers and listeners alike. In the last year of the war, the public life of professional musicians ground to a halt, and the bulk of swing performance shifted to amateurs, both in Prague and throughout the country. In June 1944, these rural activities resulted in the last great concert festival of the Protectorate, a competition of amateur small-town bands held at Prague's Lucerna Hall.[67] Traxler, Běhounek, and other veteran professionals served on the adjudication panel. The amateur competition was so successful that it spawned another legendary student-led effort: the Prague teenagers Lubomír Dorůžka and Milouš Vejvoda began to publish a clandestine journal for swing fans. Titled *Okružní korespondence* (*Circular Correspondence*)—and ironically abbreviated *O.K.*—it kept their far-flung readers up to date with individually typed copies distributed by bicycle around the countryside.[68]

The Protectorate ended with Germany's capitulation, but the professionals of Czech swing who had maintained their art under the pressures of Nazi occupation found a decidedly less tolerant regime in the Communists. Even before the start of the Czechoslovak Socialist Republic in February 1948, Western popular culture was viewed with increasing suspicion (ostensibly as a reflection of the betrayal at Munich in 1938), and the new regime further formalized the exclusion of all types of jazz from public life. Ultimately, every single performer faced a choice of whether to submit to state control or to abandon one's career—or homeland—entirely. Dvorský, the debonair leader of a bourgeois music empire, was reduced to the status of a copy editor when his businesses were nationalized in 1948; Traxler's elegiac song "Starý strom" (The Old Tree) was Dvorský's final song publication.[69] That same year, Traxler was blacklisted for brazenly programming Glenn Miller's "American Patrol" on a live radio broadcast; his career in ruin, he defected to West Germany on the night of December 31, 1949, and eventually settled in Canada. In 1951, the Communist authorities staged a sham "Singers' Festival" for popular artists, each of whom performed before a (supposed) prize jury: in fact, these were party functionaries tasked with removing swing musicians from public life. Zemánková—the festival's star attraction—proceeded to sing in her signature style and immediately had her performers' union card revoked; she spent several years driving tractors.[70]

The writings of Josef Škvorecký document the final chapter of swing in the Protectorate in vivid detail but with a significant degree of nostalgia for a world lost to Communist purges. A nineteen-year-old resident of Náchod in the northeastern Bohemian borderlands in 1943, Škvorecký was a high-school graduate and forced laborer for the local Messerschmidt factory.[71] He was also a passionate follower of swing, as both a listener and an amateur tenor saxophonist. Through Škvorecký's eyes, we have a rare viewpoint from a young Protectorate listener. Škvorecký gives us what the recorded and printed music cannot: the rich meanings this music had for Czech youth, especially during the late years of the Protectorate. Most of his testimony comes through in five novels (or rather, thinly veiled autobiographies) featuring his alter ego Danny Smiřický, beginning with his years as a swing-obsessed teenager around 1941 to his post-1989 return from Toronto exile; in several smaller works, such as *The Bass Saxophone*, that use a similar, but unnamed narrator; and in his nonfictional autobiographies, most important the essay "Red Music." Škvorecký's band was also called Red Music, "which in fact was a misnomer, since the name had no political connotations: there was a band in Prague that called itself Blue Music, ... so we called ours Red."[72] Not long after liberation, Škvorecký—a budding professional novelist—began to memorialize his Protectorate-era experiences with swing. In 1949, he completed a novel, *The Cowards* (*Zbabělci*), set in the final days of the war: significantly, it begins at a rehearsal of his alter ego Danny's band.[73] It would be the first of many reminiscences he employed throughout his career, portraying the tremendous emotional power that swing had for the author, often in a stream-of-consciousness style of writing that mimics improvisation. Over the first two decades of Communism and two more of Canadian exile, escapist nostalgia for this lost era pervaded his work. It is fair to say that, for his Czech (and non-Czech) readers, Škvorecký's personal vision served as the dominant narrative of Czech music and society during the Second World War for almost half a century. Only Škvorecký's generation, the *potápky* listeners who reached adulthood after the Protectorate, attempted to preserve its legacy, though now for reasons of nostalgia, resistance to Communist repression, and escapism. From the earliest days of his literary career in Prague, Škvorecký faithfully evoked the idols of his youth, and he continued to do so once he defected to Canada after the failure of Prague Spring in 1968. Zemánková appears by name in both *The Bass Saxophone* and "Red Music," but also crosses into fiction—in "Song of the Forgotten Years" and "Eine kleine Jazzmusik"—whenever female singers perform Traxler's "Wandering in Rhythm," their hit from 1941.[74] Ensconced as a leader of the Czech diaspora in Toronto, Škvorecký founded Sixty-Eight Publishers for dissident and exile literature, a series that eventually included Traxler's autobiography. Both gentlemen would be seminal in the post-Communist revival of Czech swing after 1989.

Marked by vicissitudes of tolerance, rejection, dictatorial repression, and escapist nostalgia, the popularity and success of Czech swing during the Protectorate is a history filled with ironies. A guilty pleasure for Nazi officials indulging in a "Garden of Eden," it did much to shape the identity of a young generation of Czech listeners who, despite the privations of wartime occupation, rode an international wave of Western popular culture. Ultimately, it was not the Germans who silenced their music, but rather the ideological zealots from within the Czech community itself—first the fascists at *Arijský boj* and then, with much greater efficacy, the Communists—who sought to exclude swing from a narrow, anti-cosmopolitan definition of Czech identity.

## NOTES

1. One of the most authoritative publications on Czech popular music, Kotek's *Dějiny české populární hudby a zpěvu*, vol. 2: 1918–1968, divides its wartime narrative into two chapters, titled "Swing pod hákovým křížem" (Swing beneath the Swastika) and "Hudba jako součást vzdoru a odboje proti okupantům" (Music as an Element of Defiance and Resistance against the Occupiers), 163–200. Peter Demetz's popular history, *Prague in Danger*, contains a brief section on "Protectorate Jazz" within his chapter "Terror and Resistance," 107–114. Neither text contains tangible evidence of anti-Nazi resistance. All translations are mine unless otherwise indicated.

2. Koura, *Swingaři a potápky v protektorátní noci*, 659–660; Bryant, *Prague in Black*, 114–119.

3. Michael Kater asserts that "despite all the polemics, jazz would never be officially banned" in the Third Reich. Kater, *Different Drummers*, 33.

4. The work of novelist and essayist Josef Škvorecký (discussed in detail later in this chapter) has played a central role in the discourse of Czech swing as "resistance," albeit on both sides of the question. Although he rejected the notion that the music was itself a form of protest during the Protectorate, he claimed the catharsis it provoked could become political in the face of totalitarianism: "But of course, when the lives of individuals and communities are controlled by powers that themselves remain uncontrolled ... then creative energy becomes a protest." (He almost immediately recants: "But even then, protest was one of the lesser reasons [we played]. Primarily, we loved that music that we called jazz ..."). Škvorecký, "Red Music," 83–84.

5. A brief list of these musicians' memoirs includes those of Kamil Běhounek, Lubomír Dorůžka, Zdeněk Novák, Zdeněk Petr, Josef Škvorecký, Jiří Traxler, and Inka Zemánková. Several of these are discussed in the current chapter.

6. The word *"potápka"* (pl. *potápky*) is more commonly used to indicate a species of diving bird, known as grebe in English. The origin of the term and reasons for its choice as a name for Czech swing listeners are unclear, but a variety of theories exist, mostly proposing either the outlandish (bird-like) apparel, the diving motions of the swing dances, or both. See Koura, *Swingaři a potápky v protektorátní noci*, 408–493.

7. See Kotek, *Kronika české synkopy*, vol. 1: 1903–1938, 17–39.

8. Wilson was lionized during the First Republic as one of the founders of Czechoslovakia (alongside the Czechs' "president-liberator," Tomáš Masaryk) at the Paris Peace Conference of 1919; dozens of cities named modern, arterial streets or major train stations after him (e.g., Wilsonovo nádraží, Prague), many of which remain today. See discussion in Margaret Macmillan, *Paris 1919*, 229–242.

9. Born in Dvůr Králové nad Labem, Bohemia, Dvorský derived his pseudonym from the adjectival form of "Dvůr." He legally changed his surname in 1925. Vladimír Bittner, *R. A. Dvorský*, 25.

10. The name "Melody Boys" was always rendered in English. Occasionally the full name appeared in polyglot fashion as *R. A. Dvorský a jeho Melody Boys*. Many other contemporary Czech bands followed this trend (see later in this chapter).

11. The music of Jaroslav Ježek dominated the listening experience of the 1930s: as in-house composer of the Liberated Theater (Osvobozené divadlo), he was able to trace the trends of American popular music—away from Whiteman toward Duke Ellington and Benny Goodman—with a high level of professionalism and personal creativity. His music for twenty plays and five films accompanied the political satire of the era's most iconic comedians, Jiří Voskovec and Jan Werich: after 1933, Ježek's jazz-band recordings became synonymous with anti-fascist resistance. See Holzknecht, *Jaroslav Ježek a Osvobozené divadlo*, 2nd ed.; and Cinger, *Šťastné blues*. Uggé's groundbreaking 1932 article was "Hot Jazz," which closely parallels the contemporary work of his Parisian counterparts, Charles

Delaunay and Hugues Panassié. Emanuel Uggé, "Hot Jazz," *Společenský skeč* 8–9 (1932/33): 83, reproduced in Doružka and Poledňák, *Československý jazz*, 43–47.

12. The ensemble's first concert took place on December 16, 1935. See Doružka and Poldeňák, *Československý jazz*, 47–52; and Poledňák, "Bod kristalizace," 4–13.

13. Bittner, *R. A. Dvorský*, 30–45.

14. Between 1936 and 1948, Dvorský's company published 515 song sheets (*popěvky*), consisting of a vocal part with text and, occasionally, chord symbols. Other solo and ensemble publication series were derived from this larger catalogue. Publications frequently made use of all available space to advertise other branches of the Dvorský empire, calling the consumer's attention to Ultraphon recordings, Barrandov films, and yet more sheet music. See figure 8.4.

15. The Second Republic government, led by Emil Hácha, ordered Czech citizens not to resist the Wehrmacht, for fear of widespread destruction and loss of life. This potentially treasonous directive has been hotly debated ever since; it became one of the charges against Hácha in postwar Czechoslovak tribunals. See Bryant, *Prague in Black*, 41–45 and 253.

16. Koura, *Swingaři a potápky v protektorátní noci*, 640; 644. On September 18, 1939, von Gregory's section became Abteilung IV of the Reichsprotektor's office, responsible for censorship and control of all propaganda, film, literature, music, and art.

17. Pokorný, "Práce pro Říši a Národní odborová ústředna zaměstnanecká," 45–50. For more on forced labor and NOÚZ, see below.

18. September 28 is St. Wenceslas's Day (a.k.a. Svatý Václav, the patron saint of Bohemia) and October 28 is the anniversary of Czechoslovak independence. Prior public demonstrations of Czech nationalism (however subdued) occurred in Prague on May 6 and 7 to commemorate the reburial of the Czech romantic poet Karel Hynek Mácha and on June 6 for Jan Hus Day. Smaller commemorative acts occurred on April 20 (for Masaryk, deliberately on Hitler's birthday), September 30 (the first anniversary of the Munich Agreement), and December 28 (Woodrow Wilson's birthday), 1939. Opletal died of his wounds on November 11. See discussion in Demetz, *Prague in Danger*, 47–51 and 77–82.

19. Josef Škvorecký reasoned that the Germans' "rule in Bohemia was less conspicuously bloody" due to its status as "a heavily industrialized country, famous for its armament factories, and the Nazis needed to maintain production…" Škvorecký, "I Was Born in Náchod…," 26. See also Bryant, *Prague in Black*, 76–84.

20. The 1938 late summer season in the modern industrial town of Zlín—a cosmopolitan hub for young international workers, thanks to the Báťa Shoe Company—served to cement the place of swing within Czech popular culture and witnessed the start of many solo careers, most notably that of Zemánková. When the musicians returned to Prague in early 1939, the best players joined Blue Music, which also provided the first professional engagements for Traxler and Běhounek. See the discussion in Suchý, *Inka Zemánková*, 18–32.

21. Koura, *Swingaři a potápky v protektorátní noci*, 483–489; Kotek, *Dějiny*, 165. Dance classes were still permitted, however, and thus hundreds of Czech youth sought refuge in studios across the Protectorate.

22. Koura, *Swingaři a potápky v protektorátní noci*, 552.

23. Traxler, *Já nic, já muzikant*, 224–225.

24. Národní Archiv, fond 114, sign. 114-312-1, karton 311; Prague SD daily report 174/40 (July 30, 1940), 2. Quoted in Koura, *Swingaři a potápky v protektorátní noci*, 676.

25. Bryant, *Prague in Black*, 50–57.

26. Ibid., 18.

27. Cohen, *The Politics of Ethnic Survival*, 100–108.

28. Demetz, *Prague in Danger*, 22–26 and 44–46.

29. Ibid., 33–39. This included the German-Liberal newspapers *Prager Presse*, *Deutsche Zeitung Bohemia*, and *Prager Tagblatt*; and albeit temporarily, the Czech-fascist *Vlajka* (see further discussion later in this chapter).

30. Koura, *Swingaři a potápky v protektorátní noci*, 641. According to Zdeněk Novák, the majority of Halla's group, Swing Rhythm, was comprised of Prague Jews, most of whom emigrated during the Second Republic. See Novák, *Swing a svoboda za mřížemi*, 21–24. Blue Music continued for approximately a year longer under the directorship of drummer Jan Rychlík and pianist Jiří Verberger, after which point its members were absorbed into other ensembles.

31. Fischerová sang with both Dvorský and Blue Music. Nothing further is known about the fate of Fischerová in the Protectorate, as her name does not appear in the documentation of the Jewish Museum in Prague. Three recordings of her voice survive, one potentially from as late as 1940. Traxler, *Já nic, já muzikant*, 133; email from Gabriel Gössel, August 10, 2016.

32. Koura, *Swingaři a potápky v protektorátní noci*, 642; and Novák, *Swing a svoboda za mřížemi*, 22–23.

33. Traxler, *Já nic, já muzikant*, 195–196.

34. Ibid., 102. Traxler recalled only three German Bohemian jazz musicians who ever wore a swastika on their lapels. Ježek's former jazz pianist from the Liberated Theater, Harry von Noé, was also conscripted into the Wehrmacht. Having survived the war, he was ostracized as a collaborator and forcibly expelled to Austria in 1945.

35. Koura, *Swingaři a potápky v protektorátní noci*, 660.

36. *Vlajka*, the mouthpiece of the Czech nationalist/anti-Semitic movement of the same name, began its run in 1928 and, after a brief closure at the end of the First Republic, operated from June 1939 to July 1942 (when its publishers were sent to Dachau). On September 10, 1939, its authors attacked Dvorský for having used a Jewish-owned advertising firm, Rotterův reklamní ateliér, for the design of his iconic logo, seen in Figure 8.1 and Figure 8.3; quoted in Kotek and Hořec, *Kronika české synkopy*, vol. 2: 1939–61, 65. *Arijský boj* began publication on May 18, 1940, and continued weekly until April 15, 1945. It regularly featured racially motivated attacks on swing, whose practitioners were castigated as "false Jewish musicians"

(*židovští falešní muzikanti*): "Instead of art, the Jews in music have given jazz as a substitute—their racial pig swill" (*Místo umění dali Židé v hudbě náhradou jazz— své rasové svinstvo*). "Falešní proroci," *Arijský boj* 1/11 (July 27, 1940): 2, quoted in Koura, *Swingaři a potápky v protektorátní noci*, 92. For other examples see Koura, *Swingaři a potápky v protektorátní noci*, 448–451; and Brabec, "Antisemitská literatura v době nacistické okupace."

37. For further discussion of *Arijský boj*, see below.

38. The phrase "saxofonová generace" first appeared in a recorded dialogue by the comedians Jiří Voskovec and Jan Werich as early as 1934. The first known mention of *potápky* in print dates from March 20, 1940, though the movement itself predates the occupation. See Koura, *Swingaři a potápky v protektorátní noci*, 408–493, especially 447 and 483.

39. Traxler, *Já nic, já muzikant*, 36–41.

40. This was a pivotal encounter, for soon Ježek's own swing band would record two more Traxler originals. In April 1938, Ježek approached Traxler as a possible assistant conductor for the Liberated Theater, but it was not to be; the theater closed in October 1939 and Ježek fled into American exile the following January. Ibid., 83; 105; 108–109; 129–132.

41. "Bylo to k neuvěření, ale teď jsem se přece jenom dozvěděl, nač náš zaměstnavatel, perfektně a bez přízvuku česky mluvící nacista, tak dlouho čekal." Ibid., 137.

42. Dorůžka and Ducháč, *Karel Vlach*, 28–48.

43. Dvorský published five songbooks devoted exclusively to Traxler's music between 1939 and 1946. In the first three seasons, Traxler's hit swing numbers included "Všemu se usmívám" (I Smile at Everything), "Bloudění v rytmu" (Wandering in Rhythm), "To si pamatuj" (Remember This), and "Bláznivý den" (Crazy Day).

44. Dorůžka and Poledňák, *Československý jazz*, 60. The concerts' name probably also references the season of Epiphany, the "Feast of the Three Kings" (*Svátek Tří králů*).

45. "Nikdy více!" In his autobiography, Traxler's sole caption below the poster for the "Monstre Show" is "Hrůza!" (Horror!). Traxler, *Já nic, já muzikant*, 168–170.

46. The song was later included in the anthology *Meine Lieblingsschlager* (Berlin: Peter Schaeffers Musikverlag, 1942), along with other German-language hits of the season.

47. Peter Kreuder, Peter Igelhoff, Michael Jary, and Hans Carste are mentioned in Traxler, *Já nic, já muzikant*, 172 and 474. The recordings of Willy Berking, Eugen Jahn, Horst Winter, Tullio Mobiglia, Die Piccolominis, and a German-language version by Dvorský are listed on undated documents in the composer's personal papers. Traxler, *Já nic, já muzikant*, 172, and personal interview, 2010.

48. The composer describes in detail his rejection of offers to arrange music for Peter Kreuder and his deliberate evasion of summons to work for the Deutsches Tanz- und Unterhaltungsorchester, a Berlin ensemble that had relocated to Prague

in 1943, in Traxler, *Já nic, já muzikant*, 222–226. See also Kater, *Different Drummers*, 168–170.

49. A full account of Zemánková's early life is given in Suchý, *Inka Zemánková*, 10–18.

50. Běhounek, *Má láska je jazz*, 114.

51. Škvorecký, "Red Music," 90; see also Koura, *Swingaři a potápky v protektorátní noci*, 531–544.

52. Koura, *Swingaři a potápky v protektorátní noci*, 451 and 592; Dorůžka and Poledňák, *Československý jazz*, 64–65.

53. Cf. the role of *Arijský boj* in the arrest of *potápka* leader Robert Guttmann, later in this chapter.

54. Bryant, *Prague in Black*, 132–133.

55. Excerpts of Heydrich's speech of October 2, 1941, before the leading Protectorate government bureaucrats at Prague's Černín Palace, are particularly revealing. "There are things that divide my task here into two rather large and clear stages or areas of responsibility. The one is the preliminary, wartime task and the second is the introduction of a farsighted, final task. The first one, the preliminary task, is dictated by the necessity of wartime leadership. Thus, I need peace in the region, so that the worker, the Czech worker, will work at full strength toward the German war effort and so that, in view of the huge presence of armaments industries here, we do not interrupt the supply and development of armaments. This includes giving the Czech workers something to eat of course—if I may say so, so that they can fulfill their work. But one should also pay close attention that the Czech does not follow his instincts to exploit the emergency situation of the Reich in order to extract his own private, Czech benefit. This preliminary task requires firstly that we show the Czechs once and for all who is master of the house, so that he knows fully that here, German interests dictate [policy] and the Reich is the top priority....

"Gentlemen, the final solution will have to include the following: that this region must finally be settled with Germans. This region forms part of the heart of the Reich and we can never tolerate—as the development of German history shows—that any dagger-thrusts against the Reich ever come from this region again. Regarding the ultimate Germanization of this region, I do not wish to say: We should now use the old methods of making this Czech garbage German, but rather quite plainly: it starts today with things that can already be done in a disguised manner. To gain an overview of what part of the people in this region is Germanizable, I have to take stock of its racial-*völkisch* makeup. To this end, I must have the opportunity, through various methods and by the most circuitous back-routes, to someday scan the völkisch and racial aspect of the entire population. Whether this is with the Waffen-SS mobile x-ray unit [*Röntgensturmbann*], by examining a school, or whether I racially overwhelm the youth by establishing a form of labor service—I must have a complete picture of the people and then I will be able to say that the population appears to be such and such. There are the following [types of] people: some are racially pure and favorably inclined, which makes it easy—these we can Germanize. Then we have the others who are the opposite: racially inferior and hostile. I have to get these people out. There is a lot of room in the East. Then in between there lies a middle layer, which I have to test thoroughly. In this layer there are the racially inferior but favorably inclined, and the racially pure but hostile ones."

("Das sind Dinge, die meine Aufgabe hier in zwei ganz grosse und klare Etappen und Aufgabengebiete teilen. Das Eine ist die kriegsmässige Nahaufgabe und das Zweite ist die Einleitung einer weitsichtigen Endaufgabe. Die erste, die Nahaufgabe ist diktiert von den Notwendigkeiten der Kriegsführung. Ich brauche also Ruhe im Raum, damit der Arbeiter, der tschechische Arbeiter, für die deutsche Kriegsleistung hier vollgültig seine Arbeitskraft einsetzt und damit wir bei dem riesigen Vorhandensein von Rüstungsindustrien hier den Nachschub und die rüstungsmässige Weiterentwicklung nicht aufhalten. Dazu gehört, dass man den tschechischen Arbeitern natürlich das an Fressen geben muss—wenn ich es so deutlich sagen darf, dass er seine Arbeit erfüllen kann. Es gehört aber auch dazu aufzupassen, dass der Tscheche nach seiner Eigenart nicht diese Notlage des Reiches benutzt, um für sich privaten und eigenen tschechischen Sondernutzen herauszuholen. Diese Nahaufgabe setzt voraus, dass wir zunächst einmal den Tschechen zeigen, wer Herr im Hause ist, dass er genau weiss, hier diktiert das deutsche Interesse und hier ist letzten Endes entscheidend das Reich....

"Meine Herren, die Endlösung wird folgendes mit sich bringen müssen: dass dieser Raum einmal endgültig deutsch besiedelt werden muss. Dieser Raum ist ein Herzstück des Reiches und wir können nie dulden,—das zeigt die Entwicklung der deutschen Geschichte—dass aus diesem Raum immer wieder die Dolchstösse gegen das Reich kommen. Zur endgültigen Eindeutschung dieses Raumes will ich nicht etwa sagen: Wir wollen nach alter Methode nun versuchen, dieses Tschechengesindel deutsch zu machen, sondern ganz nüchtern: das setzt schon bei den Dingen an, die heute bereits getarnt eingeleitet werden können. Um zu übersehen, was von diesen Menschen in diesem Raum eindeutschbar ist, muss ich eine Bestandsaufnahme machen in rassisch-völkischer Beziehung. D.h. also, ich muss durch die verschiedensten Methoden, mit den verschiedensten Hintertürchen die Gelegenheit haben, diese Gesamtbevölkerung einmal 'völkisch und rassisch' abzutasten. Ob mit dem Röntgensturmbann, durch Untersuchung einer Schule oder ob ich die Jugend bei der Bildung eines angeblichen Arbeitsdienstes rassisch überhole – ich muss ein Gesamtbild des Volkes haben und dann kann ich sagen, so und so sieht die Bevölkerung aus. Da gibt es folgende Menschen: Die einen sind gutrassig und gutgesinnt, das ist ganz einfach, die können wir eindeutschen. Dann haben wir die anderen, das sind die Gegenpole: schlechtrassig und schlechtgesinnt. Diese Menschen muss ich hinausbringen. Im Osten ist viel Platz. Dann bleibt in der Mitte nun ein Mittelschicht, die ich genau durchprüfen muss. Da sind in dieser Schicht schlechtrassig Gutgesinnte und gutrassig Schlechtgesinnte.") Printed in Kárný and Milotová, eds., *Protektorátní politika Reinharda Heydricha*, doc. 9, 106, 109. For a more complete discussion of Heydrich's Germanization program, see Bryant, *Prague in Black*, 139–166.

56. Bryant, *Prague in Black*, 167–172.

57. Kotek and Hořec, *Kronika české synkopy*, vol. 2, 1939–61, 72–78.

58. The most noteworthy of these was Michael Jary's recording of Traxler's "Peter, Peter, wo warst du heute nacht." Several of his arrangements appear on the CD *Navzdory osudu/In Defiance of Fate* (Radioservis CD ŽMP006, 2003).

59. Coco Schumann detailed his experiences as drummer for the Ghetto Swingers in *The Ghetto Swinger*, 37–52. Schumann recounted that Weiss, although initially selected by Josef Mengele to survive, voluntarily requested to stay with his parents. According to Dorůžka, Weiss perished on his twenty-fifth birthday, September 28, 1944. Dorůžka, "Jazzman Fritz Weiss navzdory osudu."

60. Koura, *Swingaři a potápky v protektorátní noci*, 496–499.

61. As the Zlín newspaper *Svět* crowed, "Mathematics instead of swing!" ("Místo swingu matematiku!"), quoted in ibid., 700.

62. The entire edict is reprinted in Kokošková, Pažout, and Sedláková, eds., *Pracovali pro Třetí říši*, 136–138. See also Koura, *Swingaři a potápky v protektorátní noci*, 704.

63. *Im Totaleinsatz: Zwangsarbeit der tschechischen Bevölkerung für das Dritte Reich*, Exhibition Catalogue. See, for example, Bittner, *R. A. Dvorský*, 55; Dorůžka and Ducháč, *Karel Vlach*, 44–45; Traxler, *Já nic, já muzikant*, 225–226.

64. Dorůžka and Ducháč mention that "Several musicians ... paid for it with their life" ("Někteří hudebníci ... to zaplatili životem"), though they offer no documented examples. Dorůžka and Ducháč, *Karel Vlach*, 44.

65. "To tenkrát potkalo většinu našich profesionálních muzikantů. Protestovat nešlo, ale na druhé straně tu byl pocit, že se hraje pro lidi, kteří v daném okamžiku asi nejvíc potřebují slyšet v nepřátelském prostředí české písničky a své oblíbené zpěváky. Však oni na nás byli pyšní!" Quoted in Suchý, *Inka Zemánková*, 47.

66. Bittner, *R. A. Dvorský*, 59; Dorůžka and Ducháč, *Karel Vlach*, 45.

67. The program is reproduced in Kotek and Hořec, *Kronika české synkopy*, vol. 2: 1939–61, 88–89.

68. Several excerpts of *O.K.* are reproduced in Kotek and Hořec, *Kronika české synkopy*, vol. 2: 1939–61, 87–92. Dorůžka became one of the most important historians of jazz through the years of Communist Czechoslovakia.

69. Dvorský was arrested in 1953 for attempting to defect to the West; he was incarcerated for three years. See Bittner, *R. A. Dvorský*, 61–71.

70. For details of Zemánková's later career (including a documentary reconstruction of the events at the Singers' Festival), see Suchý, *Inka Zemánková*, 52–69.

71. Škvorecký, "I Was Born in Náchod," 28.

72. Škvorecký, "Red Music," 83. The five "Danny novels" are, in order of completion: *The Cowards*, 1949; *The Miracle Game*, 1972; *The Swell Season*, 1975; *The Engineer of Human Souls*, 1977; and *Ordinary Lives*, 2004. *The Bass Saxophone*

was written in 1967. Náchod's more accomplished band, led by Miroslav Zachoval, competed in the June 1944 festival at Lucerna Hall; Škvorecký's band focused on Dixieland revival with Bob Crosby as their model. For a detailed examination of popular music life in Protectorate-era Náchod, see Škvorecký and Mědílek, *Swing na malém městě*.

73. Škvorecký, *The Cowards*, 11–32. In the scene, the band rehearses "Annie Laurie," "Bob Cats," and "Riverside Blues."

74. Škvorecký, "Song of the Forgotten Years," 248–259; and Škvorecký, "Eine kleine Jazzmusik," 109–127.

## BIBLIOGRAPHY

Běhounek, Kamil. *Má láska je jazz*. Toronto: Sixty-Eight Publishers, 1986.
Bittner, Vladimír. *R. A. Dvorský: král české taneční hudby*. Prague: Editio Praga, 1998.
Brabec, Jiří. "Antisemitská literatura v době nacistické okupace." *Revolver Revue* 50 (2002). Accessed December 29, 2017. http://www.revolverrevue.cz/antisemitska-literatura-v-dobe-nacisticke-okupace-1939-1945.
Bryant, Chad. *Prague in Black: Nazi Rule and Czech Nationalism*. Cambridge, MA: Harvard University Press, 2007.
Cinger, František. *Šťastné blues, aneb Z deníku Jaroslava Ježka*. Prague: BVD, 2006.
Cohen, Gary B. *The Politics of Ethnic Survival: Germans in Prague, 1861–1914*. Princeton, NJ: Princeton University Press, 1981.
Demetz, Peter. *Prague in Danger: The Years of German Occupation, 1939–45: Memories and History, Terror and Resistance, Theater and Jazz, Film and Poetry, Politics and War*. New York: Farrar, Straus, and Giroux, 2008.
Dorůžka, Lubomír. "Jazzman Fritz Weiss navzdory osudu." Accessed July 26, 2017. https://www.holocaust.cz/zdroje/clanky-z-ros-chodese/ros-chodes-2004/brezen-9/jazzman-fritz-weiss-navzdory-osudu/.
Dorůžka, Lubomír, and Miloslav Ducháč. *Karel Vlach: 50 let života s hudbou*. Prague: Ekopress, 2003.
Dorůžka, Lubomír, and Ivan Poledňák. *Československý jazz: minulost a přítomnost*. Prague: Supraphon, 1967.
Holzknecht, Václav. *Jaroslav Ježek a Osvobozené divadlo*. 2nd ed. Prague: ARSCI, 2007.
*Im Totaleinsatz: Zwangsarbeit der tschechischen Bevölkerung für das Dritte Reich*. Exhibition Catalogue. Prague: Deutsch-Tschechischer Zukunftfonds, 2008.
Kárný, Miroslav, and Jaroslava Milotová, eds. *Protektorátní politika Reinharda Heydricha*. Prague: Archivní správa MV ČR, 1991.
Kater, Michael. *Different Drummers: Jazz in the Culture of Nazi Germany*. New York: Oxford University Press, 1992.
Kokošková, Zdeňka, Jaroslav Pažout, and Monika Sedláková, eds. *Pracovali pro Třetí říši: edice dokumentů*. Prague: Scriptorium, 2011.
Kotek, Josef. *Dějiny české populární hudby a zpěvu*. Vol. 2: 1918–1968. Prague: Academia, 1998.

———. *Kronika české synkopy: půlstoletí českého jazzu a moderní populární hudby v obrazech a svědectví současníků*. Vol. 1: 1903–1938. Prague: Editio Supraphon, 1975.

Kotek, Josef, and Jaromír Hořec. *Kronika české synkopy: půlstoletí českého jazzu a moderní populární hudby v obrazech a svědectví současníků*. Vol. 2: 1939–61. Prague: Supraphon, 1990.

Koura, Petr. *Swingaři a potápky v protektorátní noci: česká swingová mládež a její hořkej svět*. Prague: Academia, 2016.

Macmillan, Margaret. *Paris 1919: Six Months That Changed the World*. New York: Random House, 2001.

*Navzdory osudu/In Defiance of Fate*. Orchestr Emila Ludvíka in arrangements by Fritz Weiss. Radioservis CD ŽMP006, 2003.

Novák, Zdeněk. *Swing a svoboda za mřížemi*. Prague: Granit, 2004.

Pokorný, Jiří. "Práce pro Říši a Národní odborová ústředna zaměstnanecká." In *Museli pracovat pro Říši. Nucené pracovní nasazení českého obyvatelstva v letech druhé světové války*, edited by Zdeňka Kokošková, Stanislav Kokoška, and Jaroslav Pažout, 45–50. Prague: Státní ústřední archiv, 2004.

Poledňák, Ivan. "Bod kristalizace." *Taneční hudba a jazz* (1963): 4–13.

Schumann, Coco [Heinz Jakob]. *The Ghetto Swinger: A Berlin Jazz Legend Remembers*. With Max Christian Graeff and Michaela Haas. Translated by John Howard. Los Angeles: DoppelHouse, 2016.

Škvorecký, Josef. "Eine kleine Jazzmusik." In his *Sedmiramenný svícen*, 109–127. Prague: Naše vojsko, 1964.

———. "I Was Born in Náchod..." In *Talkin' Moscow Blues: Essays about Literature, Politics, Movies, and Jazz*, edited by Sam Solecki, 15–63. Toronto: Lester & Orpen Dennys, 1988.

———. "Red Music." In *Talkin' Moscow Blues: Essays about Literature, Politics, Movies, and Jazz*, edited by Sam Solecki, 83–98. Toronto: Lester & Orpen Dennys, 1988.

———. "Song of the Forgotten Years." Translated by George Theiner. In *When Eve Was Naked: A Journey through Life*, 248–259. Toronto: Key Porter, 2000.

———. *The Cowards*. Translated by Jeanne Němcová. New York: Penguin, 1972.

Škvorecký, Josef, and Boris Mědílek. *Swing na malém městě*. Prague: Ivo Železný, 2002.

Suchý, Ondřej. *Inka Zemánková: Dívka k rytmu zrozená*. Prague: Ikar, 2006.

Traxler, Jiří. *Já nic, já muzikant*. Toronto: Sixty-Eight, 1980.

BRIAN S. LOCKE is Professor of Musicology at Western Illinois University. He is author of *Opera and Ideology in Prague: Polemics and Practice at the National Theatre, 1900–1938*.

# NINE

# A MUSICAL REEDUCATION

Music-Making in America's German POW Camps and the Intellectual Diversion Program

KELSEY KRAMER MCGINNIS

THE STORIES OF MUSIC-MAKING BY German POWs in America have been largely overlooked partly because of a lack of documentation, and partly because these prisoners were, for the most part, treated well. Unlike those in ghettos and concentration camps, their stories seem far less compelling and moving than the best-known accounts of music-making in captivity during World War II by those imprisoned by the Nazi regime in Europe. Historians have endeavored to document the role and meanings of music-making for prisoners in ghettos such as Terezín (Theresienstadt), where music-making was encouraged so that the camp's orchestra could be featured in propaganda films.[1] Narratives of music-making in captivity during World War II, moreover, have been popularized by films like *Playing for Time*, which tells the story of a female orchestra in Auschwitz, and *Paradise Road*, based on the story of the "vocal orchestra," a group of female inmates in a Japanese prison camp.[2] These dramas resonate with audiences not only because of the desire to uncover and address the atrocities of World War II, but also because of the symbolic significance of music-making in the face of violence and terror.

In stark contrast, German POWs were well fed, comfortably housed, and allowed to work for wages that they could use to purchase commodities such as records, beer, and cigarettes, and their treatment was carefully monitored by the International Committee of the Red Cross and the YMCA. The internment of roughly 375,000 German POWs has become a footnote in the story of America's involvement in World War II, and the history of music-making in captivity during World War II currently excludes the stories of German POWs interned in the United States.[3] Anecdotal evidence in historical scholarship on German POW camps suggests that most large camps in the United States had vibrant musical cultures. Camps often had their own orchestras, choirs, theater troupes, and chamber ensembles. Unfortunately, there have been few attempts to document musical activity in individual camps, perhaps because most camps were demolished after the war, and much of the documentary evidence associated with them appears not to have survived. Their story is nevertheless worth reconstructing; it illuminates the little-known systematic attempts of the US military to reeducate German POWs through a variety of media, including music, and it reveals the significant role of music in the expression of Germanness and the formation of community among POWs.

This chapter discusses music-making in German POW camps in the United States during World War II from two perspectives: (1) the development and planned implementation of the Intellectual Diversion Program (IDP), a reeducation initiative whose architects sought to incorporate music in the "reorientation" of German POWs, and (2) its actual role in the daily lives of German POWs interned in Iowa's Camp Algona, one of the few POW camps with a well-documented musical culture. The documentary evidence of music-making in German POW camps during World War II held in the Special Projects Division (SPD) files and in Iowa's Camp Algona suggests that while the US military struggled to understand and harness the "power" of music for reeducation, German POWs forged musical subcultures within their camps that reflected their musical pasts and allowed them to continue participating in a familiar, beloved cultural heritage.[4] This chapter thus illuminates the disconnection between military attempts to promote American culture (specifically music) through the IDP and the organic development of musical life in places such as Camp Algona.

## THE POW CAMP SYSTEM IN THE UNITED STATES

The US State Department had strongly opposed Britain's requests to send Axis POWs to America, but as Allied troops advanced against the Germans and Italians, captured soldiers completely overwhelmed the capacity of Allied POW camps in Europe.[5] In August 1942, the State Department agreed to receive an "emergency batch" of 50,000 prisoners. As an Allied victory began to seem imminent, the task of housing hundreds of thousands of POWs became a logistical challenge rather than a security concern. Eventually, 425,000 Axis POWs (370,000–375,000 of them German) were sent to America.[6] POW camps in Britain, the United States, and Germany were subject to the stipulations of the 1929 Geneva Convention.[7] Therefore, POWs in these camps were to be treated humanely, "protected . . . against acts of violence, from insults and from public curiosity," and "lodged in buildings . . . entirely free from damp, and adequately heated and lighted." They further were to be provided a food ration "equivalent in quantity and quality to that of the depot troops." The convention also had provisions requiring opportunities for recreation, the free practice of their religion, and other "intellectual pursuits," a provision that would later be repurposed by the US government to sidestep the anti-indoctrination clause.[8]

The first POWs in the United States were housed in the Civilian Conservation Corps (CCC) camps, but additional camps were required to accommodate the influx of prisoners. In September 1942, the US War Department began repurposing existing military posts as POW camps in Tennessee, Missouri, Texas, North Carolina, Massachusetts, Maryland, Georgia, Wisconsin, Mississippi, and Oklahoma.[9] The estimated combined capacity of these camps was 144,000, which was still not enough. Therefore, the Army Corps of Engineers and the Army Service Forces began to survey vacant land across the country in search of additional locations for POW camps.[10] Ultimately, the Provost Marshal General's Office (PMGO) elected to build new camps in regions that were in need of agricultural or industrial labor. POWs were sent to camps in almost every state, where they worked in corn fields, canneries, and logging companies.[11]

Newly constructed camps such as Iowa's Camp Algona were built quickly, sometimes receiving prisoners before the facilities were complete. Camp Algona's POWs worked in corn and hemp fields across the state of Iowa; they were also shipped to other regional branch camps in Minnesota and South Dakota. While the first priority of the commanders of these camps was the efficient and safe oversight of POW labor, officials in Washington, DC, began to see these camps as potential "schools" of democracy, opportune settings in which to begin the "reorientation" of the German soldier.

## THE SPECIAL PROJECTS DIVISION AND POW REEDUCATION

In March 1944, just one month before the first German POWs arrived in Algona, the US War Department and the Special War Problems Division of the State Department officially proposed a joint strategy for the reeducation of German POWs. Historian Ron Robin notes that "a basic premise of the master plan was that instead of discrediting National Socialism, American authorities should foster respect for the American alternative."[12] The joint strategy focused primarily on promoting a positive image of America, Americanism, and democracy. This initiative, the Intellectual Diversion Program (IDP, overseen by the Special Projects Division of the Provost Marshal General's Office), was introduced partly in response to the increasingly negative public attitudes toward German POWs, attitudes fueled by critiques and accusations reported in the print media and by radio commentators of "alleged 'coddling' of POWs and the 'domination' of German camps by strident, harsh Nazi cliques."[13] But the accusations of coddling the enemy were of secondary concern; the PMGO and the architects of the IDP were keenly aware that the 375,000 German POWs held in the United States would be returned to Germany at the end of the war, and that their impressions of America would impact German–American relations in a postwar world.

The IDP was a national experiment with varied results; it has been described as "belated and poorly orchestrated" and "a reflection of domestic power struggles."[14] Many of the individuals tasked with creating and overseeing the IDP were intellectuals with liberal arts backgrounds: Lt. Col. Edward Davison, chief of the Special Projects Branch, was a university professor and a poet; Howard Mumford Jones, one of the first staff members hired for the reeducation program, was a professor of English literature at Harvard.[15] Their approach seems to have been influenced by a desire to demonstrate the value of the humanities in general. Robin has suggested that the IDP was conceptualized partly as "an attempt to counteract the notion that humanities were 'archaic' and 'trivial' by proving that hardened Nazis could be transformed when exposed to college-type Western Civilization courses and reading material . . . to recreate the intellectual climate of the liberal arts college behind barbed wire."[16]

American historians such as Robin have explored and documented the history of the internment of German POWs in America and the SPD's reeducation project, but none of them have closely examined musical life in individual camps. Furthermore, until now there has been no focused exploration of the US military's attempts to incorporate music in its reeducation initiative. While the top-down policies and initiatives of the SPD were technically applied to every POW camp in the United States, the fact remains that oversight of the prisoners was often loose and haphazard. There was a shortage of camp personnel and staff, and ultimately concerns about security, morale, and labor superseded those regarding recreation and reeducation, particularly as they related to musical activity. The internal documents of the SPD reveal much about the beliefs and philosophies of those attempting to harness the power of music for reeducation, but the distance between those designing the IDP and the men making music in individual camps may have, in some cases, rendered reeducation through music a theoretical and largely unpractical pursuit.

## THE AIMS OF REEDUCATION AND THE ROLE OF MUSIC

At the heart of the US POW reeducation initiative was the promotion of the American way of life, rather than the defamation of Germany.[17] An internal memo of the Special War Problems Division entitled "Indoctrination of German Prisoners of War" (March 2, 1944), moreover, expressed the belief that successful reeducation would require a "show don't tell" strategy that showcased the best of American character: "The most powerful means of indoctrination would be by example. We should endeavor to show the Germans by our general treatment of them that we are fair, honest, humane but first, jealous of liberties but quick to punish those who infringe on the liberties of others, efficient and loyal to our own institutions and ideals."[18]

In the same memo, it was specifically noted that German POWs seemed to harbor negative prejudices toward American culture and that these prejudices ought to be directly combatted through the reeducation program: "There are among the German prisoners some who regard this country as an uncultured, materialistic nation inferior to any European country.... An indoctrination campaign should endeavor to reach the Germans by presenting to them in so far as is possible in the circumstances the best aspects of American life and institutions."[19]

Negative perceptions of American institutions and culture seem to have been among the chief concerns of those charged with the design of a reeducation program. This, of course, echoes the long-standing concerns of those in the American musical community that American composers and performers had yet to garner the respect of the European musical elite. And indeed, the architects of the IDP sought, at least in part, to promote American music and musical institutions to German POWs in an attempt to demonstrate that the American way of life could produce musical culture and talent on par with that in Europe (specifically Germany).

Yet the role of music in the reeducation program was never entirely clarified. It was not until the end of the war, in April 1945, that the SPD apparently compiled a music pamphlet, the purpose of which was "to give the German prisoners of war an idea of the background and quality of American symphony orchestras, and to offset the common idea of prisoners that America is a wasteland of culture. The pamphlet is designed to be included in record albums, pursuant to paragraph 4, Special Projects Secret Letter No. 5 dated February 5, 1945, and also to be placed in camp libraries."[20]

"Special Projects Secret Letter No. 5" was the initial invitation for camp personnel to submit the names of works and artists so that notes could be provided. Rather than create a uniform set of notes and biographies to send to each camp, the SPD asked American military staff to determine which works would be of interest or use in their individual camps. Within months of the circulation of Letter No. 5, the SPD changed course and decided instead to produce a uniform brochure to be sent to all camps and included as an insert in distributed recordings. The uniform brochure may not have been distributed at all, but the intended content demonstrates the continued interest of the SPD in showcasing American ensembles and musicians. To say that the purpose of the pamphlet was to "offset the common idea of prisoners that America is a wasteland of culture" is to reiterate the concerns outlined in earlier SPD memos regarding the overall vision and goals of the IDP. Even if attempts to create a "musical curriculum" or uniform plan for the use of music failed, it is clear that SPD staff considered music to be a tool that could be used to convince the Germans that the American way of life could produce musical excellence.

The SPD's musical efforts focused almost exclusively on the distribution of records and information about the recordings, American ensembles, and American conductors. There appears to have been little effort put toward the distribution of scores, sheet music, and instruments. The YMCA, not the SPD, is credited with furnishing many of the instruments, scores, and records in camps throughout the United States. In March 1945, the YMCA had assembled roughly four hundred boxes of records that were circulated throughout POW camps. During a conference with the SPD, Andre Vulliet, a spokesman for the Works Progress Administration (WPA), stated that "the records were chosen as to include in each box a group of records which would appeal to different tastes. This resulted in mixing classical and semi-classical records and also composers of all nationalities ... to show that music was universal."[21] This shared vision and ideology may have been one reason why YMCA representatives were allowed liberal access to the camps and to the POWs themselves.[22] The strategies of the SPD reveal the staff's unawareness of the participatory nature of music-making and the enthusiasm of German POWs for the formation of choirs, orchestras, and operetta troupes. As will become clear in the coming discussion of the case study of Camp Algona, the most significant musical activities for the POWs on the ground seem to have been live concerts and productions by their own ensembles. Records were often used as backgrounds for social events (though record concerts were also common), and radio broadcasts were useful only in large camps that had managed to obtain radios or high-quality public address systems.

Regardless of the relative success of the SPD in organizing a strategy for the use of music, the ability of the division to influence musical activity among POWs relied solely on the actions of camp commanders and American staff in each camp. Ultimately, the daily operations of a particular camp determined whether SPD curricula and materials made their way into the hands of the POWs themselves. Each one of the hundreds of POW camps across the country had its own social climate and operational challenges. Thus, to begin truly to understand the reality of musical life in a German POW camp, it is necessary to consider individual camps as case studies. Through the lens of local archives and local history, it becomes clear that musical life depended on the skills and interests of the POWs themselves and the social and cultural climate of each camp.

## CAMP ALGONA AND THE MUSICAL LIVES OF GERMAN POWS

As most of America's POW camps were either demolished or returned to their peacetime military functions almost immediately after the last POWs returned to Europe, collections of artifacts and documents from individual camps are difficult to find. When such collections exist, it is usually because of the strong interest of a community in preserving the memory of a POW camp and its effects on wartime life for civilians. Such is the case with north-central Iowa's Camp Algona, a large camp that housed more than ten thousand German POWs during the final years of the war. Because of the work of a group of volunteer historians, there exists a large body of documents and artifacts from the camp.[23] Fortuitously, this archive includes the most extensive known collection of musical material from any individual POW camp. By searching out the story of the development of musical life in Camp Algona, it is possible to consider music-making in an individual camp alongside the SPD's musical directives and mission. While this one camp should not be taken as a completely generalizable sample of life in every POW camp (or even most), the study of it *does* provide useful insight into the limits of the SPD's top-down approach.

On September 25, 1943, the town of Algona finalized a contract for the construction of Camp Algona. Five days later, work was underway on the barracks and facilities to house three thousand POWs and five hundred officers and guards. The community's response to the news was mixed; some citizens hoped that the temporary increase in population would bring an economic boost, while others complained that the camp was a waste of good farmland. Concerns about the new POW camp had little to do with the German prisoners themselves. The community actually saw the presence of POWs as a solution to the acute labor shortage and possibly as a source for a sorely needed economic stimulus, while any reluctance to embrace the contract seems to have been related either to a strain on community resources or to the influx of *American* military personnel.[24] Many were concerned about the presence of numerous transient workers and military employees and the impact they would have on Algona's social life. In an editorial, one Algona resident reported that a Wyoming town had been overrun by the employees of its POW camp and implied that the men involved in running the establishment were of poor character (suggesting that the same would be true of the men brought in to run the camp in Algona).[25]

Despite the misgivings of a few vocal citizens, it was generally accepted that housing POWs was a civic obligation and part of the war effort. Families of American POWs in Germany believed that mutual adherence to the Geneva Convention was the best way to protect their loved ones, and that mistreatment here could lead to retaliation abroad.[26] In December 1943, Algona resident Alden Reid published an editorial in the Des Moines *Morning Register* proposing that, in the interest of fostering good will between Americans and Germans, Iowans ought to consider the Golden Rule to be the standard of POW treatment. Reid suggested that the POW camp presented the opportunity to facilitate cultural diplomacy and exchanges between Americans and Germans that would foster trust and ease tense international relationships. He argued that it was important that the Germans return to their homeland after the war with a "friendly feeling" toward America:

> A contributor to the Open Forum charges that our government is "wasting money like water in building these elaborate (prison) camps" instead of making them "wire enclosures as our boys have." Perhaps there has been poor judgment in choosing the location of and general plan of some of these camps. But this contributor feels that if we would have these prisoners return to their own countries after the war with a friendly feeling toward our way of life, we can accept nothing less than the Golden Rule. This contributor writes as one who has been deferred, but also as one who is anxious to see the causes of war destroyed.[27]

The story of Camp Algona's formation, operation, and decommissioning at the end of the war begins against this backdrop of American anticipation and preparation for the arrival of thousands of German POWs. The background is significant because the social climate of and daily life in the camp were undoubtedly influenced by the local community's interest in fostering positive relationships with the POWs. While civilians were not regularly allowed in the camp, they were granted access surprisingly often, whether to attend religious services and sing as part of the church choir, or to participate in the POWs' Christmas production in December 1945.

During Camp Algona's short lifespan (April 1944 to February 1946), the camp's network of thirty-four branches housed and employed approximately ten thousand German soldiers. Life for the first arrivals was difficult; the camp was not fully constructed, there was little to no recreational activity, and the American staff struggled to organize the new arrivals. But by the time the first issue of the camp's newspaper, the *Drahtpost*, was printed in October 1944, a vibrant musical culture had emerged, much of it on the initiative of the prisoners themselves. POWs in Camp Algona pooled their wages to purchase essential materials: phonographs, records, replacement needles, instruments, reeds, and sheet music. A group of men donated $750 to purchase a used grand piano (each individual made roughly eighty cents a day as an agricultural laborer). They also contributed to the purchase of a set of drums and supplies for the theater group's costumes and elaborate stage setting. The coordination of the delivery of supplies was up to the American personnel (who seem to have been very accommodating). However, the activities and performances themselves were coordinated completely by POWs. The two principal coordinators of musical activity at Camp Algona were Willi Schwoebel and Johannes Bresseler, the conductors of the orchestra and choir, respectively. The American staff allowed them a great deal of freedom in the planning of concerts and the selection of music, partly because both men got along well with the camp's commander. They dedicated most of their free time to planning, rehearsing, and publicizing performances. Schwoebel often wrote out each individual part for the orchestra by hand.

The first live instrumental performances in Camp Algona are documented in correspondence between individual musicians and their families. On September 12, 1944, Heinz Lepinat wrote to his wife: "We have a small band in which I play the violin. I am trying very hard to perfect my playing. Perhaps it is possible for you to send me some good music lessons for violin and piano as well as the sonatas of Diabelli for piano." Another letter dated September 22, 1944, makes the earliest mention of an orchestra concert: "The day after tomorrow we are putting on a production with the title 'Comrades Play for Comrades,' in which your Heinzelmann will play, together with six buddies. There are one trumpet, two clarinets, two violins and one pianist. A set of drums will probably be added."[28] This small ensemble practiced each evening from 7 p.m. to 8:30 p.m., and members were added as new POWs arrived and more instruments became available. Between October 1944 and January 1945, the orchestra's musicians gave ten performances: four performances of the same program with a trivia contest (giving everyone the chance to showcase his musical knowledge), one private concert for the fifth company on November 12, two performances of a program on the theme "Music and Rhythm" on November 17 and 18, two private performances for the sixth and seventh companies on November 19 and 26, and one joint performance with the choir for the Christmas pageant (incidental and accompanying music). These musical events were referred to as "evenings of comradeship"; some programs were open to all POWs, and others were restricted to individual companies.[29]

Although incomplete, the extant concert programs from Camp Algona reveal a predominance of German folksongs, chamber music, lieder, and standard orchestral works. The first choir concert, given on December 12, 1944, and repeated several times shortly thereafter, included Beethoven's "Die Himmel rühmen" and "Hymne an die Nacht," Wagner's "Pilgerchor" from *Tannhäuser*, and Schubert's "Der Lindenbaum." The musical selections alternated with readings of poetry by Gottfried Keller and Joseph Eichendorff. While a theme of homesickness and longing appears to have unified the concert (given the inclusion of the "Pilgerchor," the poems "Heimweh" and "Abschied" by Eichendorff, and a choral arrangement of "Verlassen" by Thomas Koschat), the works chosen were mostly standard repertoire that the choir could quickly prepare and the audience would recognize. The concert was not overtly patriotic or even nationalistic, but unmistakably *German*, a sentimental and comforting experience and an affirmation of German art and culture. The camp's orchestra programs also primarily featured German favorites, often arranged by the orchestra's conductor, Willi Schwoebel.

On February 5, 1945, the orchestra gave a performance entitled "Something for Everyone," which included the overture from Flotow's opera *Alessandro Stradella*, Johann Strauss's "Kaiserwalzer," and medleys of music from Lehár's *Die lustige Witwe* and Strauss's *Die Fledermaus*. The review in the camp newspaper praised the orchestra's performance and referred both to the sentimental value of the music and to the link between the repertoire and the homeland.

A month later, the orchestra gave a request concert for which each barrack in the camp was allowed three requests (though additional requests inevitably poured in, leading to the decision to give two separate concerts to accommodate the number). The requests included the overture from Weber's *Der Freischütz*; Carl Teike's march, "Alte Kameraden"; and Lehár's sentimental love song, "Gern hab ich die Frau'n geküsst" (Girls were Made to Love and Kiss). It is difficult to imagine the overture to *Der Freischütz* rearranged for an orchestra of no more than seventeen musicians (three violins, one cello, one flute, one viola, one clarinet [two if one of the saxophone players switched instruments], one tenor saxophone, one alto saxophone, one c-melody saxophone, two trumpets, one trombone [and sometimes a bass trombone played by one of the percussionists], an array of percussion instruments [two percussionists regularly played with the ensemble], one accordion, and one piano). The limitations of the ensemble, and particularly of the brass section, made it difficult for Schwoebel to reproduce the richness of the horn parts for the beginning of Weber's overture. Even so, he refused to set aside requests like this one, and the audience was reportedly pleased with the arrangements and appreciated his efforts.

The determination with which the camp musicians sought to retain a sense of order and normalcy by engaging in musical activity took on many forms and fulfilled many functions in preserving their core identity nationally and spiritually, while also reminding them that they were still soldiers at war with their captors. It is striking how much freedom and control the POWs exercised in organizing these efforts and framing them to exert powerful effects on their fellow German soldiers. The framing of musical activity in Camp Algona extended beyond live performances to the numerous record concerts planned by the POWs. In October 1944 (as the orchestra was beginning to plan performances), there was a sudden influx of "record concerts." POWs saved money to purchase a record (always of German music) through the camp's canteen store and planned concerts that were either open to the "public" or closed to a specific military company. Record concerts often included carefully sequenced musical selections alternating with speeches or poetry readings, and others were serious presentations of well-known masterworks by Beethoven. For the POWs in Camp Algona, record concerts offered welcome opportunities to appreciate familiar masterpieces that were out of reach for the camp's small orchestra to perform.

In June 1945, Bresseler, the camp's choir director, planned a record concert featuring Beethoven's Ninth Symphony played by the Vienna Philharmonic.[30] The concert began with a lecture on Beethoven's life, emphasizing the deafness which famously had robbed him of his hearing before he finished the work. In his lecture, Bresseler reminded the men of the "suffering and darkness" from which the work emerged, as if to suggest that if Beethoven, the musical genius, could face deafness, the German people could face their fate as well. Interestingly, the concert was given on the Christian holiday of Pentecost, a spiritual connection that was not overlooked by the *Drahtpost* reviewer, who wrote: "Pentecost is probably the right time for this work, this song to joy that comes from so much suffering and darkness . . . Everyone had to do the decisive thing . . . listening with all inner power. Those who have done it have experienced Pentecost, in spite of everything."[31]

This record concert was presented as both a musical and spiritual event; the act of partaking in the performance of Beethoven's Ninth Symphony was equated with a spiritual ritual or act of devotion. Like the disciples on Pentecost who first received the Holy Spirit, the men who truly "listened with inner power" were thought to have received a spirit of renewed hope and determination. Beethoven's Ninth was a symbol of hope and a signal of a new era for the German people. In addition to underscoring the spiritual meaning of Pentecost, the concert emphasized the parallels between the challenges now facing Germany and those faced by Beethoven himself.

Musical events were also powerful reminders of the continuing state of war and reinforced the bonds of military solidarity. When the men formally gathered with their military companies to attend an event, the hierarchical relationships between officers and enlisted men that existed before their capture resurfaced and gave them a sense of restored order and normalcy.[32] These soldiers who had spent years in the German army still identified strongly with the practices and decorum of military life. While daily life in Camp Algona was at times monotonous and quite "civilian," POWs were acutely aware of the fact that they were still "at war."[33] On New Year's Eve 1944, the POWs presented a record concert featuring Beethoven's *Eroica* Symphony, a monumental work that, according to the *Drahtpost*, had the power to "give everyone strength."[34] Many of the POWs in Camp Algona took for granted the very real spiritual influence of great German music. On this occasion, Beethoven's *Eroica* Symphony was a rallying point, an inspirational work meant to encourage the men to believe in the eventual triumph of the German nation. Their persistence in finding this solidarity through music endured even when it became more difficult to rally participation. During the spring and summer months, the orchestra and choir were depleted, as some men were sent to branch camps for agricultural labor, and those who remained at the base camp spent long days in the fields. To maintain the frequency of live musical performances, the reduced number of camp musicians gave chamber concerts. During the spring and summer of 1945, there were six evening chamber concerts, during which soloists had the opportunity to perform favorite recital pieces, and poetry enthusiasts could select and read classic German poetry. While it is likely that (as for the orchestral and choral concerts) works were selected partly because of familiarity, certain chamber concerts of 1945 can be more clearly connected to emotional responses to events of the war. The second concert in the series, given on May 6, took place shortly after the death of Hitler (April 30) and just two days before V-E day. The concert program included readings of poetry; solo performances of Schubert's "Der Lindenbaum," "Der Wegweiser," and "Ständchen," and the slow movement from Mozart's Violin Sonata in F Major, K. 13; and ended with Mozart's *Eine kleine Nachtmusik*, K. 525. In spite of the spirited final selection, the framing of the concert seems to have been intentionally somber, a direct response to crushing reports of defeat. The concert began with a poetry reader seated at the piano in a completely darkened hall, followed immediately by the "mournful" slow movement from Mozart's string quartet. The connection between the tone of the program and the events of the war was made explicit by the editorial staff of the *Drahtpost* in their review of the evening: "The men of the base camp were able to spend an evening with music, song, and poetry which certainly allowed them to forget their present circumstances.... Perhaps some asked themselves beforehand if today is the time for the elegant and joyful beauty of such music; afterwards no one did.... In times past such things may have been concerts, art and literature. For us now, they are a piece of home, the purest, perhaps, that we have."[35]

Reviews in the *Drahtpost* provide evidence of the perceived functionality of music in this setting as a facilitator of emotional participation. Although the dominance of Austro-German repertoire in the programs of the choir and orchestra is somewhat expected, the framing of certain concerts seems to have been, at times, a way to reinforce communal bonds, express solidarity, and even celebrate German culture.[36]

## CAMP ALGONA'S MUSICAL LIFE AND THE SPECIAL PROJECTS DIVISION

This cursory examination of musical life in Camp Algona illuminates the organic, self-directed nature of the activities of the camp's orchestra, choir, and chamber musicians. The selection of music and planning of performances was left entirely to the POWs themselves. There is no evidence that American camp personnel interfered in the musicians' activities. On the contrary, it seems that Lieutenant Colonel Arthur Lobdell, the camp's commander, encouraged musical activity by allowing YMCA representatives regular access to the camp to supply instruments and scores, by allowing POWs to purchase recordings of their choice, and by trying to prevent musicians from being transferred to other branch camps to preserve the small ensembles.

Camp Algona was by definition a "large" camp, housing up to three thousand POWs at a time, so the loose oversight of musical activity was not due to a lack of awareness or involvement of the SPD. On the contrary, Camp Algona had its own assigned officer from the IDP, Captain Gunner Norgaard, tasked with overseeing all recreational activities and implementing the IDP. So serious was his charge that the staff of the SPD in Washington specified that Norgaard was not to be given other administrative or managerial duties in Camp Algona, in spite of a staffing shortage.[37] Norgaard was fluent in German and had attended an intensive training program in which he studied POW psychology, Nazi propaganda, and German history and politics.[38] He read every issue of the camp's newspaper, the *Drahtpost*, and spent a substantial amount of his time cultivating relationships with the POWs. He saw all the memos and directives from the SPD and was certainly aware of the fact that the division specifically encouraged the promotion of American music.

In late February 1945, Captain Alexander Lakes, an inspector from the SPD, spent two days observing activities and evaluating the implementation of the reeducation program in Camp Algona. Lakes concluded that the camp staff was too naive and trusting to realize that the "Nazi" prisoners were running the camp "in plain sight." In his report, Lakes wrote "[Commander] Lobdell apparently is being duped by a show of German efficiency and was advised accordingly." Lakes also had a number of concerns about the POWs' creative activities. He complained that there was an alarming lack of American music in the camp and that there were no American stage offerings.[39]

After Lakes's departure, there is no evidence that American music made its way into the programs of the orchestra, choir, or chamber ensembles. In fact, shortly after Lakes's visit, the choir gave a concert featuring exclusively German *Volkslieder*. Furthermore, there is little evidence that Norgaard or Lobdell made any serious effort to encourage inclusion of American music in the programs of the orchestra and choir (nor does it seem that they asked the YMCA for help in this endeavor). In his biography of Lt. Col. Lobdell and the accompanying history of Camp Algona, George Lobdell (Arthur Lobdell's nephew) argues that the preservation of the camp's positive morale and social climate was of the utmost importance to Lobdell and Norgaard. Their interest in security, peaceful camp-community relations, and contentment among the POWs apparently made them reluctant to interfere in well-functioning, organic activities, even when orders from Washington urged them to do so.[40]

In light of the vibrancy and communal nature of musical life in camps like Camp Algona, the SPD's emphasis on the distribution of information *about* American musicians and ensembles or recordings of American music seems misguided. The instructional pamphlet designed (or reportedly designed) by the SPD did little to encourage *participation in* American music; rather, it aimed to demonstrate that America was capable of producing excellent musicians and music. Although the SPD sought to deliver information about American music through such text-based educational materials, music was a participatory act and a source of social organization in Camp Algona, and the music performed and enjoyed was that which was already valued and familiar to the POWs. Herein may be the root of the disconnect between the SPD's musical ideas and the musical activities that emerged in the camps. The archival records of the SPD provide fascinating insights into the US military's perception of the "usefulness" of music and its role in reeducation, particularly for the promotion of "Americanism." Ultimately, though, these records tell us much more about American concerns about German perceptions of American culture than they do about the daily lives of German POWs.

The archival documentation surviving from Camp Algona suggests that the story of music-making in America's German POW camps appears to be comprised of two separate narratives: the account of the US military's attempts to grapple with American musical identity and somehow promote American music to German POWs, and the story of German musicians and their cultivation of musical life in captivity. In examining both narratives, it becomes clear that military interests were sometimes at odds with the goals and vision of the intellectuals tasked with designing a reeducation curriculum. The interests and concerns of individual camp commanders (morale, camp-community relations, camp culture) seem at times to have superseded the grander plans for reorientation expressed in the memos and directives of the SPD. Communication between the SPD and camp commanders (the memos regarding the pamphlet about American music and musicians, for example) reveals that the design and implementation of a reeducation plan involving music proved to be a logistical challenge, and that SPD personnel may have lacked the musical knowledge (and resources) necessary to formulate a coherent set of directives and curricula. Furthermore, archival evidence suggests that the musical training, preferences, and tastes of the POWs themselves seem to have been far more influential than the promotional records and literature designed to encourage the appreciation of American music. Ultimately, in spite of American efforts to control and harness its power and agency, music served a crucial and almost subversive role in upholding the POWs' strong ties to their culture, reminding them of the homeland for which they were fighting.

## NOTES

1. See, for example, the collaborative digital project "Music and the Holocaust" (www.holocaustmusic.ort.org), an online database of composers, musical works, and camps with documented musical activity.

2. *Playing for Time*, directed by Daniel Mann and Joseph Sargent (1980, CBS); *Paradise Road*, directed by Bruce Beresford (1997, Fox Searchlight).

3. The definitive scholarship on the subject includes the following: Arnold Krammer, *Nazi Prisoners of War in America*; Ron Robin, *Barbed Wire College: Reeducating German POWs in the United States during World War II*.

4. The archival material utilized for this study comes primarily from two sources: the files of the Special Projects Division (SPD) housed in the National Archives in College Park, Maryland (RG 389), and the Camp Algona POW Museum archive in Algona, Iowa. The files of the SPD include documentation of the operations of the office that designed and oversaw reeducation efforts in POW camps. They also include memos from individual camps detailing collections of musical scores, recordings, and radio programs. The archive of the Camp Algona POW Museum, which is curated by community members, contains an extensive collection of concert programs, concert reviews (written by German POWs), and musical scores.

5. The historical background provided here was previously included in the author's thesis (Kramer McGinnis, "The Purest Pieces of Home"). For a more exhaustive history of the internment project, see Krammer, *Nazi Prisoners of War in America*, and Robin, *Barbed Wire College*.

6. Krammer, *Nazi Prisoners of War in America*, 2–4; Holl, "Axis Prisoners of War in the Free State, 1943–1946."

7. Krammer, *Nazi Prisoners of War in America*, 18. Japan and Russia had not ratified the convention. According to Krammer and others, during the post-capture interrogation process, the threat of being sent to Russia was enough to force cooperation from the most hostile Axis prisoners.

8. International Committee of the Red Cross, "Convention Relative to the Treatment of Prisoners of War, 1929," Geneva, Switzerland.

9. These CCC camps were built during the 1930s so that unemployed residents of cities could move to rural areas for agricultural work (Krammer, *Nazi Prisoners of War in America*, 26). The Civilian Conservation Corps, originally the Emergency Conservation Work program, was initially established by the Emergency Conservation Work Act in 1933 and was overseen by the Agriculture, War, and Labor Departments.

10. Krammer, *Nazi Prisoners of War in America*, 27.

11. The role of POW labor in addressing the labor shortage in the United States during World War II is a fascinating subject that has been discussed in historical scholarship, including Arnold Krammer's *Nazi Prisoners of War in America*, Ron Robin's *Barbed Wire College*, Judith Gansberg's *Stalag U.S.A.*, as well as in a large

number of articles on specific regional camps (see bibliography). I will not spend time discussing the importance of POW labor in the United States in this chapter, but it should not be overlooked that daily life in POW camps almost always entailed labor of some kind, and that this labor is credited with keeping numerous farms and industrial businesses operational during World War II.

12. Robin, *Barbed Wire College*, 25.

13. Lobdell, *Golden Rule Challenge*, 272.

14. First quote from Thompson, "Men in German Uniform," 118; second quote from Robin, *Barbed Wire College*, 29.

15. Robin, *Barbed Wire College*, 43.

16. Ibid., 55.

17. This stands in stark contrast to the anti-German propaganda of World War I that dominated public discourse and led to the enactment of local laws outlawing the public use of the German language. For an excellent comparison of anti-German sentiment in America during World War I and World War II, see Hönicke Moore, *Know Your Enemy*.

18. Special War Problems Division, "Indoctrination of German Prisoners of War," March 2, 1944, RG 389, box 1603, file 40.

19. Ibid.

20. SPD memorandum, "Printing of Music Pamphlet," April 13, 1945, RG 389, box 1602.

21. "Memorandum for Director, Prisoner of War Special Projects Division: Report on Conference of War Prisoner's Aid, 24–25 March 1945," March 28, 1945, RG 389, box 1606, file 80.

22. For a more detailed account of the role of YMCA representatives in Camp Algona, specifically as it related to music, see Kramer McGinnis, "The Purest Pieces of Home"; and Lobdell, *Golden Rule Challenge*.

23. Kramer McGinnis, "The Purest Pieces of Home," includes a more detailed description of the musical activities and culture of Camp Algona, including discussions of specific concert programs, repertoire, etc.

24. POW camps did usually boost the economies of the towns in which they were built. The POWs themselves were not allowed the freedom to visit local businesses, but the hundreds of soldiers needed to staff the camps provided new business. The camp PX stores also relied on local businesses for their inventories of food, drinks, cigarettes, and various items requested by the POWs for art projects and activities.

25. "That Prison Camp," *Upper Des Moines* (Algona, Iowa), August 5, 1943. These concerns proved to be legitimate once the camp opened, as the behavior of American soldiers posed an ongoing problem for the community during its years of operation. In an anonymous letter to the camp commander, one Algona resident wrote: "the report is that the boys of late do not act like the general run of good soldiers that are of the same type as our own sons, nor do they act as we would want our sons to act were they near a town similar to Algona" (Lobdell, *Golden Rule*

*Challenge*, 147). A local businessman lamented, "It seems that the Algona Hotel is just about having all they can handle to keep the soldiers from tearing up the place" (Lobdell, *Golden Rule Challenge*, 147). Of course, the Germans were never allowed to visit the town without a military escort, so when they were in the presence of civilians, their behavior was closely monitored. Still, the community's perception was that the American soldiers were the bigger threat to the town's environment.

26. The same can be said of the families of German POWs held in the United States.

27. "A Different Opinion about Prison Camps," *Morning Register* (Des Moines, Iowa), December 15, 1943.

28. Luick-Thrams, *Signs of Life*, 24.

29. *Drahtpost #2*, November 19, 1944. Camp Algona's POW newspaper, the *Drahtpost*, is preserved in the files of the Camp Algona POW Museum in Algona, Iowa.

30. Probably a recording made in 1935 of the Vienna Philharmonic, conducted by Felix Weingartner.

31. *Drahtpost #15*, June 3, 1945.

32. This desire to return to strict military order and hierarchal organization was observed by some of the camp staff and the POWs' employers. In branch camps, for example, senior POW noncommissioned officers served as spokesmen and commanders for teams of laborers. "The spokesmen often demanded military-style obedience, and prisoners rarely disobeyed." See Simmons, *Swords into Plowshares*, 28.

33. Neitzel and Welzer describe the German army as a "community of destiny," a massive military group that was unified by a complex German nationalism that combined political ideology and "a metaphysical, abstract cult of war" created by writers, philosophers, and political opportunists. The military was an occupation *and* a fulfillment of one's duty and destiny as a German. Even the POWs who did not identify as vehement "Nazis" were heavily influenced by German military culture. As a result, POWs in Camp Algona preferred to preserve the safe and familiar military organization and hierarchy. See Neitzel and Welzer, *Soldaten*.

34. *Drahtpost #4*, December 1944.

35. *Drahtpost #14*, May 13, 1945.

36. The *Drahtpost* appears to have been particularly influential in Camp Algona and its branch camps in terms of framing musical programs. While some musical programs seem to have been framed explicitly by the musicians themselves, others were assigned particular narratives by the reviewers for the *Drahtpost*. It is important to note that these reviews were also written for the benefit of men in branch camps who were unable to attend. Thus, we can imagine that such reviews allowed POWs to participate by reading the program descriptions and imagining the sounds of familiar music and the emotional climate of the concert hall (and of the base camp in general).

37. Lobdell, *Golden Rule Challenge*, 273.
38. Ibid., 272.
39. Ibid., 272.
40. Furthermore, Norgaard came to believe that news and film were the two most effective tools for reeducation and chose to focus on regular screening of news reels and approved films.

BIBLIOGRAPHY

Applegate, Celia. "What is German Music: Reflections on the Role of Art in the Creation of the Nation." *German Studies Review* 15 (1992): 21–32.

Applegate, Celia, and Pamela Potter, eds. *Music and German National Identity*. Chicago: University of Chicago Press, 2002.

Bartlett, Wes. "A Collection of Memories of the Algona Prisoner of War Camp, 1943–1946." Self-published, 1994.

Billinger, Robert D., Jr. "Behind the Wire: German Prisoners of War at Camp Sutton, 1944–1946." *North Carolina Historical Review* 61 (1984): 481–509.

Buecker, Thomas R. "Prisoner of War Mail at the Fort Robinson Camp during World War II." *Nebraska History* 91 (2010): 58–65.

Carr, Gilly, and Harold Mytum. *Cultural Heritage and Prisoners of War: Creativity Behind Barbed Wire*. New York: Routledge, 2012.

Cepuch, Stefanie. "The Public and the POWs: Reaction to the Release of the German Prisoners of War for Agricultural Labour." *Canadian Papers in Rural History* 9 (1994): 323–335.

Corbett, William P. "A German Odyssey: The Journal of a German Prisoner of War." *Chronicles of Oklahoma* 71 (1993): 462–463.

Ehrmann, Henry W. "An Experiment in Political Education: The Prisoner-of-War Schools in the United States." *Social Research* 14 (1947): 304–320.

Fackler, Guido. "Music in Concentration Camps: 1933–1945." *Music and Politics* 1 (2007): 1–25.

Fahey, John. "John Fahey on 'Reeducating' German Prisoners during World War II." *Oregon Historical Quarterly* 93 (1992): 368–393.

Fauser, Annegret. *Sounds of War: Music in the United States during World War II*. New York: Oxford University Press, 2013.

Fincher, Jack. "By Convention, the Enemy Never Did Without." *Smithsonian* 26 (1995): 126–143.

Gansberg, Judith M. *Stalag, U.S.A.: The Remarkable Story of German POWs in America*. New York: Crowell, 1977.

Gregory, Kirk. "The German World War Two Prisoner and His Experience in the United States." Ph.D. diss., California State University, 2001.

Holl, Richard E. "Axis Prisoners of War in the Free State, 1943–1946." *Maryland Historical Magazine* 100 (2005): 490–504.

Hönicke Moore, Michaela. *Know Your Enemy: The American Debate on Nazism, 1933–1945*. Cambridge: Cambridge University Press, 2010.

Hutchison, Daniel. "'We . . . Are the Most Fortunate of Prisoners': The Axis POW Experience at Camp Opelika during World War II." *Alabama Review* 64 (2011): 285–320.

Krammer, Arnold. "American Treatment of German Generals during World War II." *Journal of Military History* 54 (1990): 27–46.

———. *Nazi Prisoners of War in America*. New York: Stein and Day, 1979.

Lobdell, George. *The Golden Rule Challenge: Command of World War II German POW Camps in the Upper Mid-West*. Seattle, WA: Classic Day, 2004.

Luick-Thrams, Michael. *Signs of Life: The Correspondence of German POWs at Camp Algona, Iowa, 1943–1946*. Mason City, IA: TRACES, 2002.

Marsh, Melissa A. "Still the Old Marlene: Hollywood at the Fort Robinson Prisoner of War Camp." *Nebraska History* 86 (2005): 46–61.

McGinnis, Kelsey Kramer. "The Purest Pieces of Home: German POWs Making German Music in Iowa." M.A. thesis, University of Iowa, 2015.

Neitzel, Sönke, and Harald Welzer. *Soldaten*. New York: Alfred Knopf, 2012.

O'Donnell, Krista, Renate Bridenthal, and Nancy Ruth Reagin, eds. *The Heimat Abroad: Boundaries of Germanness*. Ann Arbor: University of Michigan Press, 2005.

Pluth, Edward. "Enemies Within: Iowa POWs in Nazi Germany." *Annals of Iowa* 62 (2003): 267–268.

Potter, Pamela. *Art of Suppression: Confronting the Nazi Past in Histories of the Visual and Performing Arts*. Berkeley: University of California Press, 2016.

———. *Most German of the Arts: Musicology and Society from the Weimar Republic to the End of Hitler's Reich*. New Haven, CT: Yale University Press, 1998.

Reiss, Matthias. "Bronzed Bodies behind Barbed Wire: Masculinity and the Treatment of German Prisoners of War in the United States during World War II." *Journal of Military History* 69 (2005): 475–504.

———. "Solidarity Among 'Fellow Sufferers': African Americans and German Prisoners of War in the United States during World War II." *Journal of African American History* 98 (2013): 531–561.

———. "The Importance of Being Men: The Afrika-Korps in American Captivity." *Journal of Social History* 46 (2012): 23–47.

Rettig, A. "A De-programming Curriculum: Allied Reeducation and the Canadian-American Psychological Warfare Program for German POWs, 1943–47." *American Review of Canadian Studies* 29 (1999): 593–619.

Robin, Ron. *Barbed Wire College: Reeducating German POWs in the United States during World War II*. Princeton, NJ: Princeton University Press, 1995.

Simmons, Dean. *Swords into Plowshares: Minnesota's POW Camps during WWII*. St. Paul, MN: Cathedral Hill, 2000.

Stahnke, Herbert H. "Ministry to German POWs at Fort Sill, 1943–1946." *Concordia Historical Institute Quarterly* 62 (1989): 119–124.

Tent, James F. *Mission on the Rhine: Reeducation and Denazification in American-Occupied Germany.* Chicago: University of Chicago Press, 1982.

Thompson, Antonio Scott. "Men in German Uniform: German Prisoners of War Held in the United States during World War II." Ph.D. diss., University of Kentucky, 2006.

Walker, Chip. "German Creative Activities at Camp Aliceville, 1943–1946." *Alabama Review* 38 (1985): 19–37.

Walker, Richard P. "The Swastika and the Lone Star: Nazi Activity in Texas POW Camps." *Military History of the West* 36 (2006): 54–88.

Zagovec, Rafael A. "Islands of Faith: National Identity and Ideology in German POW Camps in the United States, 1943–1946." *Zeitgeschichte* 29 (2002): 113–122.

KELSEY KRAMER MCGINNIS is a Ph.D. candidate in Musicology and Adjunct Lecturer in the College of Law at the University of Iowa.

TEN

# BUNKERS, CELLARS, AND ACOUSTIC MEMORY

Sonic Experiences of War and Surrender in Nazi Germany

ABBY ANDERTON

FOR MANY CIVILIANS LIVING IN Germany, the first encounter with World War II was born of sound. Whether an air raid siren signaling an impending attack, bombs crashing into a roof, or boots marching around bunkers and over cellars, war was a uniquely aural experience. Contemporary German accounts translated these sonic markers into musical metaphors, and by describing "the music of the roaring of enemy planes," or "a crescendo in the fighting," civilians resorted to the safely structured patterns of musical terminology.[1] For those huddled in enclosed spaces, aurality was both diminished and heightened. Discerning even minute changes in the city's soundscape could mean the difference between survival and annihilation. Until relatively late in the war, for many civilians, the enemy was one that could only be heard, not seen.

The Allied air war, or the bombing of German cities by American and British planes, wreaked the most destruction on urban populations. Few German cities (regardless of their military insignificance) were safe from bombs, and cellars and bunkers became ubiquitous spaces of retreat. Inhabitants found ways to pass the time underground by knitting, sewing, and reading. Soon even singing, humming, and other forms of musical performance and spectatorship fostered an atmosphere of escapism, providing a kind of sonic camouflage as bombs exploded overhead. What neither four-meter-thick concrete walls nor bombproof doors could provide was certainty; music, at the very least, provided a distraction as live performances and radio broadcasts heard during the bombing raids served a revealing escapist function. The sheer number of German memoirs that reference making and listening to music below ground reveals how these experiences were essential in building community despite the imminent collapse of the Third Reich. As Annegret Fauser notes, "the lived sonic experience" of the Second World War included not only aerial attacks, but also newly developed mass media that played a vital role in shaping civilian experiences. This wholly unique soundtrack involved, in Brian Currid's estimation, "the roar of a crowd, the echo of a goose step, the sound of march music, and the resonant voice of Adolf Hitler."[2]

By considering first the aural experiences of air raids and the "acoustic memories" of civilians who experienced them, then radio use and live performances inside the bunker, this chapter argues that music played a primary role in providing civilians with necessary forms of escape and psychological reassurance, sometimes reinforcing, sometimes transgressing notions of the "people's community" (*Volksgemeinschaft*).[3] The Volksgemeinschaft, or racial hierarchy whereby participants displayed their allegiance to the regime through flags, symbols, greetings, and memberships in various Nazi organizations, became a core principle of National Socialist ideology. Historian Ian Kershaw has noted that above all, the Volksgemeinschaft emphasized "exclusion and inclusion as decisive features of National Socialist society, with patent implications for the regime's policies of racist discrimination, persecution, and extermination."[4] For the purposes of this chapter, I use the term to describe civilians sanctioned by the state to use the bunker or cellar. From its inception, air raid shelters were spaces of exclusion, not inclusion, as forced laborers, foreign workers, and Jewish civilians were generally unwelcome to enter.[5] In this respect, musical experiences could create an alternate sense of belonging within the confines of the bunker, forging bonds between Germans regardless of their social class. But occasionally, music even provided a means to overcome mistrust and animosity toward those outside the Volksgemeinschaft.

Despite the irrefutable and widespread civilian trauma caused by the bombing, discussions of these raids lead to difficult moral questions. As historian Robert Moeller notes, the Holocaust and the air war should not be measured on the same continuum of victimhood.[6] Yet the fall of the Berlin Wall and subsequent reunification of Germany created new space for public discourse about the air war, prompting a reevaluation of the Allied attacks, as authors from Jörg Friedrich (*The Fire*) to W. G. Sebald ("Air War and Literature") explored the panoply of ways civilian suffering resounded through German culture.[7] As evidenced by personal accounts of those who lived through these raids, German victimhood played a central role in the creation and sustenance of bunker and shelter communities.

## HEARING THE ALLIED AIR WAR: SONIC EXPERIENCES OF REACHING SHELTER

Between 1940 and 1945, the Royal Air Force, later joined by the Americans, extensively bombed civilian areas of Germany. Initially, the attacks were in retaliation for the Luftwaffe's raids on Coventry and London, as Allied bombers targeted mainly industrial areas, factories, and armaments facilities. By 1943, however, the United States and Great Britain adopted a broader policy of morale bombing designed to undermine support for the Nazi war effort, exacting a staggering human and material toll. Estimates suggest that between four hundred thousand and six hundred thousand civilians died as a direct result of these raids, and upward of 70 percent of the country's homes were rendered uninhabitable.[8] Aerial warfare left its mark not only on physical spaces; British and American bombers created new "sonoric landscapes," to borrow Richard Leppert's term, with civilians dependent on the government's aural signals to warn them of impending attacks.[9]

Sonic experiences of the bombing generally centered around two sites: the bunker and the cellar. Most of the larger bunkers were constructed between 1940 and 1942 under the purview of a Reich bunker-building initiative called the Führer's Emergency Program (*Führer-Sofortprogramm*). The program played on German fears of annihilation while still upholding the guise of Nazi victory by providing a safe space to preserve the civilian workforce and morale. By 1943 the government had used some 6.7 million cubic yards of concrete to construct shelters, and although exact figures are not known, it is estimated that between two thousand and three thousand bunkers were specially constructed for civilian protection during the Second World War. (This figure does not include the thousands of repurposed spaces, such as cellars, which also served to shelter Germans from bombings.) Yet, despite the lip service paid to constructing air raid protections, by 1942 only some 0.7 percent of the total civilian population had access to the state-funded structures, usually built above ground to save money.[10]

Despite the bunker's medieval appearance and function, the most advanced were outfitted with modern amenities, including hospital wards, operating rooms, and even ventilation systems to prevent the deadly buildup of carbon monoxide. Different spaces in the bunkers were earmarked for various activities, such as music-making, demonstrating how important escapism was to the psychological well-being of bunker dwellers from the outset.[11]

In Berlin, the three largest air raid bunkers were located in the city's parks: Friedrichshain, Humboldthain, and Zoologischer Garten (hereafter abbreviated Zoo). The Zoo bunker was considered one of the finest and most formidable bunkers in Germany (fig. 10.1). Each of Berlin's major bunkers could accommodate ten thousand civilians. Some four hundred smaller, private bunkers also provided safety to city dwellers who did not secure a place in one of the larger structures. The bunker below Berlin's Hotel Adlon, reserved for hotel guests, was often filled with prominent government figures and celebrities. Nazi Party elite also had their own shelters; Göring had two in the capital alone.[12]

Fig. 10.1. Berlin, Zoo Bunker, 1946. Bundesarchiv, Picture 183–1997-0923-505 / photographer: Erich O. Krueger.

Going to the bunker was an experience born of and bathed in sound. Often the first warnings came over the radio, commonly referred to as a *Kuckuck-Ruf*, or cuckoo call, or through an air raid siren that vibrated between 300 and 400 Hz. Larger cities had thousands of sirens, since each one could be heard only within a 1,600-foot radius. With its differing tones, the siren signaled the four stages of the raid: (1) one should stay alert, (2) one should seek shelter within the next ten minutes, (3) bombing may be over, and (4) the raid is finished.[13] As one civilian wrote in her diary, "Alarm, alarm, and still alarm. You hear nothing else, see nothing else, think nothing else."[14] Each air raid meant the delicate operation of filling the bunker would begin anew, choreographed for maximum efficiency. In the frantic ten minutes between the second alarm and entry into the shelters, streams of people poured out of their homes carrying their prepacked suitcases. Families became separated from one another and cried out to find their loved ones. Bunker wardens and police monitored the bleary-eyed influx of city dwellers as they made their way through the shelter's doors. (Most of the alarms occurred at night, depriving the urban population of sleep to weaken their daytime productivity.) Some civilians had bunker passes that granted them assigned seats or private cabinets with bunk beds. Other inhabitants spent the hours sitting on wooden benches or even on their suitcases.[15] Although there remained a wide range of experiences in "bunker communities," as Gertrud Zscharnt deemed them, these populations consisted primarily of women, children, and teenagers, especially as the war progressed and all eligible men were drafted.[16]

In the bunker, civilians had nothing to do but sit and contemplate. As Jörg Friedrich notes, "The bunker occupants were prepared for the ruin of it all: city, property, state, nation—everything except for their bare skin."[17] Civilians in the bunker may have been ready for "the ruin of it all," but that was because they still had something to lose as more privileged members of the Volksgemeinschaft. Often before the bombs were dropped, a period of silence would leave civilians hypersensitive to all sound and movement. People "listened into the void," and against this backdrop of heightened anxiety, "the infernal concert" began.[18] A direct hit by a bomb would, at best, produce an earth-shattering sound as the bunker rocked back and forth, as it was designed to do, and at worst, the force of impact would injure or kill those inside.

Yet the cellar, and not the bunker, was the most common form of shelter. Accounts of cellar and bunker dwellers differ both in their descriptions of sonic warfare and in how they spent their time waiting during air raids. The cellar was run and inhabited by neighbors and had to be evacuated once the building above caught on fire; otherwise, inhabitants could die of heatstroke or suffocation. Civilians in cellars were virtually helpless, and the sound of bombs was far more intense there than in the bunkers. During one 1944 raid, a singer in the Berlin

State Opera, Frida Leider, recalled, "A shrill, whistling sound which I couldn't place was followed by a dull, uncanny rumble," as a bomb fell next to her home.[19]

Even after the all-clear siren sounded, the sonic trauma of the event left lingering resonances for both bunker and cellar inhabitants. Those buried in the rubble and still alive shouted for help as long as they could; their voice was their only chance for survival. Inversely, after particularly violent raids, still other civilians reported temporarily losing their voice. The psychological strain of being "earwitness" (to borrow Carolyn Birdsall's term) could render one unable to form words for hours, days, or even weeks.[20]

## AIR WAVES AND THE AIR WAR

Air raid sirens and bombs were not the only sounds heard in the shelter; music from the radio also mingled with the sounds of the air war. The Second World War was the first global conflict to take place on and over the airwaves. From the technology's inception in 1923, the Reich Postal Ministry controlled radio service, licensing private firms to create nine regional stations, while a tenth station, Deutsche Welle (based in Berlin), remained programmed by the state. This model allowed great variety and flexibility in what each station could broadcast. The 1932 nationalization of radio created new rules and restrictions, cutting down on illegal stations and standardizing programming. A year later, radio ownership skyrocketed after Propaganda Minister Joseph Goebbels commissioned the *Volksempfänger* (People's Receiver), an affordable set designed for civilians. German manufacturers had produced just under four million radios in 1932, and by 1939, this number jumped to nearly eleven million, making Germany the second-largest radio-listening public in Europe, just behind England.[21]

Nanny Drechsler writes in her study of radio during the Third Reich that the primary purpose of programming during the war years was "to keep up the spirits of the people in the bombed cities and in the war business according to the motto, 'Everything is better with music.'"[22] Yet as Brian Currid argues, radio in Nazi Germany did more than raise morale, functioning as "a tense, contradictory social field alternatively shaped by various forms of mass publicity," and as a medium that furthered "hegemonic modes of national fantasy."[23] Music played an integral part in establishing and maintaining this national narrative; by the outbreak of the Second World War, about 70 percent of German radio programming consisted of music.[24]

Radio was not a mere mouthpiece designed to indoctrinate. Although Nazi ideology railed against jazz, stations were careful to tailor their programming to the tastes of civilians and soldiers, broadcasting the music of Louis Armstrong and Duke Ellington, albeit under different titles and without announcing the performers' names.[25] Other popular music programming included *The Request Concert for the Wehrmacht* (*Das Wunschkonzert für die Wehrmacht*), which aired every other Sunday at 3:00 p.m. In a letter to the program expressing his gratitude, one soldier noted the program's reassuring sonic presence: "One can reflect so well with music. We are not only here, here in the bunker, we are also there and over there, everywhere where our thoughts fly.... It was not so long ago—we had no idea that we would hear something like a 'Request Concert' so soon—but we had a deep desire for it; we longed again for music and wanted to be reminded of the many beautiful hours that we had spent earlier."[26]

The *Request Concert* program forged a musical link between soldiers and their families as well as a bond among German civilians, creating what Marc Silberman called "an acoustic bridge." The broadcast even inspired the 1940 feature film *Request Concert*, which used the program as a vital component in the love story between pilot Herbert Koch and his beloved, Inge Wagner. The pair meet at the 1936 Berlin Olympics but are abruptly separated by Herbert's top-secret military mission. They are reunited several years later, if only sonically, through Herbert's musical request to the radio program: the 1936 *Olympia Fanfare*. The broadcast, which Inge hears from the comfort of her living room, gives her renewed hope that Herbert is still alive. (After a series of mishaps and misunderstandings, they are eventually reunited at the end of the film in a military hospital.)[27] The popularity of the *Request Concert* radio program and film emphasizes the importance of music in creating and maintaining the Volksgemeinschaft despite geographical distance.

Radio also came to play a crucial role in creating a sense of community in the shelters, as it was not unusual for civilians to bring their prized radios to the cellar, listening collectively to music or news bulletins (fig. 10.2). Attending performances and concerts had become nearly impossible with such frequent air raids, and radio listening partially filled in this gap. To ensure that broadcasts could continue uninterrupted during evening bombing raids, Reich Radio, the most powerful transmitter in the country, broadcast from a Berlin bunker on Masurenallee.

Even if craning their necks to hear updates about the war, by April 1945, most civilians were well aware that the front had come home to Germany. At their country house in Pausin, northwest of Berlin, soprano Frida Leider and her mother grew tired of retreating to their cellar during air raids and instead "stayed glued to the radio," trying to find news from the BBC. (Although listening to foreign stations was illegal in Germany, there were few real consequences for doing so.)[28] As the Battle for Berlin was underway, seventeen-year-old Helmut Altner was conscripted into the *Volkssturm*, the desperate militia composed primarily of young boys and old men. Rather than return to the fighting raging above, Altner

Fig. 10.2. Listening to the radio in the cellar (ca. 1940–44). Bundesarchiv, Picture 146-1981-076-29A / photographer: Unknown.

sought safety in a Spandau air raid shelter, located in a western Berlin suburb. To pass the time, the small group listened to "gentle music" on the radio, soon to be interrupted by Nazi functionaries threatening swift punishment for any Berliner who surrendered to the Russians.[29] The "Horst Wessel Song" closed the announcement, and the entire sonic intrusion struck Altner as absurd; clearly the war was lost.

### UNDERGROUND PERFORMANCES

In his research conducted in the 1940s for the British government on air raid shelter conditions, P. E. Vernon, head of the Psychology Department at the University of Glasgow, wrote a set of guidelines to minimize the psychological stress on civilians in bunkers. Activities that Vernon recommended to help pass the time underground included singing and listening to music.[30] Though his guidelines may have been for the United Kingdom, similar behaviors occurred in German bunkers as well. The terrifying sound world of the air war led civilians to crave a return to earlier and more comforting sonic experiences. Theo Findahl, a Norwegian journalist living in Berlin, recalled of his time spent inside the Zoo bunker: "The feeling of security inside the heavy concrete bunkers brings out a kind of everyday atmosphere. Quiet chitchat and humming, the ladies sit around and talk about the food prices. You hardly sense any sadness about Berlin's fate."[31] Humming, the most ubiquitous form of singing, could resonate through the bunker space, now overfilled beyond capacity. In Findahl's account, humming is a marker of both normalcy and resignation.

Beyond mere sonic distraction, however, the cellar and bunker also hosted concerts and performances. In Berlin's Humboldthain bunker, Luftwaffe auxiliary personnel spent long hours inside the tower in case of attack. Sunbathing beneath the gun turrets was a popular activity when the weather was nice, but in the winter, other distractions had to be found. In January 1945, the teenagers staged a performance of Heinrich von Kleist's *Der zerbrochene Krug* (*The Broken Jug*) in the bunker's cafeteria with costumes borrowed from the Schiller Theater. The play's protagonist, a judge named Adam, refuses to own up to his crimes despite the fact that the audience knows he is guilty, and he flees at the end of the piece. The photograph of the performance (fig. 10.3) has a macabre air of finality as the cast is framed by the bunker's concrete walls.

While taking refuge in a Hanover bunker during the spring of 1945, Jurgen Herbst, a sixteen-year-old Wehrmacht soldier, heard a performance by several Edelweiss Pirates (*Edelweißpiraten*), a pacifist group opposed to the Hitler Youth's militarist values. While listening to the musicians strum their guitars and sing a folk song about a soldier who would never return from battle, "Mädel liebst Du einen blonden Fallschirmjäger?" (Girl, Do You Love a Blonde Paratrooper?), Herbst admitted the audience soon forgot "the threat of their own death . . . mesmerized by the haunting melody of the song."[32] He was also surprised by the gravity of their performance, acknowledging that "their message was of death and sorrow, not of final victory,"[33] which Herbst heard in subversive contrast to the Nazi propaganda of his childhood.

Holidays celebrated in the bunker also included traditional music to mark and normalize the passage of time; as a child in Kaiserslautern, Siegrid Mayer spent Christmas 1944 in a city shelter. As they had no presents to exchange, the adults in the family sang Christmas carols to celebrate.[34] The community function of music extended beyond building bonds only within the Volksgemeinschaft, as it became a form of nonverbal communication that could blur the lines of mistrust and animosity toward the Germans' perceived foes. As German teenager Sitta Hohendorf hid in a Lichtenberg bunker in eastern Berlin, against protocol, the SS permitted forced laborers (*Zwangsarbeiter*) from France, Russia, Italy, and the Ukraine to enter the shelter and hide in a separate room. As Hohendorf recalled: "When the first Russian soldiers entered the bunker, we heard the forced laborers singing and dancing. They celebrated their liberation. A soldier found his sister

Fig. 10.3. Kleist's *Der zerbrochene Krug* in the Humboldthain Bunker, January 1945. Landesarchiv Berlin, F Rep. 290 (02) Nr. 0372841 / photographer: Götz Benecke.

there, who had been taken years ago for forced labor in Germany."[35] In Hohendorf's account, music fills the liminal border between war and peace, connecting German civilians and Russian soldiers with the newly liberated prisoners.

Accounts of the surrender also reveal music's psychological role for Germans in the first hours of the liberation. Now more than a form of escapism, music in the bunker represented a protective barrier that even concrete walls could not guarantee, a medium through which musicians tried to thwart the violence Soviet troops meted out to German civilians. As the Battle of Berlin raged, and after playing for wounded soldiers at a Berlin military hospital, conductor Hans von Benda and fourteen members of his ensemble, the Berlin Chamber Orchestra

(Berliner Kammerorchester), hid in Benda's cellar along with his neighbors. Passing the days and nights below ground, the group was soon isolated from all news. Left to wonder about their chances of survival, Benda later recalled:

> In those nights in the cellar, under the ear-splitting racket of Russian grenades, the decision was made—if we came out alive—to give a concert immediately. Yes, we even became the saviors of our cellar community when the Russians invaded at night, shouting, "Uri," and "You, woman." The musicians got their instruments out and played. The Russians left the woman and Uri, grinned, and vanished. After a good hour, they appeared again, bringing a large basket with bread, wurst, cheese, and butter, laughed, listened to a little more music, and vanished. It was the only cellar in our street that did not have to suffer violent deeds.[36]

Though Benda's account is almost certainly embellished (it seems highly unlikely music would have protected his neighbors from rape), postwar testimonies like his reveal music's central role in war and surrender, as acoustic experiences united cellar and bunker communities despite invasion and defeat.[37] Even if these accounts are romanticized, the fact that music and sound are foregrounded in their memories is significant. Descriptions of the end of the war consisted not only of literary accounts of the ruined urban landscape; the cease-fire also had a distinct soundscape for those who lived through it.

## CONCLUSIONS

In the postwar period, many bunkers were destroyed during the country's occupation, while still others were left intact and repurposed, too expensive to be razed. Cities converted their remaining shelters into hospitals, offices, and even hotels, in the case of Bremerhaven's Hotel Aude, a former bunker near the city's main train station.[38] More recently, the postwar bunker has actually come to house various musical activities. One tower of Hamburg's Heiligengeistfeld bunker serves as a popular venue for bands (Uebel und Gefährlich); in Aachen, the Goffartstraße bunker became a music club; and in Cologne, the massive bunker on Berliner Straße is now known as Culture Bunker Cologne, staging dance, music, theater, and comedy events. Berlin's Hohenzollerndamm bunker houses the Artist Home Initiative, featuring a gallery space, concert hall, practice rooms, and a café, all of which can be rented for public and private events.[39]

Former shelters can also serve pedagogical purposes for reenacting the sonic experiences of war, as the popular Berlin Underworld tours demonstrate.[40] In 2008, a school in Braunschweig used the 1934 bomb shelter beneath its building to re-create both the acoustic and physical experiences of an air raid for the pupils. For thirty minutes, student volunteers stood in the shelter, listening to recordings of bombings and sirens in order to, in the words of their instructor, "make history audible and palpable."[41] Surveys handed out after the exercise revealed the students felt extreme anxiety, with one student even writing, "We were afraid, some of us for the first time, really afraid."[42] This contemporary reenactment privileged sound over all other forms of experience, underscoring the fundamentally aural experience of aerial warfare.

World War II was a conflict that was not only seen but also heard in myriad ways by civilian earwitnesses. As many of these memoirs compellingly demonstrate, sonic descriptions of defeat and occupation play just as important a role as do their visual counterparts. These accounts do not fail to recall the sounds of these memories, even if written decades after the end of the war. Often because sight was impaired in these dark, confined spaces, sound took on an even greater prominence in shaping these narratives. During World War II, the cellar and bunker could not provide an infallible safeguard against bombs and soldiers, but they could provide the false security offered by collective music-making in the midst of adverse conditions. Radio listening and live performances blurred together with the sounds of aerial warfare overhead and of advancing enemy troops on the ground. Yet music's instrumentalization as an escapist tool and community-building activity could spare civilians only temporarily from the terrors of the war, for outside the shelter, the ruined city awaited.

## NOTES

1. Quoted in Brett-Smith, *Berlin '45*, 75; and Joseph Sauer quoted in Friedrich, *The Fire*, 266.
2. See Fauser, *Sounds of War*, 9; and Currid, *A National Acoustics*, 1.
3. For more concerning acoustic memories and the air war, see Maier, *Akustisches Gedächtnis*.
4. Ian Kershaw quoted in Eley, *Nazism as Fascism*, 62. For further discussion of the Volkgemeinschaft, see Eley, *Nazism as Fascism*, 59–130; and Bergerson, "Hildesheim in an Age of Pestilence."
5. Friedrich, *The Fire*, 351.
6. Moeller, "On the History of Man-Made Destruction," 103–134.
7. For more, see Friedrich, *The Fire*, 1–48; and Sebald, "Air War and Literature," in *On the Natural History of Destruction*, 1–106.
8. Moeller, "On the History of Man-Made Destruction," 107–108.
9. Leppert, *The Sight of Sound*, 17–18.
10. Evans, *Life among the Ruins*, 27; Süss, *Death from the Skies*, 176, 202; and Friedrich, *The Fire*, 346–348.

11. Süss, *Death from the Skies*, 322.

12. Stargardt, *The German War*, 113; Friedrich, *The Fire*, 348; and Arnold and Janick, *Sirenen und gepackte Koffer*, 13, 27, 44–45.

13. Friedrich, *The Fire*, 328. Concerning the Kuckuck-Ruf, see Götsch, "Mann könnte die Bomben zahlen."

14. Andreas-Friedrich, *Berlin Underground*, 115.

15. Evans, *Life among the Ruins*, 23, 31; and Friedrich, *The Fire*, 328.

16. Quoted in Arnold and Janick, *Sirenen und gepackte Koffer*, 86.

17. Friedrich, *The Fire*, 330.

18. Quoted in ibid., 439 and 443.

19. Leider, *Playing My Part*, 179.

20. For accounts of trauma, see Friedrich, *The Fire*, 441; and Süss, *Death from the Skies*, 365. Birdsall uses "earwitness" to write about civilians whose accounts of fascism are marked by the sonoric experience of sirens and bombings rather than visual destruction. Birdsall's term comes, in part, from the Elias Canetti short story, "Der Ohrenzeuge," in which the title character wants to indict individuals with sonic, rather than visual, evidence. Birdsall, *Nazi Soundscapes*, 11.

21. For more on the nationalization of radio in this period, see Hailey, "Rethinking Sound," 13–14; Currid, *A National Acoustics*, 27, 46–47; and Oster, "Rubble, Radio, and Reconstruction," 59.

22. Drechsler, *Die Funktion der Musik*, 135. "Die Menschen in den zerbombten Städten und im 'Kriegsgeschäft' bei Laune zu halten, getreu dem Motto 'Mit Musik geht alles besser,' war das Hauptanliegen der Rundfunkprogrammgestaltung in den sechs Jahren des Zweiten Weltkriegs." All translations are my own unless otherwise noted.

23. Currid, *A National Acoustics*, 59.

24. Ibid., 33, 45–46; and Drechsler, *Die Funktion der Musik*, 33.

25. Potter, *Art of Suppression*, 18, 161; and Drechsler, *Die Funktion der Musik*, 42.

26. Quoted in Drechsler, *Die Funktion der Musik*, 132. "Man kann so gut nachdenken bei Musik. Wir sind ja nicht nur hier, hier im Bunker, wir sind da und dort, überall, wo die Gedanken hinfliegen. Gerade wenn man vor all den Dingen, die uns das Leben wert machen, am entferntesten ist, fühlt man sich ihnen am nächsten. Und die verschiedene Musik hilft dazu mit. Jeder kann sich ein Stück aussuchen, der eine kann an das, der andere an jenes denken. Es ist noch nicht so lange her—wir hatten keine Ahnung, daß wir bald so etwas wie 'Wunschkonzert' hören würden—aber wir hatten ein tiefes Verlangen danach, wir sehnten uns wieder nach Musik und wollten erinnert werden an viele schöne Stunden, die wir früher verlebt hatten." See also Goedecke and Krug, *Wunschkonzerte für die Wehrmacht*, 124–125. This book is a reprint of the 1941 edition, *Wir beginnen das Wunschkonzert für die Wehrmacht*.

27. For more information about the *Request Concert* film and radio program, see Silberman, *German Cinema*, 66–80 (page 73 is quoted here). See also Heldt, "Front

Theatre," 57–80; Currid, *A National Acoustics*, 54–58; and Fritzsche, *Life and Death in the Third Reich*, 71–75.

28. Leider, *Playing My Part*, 138; Drechsler, *Die Funktion der Musik*, 100; Arnold and Janick, *Sirenen und gepackte Koffer*, 134; Currid, *A National Acoustics*, 49; Hailey, "Rethinking Sound," 13–14; Oster, "Rubble, Radio, and Reconstruction," 59; and Levi, *Music in the Third Reich*, 124.
29. Altner, *Berlin Dance of Death*, 126.
30. Süss, *Death from the Skies*, 344.
31. Quoted in Friedrich, *The Fire*, 320.
32. Herbst, *Requiem for a German Past*, 176.
33. Ibid.
34. Mayer, "Kaiserslautern, Rheinland-Palatinate," 82–83.
35. Hohendorf, "Zwangsarbeiter feierten im Bunker ihre Befreiung," 55–56. "Als die ersten russischen Soldaten den Bunker betraten, hörten wir die Zwangsarbeiter singen und tanzen. Sie feierten ihre Befreiung. Ein Soldat hat dort seine Schwester, die vor Jahren zur Zwangsarbeit nach Deutschland verschleppt worden war, wiedergefunden."
36. Benda, "Phoenix aus der Asche: Das erste Konzert nach dem Krieg," *Tagesspiegel*, May 16, 1965. "In jenen Kellernächten, unter dem ohrenbetäubenden Lärm der russischen Granaten, wurde der Beschluß gefaßt, sofort—kämen wir lebend davon—ein Konzert zu geben. Ja, wir wurden sogar die Retter unserer Kellergemeinschaft, als die ersten Russen nachts bei uns eindrangen und 'Uri' und 'Du Frau,' riefen. Die Musiker packten ihre Instrumente aus und spielten. Die Russen ließen Frau und Uri, grinsten und verschwanden. Nach einer guten Stunde erschienen sie wieder, brachten einen großen Korb mit Brot, Wurst, Käse, Butter, lachten, hörten noch ein wenig Musik und verschwanden. Es war der einzige Keller in unserer Straße, der keine Gewalttaten zu erleiden hatte." See also "Neues Leben—neue Klänge: Gespräch mit Hans von Benda," interview with Hans von Benda, *Berliner Zeitung*, May 21, 1945; and Hans von Benda Papers, E-Rep 200-44, Landesarchiv Berlin.
37. Maier, *Akustisches Gedächtnis und Zweiter Weltkrieg*, 1–22.
38. Stenek, "Hitler's Legacy in Concrete and Steel," 60–61. For more on bunkers in Northern Germany, see Foedrowitz, *Bunkerwelten*; and Schmal and Selke, *Bunker: Luftschutz und Luftschutzbau in Hamburg*.
39. For more on the Berlin bunker, see "Artist Homes: Der Bunker," accessed June 18, 2019, http://artist-homes.com; and "Der Kulturbunker vom Roseneck," *Der Tagespiegel*, February 17, 2017, www.tagesspiegel.de/berlin/bezirke/charlottenburg-wilmersdorf/berlin-schmargendorf-der-kulturbunker-vom-roseneck/19404612.html.
40. More about Berlin Underworld's bunker tours can be found at: www.berliner-unterwelten.de.
41. Bellinskies, "Geschichtsunterreicht mit Sound-Einsatz im Luftschutzkeller. Erfahrungsbericht aus der Schule," in Maier, *Akustisches Gedächtnis und Zweiter*

*Weltkrieg*, 215–222. "Wir wollten Geschichte hörbar und fühlbar machen," 218. The school was Berufsbildende Schule 5 Braunschweig (BBS5).

42. Ibid., "Wir hatten Angst, manche zum ersten Mal so richtig Angst," 221.

BIBLIOGRAPHY

Altner, Helmut. *Berlin Dance of Death*. Translated by Tony Le Tissier. Havertown, PA: Casemate, 2002.

Andreas-Friedrich, Ruth. *Berlin Underground, 1938–1945*. Translated by Barrow Mussey. New York: Henry Holt, 1947.

Arnold, Dietmar, and Christine Steer, eds. *Wie Silberfische flimmerten Bomber am Himmel: Erinnerungen an das Inferno des Krieges in Berlin-Lichtenberg, 1940–1945*. Berlin: Edition Berliner Unterwelten, 2004.

Arnold, Dietmar, and Reiner Janick, eds. *Sirenen und gepackte Koffer: Bunkeralltag in Berlin*. Berlin: Ch. Links Verlag, 2003.

Benda, Hans von. "Neues Leben—neue Klänge: Gespräch mit Hans von Benda." Interview, *Berliner Zeitung*, May 21, 1945.

———. "Phoenix aus der Asche: Das erste Konzert nach dem Krieg." *Tagesspiegel*, May 16, 1965.

Bellinskies, Jürgen H. "Geschichtsunterreicht mit Sound-Einsatz im Luftschutzkeller. Erfahrungsbericht aus der Schule." In *Akustisches Gedächtnis und Zweiter Weltkrieg*, edited by Robert Maier, 215–222. Göttingen: V&R Unipress, 2011.

Bergerson, Andrew Stuart. "Hildesheim in an Age of Pestilence: On the Birth, Death, and Resurrection of Normalcy." In *The Work of Memory: New Directions in the Study of Germany Society and Culture*, edited by Alon Confino and Peter Fritzsche, 107–135. Urbana: University of Illinois Press, 2002.

Birdsall, Carolyn. *Nazi Soundscapes: Sound, Technology and Urban Space in Germany, 1933–1945*. Amsterdam: Amsterdam University Press, 2012.

Brett-Smith, Richard. *Berlin '45: The Grey City*. London: Macmillan, 1967.

Currid, Brian. *A National Acoustics: Music and Mass Publicity in Weimar and Nazi Germany*. Minneapolis: University of Minnesota Press, 2006.

Drechsler, Nanny. *Die Funktion der Musik im deutschen Rundfunk, 1933–1945*. Musikwissenschaftliche Studien 3. Pfaffenweiler: Centaurus-Verlagsgesellschaft, 1988.

Eley, Geoff. *Nazism as Fascism: Violence, Ideology, and the Ground of Consent in Nazi Germany 1930–1945*. Abingdon: Routledge, 2013.

Evans, Jennifer. *Life among the Ruins: Cityscape and Sexuality in Cold War Berlin*. New York: Palgrave Macmillan, 2011.

Fauser, Annegret. *Sounds of War: Music in the United States during World War II*. Oxford: Oxford University Press, 2013.

Foedrowitz, Michael. *Bunkerwelten: Luftschutzanlagen in Norddeutschland*. Berlin: Ch. Links Verlag, 1998.

Friedrich, Jörg. *The Fire: The Bombing of Germany*. Translated by Allison Brown. New York: Columbia University Press, 2006.

Fritzsche, Peter. *Life and Death in the Third Reich*. Cambridge, MA: Belknap Press of Harvard University Press, 2008.

Goedecke, Heinz, and Wilhelm Krug. *Wunschkonzerte für die Wehrmacht*. Emmelshausen: Condo-Verlag, 2002.

Götsch, Horst. "Man konnte die Bomben zählen." In *Wie Silberfische flimmerten Bomber am Himmel: Erinnerungen an das Inferno des Krieges in Berlin-Lichtenberg, 1940–1945*, edited by Dietmar Arnold and Christine Steer, 48–51. Berlin: Edition Berliner Unterwelten, 2004.

Hailey, Christopher. "Rethinking Sound: Music and Radio in Weimar Germany." In *Music and Performance during the Weimar Republic*, edited by Bryan Gilliam, 13–36. Cambridge: Cambridge University Press, 1994.

Heldt, Guido. "Front Theatre: Musical Films and War in Nazi Cinema." In *Twentieth-Century Music and Politics: Essays in Memory of Neil Edmunds*, edited by Pauline Fairclough, 57–80. London: Routledge, 2016.

Herbst, Jurgen. *Requiem for a German Past: A Boyhood among the Nazis*. Madison: University of Wisconsin Press, 1999.

Hohendorf, Sitta. "Zwangsarbeiter feierten im Bunker ihre Befreiung." In *Wie Silberfische flimmerten Bomber am Himmel: Erinnerungen an das Inferno des Krieges in Berlin-Lichtenberg, 1940–1945*, edited by Dietmar Arnold and Christine Steer, 55–56. Berlin: Edition Berliner Unterwelten, 2004.

Kardorff, Ursula von. *Diary of a Nightmare: Berlin, 1942–1945*. New York: John Day, 1966.

Leider, Frida. *Playing My Part, 1888–1975*. Translated by Charles Osborne. New York: Da Capo, 1978.

Leppert, Richard. *The Sight of Sound: Music, Representation, and the History of the Body*. Berkeley: University of California Press, 1993.

Levi, Erik. *Music in the Third Reich*. New York: Saint Martin's, 1994.

Maier, Robert, ed. *Akustisches Gedächtnis und Zweiter Weltkrieg*. Göttingen: V&R Unipress, 2011.

Mayer, Siegrid. "Kaiserslautern, Rhineland-Palatinate." In *The War of our Childhood: Memories of World War II*, edited by Wolfgang E. Samuel, 80–90. Jackson: University of Mississippi Press, 2002.

Moeller, Robert G. "On the History of Man-Made Destruction: Loss, Death, Memory and Germany in the Bombing War." *History Workshop Journal* 61 (Spring 2006): 103–134.

Oster, Andrew. "Rubble, Radio, and Reconstruction: The Genre of Funkoper in Postwar Occupied Germany and the Federal Republic, 1946–1957." Ph.D. diss., Princeton, 2010.

Potter, Pamela M. *Art of Suppression: Confronting the Nazi Part in Histories of the Visual and Performing Arts*. Berkeley: University of California Press, 2016.

Purpus, Elke, Günther B. Sellen, Walter Geis, and Helmut Buchen, eds. *Bunker in Köln—Versuche einer Sichtbar-Machung*. Essen: Klartext, 2006.

Schmal, Helga, and Tobias Selke. *Bunker: Luftschutz und Luftschutzbau in Hamburg.* Hamburg: Christians, 2001.

Sebald, W.G. *On the Natural History of Destruction.* Translated by Anthea Bell. New York: Random House, 2004.

Silberman, Marc. *German Cinema: Texts in Context.* Detroit, MI: Wayne State University Press, 1995.

Stargardt, Nicholas. *The German War: A Nation under Arms, 1939–45.* London: Penguin Random House, 2015.

Stenek, Nicholas J. "Hitler's Legacy in Concrete and Steel: Memory and Civil Defence Bunkers in West Germany, 1950–1960." In *Narratives of Trauma: Discourses of German Wartime Suffering in National and International Perspective*, edited by Helmut Schmitz and Annette Seidel-Arpaci, 59–74. Amsterdam: Rodopi, 2011.

Süss, Dietmar. *Death from the Skies: How the British and Germans Survived Bombing in World War II.* Translated by Lesley Sharpe and Jeremy Noakes. Oxford: Oxford University Press, 2010.

ABBY ANDERTON is Assistant Professor of Music in the Department of Fine and Performing Arts at Baruch College. She is the author of *Rubble Music: Occupying the Ruins of Postwar Berlin, 1945–1950* (2019).

# AFTERWORD

## Trans/national Soundscapes in World War II

ANNEGRET FAUSER

"SANDY MACPHERSON'S QUIET VOICE IS very reassuring at a time when our ears are on alert for warning sirens." This comment in a 1939 letter to the editor of the BBC's listings magazine *Radio Times*—quoted in Christina Baade's contribution to the present volume—offers an entry into thinking about the roles of sound and music during World War II. What we hear when listening for acoustic signals in wartime, this British writer implies, takes on existential qualities. Macpherson's quietness not only reassured his listeners emotionally but also promised not to obscure vital sonic information from the outside world that might make the difference between death and survival. Sounds—this quotation reveals—are neither neutral nor absolute but relational. And indeed, Macpherson's quiet vocality fulfilled a function for his British listeners different from the experience of the ominous silence the German civilians enclosed in bunkers and cellars were hearing as an acousmatic void that portended "the infernal concert" of the air raids to come.[1] In this nexus of dystopian wartime normalcy, music in particular often proffered the comfort of the familiar, whether in the *Dunkelkonzerte* in wartime Vienna, Czech-language swing in German-occupied Prague, or the performances of Mozart and Schubert put on by German POWs in the United States. Music could both challenge and reinforce cultural hegemonies—on Broadway, for instance, in Rodgers and Hammerstein's *Oklahoma!*—or serve propagandistic goals by rendering suspicious Allies such as the Soviets more palatable through the soundtracks of Hollywood movies or radio programs featuring the music of Chaikovsky and Shostakovich. But especially in war zones, music could also be dangerous and distracting: in May 1940, France's Second Army—so the anecdote goes—missed the beginning of the German invasion because the senior staff of General Charles Huntziger attended a musical gala performance at Vouziers.

Only when they left the theater, as we find out in Christopher Brent Murray's contribution, could artists and audiences hear anti-aircraft fire.

Read together, the chapters in this volume generate an acoustemology of war in the mid-twentieth century, capturing how sound, music, and silence were enmeshed in the aural experiences of civilians, soldiers, and prisoners of war across Europe and the United States. Acoustemology, in Steven Feld's definition, "is about the experience and agency of listening histories, understood as relational and contingent, situated and reflexive."[2] The authors here not only focus on uncovering listening histories from witnesses of the time in the archives and in published accounts, but also treat the musical works, recordings, soundtracks, and other material residues as "audible archives" of wartime musicking.[3] What emerges from these chapters, moreover, is a window on the transnational entanglements of wartime musical practice and ideologies. The shared past of Western music—both classical and popular—had carved well-worn grooves of sonic circulation that cultural wartime practice overwrote at times, yet also often reinforced along accustomed lines.

Nowhere else in this volume does it become clearer than in the texts that address the realm of classical music and its purported universalism that, in turn, enabled Allied institutions from the BBC to the Metropolitan Opera House in New York to claim Mozart, Beethoven, Verdi, and even Wagner as their own.[4] Arresting in their balancing act of cosmopolitanism and nationalism, these institutions and their agents claimed ownership over this repertoire not in spite of its transnational circulation but because of it.[5] Such acts of appropriation became, in effect, a gesture of cultural warfare. Given its place in US concert life, Beethoven's music, in particular, served this agenda. The critic for the *Los Angeles Times*, Isabel Morse Jones, for instance, claimed his Ninth Symphony as a symbol of musical Americanism: "It is the heartbeat of democracy. Beethoven stands today, as he did 150 years ago, a prophet declaring that the spirit of man is indomitable."[6] Yet if music per se was cast as universalist and transnational, then the claim to national if not local ownership over it lay in the preservation, crystallization, or formation of extrinsic forms of identity politics in the face of hegemonic cultures, on the one hand, and in instrumentalizing a particular repertoire or form of musical practice as a marker of bounded identities, on the other. In all cases, however, these strategies depended on trans/national legibility, whether in the case of Soviet film composers translating jazz into a sonic emblem of imperialist America right after the war, or the emphasis on local practices in Vienna, as Nicholas Attfield observes, in order to create a difference to what was perceived as a totalizing German musical hegemony at the time of the *Anschluss*. Indeed, the soundscapes of Western music in World War II developed at the glocal intersection points of transnational circulation of music and localized musical practice.[7]

In her introduction to this volume, Pamela M. Potter identifies escapism as a crucial component of musical consumption in World War II. This kind of escapist use of music was predicated on the rise of audiovisual technologies such as radio, gramophone, and film during the 1930s, which created—and responded to—new forms of listening both individually and collectively.[8] Across the belligerent nations during World War II, ministries of war and propaganda as well as institutions such as national radio stations—from the BBC to the Ente Italiano per le Audizioni Radiofoniche (EIAR)—consolidated these cultural practices previously developed during the interwar years by providing morale-building music programs and by enabling locally established forms of cultural expression.[9] But while escapism indeed forms a key aspect of musicking in World War II, four additional intersecting themes emerge from the chapters in this volume that open up areas for further, provocative reflection: the role of music in prisoner-of-war camps and its connection both to national identity politics and to institutionalized structures of military entertainment; the affirmation of a compelling conventionality in consolidating national musical tropes; the opportunities for creation if not innovation that came along with the distortions of cultural life through occupation and war; and finally, the expanded acousmatic soundscape in the wake of new technologies honed to new perfection during the war.

A short quotation toward the end of Abby Anderton's discussion of music-making in German bunkers offers a fascinating glimpse of the singing and dancing of forced laborers (*Zwangsarbeiter*) as they celebrated their liberation through the Russian army. It does not disclose what music they sang, but the eyewitness intimates that it was "theirs," not German. Music indeed played (and plays) an important role in the identity politics of captivity, displacement, and diaspora. POW camps in World War II offer a number of fascinating challenges to these interpretive frameworks. For example, POWs came from both Allied and Axis nations, thus creating implicit epistemic biases how we might best engage with their musical practices, especially in comparative terms. As Emily Roxworthy pointed out in her study about Japanese American trauma in World War II, comparison fosters "hierarchies of suffering" which privilege the trauma of one group against which that of the other inevitably pales.[10]

Anderton addresses up front the moral challenges of engaging with German trauma by emphasizing that the victimhood of the air war cannot compare to the Holocaust. This ethical dilemma still seems implicitly to carry with it the fear of betraying the unspeakable trauma of the Holocaust and other atrocities perpetrated by the Axis powers if, for instance, the well-treated German POWs in the United States should become the object of sympathetic engagement. Kelsey Kramer McGinnis makes a similar point in her chapter by reflecting that discussing cultural identity of this particular group of displaced people undeniably poses a narrative predicament. Not only did the German POWs in Camp Algona, Iowa, use music to preserve their national and spiritual core identities, but they also—either actively or by sheer happenstance—lacked any active or even passive engagement with American music, thus undermining any attempt at the cultural reeducation that the Intellectual Diversion Program (IDP) of the American authorities had devised.[11] How to read the stubborn focus on their culture by German POWs, many of whom were also Nazis, indeed poses challenges, all the more because considering them as displaced people is an unfamiliar strategy. Yet the military displacement of both combat soldiers and POWs forms part of broader experiences of displacement in the twentieth century.[12] Any scholarly evaluation of French POWs' musical activities touches these moral questions as well. As Murray shows here, the musicians who were part of the French Second Army's Centre musical et théâtral (CMT)—a military entertainment unit closely connected to Pétain's government—lived in better conditions than most of the one and a half million French POWs, many of whom were imprisoned until 1945. Instead, musicians from Olivier Messiaen to Maurice Thiriet were able to pursue musical activities throughout their captivity until they were released in spring 1941. This hitherto unknown backstory that connects the destiny of musician POWs with the collaborationist CMT raises new questions, for instance, on how to frame Messiaen's military displacement and his musical production during this period, including his famous *Quatuor pour la fin du temps* (1941).

Both Murray and McGinnis also point to a barely explored phenomenon that starts to emerge in a more transnational perspective: the translation of military structures into POW communities and their cultural activities. Murray shows that the artists of the CMT were imprisoned together, in two groups, and thus transferred their military activities into POW-camp composition and performance. McGinnis, too, points to command structures that were in place, with musical events either bounded by military unit or open to the camp as a whole. As Sears A. Eldredge uncovered for the far more precarious POW camps connected to the construction of the Thailand–Burma Railway between 1942 and 1945, pre-captivity military configurations of troop entertainment—for instance in the formation of "unit concert parties" in the British Army—enabled the setup of musical and theatrical entertainment in the Pacific war theater.[13] Contrary to the POW camps discussed by Murray and McGinnis, however, the Thailand–Burma Railway camps were international, with POWs from Britain and Australia as well as the Dutch East Indies. Performances not only put the music and culture of POWs on the stage—with repertoire that reached from London's West End to Javanese court dance—but could also involve Japanese military personnel, as when a Commander Hochi, at Aungganaung in Burma, performed a kabuki-like samurai dance.[14] The typical military structures across most of the belligerent nations were easily legible on both sides of the fence, and they enabled—at least to some extent—self-directed musicking by POWs throughout the conflict, at least in those camps where the Geneva Convention held actual or nominal sway. But the transcultural example of the Thailand–Burma Railway camps also puts the homogeneity of musical and cultural life in POW camps located in Western nations into stronger relief.

If music in POW camps helped both to escape the harshness of captivity and to affirm cultural identity through performance (the latter also in Judith Butler's sense of the term), then it also relates to the second topic emerging from these chapters, the consolidation of national musical tropes and conventional musical practice.[15] A number of chapters—by Christina Baade, Peter Kupfer, Christopher Lynch, and Tony Stoller—tell stories about how the war encouraged a turn toward the familiar, whether the BBC broadcasting the recognizable sounds of the theater organ well embedded in the soundscape of British entertainment or the way in which classical music rose to new prominence during World War II, displacing avant-garde music in similar ways as it had done already in World War I. None of these choices was uncontested, however, such as when the debate in Britain turned to the issue of so-called "enemy music," or when local music was deemed to be, in the opinion of Arthur Bliss, too sentimental and saccharine. Unsurprisingly, Bliss and his fellow critics agreed with other functionaries across Axis and Allied nations in their platonic assessment of music's power: the appropriate music for the war effort was virile, rhythmic, and rousing.[16]

Where the consolidation of conventional musical tropes played a particularly crucial role was in the sonic representation of ipseity and alterity. Kupfer's discussion of Hollywood film scores reveals that their composers used time-honored compositional strategies to integrate their Russian subjects sonically into an American soundscape. Just as nineteenth-century opera composers such as Georges Bizet (in the *Pearl Fishers*), Léo Delibes (*Lakmé*), and Jules Massenet (*Thaïs*) integrated exotic alterity into the sumptuous scores of their Western soundscapes, Hollywood film composers like Daniele Amfitheatrof (*Days of Glory*, 1944), Louis Gruenberg (*Counter-Attack*, 1945), Max Steiner (*Mission to Moscow*, 1943), as well as Eric Zeisl and Herbert Stothart (*Song of Russia*, 1944), contributed to guiding US audiences into empathizing with their Russian allies by portraying them musically as quasi-American.[17] By characterizing Russians as an integral part of a musical world anchored in the familiar realm of Hollywood soundtracks—rather than sonically differentiating between friend and enemy as, for instance, in Hans Salter's score to the spy thriller *Invisible Agent* (1942)—these scores rely on conventional tropes to all but guarantee the legibility of their signification. It is not at all surprising that the majority of composers contributing to this integrated soundscape were themselves passing as American despite their immigrant origins often from countries that might otherwise raise suspicions of their loyalties.

Nonetheless, even within this hegemonic American soundscape, composers deployed shopworn musical emblems of national identity, not only where Hollywood Russians were concerned but also on Broadway, when the music of Edvard Grieg (in *Song of Norway*, 1944) or Frédéric Chopin (in *Polonaise*, 1945) served as Norwegian and Polish soundtracks, respectively.[18] Whereas these two and other works drew on familiar forms of musical representation, wartime Broadway also offered opportunities that generated new forms of theatrical entertainment. As Tim Carter shows in his chapter, Broadway creators had their finger on the pulse of their contemporaries, both by staging escapist revues and timely shows about good neighbors and by forging a new form of nationalist musical drama, not least in the dramatically integrated *Oklahoma!* (1943). Thus, how musicians and institutions responded to, and instrumentalized, shifts in their cultural environment becomes a third theme that emerges not only from exploring the music performed on stages of New York, but also from similar efforts in the wartime cities of Vienna and Prague.

In the 1930s, Brian S. Locke explains, swing became an emblem of Czech cosmopolitanism in contrast to Austro-German cultural politics. During the war, it continued to flourish both where it served to entertain Nazi officials in command performances and—especially before the assassination of Reinhard Heydrich and the subsequent repressions—in the cafés and other gathering places of Czech youths who identified as the saxophone generation. With the interdiction of American jazz—labeled as such foremost by the language in which it was sung—swing music in Prague developed its own signature, both compositionally and performatively. The celebrated singer Inka Zemánková, for instance, used the different stress patterns in Czech to create her signature rhythmic gesture. So successful were Czech swing composers that their works circulated to Berlin, as with Jiří Traxler's hit foxtrot, "Hádej, hádej . . . ," from 1940. Reading Czech swing as being part of a transnationally circulating form of music therefore allows a better understanding of the intersections between global and local instantiations as they were shaped in a precarious wartime context. But whereas Locke's focus is on repertorial and performative innovation, Nicholas Attfield's discussion of the Dunkelkonzerte revises the way in which familiar Austrian repertoire from Mozart to Bruckner was instrumentalized not only to challenge the hegemony of German culture in post-Anschluss Vienna, but also to bring new visual technologies to bear on concert performance. By turning darkness into a spectacle and thus reconfiguring a concert's audiovisual experience, the organizers at the Konzerthaus tried to reframe listening as a silhouette show, not dissimilar to the effects seen, for instance, in Walt Disney's *Fantasia* (1940) and Sergei Eisenstein's *Alexander Nevsky* (1938). Such synchronicity locates the Viennese Dunkelkonzerte less in the bounded world of the Third Reich and more in that of transnational artistic modernism. In the Dunkelkonzerte, technologies of acousmatic listening shaped by radio and the gramophone intersected in provocative ways with new forms of visual consumption in film.[19]

The contributions to this volume hint at a final point: the complex experiential field of acousmatic soundscapes. Before 1944, Viennese audiences could enjoy the Dunkelkonzerte as an entertaining novelty while the war was taking place elsewhere. The New York theatergoers and their panoply of entertainment choices that Carter evokes so eloquently at the beginning of his chapter never had to fear (or listen for) bombs and other attacks on American soil (Pearl Harbor remained the exception). Listening to music in such physical safety and even comfort differs crucially from the visceral acoustic immersion of both civilians and soldiers into air raids in Britain, Germany, Italy, Japan, or Russia. Listening the right way became a skill honed in the crucible of airborne warfare, when ears became finely tuned to the acoustic signatures of sirens, of different aircraft, bombs, and machine guns, and of music broadcast to mask, albeit insufficiently, the noise of air raids. Listening wrongly—missing or misinterpreting acoustic cues—could be at the cost of one's life.

This dystopian acousmatic skill was weaponized, toward the end of the war, by the Allied Forces, in a military-deception campaign that used false radio traffic and the broadcasting of battle sounds to give greater reality to the dummy tanks deployed in fake configurations so as to misdirect opposition forces in terms of location and intention. One American unit, the Twenty-Third Headquarters Special Troops, was inserted into the Allied front line under General George S. Patton to perform the audiovisual spectacle of an entire heavy division with their "rubber dummies, a world-class collection of sound-effects records, and all the creativity the soldiers could muster."[20] Dubbed the Ghost Army, the unit had been recruited among successful artists and sound engineers from Hollywood and elsewhere.[21] The technologies that enabled the successful sonic deception of the German army were, on the one hand, the recently developed stereophonic sound system, used for example to record the soundtrack for *Fantasia*, and, on the other, newly enhanced loudspeakers with higher fidelity.[22] This fascinating blend of performance and technology played with audiovisual perception in ways that relied on the very acousmatic skills acquired in combat and civilian exposure to air raids. Lieutenant Dick Syracuse, an American officer assigned to provide security to the Ghost Army, recalled how listening to the sound effects in the dark affected his perception: "My eyes were beginning to tell me what my ears were hearing ... Psychologically it was the most unnerving thing; I would actually begin to see tanks in the dark."[23]

The acoustemology of World War II, to return to Steven Feld's concept, reflects a complex audiovisual ecology of sound, in which trans/national listening histories intersected with local experiences in specific times and places. In this optic, multiple hegemonic repertoires—from the Austro-German canon to American jazz—became interwoven with each other, as in Prague, or splintered, as in Vienna. Claims over musical choice and ownership stood in for social, political, and even military campaigns, taking on existential importance. The chapters in this volume have opened numerous venues of inquiry, both explicitly and implicitly. Their counterpoint reflects the intricate entanglements of musical practice across and within some of the belligerent nations in the West. But it is a West that—save for a short passage in Carter's essay, which speaks to African American Broadway in World War II—remains, at least, so far as this volume is concerned, a predominantly white, heteronormative, and masculine sphere. Queering, gendering, and racing the acoustemology of World War II in these and other theaters of war would raise still more questions for future research. Nevertheless, that research must surely build on the multifaced explorations in the present volume and the provocative questions that they raise.

### NOTES

1. The trope of combat as an infernal concert reaches back to the Napoleonic Wars and was particularly prominent in descriptions of, and reactions to, the newly mechanized soundscape of World War I. See Giesbrecht, "Höllenkonzerte und Brummerlieder."
2. Feld, "Acoustemology," 14.
3. Ibid., 19.
4. On the use of German music in the wartime United States, see Fauser, *Sounds of War*, 138–141 (Beethoven) and 172–173 (Wagner); for opera, see also Fauser, "'Carmen in Khaki.'"
5. Among the scholars prominent in framing transnationalism theoretically in the past two decades are, among others, Patricia Clavin, Akira Iriye, Marilyn Lake, Jürgen Osterhammel, Pierre-Yves Saunier, Philipp Ther, and Ian Tyrrell. For excellent overviews of the field through the disciplinary perspective of history, see Macdonald, "Transnational History"; and Körner, "Transnational History: Identities, Structures, States." For a translational perspective on the transnational circulation of culture, see the essays in Bachmann-Medick, ed., *The Trans/national Study of Culture*.
6. Jones, "Beethoven Timely as War Ends." On Beethoven in the United States during World War II, see Fauser, "Beethoven in den USA" (in press).
7. Patricia Clavin discusses the role of global intersections in transnational circulation in "Defining Transnationalism," 437.
8. See, among others, Sterne, *The Audible Past*; Denning, *Noise Uprising*; and Radano and Olaniyan, *Audible Empire*.
9. As Manuela Schwartz has shown, the German occupying forces in France were careful to maintain a semblance of cultural autonomy as a deliberate strategy

of cultural bounding; see her "Die Musikpolitik der Nationalsozialisten in Vichy-Frankreich." How strongly and deliberately fascist nations in Europe reflected on the new cultural order of the continent is explored in Martin, *The Nazi-Fascist New Order for European Culture*.

10. Roxworthy, *The Spectacle of Japanese American Trauma*, 2–3.

11. It might be worth thinking about this inward turn in German POW camps in North America also in the context of US detention camps for Japanese Americans. Here, too, the conditions of captivity fostered a focus on traditional high-art. See, for example, Waseda, "Extraordinary Circumstances, Exceptional Practices." Waseda attributes the unprecedented flourishing of traditional Japanese music to two closely interconnected factors: "For the internees, music was an important means for creating hope, cohesion, resistance and a sense of identity; yet for the camp authorities, the same music was understood to be a mechanism by which resentment could be diffused and morale could be built" (172). But although Japanese internees (re-)discovered traditional musics, they were also actively partaking in (and claiming ownership of) both American popular music and Western classical music; see, for example, Reich, "'It Took Our Minds off of the Bad Things'"; Barbour, "'For the Good of Our Country'"; and Robertson, "Ballad for Incarcerated Americans."

12. Smith and Barkhof, "Introduction."

13. Eldredge, *Captive Audiences/Captive Performers*, 5–8.

14. Ibid., 117, 242–243.

15. Butler, *Bodies That Matter*, xii: "Performativity must be understood, not as a singular or deliberate 'act,' but, rather, as the reiterative and citational practice by which discourse produces the effects that it names."

16. See, for example, Fauser, *Sounds of War*, 118.

17. On the absorption of alterity into Western musical idioms for European consumption, see Locke, *Musical Exoticism*; and Boghal, "Lakmé's Echoing Jewels."

18. See the following publications which address representation of sonic alterity in American wartime music: Fauser, "Sounding the *Tricolore*"; Fauser, "Lessons in Musical Geography"; Fauser, *Aaron Copland's Appalachian Spring*, 34–40 (on *The North Star*).

19. The foundational text connecting the emergence of media technologies and their consumption is Kittler, *Gramophone, Film, Typewriter*.

20. Beyer and Sayles, *The Ghost Army*, 10.

21. Ibid., 82.

22. Goodman, *Sonic Warfare*, 41–43.

23. Beyer and Sayles, *The Ghost Army*, 111.

## BIBLIOGRAPHY

Bachmann-Medick, Doris, ed. *The Trans/national Study of Culture: A Translational Perspective*. Berlin: Walter de Gruyter, 2016.

Barbour, Alecia D. "'For the Good of Our Country': Ruth Watanabe and the 'Good That Is in Music' at the Santa Anita Detention Center." *Notes* 74, no. 2 (2017): 221–234.

Beyer, Rick, and Elizabeth Sayles. *The Ghost Army of World War II: How One Top-Secret Unit Deceived the Enemy with Inflatable Tanks, Sound Effects, and Other Audacious Fakery*. New York: Princeton Architectural, 2015.

Boghal, Gurminder Kaur. "Lakmé's Echoing Jewels." In *The Arts of the Prima Donna in the Long Nineteenth Century*, edited by Rachel Cowgill and Hilary Poriss, 186–201. New York: Oxford University Press, 2012.

Butler, Judith. *Bodies That Matter: On the Discursive Limits of "Sex."* New York: Routledge, 2011.

Clavin, Patricia. "Defining Transnationalism." *Contemporary European History* 14 (2005): 421–439.

Denning, Michael. *Noise Uprising: The Audiopolitics of a World Musical Revolution*. London: Verso, 2015.

Eldredge, Sears A. *Captive Audiences/Captive Performers: Music and Theatre as Strategies for Survival on the Thailand–Burma Railway, 1942–1945*. St. Paul, MN: Macalester College, 2014.

Fauser, Annegret. *Aaron Copland's Appalachian Spring*. New York: Oxford University Press, 2017.

———. "Beethoven in den USA—Lokale Traditionen und diasporische Identitäten während des Zweiten Weltkriegs." *Schriften zur Beethovenforschung* 30 (2019) (in press).

———. "'Carmen in Khaki': Europäische Oper in den Vereinigten Staaten während des Zweiten Weltkrieges." In *Oper im Wandel der Gesellschaft. Kulturtransfers und Netzwerke des Musiktheaters im modernen Europa*, edited by Sven Oliver Müller, Philipp Ther, Jutta Toelle, and Gesa zur Nieden, 303–329. Vienna: Oldenbourg and Böhlau, 2010.

———. "Lessons in Musical Geography: Imagining Eastern Europe in the United States during World War II." In *Music in Dark Times: Europe East and West, 1930–1950*, edited by Valentina Sandu-Dediu, 19–60. Bucharest: Editura UNMB, 2016.

———. "Sounding the *Tricolore*: France and the United States during World War II." *Cahiers de la Société québécoise de Recherche en musique* 16 (2015): 9–21.

———. *Sounds of War: Music in the United States during World War II*. New York: Oxford University Press, 2013.

Feld, Steven. "Acoustemology." In *Keywords in Sound*, edited by David Novak and Matt Sakakeeny, 12–21. Durham, NC: Duke University Press, 2015.

Giesbrecht, Sabine. "Höllenkonzerte und Brummerlieder: der Erste Weltkrieg als Musikerlebnis." In *Musik bezieht Stellung*, edited by Stefan Hanheide, Dietrich Helms, Claudia Junk, and Thomas Fleischer, 455–468. Göttingen: V&R Unipress, 2013.

Goodman, Steve. *Sonic Warfare: Sound, Affect, and the Ecology of Fear*. Cambridge, MA: MIT Press, 2010.

Jones, Isabel Morse. "Beethoven Timely as War Ends; Offering of Ninth Symphony in Bowl Was Symbolical," *Los Angeles Times*, August 26, 1945, C5.

Kittler, Friedrich. *Gramophone, Film, Typewriter*. Translated with an introduction by Geoffrey Winthrop-Young and Michael Wutz. Stanford: Stanford University Press, 1999.

Körner, Axel. "Transnational History: Identities, Structures, States." In *Internationale Geschichte in Theorie und Praxis / International History in Theory and Practice*, edited by Barbara Haider-Wilson, William D. Godsey, and Wolfgang Mueller, 265–290. Vienna: Verlag der österreichischen Akademie der Wissenschaften, 2017.

Locke, Ralph. *Musical Exoticism: Images and Reflections*. Cambridge: Cambridge University Press, 2009.

Macdonald, Simon. "Transnational History: a Review of Past and Present Scholarship," typescript, 2013, UCL Centre for Transnational History. https://www.ucl.ac.uk/centre-transnational-history/objectives/simon_macdonald_tns_review. Accessed October 16, 2015.

Martin, Benjamin J. *The Nazi-Fascist New Order for European Culture*. Cambridge, MA: Harvard University Press, 2016.

Radano, Ronald, and Tejumola Olaniyan. *Audible Empire: Music, Global Politics, Critique*. Durham, NC: Duke University Press, 2016.

Reich, Howard. "'It Took Our Minds off of the Bad Things': Japanese Internment Camp Survivors Remember the Swing Music That Helped Them Endure," *Chicago Tribune*, October 10, 2001.

Robertson, Marta. "Ballad for Incarcerated Americans: Second Generation Japanese American Musicking in World War II Camps." *Journal of the Society for American Music* 11, no. 3 (2017): 284–312.

Roxworthy, Emily. *The Spectacle of Japanese American Trauma: Racial Performativity and World War II*. Honolulu: University of Hawai'i Press, 2008.

Schwartz, Manuela. "Die Musikpolitik der Nationalsozialisten in Vichy-Frankreich." In *Kultur, Propaganda, Öffentlichkeit: Intentionen deutscher Besatzungspolitik und Reaktionen auf die Okkupation*, edited by Wolfgang Benz, Gerhard Otto, and Anabella Weismann, 55–78. Berlin: Metropol, 1998.

Smith, Angela K., and Sandra Barkhof. "Introduction: The No-Man's Land of Displacement." In *War and Displacement in the Twentieth Century: Global Conflicts*, edited by Sandra Barkhof and Angela K. Smith, 1–15. New York: Routledge, 2014.

Sterne, Jonathan. *The Audible Past: Cultural Origins of Sound Reproduction*. Durham, NC: Duke University Press, 2003.

Waseda, Minako. "Extraordinary Circumstances, Exceptional Practices: Music in Japanese American Concentration Camps." *Journal of Asian American Studies* 8, no. 2 (2005): 171–209.

ANNEGRET FAUSER is Cary C. Boshamer Distinguished Professor of Music at the University of North Carolina at Chapel Hill. She is author of *Musical Encounters at the 1889 Paris World's Fair*, the award-winning *Sounds of War: Music in the United States during World War II*, and *Aaron Copland's Appalachian Spring*.

# SELECTED WORKS

This bibliography offers an overview of work appearing since 1945 that focuses specifically on music and World War II. It is provided here as an aid for further research as well as a guide toward demonstrating the general scholarly trends discussed in the introduction. As such, it does not include the extensive work on music and the Holocaust, music under the dictatorships of the 1930s and 1940s, or the music of exiled composers and musicians. Organized geographically, it further complements the coverage of Europe and North America reflected in the essays included in this volume. (It does not include all the works cited in individual essays, which can be found at the end of each chapter.)

General

Bade, Patrick. *Music Wars, 1937–1945*. London: East & West, 2012.
Botstein, Leon. "After Fifty Years: Thoughts on Music and the End of World War II." *The Musical Quarterly* 79, no. 2 (Summer 1995): 225–230.
Osthoff, Wolfgang. "Symphonien beim Ende des zweiten Weltkriegs: Strawinsky—Frommel—Schostakowitsch" [Symphonies at the end of the Second World War: Stravinsky, Frommel, Shostakovich]. *Acta Musicologica* 60, no. 1 (1988): 62–104.
Reagen, Bernice Johnson. "World War II Reflected in Songs." *Southern Exposure* 1, no. 3–4 (Winter 1974): 170–184.

Belgium and the Netherlands

Don, Floris. *De Nachtwacht zal klinken in donkere tijden: De opera in Nederland tijdens de Tweede Wereldoorlog en de rol van Henk Badings* ["De nachtwacht" shall sound in dark times: Opera in the Netherlands during World War II and the role of Henk Badings]. Focus. Utrecht: Koninklijke Vereniging voor Nederlandse Muziekgeschiedenis, 2008.

Murray, Christopher Brent, Marie Cornaz, and Valérie Dufour, eds. *Musical Life in Belgium during the Second World War*. Special issue of *Revue belge de musicologie/ Belgisch tijdschrift voor muziekwetenschap* 69 (2013).

Paul, Charles B. "A Belgian Refugee's Memories: World War II, Sweatshop Labor, and Beethoven." *The Beethoven Journal* 13, no. 1 (summer 1998): 45–47.

Top, Stefaan. "The Flemish Broadside-Singer Hubert Geens and the Second World War." In *The Ballad Today*, edited by Georgina Boyes, 23–35. Doncaster: January Books, 1985.

Czechoslovakia

Fejtová, Olga, Václav Ledvinka, and Jiří Pešek, eds. *Evropská velkoměsta za druhé světové války: každodennost okupovaného velkoměsta—Praha 1939–1945 v evropském srovnání* [European metropolises during the Second World War: The everyday of the occupied metropolis—Prague of 1939–1945 in European context]. 24. vědecká konference Archivu hlavního města Praha, 2005. Prague: Scriptorium, 2007.

Gálová, Jana. "Hudobné vysielania v slovenskom rozhlase v rokoch druhej svetovej vojny" [Music broadcasting on Slovak radio in the years of the Second World War]. In Hommage à Miloslav Blahynka. Special issues of *Slovenská hudba: Revue pre hudobnú kultúru* 37, no. 3 (2011): 275–309.

France

Barthoulot, T., et al., eds. *Paroles et musique: les chansons et la deuxième guerre mondiale: dossier documentaire* [Words and music: Songs of the Second World War: Documentary dossier]. Archives-ressources du musée de la résistance et de la déportation. Besançon: Musée de la résistance et de la déportation, 2003.

Boswell-Kurc, Lilise. "Olivier Messiaen's Religious War-Time Works and Their Controversial Reception in France (1941–1946)." Ph.D. diss., New York University, 2001.

Bourhis, Michelle. *La vie musicale à Nantes pendant la Seconde Guerre mondiale* [Musical life in Nantes during the Second World War]. Musiques et Champ Social. Paris: L'Harmattan, 2014.

Chimènes, Myriam. "Groupe de recherche: la vie musicale en France pendant la Seconde Guerre mondiale" [Research group: Musical life in France during the Second World War]. *Bulletin de l'Institut d'Histoire du Temps Présent* 63 (1996): 13–15.

———. *La vie musicale sous Vichy* [Music life under Vichy]. Brussels: Complexe, 2001.

Chimènes, Myriam, and Yannick Simon, eds. *La musique à Paris sous l'Occupation* [Musical life in Paris under the Occupation]. Paris: Fayard, 2013.

Fulcher, Jane. "French Identity in Flux: Vichy's Collaboration and Antigone's Operatic Triumph." *Proceedings of the American Philosophical Society* 150, no. 2 (June 2006): 261–295.

———. "Musical Style, Meaning, and Politics in France on the Eve of the Second World War." *The Journal of Musicology* 13, no. 4 (Fall 1995): 425–453.

———. *Renegotiating French Identity: Musical Culture and Creativity in France during Vichy and the German Occupation*. New York: Oxford University Press, 2018.

———. "The Preparation for Vichy: Anti-Semitism in French Musical Culture between the Two World Wars." *The Musical Quarterly* 79, no. 3 (Fall 1995): 458–475.

Iglesias, Sara. *Musicologie et Occupation: science, musique et politique dans la France des "années noires"* [Musicology and occupation: Science, music, and politics in France during the "dark years"]. Paris: Editions de la Maison des sciences de l'homme, 2014.

Launchbury, Claire. *Music, Poetry, Propaganda: Constructing French Cultural Soundscapes at the BBC during the Second World War*. Modern French Identities. Oxford: Peter Lang, 2012.

Le Bail, Karine. *La musique au pas: Être musicien sous l'Occupation* [Music at a slow pace: Being a musician under the Occupation]. Paris: CNRS éditions, 2016.

Lonjon, Bernard. *Nuit et chansons: Les chanteurs français face à la Seconde Guerre mondiale* [Night and songs: French singers confronting the Second World War]. Paris: Éditions du Moment, 2011.

Matore, Daniel. "Le modernisme musical français à la fin de la Seconde Guerre mondiale" [French musical modernism at the end of the Second World War]. *Revue Internationale de Musique Française* 18 (November 1985): 69–78.

Potter, Caroline. "French Music and the Second World War." In *French Music since Berlioz*, edited by Richard Langham Smith and Caroline Potter, 281–301. Aldershot, UK: Ashgate, 2006.

Régnier, Gérard. *Jazz et société sous l'Occupation* [Jazz and society under the Occupation]. Logiques Sociales: Musiques et Champ Social. Paris: L'Harmattan, 2009.

Roust, Colin. "Communal Singing as Political Act: A Chorus of Women Resistants in La Petite Roquette, 1943–1944." *Music and Politics* 7, no. 2 (2013): 21–39.

Schwartz, Manuela. "Die Musikpolitik der Nationalsozialisten in Vichy-Frankreich" [The music policy of National Socialists in Vichy France]. In *Kultur, Propaganda, Öffentlichkeit: Intentionen deutscher Besatzungspolitik und Reaktionen auf die Okkupation*, edited by Wolfgang Benz, Gerhard Otto, and Anabella Weismann, 55–78. Berlin: Metropol, 1998.

Simeone, Nigel. "Messiaen and the Concerts de la Pléiade: 'A Kind of Clandestine Revenge against the Occupation.'" *Music and Letters* 81, no. 4 (2000): 551–584.

Simon, Yannick. *Composer sous Vichy* [Composing under Vichy]. Lyon: Symétrie, 2009.

———. "Les périodiques musicaux français pendant la Seconde Guerre mondiale" [French music periodicals during the Second World War]. *Fontes Artis Musicae* 49, no. 1–2 (January-June 2002): 67–78.

Sprout, Leslie A. "Messiaen, Jolivet, and the Soldier-Composers of Wartime France." *The Musical Quarterly* 87, no. 2 (Summer 2004): 259–304.

———. *The Musical Legacy of Wartime France*. Berkeley: University of California Press, 2013.

## Germany

De Vries, Willem. *Sonderstab Musik: Music Confiscations by the Einsatzstab Reichsleiter Rosenberg under the Nazi Occupation of Western Europe.* Amsterdam: Amsterdam University Press, 1996.

Dittmar, Jurgen. "Zur Weltkriegspropaganda in den Programmen der 'Volksunterhaltungsabende'" [World War propaganda in the programs of the "People's Entertainment Evenings"]. In *Musikalische Volkskunde—aktuell: Festschrift für Ernst Klusen zum 75. Geburtstag*, edited by Günther Noll and Marianne Bröcker, 185–203. Bonn: Wegener, 1984.

Elbers, Winfried. "Das Soldatenlied als publizistische Erscheinung. Wege und Wirkungen der Liedpublizistik im deutschen Weltkriegsheer" [The soldier's song as a publishing phenomenon: Methods and effects of song publishing in the German World War military]. Ph.D. diss., Universität Münster, 1963.

Frommann, Eberhard. *Die Lieder der NS-Zeit: Untersuchungen zur nationalsozialistischen Liedpropaganda von den Anfängen bis zum Zweiten Weltkrieg* [Songs of the Nazi era: Examinations of National Socialist song propaganda from the beginnings until the Second World War]. PapyRossa-Hochschulschriften 26. Cologne: PapyRossa, 1999.

Haken, Boris von. "'Vom lieben Gott': Hans Heinrich Eggebrecht und die Debatte über seinen Einsatz bei der Feldgendarmerie" [For the love of God: Hans Heinrich Eggebrecht and the debate over his deployment in the field police]. *Die Musikforschung* 66, no. 3 (2013): 247–264.

Heister, Hanns-Werner. "Zwischen Anziehen und Ablenken: Zu Wirkungen und Funktionen von Musik in der nazistischen Besatzungspolitik" [Between attraction and distraction: On the effects and functions of music in Nazi occupation policy]. In *Besatzungsmacht Musik. Zur Musik- und Emotionsgeschichte im Zeitalter der Weltkriege (1914–1949)*, edited by Sarah Zalfen and Sven Oliver Müller, 159–186. Bielefeld: transcript Verlag, 2012.

Hirt, Alexander. "Die deutsche Truppenbetreuung im Zweiten Weltkrieg: Konzeption, Organisation und Wirkung" [German troop entertainment in the Second World War: Conception, organization, and effect]. *Militärgeschichtliche Zeitschrift* 59, no. 2 (2000): 407–434.

Leibovitz, Liel, and Matthew Miller. *Lili Marlene: The Soldiers' Song of World War II.* New York: W. W. Norton, 2009.

Müller, Sven Oliver. "Political Pleasures with Old Emotions? Performances of the Berlin Philharmonic in the Second World War." *International Review of the Aesthetics and Sociology of Music* 43, no. 1 (2012): 35–52.

Murdoch, Brian O. *Fighting Songs and Warring Words: Popular Lyrics of Two World Wars.* London: Routledge 1990.

Präger, Ulrike. "Music in the Sudeten-German Expulsion." *Ethnomusicology Review* 16 (January 2011): [n.p.].

Protte, Katja. "Mythos 'Lili Marleen'—Ein Lied im Zeitalter der Weltkriege" [The myth of "Lili Marleen"—A song in the time of World Wars]. *Militärgeschichtliche Zeitschrift* 63 (2004): 355–400.

Walter, Michael. "Lili Marleen: Germanische Hegemonie oder Kriegsbeute?" [Lili Marleen: Germanic hegemony or war booty?]. In *Besatzungsmacht Musik. Zur Musik- und Emotionsgeschichte im Zeitalter der Weltkriege (1914–1949)*, edited by Sarah Zalfen and Sven Oliver Müller, 279–297. Bielefeld: transcript Verlag, 2012.

Hungary

Grymes, James A. "'Dohnányi Was Not—and Could Not Have Possibly Been—a War Criminal': The Hungarian Defense of Ernő Dohnányi, 1945–1949." *Studia Musicologica: An International Journal of Musicology of the Hungarian Academy of Sciences* 54, no. 3 (2013): 301–317.

Hirsch, Eric. "Voices from the Black Box: Folk Song, Boy Scouts, and the Construction of Folk Nationalist Hegemony in Hungary, 1930–1944." *Antipode* 29, no. 2 (1997): 197–215.

Porter, Monica. *Deadly Carousel: A Singer's Story of the Second World War*. London: Quartet, 1990.

Willson, Rachel Beckles. "'Behold! The Long-Awaited New Hungarian Opera Has Been Born!' Discourses of Denial and Petrovics's *C'est la guerre*." *Central Europe* 1, no. 2 (2003): 133–145.

Poland

Kwiatkowski, Maciej-Józef. "Muzyka w Polskim Radio w czasie II wojny światowej" [Music on Radio Poland during World War II]. *Ruch Muzyczny* 12 (June 1981): 3–4.

Markiewicz, Leon. "Z życia muzycznego w obozach oficerów polskich podczas drugiej wojny światowej" [Musical life in the POW camps for Polish officers during World War II]. *Zeszyty naukowe Państwowej Wyższej Szkoły Muzycznej w Katowicach* 7 (1969): 3–10.

Michałowski, Kornel. "Z tradycji myśli muzycznej w Poznaniu XIX wieku: Z historii muzykologii poznańskiej—Muzykologia niemiecka w Poznaniu w latach II wojny światowej" [Traditions of musical thought in 19th-century Poznan: History of Poznan musicology—German musicology in Poznan during World War II]. In *Muzykologia na Uniwersytecie im. Adama Mickiewicza w Poznaniu w latach 1974–1999: Tradycje, działalność i dokumentacja*, edited by Jan Steszewski, Maciej Jabłonski, and Danuta Jasińska, 15–59. Uniwersytet im. Adama Mickiewicza w Poznaniu 5. Poznań: Wydawnictwo Naukowe UAM, 1999.

Naliwajek-Mazurek, Katarzyna. "Music and Its Emotional Aspects during the Nazi Occupation of Poland." In *Besatzungsmacht Musik. Zur Musik- und Emotionsgeschichte im Zeitalter der Weltkriege (1914–1949)*, edited by Sarah Zalfen and Sven Oliver Müller, 207–224. Bielefeld: transcript Verlag, 2012.

Naliwajek-Mazurek, Katarzyna, and Elżbieta Markowska. *Okupacyjne losy muzyków: Warszawa 1939–1945* [The fate of musicians under the Nazi occupation: Warsaw 1939–1945]. Warszawa: Towarzystwo imienia Witolda Lutosławskiego, 2014.

Nikol'skaja, Irina. "Wojna z faszyzmem a drogi polskiej i radzieckiej twórczości symfonicznej" [The Second World War and Soviet and Polish symphonic works]. In *Z zagadnień poznawczych, kulturowych i dydaktycznych muzyki* 1 (1987): 9–20.

Socha, Ziemowit. "Zakazane piosenki w przestrzeni publicznej okupacyjnej Warszawy: Ujęcie socjologii historycznej" [Forbidden songs in the public space of Nazi-occupied Warsaw: A historical-sociological perspective]. *Muzyka* 59, no. 1 (2014): 61–76.

Tamura, Susumu. "Dai 2 ji sekaitaisen chu no Poland ongakubunka. Poland gendai ongakushi kenkyu ni yosete" [Music culture in Poland during World War II: A contribution to the investigation of the history of contemporary Polish music]. *Bulletin of Tokyo College of Music* 1 (1976): 41–72.

Zimniak, Henryk. "La vie musicale allemande dans le 'Pays de la Warta' (1939–1945)" [German musical culture in the Wartheland (1939–1945)]. *Polish Western Affairs* 24, no. 2 (1983): 215–243.

Scandinavia

Kvideland, Reimund. "Singen als Widerstand in Norwegen während des Zweiten Weltkriegs" [Singing as resistance in Norway during the Second World War]. In *Musikalische Volkskultur und die politische Macht*, edited by Günther Noll, 369–381. Musikalische Volkskunde 11. Essen: Blaue Eule, 1994.

Lindberg, Boel. "'Exportera den där Hitlermusiken till Tyskland': Brev till Radiotjänst om musiken i svensk radio under andra världskriget" ["Export that Hitler music to Germany!" Listener mail about music programs of the AB Radiotjänst during World War II]. In *Fruktan, fascination och frändskap: Det svenska musiklivet och nazismen*, edited by Greger Andersson and Ursula Geisler, 145–178. Malmö: Sekel, 2006.

Välimäki, Susanna. *Miten sota soi? Sotaelokuva, ääni ja musiikki* [How does the war sound? War films, sound, and music]. Tampere: Tampereen Yliopistopaino/Tampere University Press, 2008.

Wasserloos, Yvonne. "Protestgesang und verbotener Klang: Alsang und Lili Marleen in Kopenhagen 1940–1943" [Protest song and forbidden sound: Alsang and Lili Marlene in Copenhagen, 1940–1943]. *Moderne Stadtgeschichte (MSG)* 1 (January 2017): 84–99.

Spain

Iglesias, Iván. "(Re)construyendo la identidad musical española: el jazz y el discurso cultural del franquismo durante la Segunda Guerra Mundial" [(Re)constructing

Spanish musical identity: Jazz and the cultural discourse of Francoism during World War II]. *Historia Actual Online* 23 (Fall 2010): 119–135.

Moreda Rodríguez, Eva. "Italian Musicians in Francoist Spain, 1939–1945: The Perspective of Music Critics." *Music and Politics* 2, no. 1 (2008): 82–91.

Soviet Union

Ament, Suzanne. "Sing to Victory: The Role of Popular Song in the Soviet Union during World War II." Ph.D. diss., Indiana University, 1996.

Arkin, Yefim. "Narodnaya pesnya Velikoy Otechestvennoy voynï" [Russian songs of World War II]. In *Narodnaya kul'tura Sibiri: Materialï X nauchno-prakticheskogo seminara Sibirskogo Regional'nogo Vuzovskogo Tsentra po Fol'kloru*, edited by Tat'yana Georgiyevna Leonova, 276–279. Omsk: Omskiy Gosudarstvennïy Pedagogicheskiy Universitet, 2001.

Aydarov, Nadim Zhavdetovich. "Blokadnaya epopeya Zh.K. Aydarova: Pis'ma iz goroda-fronta" [The Siege Epopee written down by Zhavdet Aydarov: Letters from the city in combat]. *Musicus* 3, no. 43 (2015): 50–57.

Bric'na, O.Ju. "Osoblyvosti pozvytku narodnoj pisennosti velykoj vitcyznianoj vijny" [Peculiar developments in the folksongs of the Second World War]. *Narodna Tvorchist' ta Etnografiya* 29, no. 3 (May–June 1985): 20–28.

Glushakov, Yaroslav Vladimirovich. "'O. K. Great Britany and Russian Soviet Land!': nuzhno li miru boyat'sya sovetskikh pesen perioda Vtoroy mirovoy voynï—Tsena Pobedï" ["O. K. Great Britany and Russian Soviet land!": Should the World Be Afraid of the Soviet World War II songs—The price of victory]. *Muzïkovedenie* 7 (January 2015): 10–16.

Ivanova, Svetlana Vyacheslavovna. "Zhenskoye litso Velikoy Otechestvennoy..." [The female face of the Great Patriotic...]. *Muzïkal'naya Akademiya: Yezhekvartal'nïy Nauchno-Teoreticheskiy i Kritiko-Publitsisticheskiy Zhurnal* 2 (January, 2010): 135–139.

Kyrdan, B.P. "Masovni pisni i fol'klor periodu velykoj vitcyznianoj vijny" [Mass songs and folklore of World War II]. *Narodna Tvorchist' ta Etnografiya* 29, no. 3 (May–June 1985): 3–12.

Lange, Vladimir. "Muzïka v Ufe v godï Velikoy Otechestvennoy Voynï" [Music in Ufa during World War II]. In *Ocherki po istorii bashkirskoy muzïki*, edited by Yelena Karpova, 44–54. Ufa: Gosudarstvennïy Institut Iskusstv, 2001.

"Muzï ne molchali" [The muses were not silent]. *Muzïkal'naya Zhizn': Muzïkal'nïy Kritiko-Publitsisticheskiy Illyustrirovannïy Zhurnal* 4 (January 2001): 2–26.

Nazar, Natal'ya. "Geroiko-patrioticheskaya tema v ukrainskoy sovetskoy simfonii: Na materiale proizvedeniy, posvyashchennïkh Velikoy Otechestvennoy voyne" [Heroic-patriotic themes in Soviet Ukrainian symphonies: Works commemorating the Second World War]. Ph.D. diss., Kievskaya Gosudarstvennaya Konservatoriya im. P. I. Chaykovskogo, 1988.

———. "Tema podviga sovetskogo naroda v Velikoy Otechestvennoy voyne v tvorchestve Borisa Lyatoshinskogo" [The heroics of the people during the Second World War in Boris Lyatoshinskiy's works]. In *Boris Nikolayevich Lyatoshinsky*, edited by Marianna Kopitsa, 112–117. Kiev: Muzichna Ukraïna, 1987.

Nikol'skaja, Irina. "Wojna z faszyzmem a drogi polskiej i radzieckiej twórczości symfonicznej" [The Second World War and Soviet and Polish symphonic works]. In *Z zagadnień poznawczych, kulturowych i dydaktycznych muzyki* 1 (1987): 9–20.

Olesenyuk, Yevgeniy, Vladimir Dragomir, and Igor' Fyodorov, eds. *Velikiy podvig: VUZï Moskvï v godï Velikoy Otechestvennoy Voynï* [Great sacrifice: Moscow institutions of higher education during World War II]. 3 vols. Moscow: Moskovskiy Gosudarstvennïy Tekhnicheskiy Universitet imeni N. Baumana, 2001.

Osipova, Yelena Pavlovna. *Vtoraya mirovaya voyna v tvorchestve kompozitorov Sredney Azii i Kazakhstana* [Reflections of World War II in the music of composers from Central Asia and Kazakhstan]. Ashgabat: Ïlïm, 1994.

Ozhigova, Margarita Petrovna, Konstantin Anatol'yevich, and Galina Vasil'yevna. "Vospominaniya o blokade Leningrada" [Remembering the Siege of Leningrad]. *Yuzhno-Rossiyskiy Muzïkal'nïy Al'manakh* 1:18 (January, 2015): 80–93.

Pravdjuk, Oleksandr A. "Velyka vitcyznjana vijna v pisennij tvorchosti narodu" [World War II in traditional song]. *Narodna Tvorchist' ta Etnografiya* 29, no. 1 (January–February 1985): 20–29.

Varul', Dar'ya Alekseyevna, and Anastasiya Nikolayevna Tsvetkova. "Konservatoriya v preddverii Pobedï: Po arkhivnïm dokumentam 1944–45 gg" [The conservatory on the eve of victory: From archival documents of 1944–45]. *Musicus* 2, no. 42 (2015): 11–13.

Velichko, Artyom Tagiyevich. "Dmitry Shostakovich: Pervïe dni voynï" [Dmitry Shostakovich: The first days of World War II]. *Musicus* 3, no. 43 (2015): 3–6.

Yareshko, Aleksandr Sergeyevich. "Narodnïe pesni velikoy Otechestvennoy voynï: K probleme izucheniya" [Russian popular songs of World War II: The problem of investigation]. *Muzïkal'naya Akademiya: Yezhekvartal'nïy Nauchno-Teoreticheskiy i Kritiko-Publitsisticheskiy Zhurnal* 2 (January 2015): 18–25.

United Kingdom & British Colonies

Baade Christina. "'The Dancing Front': Dance Music, Dancing, and the BBC in World War II." *Popular Music* 25, no. 3 (October 2006): 347–368.

———. *Victory through Harmony: The BBC and Popular Music in World War II*. New York: Oxford University Press, 2012.

Beith, Richard. "The November 1943 London Production of Smetana's *The Bartered Bride* (Prodaná Nevěsta)." *Journal of Czech and Slovak Music: The Journal of the Dvořák Society* 26 (January 2017): 63–76.

Dee, Constance R. "Music and Propaganda: Soviet Music and the BBC during the Second World War." Ph.D. diss., University of Manchester, 2007.

Eliot, Karen. *Albion's Dance: British Ballet during the Second World War*. New York: Oxford University Press, 2016.

Green, Anthony. "For the Boys beyond the Blue: Bengal Services Entertainment Association 1942–1944." *Popular Entertainment Studies* 5, no. 1 (2014): 100–127.

Guthrie, Kate. "Propaganda Music in Second World War Britain: John Ireland's Epic March." *Journal of the Royal Musical Association* 139, no. 1 (2014): 137–175.

———. "Soundtracks to the 'People's War.'" *Music & Letters* 94, no. 2 (2013): 324–333.

———. "Vera Lynn on Screen: Popular Music and the 'People's War.'" *Twentieth-Century Music* 14, no. 2 (2017): 245–270.

Hayes, Nick. "More Than 'Music-While-You-Eat'? Factory and Hostel Concerts, 'Good Culture' and the Workers." In *"Millions Like Us?" British Culture in the Second World War,* edited by Nick Hayes and Jeff Hill, 209–235. Liverpool: Liverpool University Press, 1999.

Korczynski, Marek, Michael Pickering, Emma Robertson, and Keith Jones. "'We Sang Ourselves through That War': Women, Music and Factory Work in World War Two." *Labour History Review* 70, no. 2 (2005): 185–214.

Leventhal, F. M. "'The Best for the Most': CEMA and State Sponsorship of the Arts in Wartime, 1939–1945." *Twentieth Century British History* 1, no. 3 (1990): 289–317.

Mackay, Robert. "Being Beastly to the Germans: Music, Censorship, and the BBC in World War II." *Historical Journal of Film, Radio, & Television* 20, no. 4 (October 2000): 513–525.

———. "Leaving out the Black Notes: The BBC and 'Enemy Music' in the Second World War." *Media History* 6, no. 1 (2000): 75–80.

———. "Safe and Sound: New Music in Wartime Britain." In *"Millions Like Us?" British Culture in the Second World War,* edited by Nick Hayes and Jeff Hill, 179–208. Liverpool: Liverpool University Press, 1999.

Mathis, Ursula. "Politique 'via ether': La chanson française de la B.B.C. pendant la Seconde Guerre mondiale" [Politics 'via Ether': French song on the BBC during the Second World War]. In *1789–1989: Musique, histoire, démocratie,* edited by Antoine Hennion, 483–498. Recherche, musique et danse 6–8. Paris: Maison des Sciences de l'Homme, 1992.

Merriman, Andrew. *Greasepaint and Cordite: The Story of ENSA and Concert Party Entertainment during the Second World War.* London: Aurum, 2013.

Morris, John. *Culture and Propaganda in World War II: Music, Film and the Battle for National Identity.* International Library of Twentieth Century History. London: I. B. Tauris, 2014.

Murdoch, Brian O. *Fighting Songs and Warring Words: Popular Lyrics of Two World Wars.* London: Routledge, 1990.

Nicholas, Siân. "The People's Radio: The BBC and Its Audience, 1939–1945." In *"Millions Like Us?" British Culture in the Second World War,* edited by Nick Hayes and Jeff Hill, 62–92. Liverpool: Liverpool University Press, 1999.

Page, Martin. *Kiss Me Goodnight, Sergeant Major: The Songs and Ballads of World War II.* London: Hart-Davis, McGibbon, 1973.

Studdert, Will. "'We've Got a Gig in Poland!' Britain and Jazz in World War II." *Jazz Research Journal* 7, no. 1 (2013): 79–111.

Weingärtner, Jörn. *The Arts as a Weapon of War: Britain and the Shaping of the National Morale in the Second World War.* London: Tauris, 2012.

Whiteley, Sheila. "'When You Wish upon a Star': Nostalgia, Fairy Stories and the Songs of World War II." In *Souvenirs, souvenirs: La nostalgie dans les musiques populaires*, edited by Hugh Dauncey and Christopher Tinker. Special issue of *Volume! La revue des musiques populaires*. 11, no. 1 (2014): 83–97.

United States and Canada

Akerbergs, Ilze. "Rhythms for a Common Purpose: A Look at Laura Boulton's Ethnographical Films on the Peoples of Canada during World War II." *Resound: A Quarterly of the Archives of Traditional Music* 17, no. 3–4 (July–October 1998): 1–6.

Anderson, Alan. *The Songwriter Goes to War: The Story of Irving Berlin's World War II All-Army Production of "This Is the Army."* Pompton Plains, NJ: Limelight, 2004.

Andrews, Maxene, and Bill Gilbert. *Over Here, Over There: The Andrews Sisters and the USO Stars in World War II.* New York: Kensington, 1993.

Barbour, Alecia D. "'For the Good of Our Country': Ruth Watanabe and the 'Good That Is in Music' at the Santa Anita Detention Center." *Notes* 74, no. 2 (2017): 221–234.

Beegle, Amy. "American Music Education 1941–1946: Meeting Needs and Making Adjustments during World War II." *Journal of Historical Research in Music Education* 26, no. 1 (October 2004): 54–67.

Brown, Sheldon. "The Depression and World War II as Seen through Country Music." *Social Education* 49, no. 7 (July 1985): 588–595.

Bush, John. *The Songs That Fought the War: Popular Music and the Home Front, 1939–1945.* Waltham, MA: Brandeis University Press, 2006.

Carter, Tim. *Rodgers and Hammerstein's Carousel.* Oxford Keynotes. New York: Oxford University Press, 2017.

Fauser, Annegret. "'Dixie Carmen': War, Race, and Identity in Oscar Hammerstein's *Carmen Jones*, 1943." *Journal of the Society for American Music* 4, no. 2 (2010): 127–174.

———. *Sounds of War: Music in the United States during World War II.* New York: Oxford University Press, 2013.

Genne, Beth. "'Freedom Incarnate': Jerome Robbins, Gene Kelly, and the Dancing Sailor as an Icon of American Values in World War II." *Dance Chronicle* 24, no. 1 (2001): 83–103.

Giddins, Gary. *Bing Crosby: Swinging on a Star—The War Years, 1940–1946.* New York: Little, Brown, 2018.

Goble, J. Scott. "Nationalism in United States Music Education during World War II." *Journal of Historical Research in Music Education* 30, no. 2 (2009): 103–117.

Griffin, Farah Jasmine. *Harlem Nocturne: Women Artists and Progressive Politics during World War II.* New York: Basic Civitas, 2013.

Heberling, Lynn O'Neal. "Soldiers in Greasepaint: USO-Camp Shows, Inc., during World War II." Ph.D. diss., Kent State University, 1989.

Hickerson, Joseph C., and Jennifer L. Davis, eds. *World War II Collections in the Archive of Folk Culture*. Library of Congress Folk Archive Finding Aid 15. Washington, DC: Library of Congress, 1995.

Jones, John Bush. *The Songs That Fought the War: Popular Music and the Home Front, 1939–1945*. Hanover, NH: University Press of New England, 2006.

Keesing, Hugo. *World War II's Distaff Army: An Annotated Index of Original Songs about WACs and Nurses*. Columbia, MD: Keesing Musical Archives, 1996.

———. *Yankee Doodle Girl: Sheet Music's Depiction of Women in the Military during World War II*. Columbia, MD: Keesing Musical Archives, 1996.

Marvin, Roberta Montemorra. *The Politics of Verdi's Cantica*. Farnham, Surrey: Ashgate, 2014.

Moon, Krystyn R. "'There's No Yellow in the Red, White, and Blue': The Creation of Anti-Japanese Music during World War II." *Pacific Historical Review* 72, no. 3 (2003): 333–352.

Parker, Nancy. "MEJ and World War II: A Review of Music Educators Journal (1940–42)." *Music Educators Journal* 95, no. 2 (2008): 69–74.

Plank, Steven. "Music and the Armed Services Edition." *Notes: Quarterly Journal of the Music Library Association* 75, no. 1 (2018): 39–52.

Robertson, Marta. "Ballad for Incarcerated Americans: Second-Generation Japanese American Musicking in World War II Camps." *Journal of the Society for American Music* 11, no. 3 (2017): 284–312.

Schofield, Mary Anne. "Marketing Iron Pigs, Patriotism, and Peace: Bing Crosby and World War II—A Discourse." *Journal of Popular Culture* 40, no. 5 (2007): 867–881.

Sheppard, W. Anthony. "An Exotic Enemy: Anti-Japanese Musical Propaganda in World War II Hollywood." *Journal of the American Musicological Society* 54, no. 2 (Summer 2001): 303–357.

Simmonds, Rae Nichols. "The Use of Music as a Political Tool by the United States during World War II." Ph.D. diss., Walden University, 1994.

Smith, Kathleen E. R. *God Bless America: Tin Pan Alley Goes to War*. Lexington: University Press of Kentucky, 2003.

Sullivan, Jill M. *Bands of Sisters: U.S. Women's Military Bands during World War II*. American Wind Band Series. Lanham, MD: Scarecrow, 2011.

———. "Music for the Injured Soldier: A Contribution of American Women's Military Bands during World War II." *Journal of Music Therapy* 44, no. 3 (2007): 282–305.

———. "Women Music Teachers as Military Band Directors during World War II." *Journal of Historical Research in Music Education* 39, no. 1 (October 2017): 78–105.

Sumner, Carolyne. "Writing for CBC Wartime Radio Drama: John Weinzweig, Socialism, and the Twelve-Tone Dilemma." *Intersections* 36, no. 2 (January 1, 2017): 77–88.

Townshend, Pete. *Pearl Harbor Jazz: Change in Popular Music in the Early 1940s*. Jackson: University Press of Mississippi, 2007.

Tucker, Sherrie. *Dance Floor Democracy: The Social Geography of Memory at the Hollywood Canteen*. Durham, NC: Duke University Press, 2014.

———. *Swing Shift: "All-Girl" Bands of the 1940s*. Durham, NC: Duke University Press, 2000.

Waseda, Minako. "Extraordinary Circumstances, Exceptional Practices: Music in Japanese American Concentration Camps." *Journal of Asian American Studies* 8, no. 2 (2005): 171–209.

Way, Chris. *The Big Bands Go to War*. Edinburgh: Mainstream Publishing, 1991.

Whiteley, Sheila. "'When You Wish upon a Star': Nostalgia, Fairy Stories, and the Songs of World War II." In *Souvenirs, souvenirs: La nostalgie dans les musiques populaires*, edited by Hugh Dauncey and Christopher Tinker. Special issue of *Volume! La revue des musiques populaires*. 11, no. 1 (2014): 83–97.

Widmaier, Tobias. "'The Kaiser's Got the Blues' und 'Fuehrer's Swan Song': Amerikanische Song-Produktion im Ersten und Zweiten Weltkrieg" ["The Kaiser's got the blues" and "Fuehrer's Swan Song": American song production in the First and Second World Wars]." In *Musik, Wissenschaft und ihre Vermittlung: Bericht über die internationale musikwissenschaftliche Tagung der Hochschule für Musik und Theater Hannover*, edited by Arnfried Edler and Sabine Meine, 335–340. Publikationen der Hochschule für Musik und Theater Hannover 12. Augsburg: Wissner, 2002.

Wolfe, Charles K., and James E. Akenson. eds. *Country Music Goes to War*. Lexington: The University Press of Kentucky, 2005.

Young, William H., and Nancy K. Young. *Music of the World War II Era*. American History through Music. Westport, CT: Greenwood, 2008.

## Yugoslavia

Ceribašić, Naila. "Heritage of the Second World War in Croatia: Identity Imposed upon and by Music." In *Music, Politics, and War: Views from Croatia*, edited by Svanibor Pettan, 109–129. Zagreb: Institut za Etnologiju i Folkloristiku, 1988.

Križnar, Franc. "Glasba na Slovenskem in druga svetovna vojna: Skica za studio" [Music in Slovenia during World War II: Sketch for a study]. *Borec* 49, no. 555–556 (1997): 61–117.

———. *Slovenska glasba v narodnoosvobodilnem boju* [Slovenian music in the National Liberation War]. Ljubljana: Filozofska Fakulteta, 1992.

———. "Slovenska glasba v narodnoosvobodilnem boju (1941–1945)" [Slovene music during the National Liberation War, 1941–45]. *Zgodovinski časopis* 51, no. 2 (1997): 235–239.

Kuret, Primož. "Die Bedeutung der Musik in der slowenischen Widerstandsbewegung" [The significance of music in the Slovenian resistance movement]. *Glasbeno-pedagoški zbornik Akademije za Glasbo v Ljubljani* 22 (January 2015): 284–289.

Radmanović, Mirko. "Žrnovnicka muzika u narodnooslobodilačkom ratu" [The music of Zrnovnica in the National Liberation War]. *Vojnoistorijski Glasnik* 33, no. 3 (1982): 181–200.

Strajnar, Julijan. "Vloga ljudske glasbe med narodnoosvobodilnim bojem" [The role of traditional music in the National Liberation War]. *Traditiones* 15 (1986): 181–189.

# INDEX

Note: Page numbers in *italics* indicate illustrations or musical examples.

acoustemology, 264, 265, 269–70
*Across the Pacific* (film), 141
Action Française, 175, 186
Adams, G. D., 45
Adorno, Theodor, 14, 58
Affron, Charles and Mirella Jona, 112
African American performers, 132–33, 136, 270
Afritsch, Gretl, 160
air raid shelters in Nazi Germany: sonic experiences of, 15, 18–19, 246–57, 263; as spaces of exclusion, 247. *See also* bunkers; cellars
air raid sirens, 15, 36, 246, 250–51, 257, 263, 269
Akoka, Henri, 178, 182–83
Aleksandrov, Grigory, 78, 97–98
*Alerte aux champs* (film), 186
*Alexander Nevsky* (film), 268
Aliens Act (Britain, 1905), 72n26
alterity: coded in World War II films, 78, 79, 93; sonic representation of, 267
Altner, Helmut, 252–53
Amadeus Quartet, 62
*American Music*, 9
American Theatre Wing, 133
Amery, Leopold, 39
Amfitheatrof, Daniele: *Days of Glory* film score, 77, 81–82, 267
*Anchors Aweigh* (film), 140, 146n27
Anderson, Ben, 48n4
Anderson, Maxwell: *The Eve of St. Mark*, 131, 133

Anderson, W. R., 34
*Annales musicologiques*, 175
anti-Semitism: in Britain, 62, 71, 72n26; in Nazi Germany, 247; in Vichy France, 185, 186
Antonín, Rudolf. *See* Dvorský, R. A.
*Arijský boj*, 206, 210, 212, 213, 216, 219–20n36
Arlen, Harold: *Bloomer Girl*, 140, 146n25
*Arlequinades*, 176, 180
Armstrong, Louis, 251–52
Army Corps of Engineers, 228
Army Service Forces, 228
Atkinson, Brooks, 131, 133
Auric, Georges, 191n45
Austria: *Anschluss*, 150, 152–53, 264; Dunkelkonzerte during World War II, 18, 148–62, 263, 268–69; postwar reconstruction of, 70. *See also* Vienna
Ayers, Lemuel, 146n25

Baade, Christina, 11, 56, 58–59, 60
Baccaloni, Salvatore, 119, *120*
Bach, Johann Sebastian: *Art of Fugue*, 157; BBC wartime programming of, 60, 65, 67; *Der Streit zwischen Phoebus und Pan*, 113; "Vor Deinen Thron tret' ich hiermit," 157
Bach Society, 6
Baker, Josephine, 176
Balanchine, George, 145n14
ballet, 132, 133, 140, 144n4
Ballet Russe de Monte Carlo, 132

289

Balmer, Yves, 190n35
Barlach, Ernst, 2
Barrès, Maurice, 175
Barta, Erwin, 152
"Battle Hymn of the Republic, The," 97
Bayreuth Festival, 157
BBC (British Broadcasting Corporation): bombing destruction of St. George's Hall, 40, 47; Compton organ of, 30, 31–32, 33, 40, 41, 47; Continuous Survey of Listening, 61; crooner ban, 42, 43; Daily Listening Barometer, 61; Dance Band Policy Committee, 43; distinction between serious and popular music at, 58–59; *Forces Music Club*, 60; Forces Programme, 38, 45, 60, 67; General Forces Programme, 46, 60; Genome project, 59, 64, 66–68; Gramophone Department, 58; gramophone record requests shows, 47; Home Service, 60, 67; importance of audience size, 67–68; Light Programme, 47; listeners in Nazi Germany, 252–53; live concert broadcasts, 69; Middle East Service, 38; musical uplift mission, 29–30, 41–42, 46, 57, 265; North American Service, 38; Outside Broadcasting Unit, 31; Overseas Service, 39, 58; policy toward collaborators, 57, 63; postwar policies, 69–71; programming as ideological battleground, 11, 17, 29–30, 41–46; programming changes, 46; programming of classical music by "enemy aliens," 17, 56–71, 264, 267; programming of light classical music, 58–59; theater organ programming, 27–48, 59–60, 263; Theatre Organ Committee, 43–44; Third Programme, 57; wartime programming of newly composed music, 68–69
Beauplan, Amadée de: "Le secret," 180
Bechstein, Carl, 61
Beecham, Sir Thomas, 70, 112, 128n8
Beethoven, Ludwig van: BBC wartime programming of, 67, 71; choral works of, 234; *Fidelio*, 115–17; Symphony no. 3, 236; Symphony no. 5, 60–61, 65, 99; Symphony no. 7, 69; Symphony no. 9, 236, 264; transnational identity of, 264; wartime performances in Vienna, 164n27

Běhounek, Kamil, 204, 206, 208, 209, 214, 217n5, 218n20; "Má láska je jazz," 209–10; "Ráda zpívámhot," 209
Beiswanger, George, 140
Belgium, occupied, musical activity in, 10
Bellows, George, 2
Belmont, Eleanor Robson, 128n6
Benda, Hans von, 255–56
Beneš, Edvard, 202
Bennett, Robert Russell, 138, 146n25
Bentley, Eric, 140
Berend, Ivan, 5
Berking, Willy, 220n47
Berlant, Lauren, 28–29, 36, 45–46
Berlin, Irving: *Annie Get Your Gun*, 141; *This Is the Army*, 136–37, 145n16; *Yip Yip Yaphank*, 137
Berlin Chamber Orchestra (Berliner Kammerorchester), 255–56
Bernstein, Leonard: *Fancy Free*, 140; *On the Town*, 136, 140–41
Biancolli, Louis, 117
Bick, Sally, 92
Binkau, Guido, 164n27
Birdsall, Carolyn, 251, 258n20
Bizet, Georges: *The Pearl Fishers*, 267
Bjoerling, Jussi, 113
Black, Gregory, 88
Blaschke, Hanns, 153
Bliss, Arthur, 29–30, 31, 43, 44, 62, 67, 68, 267
Bliss, Cornelius N., 111, 112
Bloch-Bauer, Gustav, 164n23
*Blossom Time* (operetta), 138
Blue Music ensemble, 204, 206, 208, 218n20, 219nn30–31
Bodanzky, Artur, 112
Bogart, Humphrey, 141
Böhm, Karl, 151
Botstein, Leon, 9–10
Botstiber, Hugo, 164n23
Boulanger, Lili: *Nocturne* and *Cortège*, 179
Boulanger, Nadia, 177, 178–79, 183–84
Boult, Adrian, 62, 68, 71
*Boy from Stalingrad, The* (film), 77, 81
Brady, Leo, 133
Brahms, Johannes: BBC wartime programming of, 67; *Requiem*, 70; Violin Concerto, 159

Brainin, Norbert, 62
Breisach, Paul, 120
Bresseler, Johannes, 233–34, 236
Briggs, Asa, 59
*Bristol Evening Post*, 63–64
British Expeditionary Forces, 36–38, 63
Britten, Benjamin: *War Requiem*, 3
Britton, Pamela, 146n27
Broadway musicals: classical music and, 138–39; decline of vaudeville, 135; engagement with World War II, 133–34, 136–37, 139, 140–41, 268; as escapism, 18, 133; films as competition for, 133; financial investment needed for, 136; integrated, 140, 268; operetta revivals, 138; popularity of, 134–35; postwar cultural diplomacy and, 142; wartime offerings, 131–44, 263
*Brooklyn Daily Eagle*, 133
Bruch, Max: BBC ban on music of, 64, 65–66
Bruckner, Anton: as cultural symbol of the *Anschluss*, 149; *Dunkelkonzerte* performances of, 155, 268; Hitler and, 148, 162; Symphony no. 4, 155; Symphony no. 7, 148, 157; Symphony no. 9, 155
bunkers in Nazi Germany, 13, 15, 18–19, 246–48, 249, 250–57, 263, 265; Berlin locations, 248, 249, 254, 256; construction of, 248; forced laborers in, 254–55, 265; holidays in, 254; life in, 250; live performances in, 246, 247, 253–56, 257; postwar destruction or repurposing of, 256–57; radio broadcasts from, 252; *Volksgemeinschaft* ideology and, 247
Busch, Fritz, 112
Busoni, Ferruccio, 64
Büsser, Henri, 177
Butler, Judith, 267, 271n15

Camp Algona (Iowa POW camp), 227, 266; chamber concerts, 237; Christmas pageant, 234; concert programs, 234–35; construction of, 228; daily life for POWs, 233–34, 236; local concerns about, 232–33, 241–42n25; poetry readings, 235–36, 237; POWs housed, 233, 238; prisoner musical activities, 231–32, 233–37; record concerts, 235–36; Special Projects Division and, 237–39
Canada in World War II, 38
Canetti, Elias: "Der Ohrenzeuge," 258n20

Capra, Frank, 131
Carroll, Michael Thomas, 34
Carste, Hans, 220n47
Casadesus, Henri, 176, 180
Casadesus, Jacqueline, 176, 180
cellars in Nazi Germany, 18, 246–48, 250–52, 253, 254, 256, 263; differences from bunkers, 250–51; life in, 251; live performances in, 246, 247, 253–56, 257; postwar use for pedagogical purposes, 256–57; radio listeners in, 252, 253, 257
Ceriani, Davide, 128n1
Chabrier, Emmanuel: *Marche joyeuse*, 179
Chaikovsky, Pyotr: in American popular culture, 82; BBC radio theater organ performances of, 42, 263
Challan, Henri, 177, 179–80, 183, 184, 185, 192n78
*chariot d'Arlequin, Le* (play), 186
Charle, René, 178, 179, 182–83
Chatelain, Simeone, 180
Chauffeté, Virginie, 189n32
*Chauve-Souris* (revue), 146n19
Chávez, Carlos, 84
Chevalier, Maurice, 57, 176
Chiaureli, Mikhail, 98
Chimènes, Myriam, 10
Chodorov, Edward, 83–84
Chopin, Frédéric, 138, 268
Churchill, Winston, 77
*Circus, The* (film), 84
Civilian Conservation Corps (CCC) camps, 228, 240n9
CMT (Centre musical et théâtral de la IIe armée), 172–87; administration of, 178; Nadia Boulanger and, 178–79; formation of, 172–73; founders of, 174–76; future research avenues, 186–87; last performance and role in Battle of France, 180–82, 186; legacy after dissolution, 182–86; members as German prisoners, 173, 182–85, 266; members considered "*sanitaires*," 184; members' early release from captivity, 173, 183–85, 186, 187; members of, 177–78; musical programs and concerts, 178–80; obligatory service and, 187; purposes of, 176–77; Vichy propaganda and, 173, 178, 183–85, 186
Cold War, music scholarship on, 3, 6–7, 9

concentration camps: sadistic use of music in, 4; scholarship on music in, 10; slave labor in, 19; Theresienstadt, 206, 209, 213, 226
*Conspiracy of the Doomed* (film), 78, 93–94, 95, 96
Cooke, Richard, 133–34, 135
Cooper, Emil, 112
Cooper, Gary, 141
Copland, Aaron: Americana-themed ballets of, 88, 132, 133; BBC wartime programming of, 68; *Of Mice and Men* film score, 92; *The North Star* film score, 77, 84, 85, 86–88, 91, 92–93; nostalgia in music of, 92; "Younger Generation," 84, 85, 86–87
copyright issues, 63
Cortot, Alfred, 176, 177, 178, 190n40
Council for the Encouragement of Music and the Arts (CEMA), 57
*Counter-Attack* (film), 77, 80, 267
Courteline, Georges: *Un client sérieux*, 179
Courville, Louise de, 175
Courville, Maurice, Comte de, 175
Courville, Xavier de, 174, 175–76, 178, 179, 180–81, 182, 186, 191n46
Coward, Noël: *Blithe Spirit*, 131
Crawford, Cheryl, 136
Crawford, Jessie, 44
Crosby, Bing, 144n5
Crosby, Bob, 224n72
Crouse, Russel: *Life with Father*, 135; *Strip for Action*, 131, 132
Currid, Brian, 247, 251
Curtiz, Michael, 77
Czechoslovakia: Czech fascists in, 206, 212, 213, 216, 219n34; forced labor in, 214; Czech-German relations in, 205, 206, 212, 219n34; First Republic (1918–1938), 200, 201–2; as "Garden of Eden" for German officials, 199, 200, 204–5, 216, 268; German annexation of Sudentenland, 199, 202, 205; Heydrich's assassination, 200; Jews in, 205–6, 209, 212–13, 219–20n36; popular music under German occupation, 10, 17–18, 199–216, 263, 268; as Socialist Republic, 214–16
Czech swing, 18, 199, 201–2, 204–16, 263; amateur performers, 214; under Communists, 214–16; core listenership, 206; criticism of, 206, 210, 212, 213; Czech vowel length and rhythmic style in, 209, 268; as emblem of cosmopolitanism, 200, 205, 216, 268; German attitude toward, 204–5; during *Heydrichiáda* and total war, 212–16; musicians, 202, 204–10, 212; rise under German occupation, 207–12; Škvorecký's writings about, 215–16

*Daily Mail*, 34
Dassary, André, 178
David, José, 187
Davies, Henry Walford, 62
Davies, Joseph, 82–83
Davison, Edward, 229
*Days of Glory* (film), 77, 80–82, 267
Debussy, Claude, 6, 180; *Petite suite*, 179
*Degenerate Music* exhibition, 1938, 199
Delaunay, Charles, 217–18n11
Delibes, Léo: *Lakmé*, 267
Demetz, Peter, 216n1
de Mille, Agnes, 132, 135, 146n25
Derenne, Paul, 179
Deutsches Tanz- und Unterhaltungsorchester, 220–21n48
Deutsche Welle, 251
d'Indy, Vincent, 175, 176
Disney, Walt, 268
diversion and escapism, music as: in air raid shelters, bunkers, and cellars, 13, 246, 247, 251–53, 255–56, 257; audiovisual media and, 4, 15, 16, 29, 33–34, 246, 247, 251–53, 255, 257, 265; in Austria after the *Anschluss*, 152, 162; Broadway shows, 18, 134, 268; Czech swing, 204–16; importance to morale, 3, 11; in POW camps, 13, 18, 227–29, 238; theater organ and, 30, 31
Dix, Otto, 2
Dobrenko, Evgeny, 78
Doctor, Jenny, 62, 68, 69
Doherty, Thomas, 88
Dorůžka, Lubomír, 214, 217n5
Downes, Olin, 112, 134, 138
*Drahpost*, 233, 236, 237, 238, 242n36
Drake, Alfred, 141
Drechsler, Nanny, 251
Dreiblatt, Martha, 141
Dreyfus Affair, 186
Duke, Vernon, 135; *Cabin in the Sky*, 136; *The Lady Comes Across*, 136, 145n14

Dümling, Albrecht, 10
Dunayevsky, Isaak: "Song of the Motherland," 84, 97–98, 102n41, 104n69
Dunham, Katherine: *Tropical Revue*, 136
*Dunkelkonzerte*, 18, 148–62, 263, 268–69; conventional image of, 149–50; darkness component of, 157–61; as entertaining novelty, 159–60, 268; inception of, 154–55; performances outside Vienna, 161; popularity of, 160–61, 162; practicalities of, 158
Dupré, Marcel, 177
Dürauer, Friedrich, 154–55, 158, 159, 166n44
Duruflé, Maurice, 12
Dvořák, Antonín: Piano Concerto, 157, 158
Dvorský, R. A., 200, 201–2, 204, 206–9, 214, 217n9, 219n31, 219n36; attempted defection of, 223n69; under Communists, 215; expansion into swing, 207–8; fascist attacks on, 206; publishing company of, 202, 203, 207–8, 210–11, 218n14, 220n43
Dyer, Richard, 35

*Early to Bed* (musical), 139
Echourin, Henri, 178, 179, 180, 182–83
Edelweiss Pirates, 254
Eggerth, Marta, 138
Eichendorff, Joseph, 234
Eichmann, Adolf, 212
Eisenstein, Sergei, 268
Eisler, Hanns: "Solidarity Song," 160, 161
Eldredge, Sears A., 266
Elgar, Edward, BBC wartime programming of, 60, 66, 67, 71
Ellington, Duke, 217n11, 251–52
"enemy aliens," BBC programming of classical music by, 17, 56–71, 264, 267
Ente Italiano per le Audizioni Radiofoniche (EIAR), 265
Entertainments National Service Association, 57
escapism. *See* diversion and escapism, music as
Estrin, Marc: *The Education of Arnold Hitler*, 148, 149

*Family Favourites*, 47
*Fantasia* (film), 268, 269
Fauré, Gabriel, 180; *Nocturne*, 179
Fauser, Annegret, 11, 13, 122, 246–47

Faÿ, Bernard, 180, 181–82, 191n58
Feld, Steven, 264, 269
Ferraris, Adalgiso, 64
films: American and Soviet World War II films, 17, 77–100, 263, 267; American prewar portrayal of Russians, 79; conventional tropes in, 267; diegetic performances of Russian music, 80–81, 84, 86–88; as escapism, 4, 265; importance of music in 1940s films, 78–79; introduction of technology, 14–15; propaganda, 12, 16, 17, 79, 98, 100, 263; Soviet productions, 77–78, 79; underscoring in, 81–83, 88, 92–93, 97–98; wartime offerings, 132, 133, 138, 140, 141
Findahl, Theo, 253–54
Fischerová, Edith, 206, 219n31
Fishman, Sarah, 185
Fitzgerald, Ella, 209
Flagstad, Kirsten, 113, 116
Flotow, Friedrich von: *Alessandro Stradella*, 235
*Follow the Girls* (musical), 139
Foort, Reginald, 30, 31, 32, 32, 34–35, 40–41, 42, 43, 47, 51n67
Foot, Robert, 29
*Forces Music Club* (radio program), 60
44th Street Theatre playlist, 136, 137, 141
Fournier, Jean, 178, 179
"fox-polka," 201
foxtrots, 209, 212, 268
*Foyers du soldat*, 176
Françaix, Jean, 179
France, occupied: anti-Semitism in, 185, 186; German invasion, 180–82, 263–64; musical activity in, 10, 11–12, 18, 172–87; prisoner-of-war camps in, 173, 182; resistance and collaboration in, 12, 18, 57, 63, 69, 173, 178, 181, 183–86; Vichy regime, 11, 12, 18, 63, 71, 173, 178, 181, 183–85, 186
Franck, César, 180
Frank, Karl Hermann, 205
Frankfurt School, 14
Freemasonry, 119–21
Friedrich, Jörg, 250; *The Fire*, 247
Friml, Rudolf: *The Vagabond King*, 138
Frost, Phyllis, 34
Fulcher, Jane, 10, 11–12, 175
Furtwängler, Wilhelm, 190n40

Gabčík, Jozef, 212
Gallois-Montbrun, Raymond, 178, 182–83, 184, 186; *Trois mélodies sur trois poèmes de Jean Mariat*, 185
Gandhi, Mahatma, 39
Garnham, Alison, 61, 69
Gatti-Casazza, Giulio, 112–13, 128n1
Gemblaco, Franchois de: *Par un regart des deux biaulx yeux riant*, 179
Geneva Convention stipulations for POWs, 227–28, 232, 240n7, 267
Germanocentric canon of art music, World War II and, 10, 17, 63–68, 111
Germany: attacks on American popular music and jazz, 199; bunker building project, 248; German POWs in America, 226–39; music in, 9–10; pacifists in, 254; Nazi propaganda about Mozart, 119–21; postwar reconstruction of, 70; radio broadcasting during Allied bombing campaign, 247, 251–53, 257; refugees from, 15–16; sonic experiences in air raid shelters, bunkers, and cellars, 15, 18–19, 246–57, 263; *Totaleinsatz* (Total War), 214; victims' experiences, 12–13; *Volksgemeinschaft* ideology, 247. *See also* Austria; concentration camps; Czechoslovakia; France, occupied
Gershwin, George: *Porgy and Bess*, 136, 138, 142
Gershwin, Ira, 84, 87
Geutebrück, Ernst, 152
Ghetto Swingers, the, 213, 223n59
Gier, Christina, 9
Gilbert and Sullivan operettas, 58, 61
Gilliam, Bryan, 149, 157–58
Giono, Jean: *Le Serpent d'étoiles*, 185
Gitton, Jean, 184, 192n78
Gleason, Jackie, 139
Globocnik, Odilo, 154
Glover, C. Gordon, 42
Gluck, Christoph Willibald, 176
Goebbels, Joseph, 138, 149, 151, 155, 157, 251; Sportpalast speech, 214
Goldwyn, Samuel, 83–84
Goodman, Benny, 138, 217n11
Goossens, Eugene, 128n8
Gordon, Max, 141

Göring, Hermann, 248
Goué, Émile, 192n78
Gounelle, Claude, 181
Gounod, Charles, 179
Goutard, Alphonse, 181
Gouts, Suzanne, 180
Graf, Herbert, 117
Grant, Cary, 131
Graves, Sir Cecil, 29, 43, 45
Grayson, Kathryn, 140
Green, Johnny: *Beat the Band*, 131, 132
Greenway, Rob, 60
Gregory, Karl von, 202, 218n16
Grieg, Edvard, 138, 268
Grosz, Georg, 2
Gruber, Ludwig, 152
Gruenberg, Louis: *Counter-Attack* film score, 77, 80, 267
Gruppe für kulturpolitische Angelegenheiten, 202
Guilbert, Yvette, 180
Guttmann, Robert, 213

Haasbauer, Anton, 153–54
Hácha, Emil, 205, 218n15
Haerdtl, Heinrich, 160, 168n75
Hall, Henry, 32
Halla, Milan, 205–6, 219n30
Hammerstein, Oscar, II: *Carmen Jones*, 136, 144n5, 145n12; *Carousel*, 141; *Oklahoma!*, 132, 134, 135, 138, 139–40, 141–42, 263, 268; *Show Boat*, 136
Handel, Georg Frideric: Largo, 35
Harden, Harry, 205
Hart, Lorenz: *By Jupiter*, 131
Hart, Moss: *Winged Victory*, 136, 137
Hasenöhrl, Franz: Piano Concerto, 152
Haydn, Franz Joseph, BBC wartime programming of, 67
Hays Production Code, 80
Hebbel, Friedrich: "Requiem," 157
Hegarty, Marilyn, 139
Helburn, Theresa, 132, 134, 140
Heller, Friedrich C., 148
Hellman, Lillian, 83–84, 88, 102n37
*Hellzapoppin'* (Broadway revue), 135, 136, 142
Henlein, Konrad, 205
*Henry V* (film), 57

Henry Wood Promenade Concerts, 69
Herbst, Jurgen, 254
Hess, Myra, 57, 69
Heydrich, Reinhard, 18, 200, 212–13, 221–23n55
*High Kickers* (revue), 144n5
Hill, Ralph, 42, 56, 63–64, 65
Hines, Earl "Fatha," 132
historiography of twentieth-century music, 5–6
Hitler, Adolf, 120, 138, 148, 149, 162, 164n19, 184, 202, 212, 237
Hobsbawm, Eric: *The Age of Extremes*, 5
Hochi, Commander, 266
Hochstetter, Armin Caspar, 153, 164n23
Hohendorf, Sitta, 254–55
Holm, Celeste, 146n25
Holocaust, music of the, 10, 19
"home front" concept, 1, 2–3
Honegger, Arthur, 12
Hope-Jones, Robert, 30
Hopkins, Harry, 83
"Horst-Wessel-Lied," 70, 253
Hot Kvintet, 204
House Committee on Un-American Activities, 101n29
Howard, Michael, 14
Howe, James Wong, 83–84
Hruby, Viktor: *Phantastisches Scherzo*, 152
Humperdinck, Engelbert, 64
Huntziger, Anne, 178, 183
Huntziger, Charles, 172–83; Battle of France and, 180–82, 186, 263–64; CMT and, 172–73, 177–82, 186–87; family background, 174; political sympathies and aesthetic views of, 173, 174–77; as Vichy's war minister, 183, 186
Huntziger, Léon-Jacques, 174
Hurok, Sol, 132, 133

Igelhoff, Peter, 220n47
Incorporated Society for Musicians (ISM), 62, 63
India during World War II, 39, 50n55
Indian National Congress, 39
Institute for Youth Education in Bohemia and Moravia, 213
"integrated musical" concept, 140, 268
Intellectual Diversion Program (IDP), 227, 228–29, 238, 266

International Committee of the Red Cross, 226
"Internationale," 84
internationalism of classical music, 4, 15, 82, 112, 115, 117, 119–23, 264
*In the Rear of the Enemy* (film), 141
"intimate public": Berlant's use of, 28–29, 36, 45–46; Loviglio's use of, 28–29, 34, 45
*Invisible Agent* (film), 267
Iowa, German POW camps in, 18, 19, 226–39, 263, 266
ipseity, sonic representation of, 267
Ireland, John, 67
*Iron Curtain, The* (film), 100n8
Italy, Fascist, 12

Jahn, Eugen, 220n47
Japanese American detention camps, 271n11
Jary, Michael, 209, 220n47, 223n58
jazz. *See* popular music
Jewish Culture League, 10
Ježek, Jaroslav, 202, 207, 217n11, 219n34, 220n40
Jindra, Alfons, 209; "*Dávka k rytmu zrozená*," 210
Johnson, Edward, 111, 112, 115, 121–22, 123, 129n18
Johnson, Hall: *Run, Little Chillun*, 136
Jones, Howard Mumford, 229
Jones, Isabel Morse, 264
*Journal of Musicological Research*, 9
Juilliard Foundation, 112

Kabasta, Oswald, 151
Kalatozov, Mikhail, 78, 94, 103n58
Kane, Brian, 149, 158
Karel Vlach Orchestra, 204, 207–8, 213, 214. *See also* Orchestr Karla Vlacha.
Kastendieck, Miles, 133
Kaye, Danny, 131
Kazakhstan, 78
Kédroff, Nathalie and Irène, 179
Keller, Gottfried, 234
Keller, Hans, 61, 62
Kelly, Gene, 140
Kenez, Peter, 93, 98
Kent, Arthur, 114
Kern, Jerome: *Show Boat*, 136, 138

Kerr, Walter, 133
Kershaw, Ian, 247
Kesselring, John: *Arsenic and Old Lace*, 131
Khachaturyan, Aram: *The Secret Mission* film score, 78, 96
Kienzl, Wilhelm, 157
*Kinematograph Weekly*, 35
Kiprensky, Orest, 103n48
Kleist, Heinrich von: *Der zerbrochene Krug*, 254, 255
Knox, Collie, 34
Kobau, Ernst, 151, 154
Kollwitz, Käthe, 2
Komzák, Karel, 164n27
Königer, Paul, 164n27
Koppes, Clayton, 88
Korda, Zoltan, 77
Korstvedt, Benjamin, 148–49
Koschat, Thomas, 234
Kotek, Josef, 216n1
Koussevitzky, Serge, xi, 122
Kraft durch Freude (leisure organization), 150, 160
Kreisler, Fritz, 64
Kreuder, Peter, 220–21nn47–48
Kronenberger, Louis, 102n37
Kubiš, Jan, 212
Kulenkampff, Georg, 159
Kullman, Charles, 117

Labusquière, Jean, 178, 179, 183–84
Lacaille, Henri, 181
Lakes, Alexander, 238
Langhamer, Claire, 47
Langner, Lawrence, 134
Lanner, Joseph, 152
Lanvin, Jeanne, 178–79
La Petite Scène, 176, 180
Launchbury, Claire, 58, 69
Laurence, Paula, 139
Lebedev-Kumach, Vasiliy, 102n41
Lebon, Henri, 179
Le Boterf, Hervé, 188n1
Lee, Gypsy Rose, 131
Legge, Walter, 66
Lehár, Franz: "Gern hab ich die Frau'n geküsst," 235; *The Merry Widow (Die lustige Witwe)*, 138, 235; Nazism and, 145–46n18

Leider, Frida, 251, 252
Leinsdorf, Erich, 122
Leonard, Kendra Preston, 48n9
Leoncavallo, Ruggero, 64
Lepinat, Heinz, 234
Leppert, Richard, 248
Lerner, Neil, 92
Levi, Erik, 119
Lewis, Wyndham, 2
Liberated Theater, 217n11, 220n40
Lindsay, Howard: *Life with Father*, 135; *Strip for Action*, 131, 132
Lobdell, Arthur, 237–38
Lobdell, George, 238
Loewe, Frederick, 135
Logan, Joshua, 135
Lombardo, Guy, 131
Lombarès, Michel de, 181
London Philharmonic Orchestra, 69
Lovett, Martin, 62
Loviglio, Jason, 28–29, 34, 45
Ludvík, Emil, 204, 213
Lully, Jean-Baptiste, 176; *Le mariage forcé*, 180
Lunacharsky, Anatoly, 117
Lynn, Vera, 40, 57

Macho, Gustav, 161, 162
Maclean, Quentin, 35
Macpherson, Sandy, 41, 263; BBC radio programs, 27–28, 32–48, 59–60; broadcasts from emergency theater organ sites, 40–41, 44; Canadian origins of, 27, 35; Christmas message of, 36; as Empire Cinema organist, 35; music programming choices, 29, 35, 39–40, 43–44; on-air persona, 27–28, 34–36, 39, 47–48; post-bag of, 37; post-war BBC career, 47; requests and messages included in programs, 27–28, 29, 36–41, 44–45, 46–47; signature tune "I'll Play to You," 39
Madden, Cecil, 38
magic lantern shows, 159
Mahler, Gustav, 152
Maison, René, 116
Malina, Jaroslav, 205, 212
*Manila Calling* (film), 141
Marivaux, Pierre, 176
Mark, Karl, 160, 161–62

Marr, Andrew, 61–62
Martinon, Jean, 178, 182–83, 186; *Requiem*, 185
Marvin, Roberta Montemorra, 12
Masaryk, Tomáš, 217n8
Mascagni, Pietro, 64
Massenet, Jules: *Thaïs*, 267
Massine, Léonid, 132
Massis, Henri, 174–75, 176, 177, 180; *Manifeste d'intellectuels français pour la défense de l'Occident*, 175, 181, 191n58
Matisse, Henri, 132
Maurras, Charles, 174–75, 187
May Act (1941), 139
Maybrick, Michael: "The Holy City," 35
Mayer, Siegrid, 254
McCracken, Joan, 146n25
McLaughlin, Robert, 77, 78
*Meeting at the Elbe* (film), 78, 79, 96–98, 99
Mendelssohn, Felix: BBC wartime programming of, 67; scarcity of 1930s performances in Vienna, 152
Mengele, Josef, 223n59
Merman, Ethel, 139, 146n23
Messiaen, Olivier, 12; in CMT troupe, 172, 177–78; as prisoner-of-war, 182–83, 266; *Quartet for the End of Time*, 18, 57, 172, 182, 183, 185, 190n35, 266; release from captivity, 185, 186
Metcalfe, Jean, 47, 53n93
Metropolitan Opera Guild, 113
Metropolitan Opera House (New York): ballet performances, 132; democratization of opera, 112, 122; engagement of foreign conductors, 112, 115–17; exiled artists at, 115–17; live radio broadcasts, 112; "Metropolitan Auditions of the Air," 113; Mozart revival at, 119–21; opera in English, 113, 128n1, 128n8; postwar labor disputes, 123; promotion of American artists, 112–13, 115; repertoire, 1935–45, 123–28; ticket price reduction, 112, 113; World War II programming of Italian and German works, 17, 111–28, 264
Middleton, C. H., 34
Mikoyan, Nami, 96
Milanov, Zinka, 113
Milestone, Lewis, 77, 83–84, 92
military music, 2–3, 9
Miller, Charles, 138

Miller, Glenn: "American Patrol," 215
*Mission to Moscow* (film), 77, 82–83, 267
Mobiglia, Tullio, 220n47
Moeller, Robert, 247
Molière, 176
Molotov–Ribbentrop Pact, 80
Montemorra, Anthony Joseph, *viii*, x
Monteverdi, Claudio, 176; *Il ritorno d'Ulisse in patria*, 186
morale, wartime: Allied bombing campaign and, 248, 251; BBC programming and, 28–29, 36–38, 41–43, 56; French, 172, 175; French CMT troupe and, 176; in German-occupied Czechoslovakia, 214; improving, 11, 48n4; national radio stations and, 265; POW camps in United States and, 229, 238, 239; Soviet films and, 78
Moravec, Emanuel, 213
"Moscow in May" (Soviet march), 84, 102n41
Mostel, Zero, 137–38
Mozart, Wolfgang Amadeus, 180; arias by, 179; "Das Bandel," 180; BBC wartime programming of, 60, 65, 67, 71; *Dunkelkonzerte* performances of, 155, 157, 166n52, 268; *Eine kleine Nachtmusik*, K. 525, 237; Metropolitan Opera wartime performances, 119, 120–21, 129n18; music performed by German POWs in American war camps, 237, 263; Nazi propaganda about, 119–21; *Regina Coeli*, 155; *Requiem*, 157; Violin Sonata in F Major, K. 13, 237; *Die Zauberflöte*, 113, 121
Muni, Paul, 80
Munich Agreement, 205
*Musical Times*, 34
Mussolini, Benito, 73n44, 175, 205
Mussorgsky, Modeste: *Boris Godunov*, 117, 118

Nakladatelství R. A. Dvorský, 202, 203, 207–8, 210–11, 218n14, 220n43
Nash, Paul, 2
nationalism. *See* patriotism and national identity
National Professional Employment Center, 202
National Service Act, 47
Nehru, Jawaharlal, 39
Neitzel, Sönke, 242n33

Nettl, Paul, 119
*Neues Wiener Tagblatt*, 154
Neurath, Konstantin von, 202, 205, 212
New Opera Company, 136, 138
*New Priorities of 1943* (revue), 138
*New Sound: International Journal of Music*, 9
*New York Times*, 131, 132, 134, 141
Nichols, Lewis, 134, 146n19, 146n23
Nicolls, Basil, 33, 43, 67
Niesen, Gertrude, 139
Nisnevich, Anna, 82
Nissel, Siegmund, 62
Noé, Harry von, 219n34
Norgaard, Captain Gunner, 238, 243n40
Noriega, Manuel, 3
*North Star, The* (film), 77, 79, 83–84, 86–88, 89–90, 92–93, 97
*Nouveau Temps, Les*, 185
Novák, Zdeněk, 217n5, 219n30
Nuremberg Race Laws, 205

Offenbach, Jacques, 191n46; *Les deux aveugles*, 179; *Gaîté parisienne*, 132; *La Vie parisienne*, 138
Office of War Information (OWI), 79–80
*Of Mice and Men* (film), 92
*Okružní korespondence*, 214
Olivier, Laurence, 57
O'Neill, Eugene, 134, 140
opera, politics of publicity during wartime, 17, 111–28
*Opera News*, 113–14, 115–16, 117, 119, 121, 122, 123
Operation Anthropoid, 212
Opletal, Jan, 202
*Orchestral Half Hour* (radio program), 60
Orchestr Gramoklubu, 202, 206, 207
Orchestr Karla Vlacha, 207. *See also* Karel Vlach Orchestra.
Orelio and Pedro, 132–33
Orlova, Lyubov', 97
Osten, Harry, 205
*Österreichische Volks-Zeitung*, 155, 159–60
Owen, Wilfred, 2, 56
*Oy Is Dus a Leben!* (Yiddish musical), 131

Pach, Walter, 157
Paillat, Claude, 181, 190n40
Panassié, Hugues, 217–18n11

Panizza, Ettore, 112
Pappen, Franz von, 151
Paquin, Colonel, 181, 182
*Paradise Road* (film), 226
Paris Conservatory, 178, 184, 185–86, 192n87
Parkington, Dorothy, 138
Parry, Sally E., 77, 78
Pasquier, Etienne, 178, 180, 182–83, 185
patriotism and national identity: Austrian, 152–53, 155; Broadway musicals and, 137, 139–40; classical music and, 57, 115, 123, 264, 267; Czech, 200, 201, 204–5, 216; French culture and, 175, 177; Nazi ideology and, 122, 206, 242n33; politics of, 265–66, 271n11; POW camps and, 228–29, 235, 238, 239, 265–66, 267, 271n11; precariousness of, 13, 264; radio programming and, 15, 57; wartime morale and, 2, 9
Patton, George S., 269
Paul, Walter, 206
Payne, Jack, 32
Peck, Gregory, 82
Penderecki, Krzysztof: *Threnody to the Victims of Hiroshima*, 3
Performing Rights Society, 63
Pergolesi, Giovanni Battista: *La serva padrona*, 119, 120
Permoser, Manfred, 149, 152
Pétain, Philippe, 173, 174, 183, 184, 185, 266
Peters, Susan, 82
Peter Schaeffers Musikverlag, 209
Petr, Zdeněk, 217n5
phantasmagorias, 159
*Phoebus and Pan* (opera adapted from Bach), 113, 128n8
Piccolominis, Die, 220n47
Picon, Molly, 131
Pinza, Ezio, 117, *118*
*Playing for Time* (film), 226
Pokrass Brothers, 102n41
Poland, occupied, musical activity in, 10
Polignac, Marie-Blanche de, 179, 181
Pollock, Lew: "The Yanks Are Coming Again," 137–38
*Polonaise* (operetta), 138, 268
popular music: classical adaptations, 42; Czech, during German occupation, 10,

17–18, 199–200, 202–16; Czech, interwar, 201–2, 207; "enemy aliens" and, 57–58; internationalization of American, 15, 17–18; scholarship on, 7, 8, 9, 11; Soviet postwar use of jazz as imperialist symbol of America, 94, 95, 96, 98, 264
Porter, Cole, 135; *Let's Face It!*, 131; *Mexican Hayride*, 142; *Panama Hattie*, 139; Rodgers on, 145n11; *Seven Lively Arts*, 138; *Something for the Boys*, 139, 146n24
*potápky*, 200, 206, 210, 213, 216, 217n6, 220n38
Potter, Pamela, 149
Potter, Sewall Bennett, ix–x, *viii*
Poulenc, Francis, 12; *Les Animaux modèles*, 69; BBC wartime programming of, 68; *Figure Humaine*, 69
*Pride of the Yankees* (film), 141
Prieberg, Fred, 10
prisoner-of-war camps in Burma, 266–67
prisoner-of-war camps for French soldiers, 18, 57, 173, 182–85, 187, 265, 266
prisoner-of-war camps in United States, 18, 19, 226–39; construction of, 228; German military culture and, 236, 242n33; musical activities in, 231–37, 263, 265–66; POW labor, 228, 232, 241n11, 241n24; POW reeducation aims, 228–31, 238–39, 266; Special Projects Division, 228–31
*Prisonnier en Allemagne*, 185
Prokofiev, Sergei: *War and Peace*, 16
protest music, 3, 4
Puccini, Giacomo, 64; BBC wartime programming of, 66; *Madama Butterfly*, 112, 128n3
Pushkin, Alexander, 103n48

Quit India movement, 39

R. A. Dvorský and his Melody Boys, 201–2, 203, 217n10
Rachmaninoff, Serge: Prelude in C-sharp Minor, 44
radio broadcasting, 4, 14–15; accessibility of, 16–17; censorship under German occupation, 202; as connector between home front and war front, 16, 36–38; as diversion or escapism, 4, 16, 29, 33–34, 247, 251–53, 265; "enemy alien" classical musicians and, 15, 17, 56–71, 267; "intimate public" of, 28–29, 34–35, 36, 40, 45, 47–48; Metropolitan Opera, 112; in post-*Anschluss* Austria, 151, 160, 169n81; programming controversies, 17, 29–30, 41–47; propaganda and, 265; theater organ programs, 27–47
*Radio Times*, 33, 35–36, 40, 42, 59, 64, 65, 66, 67, 263
Ratoff, Gregory, 77
Raupenstrauch, Roland, 158
Red Ace Players, 207
Reger, Max: "Requiem," 157
Reich Radio, 252
Reichwein, Leopold, 164n20
Reid, Alden, 232–33
Reiner, Fritz, 112, 138
Remarque, Erich Maria, 56; *All Quiet on the Western Front*, 2
*Request Concert* (film), 252
*Request Concert for the Wehrmacht* (radio program), *The*, 252
resistance, music used as, 12, 18, 65, 200, 207, 209, 217n4, 217n11
Rethberg, Elisabeth, 117
*Rêve de Cinyras, Le*, 176
*Revue critique*, 174–76
*Revue universelle*, 174–75
Rhythmaires, the, 144n5
Rice, Elmer, 141
Richardot, Jean-Pierre, 181
Richter, Klaus, 209
Riggs, Lynn: *Green Grow the Lilacs*, 132
Rischin, Rebecca, 190n35
Rivain, Jean, 175–76
Rivain, Marie-Ange, 175–76
*rivière enchantée, La* (film), 186
Robbins, Jerome, 140
Robin, Ron, 228, 229
Rodgers, Richard, 135; *Carousel*, 141; *By Jupiter*, 131; *Oklahoma!*, 132, 134, 135, 138, 139–40, 141–42, 263, 268; on Porter, 145n11
Rogers, Roy, 132
Roissard de Bellet, Guy, 185; *La nuit des bergers*, 185
Romberg, Sigmund, 135; *The Student Prince*, 138
Romm, Mikhail, 78, 100n11
Ronell, Ann: *Count Me In*, 131, 133, 144n4
Roosevelt, Eleanor, 122

Rose, Billy: *Seven Lively Arts*, 138
Rose, David, 136
Rosenberg, Isaac, 56
Rouche, Jacques, 69
Rousseau, Emile, 178
Roxworthy, Emily, 265
Ruby, Edmond, 178, 181
*Russkiy Vopros* (film), 100n11
Rychlík, Jan, 219n30

Salkow, Sidney, 77
Salter, Hans: *Invisible Agent* film score, 267
*Sandy Calling India* (radio program), 27, 39, 46
*Sandy Calling the Middle East* (radio program), 27, 38, 39–40, 44, 45, 46–47
*Sandy's Half-Hour for Canada* (radio program), 27, 38
*Sandy's Half-Hour* (radio program), 27, 36–38, 40, 45–47
Sanos, Sandrine, 175
Sargent, John Singer, 2
Sargent, Malcolm, 69
Sassoon, Siegfried, 2, 56
*saxofonová generace*, 206, 220n38, 268
Sayao, Bidú, 119, 120
Scapini, Georges, 183, 192n78
Schaffer, Pierre, 12
Schallert, Edwin, 88
Scheck, Raffael, 184
Schidlof, Peter, 62
Schirach, Baldur von, 153, 155–56, 159
Schmidt, Franz: Organ Toccata in C major, 152
Schoenberg, Arnold, 6, 68, 152
Schola Cantorum, 175
Schrammel, Johann: "Wien bleibt Wien," 152
Schubert, Franz, 179; BBC wartime programming of, 67; *Great* Symphony in C major, 157; "Der Lindenbaum," 234, 237; music performed by German POWs in American war camps, 237, 263; "Ständchen," 237; Symphony no. 3, 164n27; *Unfinished* Symphony, 152; "Der Wegweiser," 237
Schumann, Coco, 223n59
Schumann, Robert: BBC wartime programming of, 67; *Traümerei*, 44
Schwartz, Manuela, 270–71n9
Schwoebel, Willi, 233–35

Seaton, Jean, 62
Sebald, W. G.: "Air War and Literature," 247
Second Viennese School, 68
*Secret Mission, The* (film), 78, 96
Sedaine, Michel-Jean, 176
Seidlhofer, Bruno, 157
sentimentality, 29, 42–43, 44–47, 48n4, 56–57, 267
Shaw, Tony, 96–97
Shebalin, Vissarion: *Conspiracy of the Doomed* film score, 78, 94
Sheppard, W. Anthony, 79
Sherriff, R. C., 56
Shostakovich, Dmitry: film scores of, 263; *Leningrad* Symphony, 16, 57, 104n64, 131; *Meeting at the Elbe* film score, 78, 97–98; Symphony no. 1, 132
Shubert brothers, 136
Shull, Michael, 79
Sibelius, Jean: BBC wartime programming of, 60, 66, 67; *Finlandia*, 65
Siegl, Otto: *Concerto grosso antico*, 152
Silberman, Marc, 252
*Silent Film Sound & Music Archive*, 48n9
Simon, Yannick, 10, 173, 183
Sinatra, Frank, 140, 146n27
*Sing Out, Sweet Land* (musical), 141
Sixty-Eight Publishers, 216
Škvorecký, Josef, 217nn4–5, 218n19; *Zbabělci*, 215–16
Slavík, Karel, 204, 206
Société de Musique d'Autrefois, 175
*Song of Norway* (operetta), 138, 268
*Song of Russia* (film), 77, 82, 267
"Song of the Motherland" (Soviet march), 84, 97–98, 102n41, 104n69
sonic dimensions of warfare and incarceration, 13, 15, 18–19, 246–57, 263–70
sound recordings: communities created through, 16; Czech swing and, 201, 202, 204, 207, 217n11, 218n14, 220n47; as escapism, 4, 265; industry expansion, 14–15; of popular music during World War I, 9; in POW camps, 231, 233, 235–36, 239
Soviet Union: film production, 77–78; portrayal in American wartime films, 77, 79–93, 263, 267; postwar clampdown on Western influences, 78; postwar portrayal

of Americans in films, 79, 93–100; postwar use of jazz as imperialist symbol of America, 94, 95, 96, 98, 264; scholarship on World War II music in, 10; United States' wartime alliance with, 17, 80, 117, 267

Special Projects Division (SPD), 227, 228–32, 237–39

Sprout, Leslie, 10, 12, 173

Stacey, Jackie, 31

Stage Door Canteen, 133

Stalin, Joseph, 88

*Star, The*, 34

Starr, Frederick, 94

Steber, Eleanor, 113, *114*

Stein, Philipp, 169n81

Steiner, Max: *Mission to Moscow* film score, 77, 83, 267

Stern, Tony: "The Yanks Are Coming Again," 137–38

Stevens, Risë, 113

Stoloff, M. W.: *The Boy from Stalingrad* film score, 77

Stothart, Herbert: *Song of Russia* film score, 77, 82, 267

Stransky, Felix, 164n23

Straus, Oscar, 65

Strauss, Johann (father): BBC postwar programming of, 70; wartime performances in Vienna, 152

Strauss, Johann (son): BBC postwar programming of, 70; BBC wartime programming of, 67; *Die Fledermaus*, 235; "Kaiserwalzer," 235; *Rosalinda (Die Fledermaus)*, 136, 138; wartime performances in Vienna, 152

Strauss, Richard: BBC postwar programming of, 70–71; BBC wartime programming of, 61, 64, 66–67, 71; *Don Juan*, 70; *Ein Heldeleben*, 71

Stravinsky, Igor, 6, 12, 84, 138, 179

Strecker, Heinrich, 152

Street, Sean, 61

Streicher, Jean-Claude, 181, 188n1

Streicher, Theodor, 157

Sullivan, Arthur: "The Lost Chord," 35

*Sunday Pictorial*, 27, 29, 40

swing. *See* Czech swing

Swing Rhythm ensemble, 219n30

Syracuse, Dick, 269

Szell, George, 112

Taruskin, Richard, 104n64

Taylor, Deems, 122

Taylor, Robert, 82

Tchaikovsky, Pyotr. *See* Chaikovsky, Pyotr

technology: in World War I, 1, 9, 14; in World War II, 1, 3, 4, 13, 14–15

Teike, Carl: "Alte Kameraden," 235

Thacker, Toby, 70

Thailand–Burma Railway, 266–67

Thalben-Ball, George, 43–44

Thatcher, R. S., 63

theater organs: BBC listeners' opinions of, 41–42, 46, 51n69; BBC programming of, 27–47, 267; BBC's Compton organ, 30, 31–32, 33; Bliss's opinion of, 29–30; as entertainment, 31; history of, 30; Moller organ owned by Foort, 32, *32*, 40–41, 47, 51n67; as one-man orchestras, 30–31, 33–34; sentimentality and, 42–43; viewed as threat to wartime morale, 41–46

Théâtre aux Armées, 175, 176–77

Theatre Guild, 134, 139–40

Thiriet, Maurice, 178, 180, 182–83, 184, 185, 186, 192n78, 266

Thomson, Virgil, 181

Thorborg, Kerstin, 117

Tierney, Harry: *Irene*, 142

*Times* (London), 30

Todd, Michael: *Star and Garter*, 131, 132, 142

Toland, Gregg, 83

*Top-Notchers* (revue), 137–38

torture, music used as, 3, 4

Toscanini, Arturo, 12, 131

Tourneur, Jacques, 77

transnationalism, 58, 264, 266, 268–69, 270n5

Traxler, Jiří, 200, 204, 206, 207–9, *208*, 214, 218n20, 219n34, 220n40; "Bloudění v rytmu," 210, *211*; defection of, 215; "Hádej, hádej . . ." ("Peter, Peter, wo warst du heute nacht?"), 209, 223n58, 268; memoirs of, 207, 208–9, 217n5; songs by, 220n43; "Starý strom," 215

Trio Pasquier, 185

Troller, Paul, 181

Tucker, Richard, 113

Tucker, Sherrie, 11
*Two-Way Family Favourites* (radio program), 47

Uggé, Emanuel, 202, 207; "Hot Jazz," 217n11
Uhl, Alfred, 164n27; Double Fugue for Orchestra, 152
Ullswater Committee, 62
Ultraphon record label, 202, 207, 208, 218n14
"Umorilas" (Russian folk song), 86–87, *86–87*
United Kingdom in World War II: anti-Semitism and, 62, 71, 72n26; bombing destruction in, 40, 47, 69; classical music's role in, 57–58, 267; everyday private life in, 28, 33; internment of "enemy aliens," 61–62, 71; as "People's War," 35–36, 46, 47; theater organ broadcasts, 27–47. *See also* BBC
United States: Broadway theater and musicals during wartime, 131–44, 268, 269; European reception of American classical music, 230, 238–39; Japanese American detention camps, 271n11; military music in, 2–3; musical identity of, 11; politics of opera publicity during wartime, 17, 111–28; portrayal of Russians in wartime films, 77, 79–93, 100, 263, 267; prisoner-of-war camps in, 18, 19, 226–39, 265–66; safety from wartime bombing attacks, 269; Soviet postwar portrayal of, 79, 93–100, 264
USO, 142, 146–47n30

Vaughan Williams, Ralph, 66, 67; BBC wartime programming of, 71
Vejvoda, Milouš, 214
Verberger, Jiří, 219n30
Verdi, Giuseppe, 64; BBC wartime programming of, 66; *Cantica—Inno delle nazioni*, 12; *La Traviata*, 66
Vernon, P. E., 253
Vienna: assertion of cultural identity after *Anschluss*, 152–54, 161–62, 264, 268–69; concert funding after *Anschluss*, 150–51, 163n17; *Dunkelkonzerte* in, 18, 148–62, 263, 268–69; postwar, 68; pre-1944 safety of, 269; rivalry with Berlin, 153, 154; symphony orchestra schedule, 1940/41 season, 155, *156*; symphony orchestra repertory, 1938–45, 151–52

Vlach, Karel, 204, 206, 207–8, 213, 214
*Vlajka*, 206, 219n36
Voskovec, Jiří, 217n11, 220n38
Vuillermoz, Jean, 192n78
Vulliet, Andre, 231

Wade, Martyn: *Hide the Moon*, 64
Wagner, Oskar: Symphony in C minor, 152
Wagner, Richard: BBC postwar programming of, 70; BBC wartime programming of, 66–67, 71; English-language productions of operas, 128n1; *Die Meistersinger*, 57; *Parsifal*, 157, 158; *Ride of the Valkyries*, 60; *Tannhäuser*, 67, 234
Wallenstein, Alfred, 138
*Wall Street Journal*, 133–34
Walter, Bruno, 112, 115–17, 120
Walton, William: *Agincourt Suite*, 57
Wanausek, Camillo, 160
Warlop, Michel, 183
Waseda, Minako, 271n11
Watkins, Glenn, 8
Watt, John, 32, 33, 35, 43, 44, 47
Webb, Clifton, 131
Weber, Carl Maria von: *Der Freischütz*, 235
Weill, Kurt, 135
Weingartner, Felix, 242n30
Weisbach, Hans, 154, 158, 161
Weiss, Fricek, 209, 213, 223n59
Weiss, Fritz, 206
Wellman, William, 100n8
Welzer, Harald, 242n33
Werich, Jan, 217n11, 220n38
White, Miles, 146n25
Whiteman, Paul, 201
*Why We Fight* (film documentary series), 101n15
*Wiener Neueste Nachrichten*, 161
Wiener Schubertbund, 158
Wilson, Woodrow, 201, 217n8
Wilt, David, 79
Winchell, Walter, 134
*Winged Victory* (Army Air Forces show), 136, 137
Winger, Otto, 164n23
Winter, Horst, 220n47
Wolf, Hugo, 164n27
Wolfram, Aurel, 154, 159
Wood, Henry, 69

Works Progress Administration (WPA), 231
World War I: anti-German feeling during, 61; concept of "home front" in, 1; music of, 2, 3, 6; music scholarship on, 3, 7–9, 13–14; post-war reckoning, 2, 56, 186
World War II: Allied bombing of German cities, 246, 247–48, 250–51; atrocities of, 1; audiovisual media as diversion during, 3, 4, 11, 16, 29, 33–34, 246–47, 251–57, 265; audiovisual media coverage of, 1–2; avenues for music scholarship, 10–16, 19–20; Battle for Berlin, 252–53; collaboration with German authorities during, 12, 57, 63, 68, 69, 70, 173, 181, 183–85, 186, 202, 206, 209, 212–14, 219n34, 266; events of 1942 for British forces, 42; geographical and temporal definition of, 4–5; Ghost Army Allied military-deception campaign, 269; Indian Army in, 50n55; music scholarship on, 3, 6, 7, 9–10; post-war anti-war sentiment, 3, 4; resistance during, 12, 18, 65, 200, 202, 207, 209, 212–13, 217n4, 217n11; role of music in, 5–6; *Totaleinsatz*, 214. *See also specific names, countries, and topics*

Wright, K. A., 64
Wurlitzer, Farny and Howard, 30
Wyler, William, 83

"Yankee Doodle Dandy," 97
*Yanks Are Coming, The* (film), 138
YMCA, 226, 231, 238
Youngblood, Denise, 96–97
Yugoslavia, occupied, musical activity in, 10

Zachoval, Miroslav, 224n72
Zeisl, Eric: *Song of Russia* film score, 267
Zemánková, Inka, 200, 204, 208, 209–10, 210, 212, 218n20; Czech-language rhythmic style of, 209, 268; fascist attacks on, 206, 210, 212; later life of, 215; memoirs of, 207, 217n5; performances in forced-labor camps, 214; in Škvorecký's writings, 216
Zhdanov, Andrey, 78, 93
*Ziegfeld Follies of 1943*, 144n5
Ziehrer, Carl Michael, 164n27; "O Wien, mein liebes Wien," 152
Zscharnt, Gertrud, 250

www.ingramcontent.com/pod-product-compliance
Lightning Source LLC
Chambersburg PA
CBHW030523230426
43665CB00010B/748